THE REVOLUTION
FROM WITHIN

THE REVOLUTION
FROM WITHIN

CUBA, 1959–1980

Michael J. Bustamante and Jennifer L. Lambe, editors

Duke University Press   Durham and London   2019

© 2019 DUKE UNIVERSITY PRESS. All rights reserved
Printed and bound by CPI Group (UK) Ltd, Croydon, CR0 4YY
Designed by Courtney Leigh Baker
Typeset in Whitman and Futura
by Westchester Publishing Services

Library of Congress Cataloging-in-Publication Data
Names: Bustamante, Michael J., editor. | Lambe, Jennifer L., editor.
Title: The revolution from within : Cuba, 1959–1980 /
Michael J. Bustamante and Jennifer L. Lambe, editors.
Description: Durham : Duke University Press, 2019. |
Includes bibliographical references and index.
Identifiers: LCCN 2018031280 (print)
LCCN 2018041257 (ebook)
ISBN 9781478004325 (ebook)
ISBN 9781478001706 (hardcover : alk. paper)
ISBN 9781478002963 (pbk. : alk. paper)
Subjects: LCSH: Cuba—History—1959–1990. | Cuba—Politics and
government—1959–1990. | Cuba—History—Revolution, 1959. |
Cuba—History—1933–1959. | Cuba—Politics and government—1933–1959.
Classification: LCC F1788 (ebook) | LCC F1788 .R428 2019 (print) |
DDC 972.9106/4—dc23
LC record available at https://lccn.loc.gov/2018031280

Frontispiece: "Entrando en la historia" (Entering History). Antonio,
"El humorismo y La Revolución: Frase hecha," *Bohemia*, February 1, 1959, 176.

Cover art: Cuba in the early 1970s.
Photograph by John van Hasselt / Corbis / Getty Images.

CONTENTS

ACKNOWLEDGMENTS

Edited volumes are necessarily collaborative, and in this lies many intellectual rewards and debts. We would like to begin by thanking all of the authors represented in this book for their enthusiasm, patience, and camaraderie along the road to publication. We trust that the final product is sufficient testament to their hard work.

This book grew out of a conference, New Histories of the Cuban Revolution, held at Yale University in 2014. We remain grateful for the generous sponsorship of numerous institutions at Yale: the Council on Latin American and Iberian Studies (a special thanks to Jean Silk, Nancy Ramírez, and especially Taylor Jardno, who played a key last-minute role), the Whitney Humanities Center, the Edward J. and Dorothy Clarke Kempf Memorial Fund, the Department of History, the Graduate School of Arts and Sciences, and the Program in Ethnicity, Race, and Migration. Brown University and New York University also contributed generous financial support. We would especially like to thank Gilbert Joseph and Stuart Schwartz, who offered advice and enthusiastic collaboration, along with the participants in that event, whose contributions have decisively shaped our understanding of the Cuban Revolution and helped revitalize the study of its past: Manuel Barcia Paz, Enrique Beldarraín, María A. Cabrera Arús, Odette Casamayor, Luciano Castillo, Michelle Chase, Walfrido Dorta, Jorge Duany, Ada Ferrer, Víctor Fowler, Reinaldo Funes, Anne Gorsuch, Lillian Guerra, Ariana Hernández-Reguant, Jesse Horst, Rachel Hynson, Marial Iglesias Utset, Iraida López, Jorge Macle, Christabelle Peters, José Quiroga, Ricardo Quiza, Rafael Rojas, Rainer Schultz, Elizabeth Schwall, Stuart Schwartz, Abel Sierra Madero, and Devyn Spence Benson. Taylor Jardno, Anne Eller, Roberto González Echevarría, Albert

Laguna, Marcela Echeverri, and Gilbert Joseph kindly served as moderators. Yale students Angelo Pis-Dudot and Fabián Fernández provided logistical support throughout the conference weekend. Lynn Roche, of the then U.S. Interests Section in Havana, and Milagros Martínez, at the University of Havana, lent their assistance and advice in the processing of visa applications. Alejandro Vázquez designed our conference poster. Steve Pitti and Alicia Schmidt-Camacho hosted all of us for dinner in their home.

This book might never have seen the light of publication had it not been for the unflagging support and guidance of Gilbert Joseph and Alejandro de la Fuente, who steered us out of many intellectual and bureaucratic cul-de-sacs. We would also like to thank Lillian Guerra, whose work represents an intellectual touchstone for all scholars of the Cuban Revolution. We are fortunate to count her as a mentor and friend. Throughout this process it has been a pleasure to work with Gisela Fosado and Lydia Rose Rappoport-Hankins at Duke University Press. We sincerely appreciate the feedback provided by anonymous reviewers, which has shaped this book in profound ways. Colleagues and mentors at our current institutions—Brown University and Florida International University—have been encouraging throughout. Andra Chastain and Timothy Lorek were kind enough to read a late draft of our introduction, and Carlos Velazco Fernández and Elizabeth Mirabal offered intellectual dialogue and personal friendship. Mylena contributed to multiple stages of the conference and book production process; Lauren Krebs helped source several images; and Ian Russell assisted with translations of several chapters. To each of them, thank you.

Finally, though we do not have the space to list them all here, we are eternally grateful to the many colleagues, friends, and family members—*aquí y allá*—who sustained us through this demanding process. We hope that they are as excited as we are to see this book in print.

PART I

Stakes of the Field

———

1. Cuba's Revolution from Within

THE POLITICS OF HISTORICAL PARADIGMS

JENNIFER L. LAMBE AND MICHAEL J. BUSTAMANTE

"When this year comes to a close," the Cuban writer Virgilio Piñera observed in the newspaper *Revolución* on November 11, 1959, "what has been written about the Revolution will comprise little more than a *novelette*, a couple short stories, a dozen poems, and a few hundred articles. No one would downplay the importance of this panoramic production about the Cuban Revolution. Nevertheless, the organic book, *the* history of the Revolution, has yet to be written."[1]

As Piñera reflected upon "the Revolution" in 1959, he was referring to the anti-Batista struggle that had unfolded *before* that year of insurgent triumph. Today, in contrast, "the Revolution" generally denotes a historical age that only *begins* with Batista's flight—for some ongoing and unbroken, for others inconclusive or even terminal. Neither could we categorize what has been written about the 1959 Revolution as a mere "novelette." Sixty years later, that event has received as much attention as any other in recent Latin American history. Moreover, as self-interested academics dependent on the "wheel of revisionism" (per Florencia Mallon), we would be hard-pressed to stand behind Piñera's plea for one "organic" book that might present "*the* History of the Revolution."[2] Certainly, the Cuban Revolution has not wanted for a constant stream of experts, churning out decades' worth of observations, analyses, and critiques.

Yet in spite of the profusion of work about the era in question—both critical and deferential, serious and superficial—our knowledge of the social, cultural, and political history of revolutionary Cuba remains fragmented and, in many places, underdeveloped. In recent years, the scholarship has gained a fresh vitality, spurred by a more receptive, if still politically constrained climate for researchers on the island, as well as the emergence of a new cohort of senior and junior scholars abroad. Nonetheless, historians continue to be challenged by a dearth of primary sources, the vagaries of archival access, and the broader politicization of the field. "In more than one respect," noted the Havana-based historian Oscar Zanetti in 2010, "the Cuban Revolution has yet to be historicized."[3] Or, as the expatriate intellectual Rafael Rojas put it in 2008, "fifty years is enough time for a historiographical school to emerge, and yet the Cuban Revolution wants for canonical studies."[4] Historical work published since then does not fully address these concerns, even as the 2009 fiftieth anniversary of the Revolution, and now the sixtieth, have brought renewed attention to what has been—and has yet to be—written of its history, particularly on the island.[5]

How can a historiographical school be simultaneously overpopulated and underdeveloped? In this context, what might it mean to write histories of the Cuban Revolution anew? This tension between analytical saturation and historiographical absence stems from the myriad ways in which history itself was central to the revolutionary project. After all, the *barbudos* not only assumed political power; they also effected, as Louis A. Pérez has written, an "appropriation of history": "Central to the claim of historical authenticity was the proposition of the triumphant revolution as culmination of a process whose antecedents reached deep into the nineteenth century."[6] The Revolution's master narrative (and the exile variations that emerged to counter it) thus yoked the past to its vision for the present, collapsing Cuban history into the teleological arc of an overdetermined future. Official discourse, in turn, helped set the stage for its scholarly counterpoint. For years, researchers have had little choice but to take revolutionary leaders at their word, either to laud or to criticize them. From official claims and statistics, they have often generalized to popular experience more broadly. Those temptations still confront scholars today.

It is this old, often intramural conversation to which more recent critics, including some represented in this volume, have been responding with renewed energy. Taking inspiration from pioneering scholars in the past, commentators across the ideological and geographical landscape have rekindled the call for a historiography that might overcome partisan differences, whatever the obstacles. Without rejecting the imperative to revisit old debates with new evidence in hand, this volume embraces the need to move beyond preexisting polemics—whether questions about the Revolution's success or failure or the root causes of its evolution over time. Nonetheless, it also challenges the idea that analytical synthesis, or apolitical scholarship, is the necessary result. *The Revolution from Within: Cuba, 1959–1980* thus meets Piñera's call for an "organic" history of the Revolution with an assertion of plurality and antiteleology—what we might characterize as an essentially historicist spirit. This emphasis on diversity, however, should not be taken for an analytical free-for-all.

What connects all of the essays in this volume is their insistence on a *Cuba-centric* approach to the first two decades of the island's post-1959 history. Decades of scholarly production have brought us sophisticated accounts of the influence of major Cold War power brokers—the United States and the Soviet Union, especially—on Cuba's revolutionary path. While gesturing to the importance of these and other transnational connections, however, these essays are instead oriented to the internal dynamics of revolutionary process. In this, they build on and open up several important areas of thematic inquiry. The authors work to further pluralize our understanding of the revolutionary state beyond its most public leaders. And, through the insights of cultural history, they seek to restore the Revolution's basic historicity and heterogeneity, highlighting the experiences of everyday actors without losing sight of the force of state power—at once overwhelming yet diffuse, persistent but also quotidian.

Yet these essays also engage, implicitly or explicitly, the political stakes of Cuban history itself. On one hand, contributors historicize the uses made of Cuba's past by the revolutionary state, dissecting the political weight with which officials invested historical narratives. Several essays capture such claims in their historical construction, as state actors fashioned the Revolution as the fulfillment of past political dreams deferred. But these works likewise compel us to consider the impact of official narratives on what is known, and knowable, about the Revolution, particularly for scholars. In that, they force a reckoning with the political uses to which academic historical knowledge about the revolutionary era can still be put.

In what follows, we further detail this volume's contributions to the field of revolutionary history at a vibrant, nodal point in its development. First, however, we try to understand the weight of official paradigms in the construction of *historiographical* narratives about the Revolution over time. How, we ask, have revolutionary processes of state formation shaped what popular, official, and, finally, academic voices have had to say about the Revolution's history? Overall, we argue that the construction of a revolutionary and counterrevolutionary canon of historical knowledge has thrown even purportedly "neutral" scholars into a polarized minefield. The political function with which the state ascribed historical knowledge has thus endowed all historical scholarship on the Cuban Revolution with an inevitably ideological cast. This, we argue, is not just a historiographical problematic but an essential historical question in its own right.

Building a Revolution: The Uses of History

In its analytical approach to official paradigms, *The Revolution from Within* can be classified as a revisionist project. But to call the essays in this collection "revisionist" begs the question: Revisionist relative to what? Most obviously, they push back on the parameters governing official narratives within Cuba's public sphere. They are not uniformly reverent; they do not celebrate the Revolution's emergence, nor sugarcoat the conflicts that came in its wake. Yet they are also invested in exploring the Revolution's lived meanings, diverse subjects, and internal complexities. These imperatives are not exclusively or even primarily targeted to antagonistic political aims.

Debates about the purpose of historical revisionism are far from new when it comes to Cuba. As we explore below, historiographical rupture in the early 1960s once represented a revolutionary response to the apolitical scholarship of the past. Historical "revisionism," however, was far from a uniform project, and the political significance ascribed to it varied considerably over time. As the bounds for ideological diversity narrowed throughout the 1960s and 1970s, heterodox perspectives on Cuba's past would be conflated with "ideological diversionism" and other political sins.[7] In Cuba today, "revisionism" continues to be read as constitutionally subversive, particularly in its presumed challenge to official narratives and the revolutionary state.

The essays in this volume thus evoke a question that has long haunted historical knowledge of the revolutionary period. Namely, can even the most rigorous accounts of Cuba's post-1959 history evolve beyond a game of opposed mirrors, one standing in the discursive and ideological space of Havana's Revolution Square, the other planted in front of Miami's Freedom Tower?[8] To return to Piñera's insightful prognostications from 1959, can scholars of the Cuban Revolution be anything but historians of a "court," beholden to one or another master narrative?[9] Should—could—historians of the Cuban Revolution find an analytical path out from under the shadow of official (and counterofficial) paradigms?

The problem is perhaps elucidated by an anecdote from a different, not unrelated context. In her essay "The Material Existence of Soviet Samizdat," Ann

Komaromi relates a joke that would have been familiar to its Russian audience. "A Soviet grandmother is having trouble interesting her granddaughter in Lev Tolstoi's beloved classic *War and Peace*," Komaromi narrates. "The problem is not that the novel is too long. It just looks too official." So the grandmother decides to get creative. Drawing on counterhegemonic visual codes, "the poor woman stays up nights retyping the work as 'samizdat,'" a term for clandestine literature in the late Soviet Union.[10] Suddenly, the classic remade with alternative trappings has become palatable—tantalizingly forbidden—to the granddaughter weary of tomes of all stripes.

Essentially subversive, samizdat drew its force and sustained relevance in the Soviet context from the fact of critique: a "resistance to mythologizing ideology in general."[11] In that, there is much that endears the concept to a volume focused on the Cuban Revolution. An enduring notion of history as critique has likewise shaped popular and scholarly accounts of Cuban history after 1959—including some of those in this volume—largely in response to the teleological narratives woven around revolutionary authority.[12] In this formulation, the "difference" of historiographical critique lies in its heterodox stance vis-à-vis Cuban political officials and institutions or, more rarely, their counterparts in the Cuban diaspora. Where Fidel Castro declared "100 Years of Struggle," for example, stretching from the first outbreak of the independence wars all the way through his revolutionary present, his critics (Cuban and not) have stressed incompatibility with—and even betrayal of—those same principles and points of origin.

The grandmother's parodic act, though, begs for another interpretation. However pleased her granddaughter might be to receive this remake of an old classic, behind the cover she will still be confronted with the same story. Tolstoi remains Tolstoi, adorned yet fundamentally unadulterated. For twenty-first-century Cubans and Cubanists, that act of mimicry masquerading as opposition would feel both immediate and significant. Trapped in the enduring terms of a Manichaean ideological field, revisionists of the present, like those of the past, find themselves hard-pressed to reach beyond fragmented half-truths, tepid deflections, and revolutionary just-so stories turned inside out.

Perhaps the correct response, then, is to aim for *post*revisionism: to claim, however dubiously, that we can transcend the political fault lines that burdened the telling of history in the past. It would be tempting, if disingenuous, to raise the shield of guild "objectivity," of historical "professionalism." Claiming scholarly "neutrality," as has long been the practice in U.S. academic historical production, seems to offer one potential response to charges of politicization.[13] Yet we are too aware of how newer scholarship might recapitulate polarized debates—how we might, in purporting to shed partisan trappings, actually endow them with renewed force. In the place of the revolutionary master narrative, do we risk erecting another, essentially mirroring, even when negating, the central tenets of official discourse?

In the early 1960s, however, Cuba's history represented genuinely *subversive* material to those who sought to build a new revolutionary society. Much as contemporary critics of the revolutionary government now claim history as a mode of critique, so revolutionary intellectuals once called for a new history to speak to a transformed present. For its most radical proponents, a new history would not only overturn the "bourgeois," pro-U.S., and nationalist mythologies they claimed to discern behind prior historiographical work. It would also respond, quite explicitly, to the demands of the revolutionary moment. As Manuel Moreno Fraginals famously declared from the vantage point of 1966, "There is a general clamor for a *new history*, for a distinct way of looking at the past."[14] Importantly, this "new history" would not just detail events immediately preceding or following 1959; it would also revisit and reinterpret the independence era and beyond.

How new would the new history be? For Moreno Fraginals, it could not stop at the rejection of old paradigms, though it would be necessary to overcome "petty polemics . . . debating Saco, Martí, Céspedes [luminaries of Cuban national thought and the long Cuban independence struggle] time and again." "Destroying the old categories" represented an act of initial but ultimately futile "iconoclasm." In their place Moreno Fraginals called for a "true history," committed by definition, that would break all "bourgeois" rules in clearing the path to a Marxist, dialectical approach: "We must head towards those truly rich sources that the bourgeoisie eliminated from our historical inheritance because they were precisely the most significant ones. And with the support of this new and essential research we must *discover* the dialectical laws of our history."[15]

That is, what defined the new revolutionary history was that its authors (both state officials and professional historians) made historical production responsive—or, critics might say, beholden—to political concerns. Undoubtedly, the commitment of revolutionary historians yielded important contributions to Cuban historiography, from new attention to marginalized "people without history" to critiques of slavery, imperialism (Spanish and U.S.), and political corruption in Cuba's past. Moreover, as Kate Quinn charts, in the 1960s historiographical ferment provoked contentious debates over how Cuba's past should be interpreted in light of its revolutionary present. These battles pitted a nationalist camp that continued to lionize Cuba's "heroes" against Marxist scholars invested in uncovering economic processes and structures. Yet by 1970, Quinn points out, this "critical historiography" was supplanted by a "culture of consent," dominated by a more conservative nationalist school.[16] For later historians, this pivot rendered earlier, more heterodox work off limits.

Also of interest for this story of shifting samizdat is the fact that many classic official texts were in fact written before 1959 and later repurposed for a revolutionary context.[17] This was true, for example, of longtime Cuban Communist Party leader Blas Roca's *Los fundamentos del socialismo en Cuba* (1943), which after 1959 helped make the argument that Cuban history led inexorably to both revolutionary struggle and socialism.[18] Yet, in hindsight, the revolutionary resurrection of this document is rather surprising. After all, Blas Roca could boast a sustained history of militancy in the Communist Party, which spanned its early years as a contestational and revolutionary force, particularly leading up to the Revolution of 1933, but also a period of comparative success when it functioned as one of a number of progressive blocs cooperating with and tolerated during Batista's only elected presidency (1940–44). It was Batista himself who legalized the Party in 1938. Subsequently, Roca's career saw the discrediting of the Communist Party for its collaboration with Batista; the resumption of anticommunist persecution in the late 1940s and under Batista's pro-U.S. dictatorship of the 1950s; and the tentative and often conflicted dance between the Communist Party and Castro's revolutionary movement well into the 1960s. And so the shifting political fault lines between Roca and his one-time ally Batista were rewritten in the revolutionary canonization of Roca's text, which had been penned at a strikingly different political juncture. The transformation from countercanon to canon thus brings us back to the samizdat Tolstoi: the *same text* (Roca) could in one context be read as counterhegemonic, only to be appropriated and made "official."[19]

When it came to the post-1959 era itself, available portrayals further entrenched new master narratives by relying, with few exceptions, on anecdote and political truisms. By virtue of proximity to the events in question, testimonies by the Revolution's leaders—whether Che Guevara's narrative of the guerrilla war or Antonio Núñez Jiménez's later account, *Marching alongside Fidel*—overshadowed academic texts.[20] Meanwhile, as insurgent achievements became "official" lore, exile counternarratives quickly emerged to refute them. Batista himself published exculpatory memoirs from exile, as did other republican-era politicians.[21] Even more influential were early U.S. academic and exile publications casting the Revolution's radicalization across 1960 and 1961 as a deviation from its "true," more moderate aims.[22]

Those who tried to escape the choice between officialist conscription and exile denunciation found themselves all too often cast into the opposing camp. By the mid- to late 1960s, a wave of foreign Marxist scholars had published some of the first analytical accounts of the Revolution's first decade in power. K. S. Karol, René Dumont, Maurice Halperin, Edward Boorstein, Leo Huberman, and Paul Sweezy remained critical of U.S. aggression and the exile community, and they were sympathetic to the Revolution's radical course.[23] But unlike the more enthusiastic fellow travelers of the Revolution's early years (e.g., C. Wright Mills, Jean-Paul Sartre, and Huberman and Sweezy themselves in an earlier book), these authors were not shy about criticizing the state's self-inflicted wounds, particularly in the economic realm.[24] Coinciding with a period of financial hardship on the island and a turn toward internal orthodoxy (in part via closer ties with the Soviet Union), these texts quickly became *non grata* in Cuba. For a time, their authors, along with many other nonconformist intellectuals from the Latin American and European left, suffered a similar fate.[25] More ambiguous in their implications were the accounts of New Left–affiliated young Americans and Latin Americans who traveled to the island in continuing solidarity with, if not outright conformity to, these political turns. These authors were often more attentive to the ways race, gender, and sexuality still divided Cubans—and their own group—along political lines.[26]

Institutionalization, followed by disillusionment and exclusion, could also endow a growing countercanon with amplified potency. Memoirs and exposés by an expanding list of collaborators turned enemies of the revolutionary state—Teresa Casuso, Carlos Moore, Rufo López Fresquet, Mario Llerena, and particularly Carlos Franqui and Heberto Padilla, whose controversial 1971 arrest fiercely divided the Revolution's admirers abroad—provided insider accounts of those who were instrumental in the Revolution's rise but had fallen afoul of its rule.[27] Though these texts circulated on the island in scarce quantities, if at all, there and in the exile community their critical portraits of state dynamics acquired allure precisely because they were taboo.

Historical texts—whether domestic or foreign, partisan, testimonial, or academic—thus evolved in revolutionary times. In the early 1960s the work of rewriting the Cuban historical tradition could be seen as genuinely subversive in appropriating past manifestos as its own. Yet in yoking originally contestational texts to an institutionalizing state, canonization carried its own risks. Over time, it made a once heterodox historiography vulnerable to the Revolution's political vicissitudes. Revisited in light of 1968, 1970, or, most decisively, 1989, what was once radical could seem tired and even hypocritical. And as historical accounts took up the revolutionary era directly, their predictably heroic qualities produced an equal but opposite denunciatory response, albeit mostly abroad.

So where does that leave us, historians conscious of the limitations of early schools, yet aware of, anxious about, or even energized by the political uses to which our own work can still be put? Can we escape the looping effects of the official historical canon? Or are our histories just Tolstoi masquerading as samizdat—a familiar oppositional fable hiding behind an attractively "revisionist" cover? To answer these questions, a further exploration of historiographical developments since the late 1960s is required. We offer such an analysis below. But we also must recognize that the enduring place of revolutionary hagiography in Cuba's public sphere imbues many of the essays in this volume, like the work of our scholarly predecessors, with a degree of contestational force. This is perhaps inevitable in a context in which historical work on the Revolution is implicitly pitted or measured against official discourse on the same.[28]

Even so, we insist on the analytical power of serious historicism. Scholars, we suggest, can best respond to the revolutionary appropriation of history (and the exile community's mirror-image replies) by taking the Revolution's historical narratives as their analytical starting rather than ending point. This work necessarily forgoes historiographical volleys lobbed from ideological safe spaces—the ivory towers of reciprocal deafness—in favor of deep engagement with Cuban sources and island colleagues. It may not be possible to break the vise grip of hagiography on one hand and wholesale denunciation on the other. Nonetheless, there is scholarly territory that lies in between.

Historical Work in Historic Times:
Past and Present Scholarly Directions

In its emphasis on a Cuba-centric, historicist approach, *The Revolution from Within* seeks to contribute to the innovative and increasingly diverse work on the Revolution being produced within and beyond Cuba. Taking advantage of a more open, if still cautious climate for academic production on the island, intellectuals and scholars have played a notable role in probing Cuba's revolutionary conjuncture anew. But these essays also draw on critical gestures advanced in previous scholarly production. They are not the first to grapple with the (im)possibilities of "rising above" (or beyond) the Revolution's politics or the ways in which ongoing events shape the contours of scholarly work.

In addition to the critical Marxists already cited, we might point to the political scientist Richard Fagen as a pioneer of Cuban revolutionary history "from within." His foundational analysis of political culture on the island, published in 1968, still offers a useful framework for understanding the patterns and structures of grassroots political mobilization.[29] Also noteworthy is the work of the anthropologist Oscar Lewis, who between 1968 and 1970 conducted research on the island at Fidel Castro's invitation. With a binational team of researchers, he examined the fate of former slum dwellers relocated to government housing after 1959. The multiple publications that resulted from that project offer a textured account of one of the Revolution's signature reforms. Moreover, they portray everyday life under socialism with a degree of detail that historians today would be lucky to duplicate.[30]

By the end of the next decade, another promising development had taken place. "Cuban Studies," driven by the work of Cuban American scholars who had left the revolutionary island in their adolescence, began to coalesce as a field in the United States. Jorge Domínguez, Carmelo Mesa-Lago, and (a bit later) Marifeli Pérez-Stable published still classic surveys of political and economic developments across the 1959 revolutionary divide.[31] Given that academic work on the revolutionary period was generally limited on the island, these studies and others filled a crucial gap, particularly in their emphasis on macropolitical process over time.[32] It was also from this intellectual ferment that some of the most enduring commitments and pioneering efforts toward scholarly engagement with the island were born.

Throughout this early period, however, historical circumstances in and outside Cuba continued to influence the production and reception of such scholarly literature. The Lewis project, for example, was forcibly shut down when Cuban authorities became concerned about its results.[33] Meanwhile, those associated with the field of Cuban Studies would confront critics on both sides of the Florida Straits. Developed in part along an area studies track, the discipline was in some ways intertwined with the geopolitics of the Cold War.[34] On the island, "Cubanology," as it was derisively called, was criticized for its alleged ties to the U.S. foreign policy establishment and purported bias against the revolutionary government.[35] For hardline exile activists, in turn, the *cubanólogos* gathered around María Cristina Herrera's Instituto de Estudios Cubanos, the more pro-Revolution magazine *Areíto*, or, later, the journal *Cuban Studies* were equally suspect, insofar as they were not opposed to, and even participated in, cautious dialogues with island colleagues and officials.[36] Yet the very seriousness of the work undertaken by these pioneering Cuban Studies scholars meant that their research—and their efforts to build scholarly communities on the island—often endured, even as they continued to weather shifting geopolitical circumstances. On the other side, their island colleagues faced not insignificant professional risks in engaging in serious academic exchange, at times critical, with their U.S. counterparts.[37]

Scholars of revolutionary Cuba working outside of the United States—in Europe, Latin America, and Canada, for instance—have tended to swim in less tumultuous political waters, and many have generated prodigious bodies of scholarship and intellectual ties to the island.[38] Nonetheless, the impact of political divisions, in the United States and abroad, was to fortify more established or safer areas of scholarly emphasis. U.S.-Cuban relations loomed particularly large, even for scholars working outside of that conflict's direct shadow. From Morris Morley (Australia) to Thomas Paterson (United States), historians depicted the "breakup" of and subsequent hostility between the United States and Cuba as *the* central telos of the Revolution's first years.[39] With the subsequent declassification of U.S. government documents, paired with revelations of the full gamut of U.S. efforts to oust Cuba's revolutionary government, the temptation to reduce the history of the Revolution to its conflict with the United States did not go away.[40] This conspicuously echoed one of the key tenets of official Cuban discourse itself. Yet the task of relaying more internally focused histories of revolutionary process still seemed not just politically fraught, but practically out of reach. With available archival sources on the period stopping in many cases in 1960, influential scholars who came up in the early Cuban Studies mold may have understandably concluded that a deeper history of the Revolution was not a viable pursuit.

In fact, it first became possible to write critical, textured histories of Cuban politics and culture not about the Revolution but about the Republic (1902–58). The backdrop to this development was the so-called Special Period, a moment of economic and existential crisis in the 1990s and early 2000s brought on by the fall of the Soviet Union. In response, the Cuban government gingerly opened its doors to foreign capital but in the process also revived some of the island's pre-1959 ghosts. Emblems of what revolutionary discourse called the "pseudo-republic"—inequality, prostitution, the U.S. dollar, Western tourism—resurfaced with a vengeance, and Cubans looked back to previous times for clues as to how to read their disorienting present. Without ignoring the weight of U.S. influence and imperialism, a generation of Cuban and foreign scholars now paid closer attention to dynamics of agency, resistance, and popular mobilization in the pre-1959 years.[41] In so doing, they drew on trends in a wider Latin Americanist and Caribbean historiography that had moved away from the flattening paradigms of dependency theory.[42] They also unearthed historical analogues to the inventive ways in which Cubans in the 1990s managed to culturally, politically, and economically "get by" (*resolver*) in unpropitious sociopolitical circumstances. Such questions had also surfaced over the course of the Lewis project decades earlier.

Nonetheless, in writing about the Republic, these scholars were also writing about the Revolution, albeit indirectly. Insofar as they complicated revolutionary mythologies about the pre-1959 past, they also put into question the historical truisms on which the Revolution's political legitimacy rested. And they were soon joined by wide-ranging, interdisciplinary treatments of the Special Period itself (and more recent years) in contiguous disciplines like anthropology and cultural studies that similarly cast revolutionary discourse into doubt.[43] If tackling understudied aspects of the 1959–89 era remained challenging, critical attention to the racial, gendered, and sexual ambiguities attending Cuba's economic and social evolution in the 1990s and beyond involved an implicit judgment on the legacies of the previous three decades.

Not long thereafter, scholars finally began to devote renewed analytical attention to the revolutionary years. This included, notably, insightful efforts to demythologize the anti-Batista insurrection.[44] But other academic publications, such as *Ideología y Revolución* (2001) and *Prensa y Revolución* (2010) by María del Pilar Díaz Castañón, also began opening up the early experiments of revolutionary governance to cultural analysis with, but not beholden to, hindsight.[45] Both titles are embedded in exhaustive press research, and *Prensa y Revolución*, an edited volume written in collaboration with several of Díaz Castañón's students, extends her expertise on the Cuban press to other scholars working on the period. Díaz Castañón's work was joined by seminal English-language publications by Alejandro de la Fuente and Lillian Guerra, which brought renewed attention to the controversies and transformations of the Revolution's first decade.[46] Guerra's work in particular represents a trailblazing effort to reconsider the emerging revolutionary state from the bottom up, with an eye to tracking hegemony as an evolving construction rather than a naturalized outcome. The Revolution, she argues, deputized ordinary citizens to act on its behalf, augmenting state control but also personal agency. Such tactics, however, engendered overt and "unintended dissidence" as much as unprecedented popular support. Other scholars have applied a similarly nuanced cultural-historical lens to the politics of gender, the body, sexuality, and race.[47]

In the field of intellectual and literary history, meanwhile, new studies of revolutionary cultural production and the state's cultural politics—particularly leading up to the repressive "gray years" (*quinquenio gris*) of the early 1970s—date in some respects to the 1990s.[48] Amid the ideological shifts of that era, the partial rehabilitation of nonconformist (but not antisocialist) artists facilitated a qualified recovery of their past experiences of censorship and marginalization, often through published memoirs.[49] Since then, however, scholars on and off the island have continued to bring fresh attention to the Revolution's controversial chapters and forgotten voices, in and beyond the world of arts and letters. Groundbreaking books by Carlos Velazco and Elizabeth Mirabal about Guillermo Cabrera Infante and Guillermo Rosales have revisited the legacies of once-revolutionary writers turned expatriates, while Jorge Fornet's *El 71: Anatomía de una crisis* (2014) provides an innovative account of the Revolution's most notorious year of intellectual repression.[50] All of these works, in turn, enter into implicit dialogue, and at times productive tension, with the wide-reaching, interdisciplinary scholarship of Rafael Rojas.[51]

This renewed attention to the Revolution's history has produced not only a corpus of monographs but also a wave of scholarly and public-facing events and mobilizations on the island.[52] For example, the Simposio Internacional sobre la Revolución Cubana, convened on multiple occasions by Cuba's Instituto de Historia, has brought together leading academics, but also former Cuban government officials as participants. Then vice president Miguel Díaz-Canel (now president) attended the first edition of the event in 2015.[53] Meanwhile, a sequence of roundtables hosted by *Temas* magazine (published since 1995), together with a provocative series of new documentary films, has helped to push conversations about understudied chapters of the Revolution's past further into the public sphere.[54] More recently, addressing a new study group on the Revolution at the Instituto Cubano de Investigación Cultural Juan Marinello, the late socialist intellectual Fernando Martínez Heredia issued a call to further historicize the Revolution beyond enduring "clichés" and oft-repeated "falsities."[55] If some of these discussions have adhered to a largely hagiographical framework, others have taken on a spirit of critical inquiry in broaching challenging and politically complicated questions.

In these ways, the intensity of recent discussions of the Cuban Revolution reflects a new horizon of scholarly possibility, as well as continued challenges. Today, those who seek to open up the Revolution to historical inquiry may not face the same risks that their predecessors once confronted. To a significant degree, scholars are no longer trying to tell the story of a historical process in the direct shadow of the Cold War. Nonetheless, historians must still navigate both structural obstacles and the political stakes of academic conversations in which they engage, given the continued mobilization of Cuba's past by the political class of its present. As they do so, insights gleaned from Cuba's own revolutionary trajectory, now entering its sixth decade, as well as cognate contexts elsewhere, may yet allow scholars of the Revolution to chart a forward-looking, rather than Sisyphean, intellectual path.

Indeed, the dynamism of conversations about the Revolution is not solely a reflection of changing political and economic circumstances in Cuba. Rather, new work has found inspiration in historical and theoretical paths forged in other contexts, from Latin America to the Soviet Union and beyond. Scholars of Cuba have been particularly influenced by a well-developed historiography on authoritarianism and populism in Latin America and the Caribbean, which has added nuance to traditionally mechanistic framings of the operations of revolutionary authority.[56] One imagines that recent trends in the study of the Soviet Union will also come increasingly to bear on Cuban conversations, from a centering of popular experience to more robust theorizations of disciplinary and political power under socialism.[57] The theoretical corpus of Michel Foucault, a longstanding but politically complicated source of inspiration for island-dwelling Cuban scholars, has already begun to inform discussions of gender, sexuality, and biopolitics in the revolutionary era.[58]

Nonetheless, the range of topics, sources, and periods has hardly been exhausted. The 1960s, for example, continue to receive far more attention than the two decades of "socialist institutionalization" that followed.[59] Responding to and building on newer work, this volume thus presents multiple and complementary interventions into ongoing debates on the Cuban Revolution. Above all, contributors capture and contribute to the growing emphasis on revolutionary process, viewed from within. As we discuss below, the most salient of their approaches to this question include a renewed interest in the conflicted and contested trajectory of state formation, a critical deployment of the major insights of cultural history, reflexive attention to the state of the Revolution's "archive," and an investment in analyzing the exceptionality (or not) of the Cuban Revolution, unbeholden to Cold War power politics.

In what follows, we have traced these themes throughout the volume in ways that occasionally range out of chronological order, but we believe that this approach best highlights the significant continuity of the essays, even across diverse moments of the revolutionary project. All told, this work cannot fully resolve the continued challenges (existential or practical) associated with writing the Revolution's history. Eras not fully covered here, such as the 1980s and 1990s, will eventually become the focus of historical scholarship in their own right. Still, while building on important trends evident in recent work, the transnational cohort of authors gathered here treat fresh topics and periods (the 1970s) with innovative sources. Most important, the volume affords an opportunity to assess the intersecting coordinates of an evolving field. "Revisionist," returning to an earlier point, may remain a label more easily worn by scholars outside the island. Yet we argue that the imperative, echoing the title and concerns of the book itself, does draw from scholarly mobilizations from within.

The "State" and the "People": Approaches to an Intractable Binary

Even more so than in other revolutionary histories, scholarship on the Cuban Revolution has been shaped by a top-down orientation. Persistent attention to Fidel, Che, and Raúl has tended to ossify their own political and ideological trajectories, though more recent biographies—including of the Revolution's leading women—point in more dynamic and nuanced directions.[60] Nevertheless, far less attention has been afforded to other state and popular actors. Several essays in this volume revisit and repopulate the history of the revolutionary state, drawing on insights from other revolutionary and Latin American contexts. Overall, they revivify the early years of revolutionary state formation, restoring the essential dynamism of this process, rescripting overdetermined outcomes (e.g., the state as leviathan), and framing it around a broader cast of characters.

Lillian Guerra's essay, for example, captures revolutionary master narratives at a pivotal moment in their elaboration, as *sierra* leaders acted out their relationship to Cuba's past for the eyes of Andrew St. George, a foreign journalist embedded with their troops. In order to garner popular support for their movement, revolutionaries began to act—the word is no coincidence—like a state: functional and socially responsible governance constructed as a deliberate, if sometimes vague, palimpsest of broken promises past. The result was a highly intertextual, if still incipient, "official discourse," which glossed distant and proximate Cuban history as the justification for its righteousness.

If Guerra allows us to see revolutionary leaders constructing an image of the state before it existed as such, other contributors seek to broaden our understanding of the Cuban state beyond the small inner circle that tends to draw the most attention. Several essays explore a variety of intermediate actors more rarely foregrounded in accounts of the Revolution's formative decades, including "everyday citizens," however difficult their perspectives might be to access. How, authors ask, did state bureaucrats and average Cubans conceive of their roles in extending state programs? What kind of agency did they exercise?

Building on the case study approach of some of her earlier work, María del Pilar Díaz Castañón captures the heterogeneous constituency that, in early 1959, positioned itself in enthusiastic support of agrarian reform. Industrialists, business owners, and even schoolchildren pooled their *centavos* to deliver a vote of confidence to the reformist politics of early 1959. Yet the very breadth of support spoke equally to the undefined character of the revolutionary project itself, a perhaps intentional vagueness that had characterized the 26th of July Movement since its battles in the mountains. Soon, it would founder over inevitable differences; as Díaz Castañón notes, "What was possible for some was not possible for others."

In a similar vein, Reinaldo Funes Monzote's essay draws our attention to one professional bloc of note: the geographers who, led by the revolutionary stalwart Antonio Núñez Jiménez, seized on the political opening afforded by 1959 to advance their own programs for managing and transforming the natural environment. The project of "geotransformation," as it was known, condensed multiple prerevolutionary academic conversations into a mandate for state action. Though many of these plans never came to fruition, they point not only to the weight of the revolutionary state (Núñez Jiménez was, ultimately, a close collaborator of Fidel Castro's) but also the stage it provided for other professional and social goals.

In the face of hyperpoliticization, then, no simple binary between the "state" and the "people" can be sustained. Rather, the volume's contributors invite us to consider how a variety of actors—bureaucrats, ordinary citizens, and semi-autonomous institutions—conceived of and responded to their interpellation by an increasingly powerful state. Solely reliant on neither consent nor coercion, revolutionary governance, they insist, drew from a potent mixture of both. A more robust analysis of the interaction between state and populace productively moves us away from notions of popular irrationality, blanket repression, or "charisma" as the sources of revolutionary longevity and instead highlights mechanisms of incorporation, experimentation, and co-optation, as well as disagreement and divergence.

As the Revolution began to radicalize, there were growing numbers of Cubans who found themselves located outside new state imaginaries. The discursive (and actual) violence of exclusion was the necessary counterpart to the task of popular incorporation, as some Cubans found their place in the new revolutionary state by questioning, informing on, and rejecting those believed not to belong. As Abel Sierra Madero argues in his essay, this interplay culminated in the 1980 Mariel boatlift, a mass exodus of 125,000 Cubans who would be stigmatized by both Cuban officials and their Miami counterparts. Sierra Madero invites us to consider how the Mariel boatlift actualized these reciprocal processes of inclusion and exclusion, conscripting some to act out the state's long-established rejection of homosexuals, political nonconformists, and those who simply wished to leave. As it became ritualized and centralized in the moment of the boatlift, the "acto de repudio" brought together a number of exclusionary discourses and practices of decades past, from a "dehumanizing" discourse of "animality" to masculinist and homophobic national imaginaries.

A Cultural History of the Cuban Revolution

Few groups more vividly confronted the interplay between inclusive and exclusive state practices and discourses than those writers, artists, and creators who found themselves swept up in the new state's embrace—with some forcibly located outside of it. It is no wonder, then, that studies of literature, film, theater, and the arts constitute an enduring area of emphasis within the historiography on the Revolution produced thus far. Yet for all of the revolutionary government's efforts to simultaneously expand arts education and reward "folklore" with patronage, revolutionary officials tended to preserve an elitist definition of *la cultura*, referring less to a mission of popular inclusion than to an ideologically charged sphere of intellectual endeavor. In general, subsequent scholarship has followed suit.[61]

Challenging this division between "high" and "low" culture as it played out after 1959, Elizabeth Schwall explores the counterpoint between two forms of dance: ballet, which is aristocratic in its origins, and cabaret, conceived of as crass and commercial. Under the guidance of the Alonso family, ballet famously morphed into an emblem of the Revolution's sophistication at home and abroad. Cabaret, by contrast, could be dismissed as a curious holdover from times past. By looking on and off stage, however, Schwall elucidates how dancers in both genres not only changed choreographic content to be relevant to the new political order but also forged spaces for "conspicuous and inconspicuous dissent."

Contributors to this volume likewise gesture toward the importance of the state-controlled "culture industries" in which many artists labored, building on Cuba's status as a modern media space prior to 1959. Alejandra Bronfman and Yeidy Rivero, for example, have historicized the precocious development of radio and television, respectively, during the republican period.[62] Scholars like José Quiroga and Lillian Guerra have also studied officials' use of these and other media after the revolutionary triumph.[63] Guerra's contribution to this volume provides a bridge in this respect, exploring how guerrilla insurgents of the 26th of July Movement mobilized foreign and domestic media to galvanize a broader audience of supporters.

Michael J. Bustamante draws our to attention to a later moment in the revolutionary state's evolving self-representation, when the origin stories of political leaders reached a peak of retrospective simplification. Such pronouncements found ubiquitous, if imperfect, analogues in a broader landscape of "memory surplus," composed of museums, films, and writings celebrating an epic struggle that, by many measures, appeared complete. Bustamante also asks whether commemorative excess turned once seductive master narratives into stale bromides, absent fresh struggles to revive earlier ambitions.

In dialogue with this introduction, both Guerra and Bustamante thus chart how the Revolution's claims to historical predetermination evolved over time and in dialogue with changing political, economic, and social realities. Ultimately, they argue, the production of official histories was never the result of a perfectly controlled conspiracy. While increasingly channeled over the 1960s and 1970s through prescriptive ideological filters, historical knowledge remained the messy outcome of diverse institutions, players, and the publics with whom they interacted. But what role, exactly, did the "public" play in this process?

We know much less about the everyday cultural practices, lifeways, and beliefs of ordinary Cubans—in short, the social universe beyond official politicization. In her essay, María A. Cabrera Arús begins to point us in tantalizing directions in her analysis of consumer options and discourses in the 1970s, at the high point of Cuban state socialism. How, she asks, did state officials and intermediate agents navigate integration into the socialist bloc in the early 1970s, with all of the challenges it seemed to offer to material practices and ideological policies of the previous decade? She suggests that they did so in contradictory yet generative ways: celebrating the technological possibilities afforded by the Soviet model while continuing to vaunt Cuba's national material traditions. Yet both groups struggled to reconcile the economic stratification that greater plenty seemed to imply, given the emphasis on egalitarian scarcity throughout the 1960s. Ultimately, it was ordinary Cubans who were left to navigate the material realities and contradictions of "socialist modernity."

In their efforts to pluralize and nuance our vision of the revolutionary experience, these essays turn to a number of novel source bases, some previously unexplored and others read newly against the grain. Since state archives have yet to be declassified in any significant way, new histories of the Cuban Revolution have relied, per Jorge Macle Cruz, on "interviews, personal experiences, existing publications, memoirs, speeches, the press, and inferences." As Macle Cruz argues in his contribution, efforts to further historicize the Revolution necessarily depend on initiatives within the island's archival sector, as librarians, archivists, and preservationists advocate for broader access to and coordination of state records. Several authors in this collection likewise wrestle with the consequences of restricted archival access and availability. Yet there is much, these essays show, that can be written and imagined from alternative sources: the dancing body, popular fashion, and, in our own work, mental hospitals and the ephemera of exile.[64] More than fodder for well-worn polemics, new archives can fundamentally alter our understanding of the Revolution, prying it open and reimagining it from the perspective of a broader range of actors and experiences.[65]

In the rush for novelty, however, we ought not discard the significant insights that can be gleaned from the Revolution's own published archive: the many (often unread) pages and issues of official newspapers, magazines, and bulletins. Throughout her published work, Díaz Castañón has worked to historicize and contextualize the press in the transition to Revolution. Here she carries that spirit to a little remembered campaign in support of agrarian reform transacted in the pages of *Bohemia*, Cuba's popular weekly. Other contributors read critically revolutionary imaginaries as they appeared in museums, the press, media campaigns, and even the arts, unearthing the silences and ambiguities built into the most official of official discourses.

Yet even at the highest levels of state policy, there are dimensions of the revolutionary experience that remain opaque to historical understanding. Christabelle Peters offers a novel mode of entry into such questions in her essay on Che Guevara's African experience. She revisits, and recasts, one of the archetypal "great men" of the Cuban Revolution through the prism of an imagined, albeit historically plausible conversation between him and Tanzanian president Julius Nyerere in 1964. What, she asks, might this tantalizing episode tell us about Che's political evolution—and Cuba's own African "shadow" life? How did dreams forged in the spirit of unbounded imagination founder on realities of continued racial exclusion at home and geopolitical impossibility? And, most important, how do we write through, around, and across the archival silences that might be forever closed?

Cuba's (Revolutionary) Exceptionality?

Peters's essay notably points us toward another enduring problematic in the literature on the Cuban Revolution: the question of exceptionality. Cuba's Revolution has sometimes been cast as a sui generis, uncategorizable phenomenon, but also (paradoxically) as a pale imitation of any number of socialist and revolutionary models with which it interacted: Russia, China, Vietnam, and more. What happens, then, when we place Cuba in dialogue with other trajectories and examine concrete paths of connection? What common thematic concerns emerge from historicizing the ties between Cuba and other sites? A historiographical orientation to "within" hardly means seeing Cuba as hermetically sealed. It also requires engaging the external influences, reference points, and international events that shaped the revolutionary everyday. From the Cold War to decolonization, the Revolution was bound up in some of the most important geopolitical transitions of the period.

Peters offers a novel response to this debate in inviting us to consider linkages, philosophical more than diplomatic, between revolutionary Latin America and decolonizing Africa. Ada Ferrer, meanwhile, orients us to a similarly plural mode of analysis, placing the vicissitudes of Cuba's revolutionary experiment alongside those of Haiti, the "other" revolutionary island and a specter that had long haunted Cuban history (and historiography). In tracing connections between these paradigm-shifting Caribbean revolutions, Ferrer draws comparisons related to the "revolutionary situation" of both islands, the geopolitical consequences of their revolutions, the politics of race and blackness, and the mutual and sometimes symbiotic attraction of Haiti and Cuba for political dissidents all over the hemisphere. She also considers the imaginative links forged between these two cases by authors, intellectuals, and the Caribbean's towering historian of revolution, C. L. R. James, after 1959.

Overall, however, this volume takes the history of the Cuban Revolution largely on its own terms, with an emphasis on internal revolutionary processes. The volume thus self-consciously forgoes the kind of great power, Cold War intrigue that has long structured debates about Cuba's revolution. Where anxious U.S. politicians and functionaries might have once occupied a starring role, Peters points to lateral South–South connections and the impact of decolonizing Africa on Che's ideological vision. The Soviet Union certainly appears here, too, but less as an imperial patron than as a source of fashion and material inspiration, as analyzed by Cabrera Arús.

And yet these essays are deeply invested in the question—or problem—of Cuba's exceptionality. Several contributors, including Alejandro de la Fuente and Rafael Rojas, consider just how different post-1959 Cuba was vis-à-vis its *own* prerevolutionary history. Is the Cuban Revolution largely a story of rupture or of continuity? Has post–Special Period Cuba reverted to the ignominious economic and social circumstances of the pre-revolutionary past? Was the difference from that past ever as great as revolutionary leaders claimed it to be? To answer questions about singularity, authors turn to other paradigm-shifting revolutions. De la Fuente, for example, offers a sustained engagement with the history and historiography of the Mexican Revolution. One point in particular stands out among the insights gleaned from the Mexican case: Cubanists, he warns, would do well to take the "coherence and effectiveness of the revolutionary state as empirical questions rather than assumptions."

In a kindred spirit, Rojas situates the problem of revolutionary exceptionality in the analytical space of historical time. Revolutions, he suggests, have long been studied as "present pasts," at once fleeting and eternal. He carries that paradox to the historical and historiographical construction of the Cuban Revolution itself. How, he asks, did it define its present through relation to its past and future? Was it two revolutions, a revolution with multiple phases, or merely the "totalizing, metahistorical" revolution stretching from the outbreak of the independence struggle all the way through the revolutionary present?

As already noted, perhaps the most influential trope informing histories of the Cuban Revolution on and off the island has been the presumption that the island's history can be understood as a function of its conflicted relationship with the United States. Faced, moreover, with the domestic archival limitations that Macle Cruz describes, it has long been easier to focus on U.S. sources that sustain this construct. Ironically, as patterns of diplomatic and economic isolation have given way in recent years to an unfolding and now fragile rapprochement, the U.S.-centric impulse has at times become, once again, the most tempting metanarrative of all. To close the volume, Jennifer Lambe offers a reflection on the contemporary stakes of historical scholarship on the Cuban Revolution in light of these developments. Diplomatic normalization with the United States after 2014, she argues, necessarily revived ancient concerns about the status of Cuban history and its archive(s). Historical narratives in all their variety—official, dissident, critical, and ambivalent—have thus become vulnerable not only to revisionism but also to external (and perhaps internal) erasure. In this regard, the project of historicizing the Revolution on its own terms is more crucial than ever.

Still, as the volume argues overall, histories of the Cuban Revolution need not cohere into a singular history. We can only imagine how the opening of new archives and sources, including those utilized by this volume's authors, may impact future debates. In their very synergies and disjunctures, these essays suggest that new historical accounts of the Revolution are necessarily composed of *histories*. Yet they will also benefit, we argue, from reflexive attention to Cuba's own analytical paradigms and understandings: historicizing the Revolution from within.

A Note on Terminology

When it comes to the Cuban Revolution, words—English, Spanish, and otherwise—are rarely innocent. The most basic categories through which we interpret Cuban history have long sparked battles along partisan and ideological lines. Take, for example, the chronological demarcations essential to any historian's work. As enshrined in a landmark two-volume publication by Cuba's Instituto de Historia (under the institutional aegis of the Communist Party), on the island the period before 1959 has come to be known as the "neocolonial" Republic, or the "shackled [*mediatizado*]," "bourgeois" Republic. Sometimes, as had previously been customary, that same period was still divided into Cuba's "First" (1902–33) and "Second" (1933–58) Republics in recognition of the wave of revolutionary upheaval that brought an end to formal (i.e., constitutional) U.S. oversight. Nonetheless it was only after 1959, with the "triumph"—another charged word—of Fidel Castro's government, that a true "Republic" was acknowledged to have been born. It perhaps goes without saying that exile chroniclers see things quite differently, alleging that 1959 (or 1960 or 1961) brought an end, not a hopeful beginning, to democratic governance on the island. Adding further complexity to the picture, the very rendering of the word "Revolution" with a capital "R," long something of a convention in the field, seems to carry ideological assumptions born of the revolutionary context.

The problem, however, runs deeper. Though we could conceivably agree to steer clear of charged words with plastic meanings—"democracy," say— scholars of the Cuban Revolution have also sparred over the term most essential to this volume's work: "revolution." As we and other contributors to this volume suggest, there is no basic agreement on whether "the Revolution" (is it even singular?) begins or ends in 1959 or how long it continues thereafter. Some, notably Rafael Rojas, have posited that the institutionalizing phase ushered in by Cuba's rapprochement with the Soviet Union marks the Revolution's terminus; others instead date it to the dissolution of that bond with the fall of the Soviet Union and the introduction of liberalizing economic measures in the 1990s. Debated as well is the degree to which the Cuban government should have a monopoly on the term—that is, whether its project, policies, and politics are the only "revolution" to which we might refer.

In recognition of our political differences, not to mention the theoretical richness provided by the same, we have opted not to impose semantic homogeneity on this volume's authors. Instead, we have encouraged them to make the terms of their own historiographical engagement as clear and rigorous as possible. This has yielded some inevitable points of disharmony and cacophony. Nonetheless, we believe that the interpretive possibilities opened up by this juxtaposition far outweigh its risks.

NOTES

1. El Escriba (pseudonym that Piñera used), "La historia de la Revolución," *Revolución*, November 11, 1959, 2.

2. Florencia Mallon, "Time on the Wheel: Cycles of Revisionism and the 'New Cultural History,'" *Hispanic American Historical Review* 79, no. 2 (1999): 332.

3. Oscar Zanetti Lecuona, "Medio siglo de historiografía en Cuba: La impronta de la Revolución," *Cuban Studies* 40 (2010): 95, 102.

4. Rafael Rojas, "La Revolución y sus historiadores," *El Nuevo Herald*, May 13, 2008, http://www.elnuevoherald.com/2008/05/13/206514/la-revolucion-y-sus-historiadores .html.

5. See, for example, Julio Rensoli Medina, ed., *La historiografía en la Revolución cubana: Reflexiones a 50 años* (Havana: Editora Historia, 2010).

6. Louis A. Pérez Jr., *The Structure of Cuban History: Meanings and Purpose of the Past* (Chapel Hill: University of North Carolina Press, 2013), 238.

7. For more on the shifting terms of revisionism, see Kate Quinn, "Cuban Historiography in the 1960s: Revisionists, Revolutionaries and the Nationalist Past," *Bulletin of Latin American Research* 26, no. 3 (2007): 378–98.

8. Revolution Square is the iconic site of official mass rallies, dating back to the 1960s and all the way through the present. The building known as the Freedom Tower, located on Biscayne Bay, was home to the U.S. government–sponsored Cuban Refugee Program in the 1960s. Today it is a national historic landmark and museum run by Miami-Dade College.

9. El Escriba, "La historia," 2.

10. Ann Komaromi, "The Material Existence of Soviet Samizdat," *Slavic Review* 63, no. 3 (2004): 609.

11. Komaromi, "The Material Existence," 618.

12. See Dipesh Chakrabarty, "History as Critique and Critique(s) of History," *Economic and Political Weekly* 26, no. 37 (1991): 2162–66.

13. For a critical history of this category, see Peter Novick, *That Noble Dream: The "Objectivity Question" and the American Historical Profession* (Cambridge: Cambridge University Press, 1988).

14. Manuel Moreno Fraginals, "La historia como arma," *Casa de las Américas*, October 1966, 21. See also Quinn, "Cuban Historiography."

15. Fraginals, "La historia como arma," 26.

16. See Quinn, "Cuban Historiography."

17. Quinn traces a similar dynamic vis-à-vis "revisionist" historians from the republic resurrected in the 1960s. See Quinn, "Cuban Historiography."

18. Blas Roca, *Los fundamentos del socialismo en Cuba* (Havana: Editorial Páginas, 1943), reprinted in 1961 and thereafter.

19. Longtime activist and intellectual Raúl Roa enacted a similar reinterpretation of previous writings in light of his new position as foreign minister in the post-1959 government. His compilation of essays *La Revolución del 30 se fue a bolina* (Havana: Instituto del Libro, 1967) redirected past writing toward a new analytical end point: that the aborted 1933 revolution against dictator Gerardo Machado, in which Roa had participated, had been "lost to the wind." He thereby advanced an influential interpretation of the 1959 Revolution as 1933's postponed fulfillment.

20. Ernesto Che Guevara, *Pasajes de la Guerra Revolucionaria* (Havana: Ediciones Unión, 1963); Antonio Núñez Jiménez, *En marcha con Fidel, 1959–1962*, vols. 1–4 (Havana: Letras Cubanas, 1982).

21. Fulgencio Batista y Zaldívar, *Cuba Betrayed* (New York: Vantage Press, 1962); Eduardo Suárez Rivas, *Los Días Iguales* (Miami: n.p., 1974).

22. Most notably, Theodore Draper, *Castro's Cuba: A Revolution Betrayed?* (New York: New Leader, 1961). See also Fermín Peinado, *Beware Yankee: The Revolution in Cuba* (Miami: n.p., 1961), a direct response to New Left intellectual C. Wright Mills's *Listen Yankee: The Revolution in Cuba* (New York: Ballantine Books, 1961). On a cognate phenomenon, see David C. Engerman, *Know Your Enemy: The Rise and Fall of America's Soviet Experts* (New York: Oxford University Press, 2009).

23. K. S. Karol, *Guerrillas in Power: The Course of the Cuban Revolution* (New York: Hill and Wang, 1970); René Dumont, *Cuba: Socialism and Development* (1964), translated by Helen R. Lane (New York: Grove Press, 1970); Maurice Halperin, *The Rise and Decline of Fidel Castro* (Berkeley: University of California Press, 1972); Edward Boorstein, *The Economic Transformation of Cuba* (New York: Monthly Review Press, 1968); Leo Huberman and Paul M. Sweezy, *Socialism in Cuba* (New York: Monthly Review Press, 1969).

24. Mills, *Listen Yankee*; Jean-Paul Sartre, *Sartre on Cuba* (New York: Ballantine Books, 1961); Leo Huberman and Paul M. Sweezy, *Cuba: Anatomy of a Revolution* (New York: Monthly Review Books, 1960).

25. Most famously, Jorge Edwards, *Persona Non Grata*, translated by Colin Harding (New York: Pomerica Press, 1973).

26. Elizabeth Sutherland, *The Youngest Revolution: A Personal Report on Cuba* (New York: Dial Press, 1969); José Yglesias, *In the Fist of the Revolution: Life in a Cuban Country*

Town (New York: Vintage Books, 1969). Caribbean and Latin American writers also offered several nuanced portraits. See Andrew Salkey, *Havana Journal* (New York: Penguin Press, 1971); Ernesto Cardenal, *In Cuba* (1972), translated by Donald D. Walsh (New York: New Directions, 1974).

27. Teresa Casuso, *Cuba and Castro* (New York: Random House, 1961); Carlos Moore, "Le peuple noir a-t-il sa place dans la Révolution cubaine," *Presence Africaine* 22 (December 1964): 177–230; Rufo López Fresquet, *My Fourteen Months with Fidel Castro* (New York: World, 1966); Mario Llerena, *The Unsuspected Revolution: The Birth and Rise of Castroism* (Ithaca, NY: Cornell University Press, 1978); Carlos Franqui, *Retrato de familia con Fidel* (Barcelona: Seix Barral, 1981); Carlos Moore, *Castro, the Blacks, and Africa* (Los Angeles: UCLA Center for African-American Studies, 1988); Heberto Padilla, *La mala memoria* (Barcelona: Plaza y Janes, 1989).

28. Cubanists are hardly the first to confront this problematic. Some of the works that have shaped our thinking on kindred historiographies include Nancy Whittier Heer, *Politics and History in the Soviet Union* (Cambridge, MA: MIT Press, 1971); Sheila Fitzpatrick, "Russia's Twentieth Century in History and Historiography," *Australian Journal of Politics and History* 46, no. 3 (2000): 378–87; Steve J. Stern, "Between Tragedy and Promise: The Politics of Writing Latin American History in the Late Twentieth Century," in *Reclaiming the Political in Latin American History*, edited by Gilbert Joseph (Durham, NC: Duke University Press, 2001), 32–77; Lynne Viola, "The Cold War in American Soviet Historiography and the End of the Soviet Union," *Russian Review* 61, no. 1 (2002): 25–34; David W. Blight, *American Oracle: The Civil War in the Civil Rights Era* (Cambridge, MA: Harvard University Press, 2011). In his contribution to this volume, Alejandro de la Fuente considers similar questions in the case of the Mexican Revolution. Since the 1990s, historians of Chile have mobilized to confront this problematic as it played out in the public sphere. See, for example, the "Manifiesto de historiadores" (Santiago, Chile, January 1999; available at http://www.archivochile.com/Ceme/recup _memoria/cememem00003.pdf), written to combat false and "manipulative" interpretations of Chile's recent authoritarian past. We are grateful to Tim Lorek for suggesting this reference.

29. Richard Fagen, *The Transformation of Political Culture in Cuba* (Stanford: Stanford University Press, 1968).

30. Oscar Lewis, Ruth M. Lewis, and Susan M. Rigdon, *Four Men: Living the Revolution: An Oral History of Contemporary Cuba* (Urbana: University of Illinois Press, 1977); Oscar Lewis, Ruth M. Lewis, and Susan M. Rigdon, *Four Women: Living the Revolution: An Oral History of Contemporary Cuba* (Urbana: University of Illinois Press, 1977); Douglas Butterworth, *The People of Buenaventura: Relocation of Slum Dwellers in Post-Revolutionary Cuba* (Urbana: University of Illinois Press, 1980).

31. For example, Jorge I. Domínguez, *Cuba: Order and Revolution* (Cambridge, MA: Belknap Press, 1979); Carmelo Mesa-Lago, *Cuba in the 1970s: Pragmatism and Institutionalization* (Albuquerque: University of New Mexico Press, 1979); Carmelo Mesa-Lago, *The Economy of Socialist Cuba: A Two-Decade Appraisal* (Albuquerque: University of New Mexico Press, 1985); Marifeli Pérez-Stable, *The Cuban Revolution: Origins, Course, Legacy* (New York: Oxford University Press, 1993).

32. For helpful early representations of the state of the field, its early contributors, and its diversity, see María Cristina Herrera, ed., "Temática cubana: Primera reunión de estudios cubanos," special issue of *Exilio: Revista Trimestral* 3, nos. 2–3, 4, no. 1 (1969–70): 279; Lourdes Casal, "The Development of Cuban Studies in the US," *Latin American Research Review* 13, no. 1 (1978): 248–54. Another topic of early work in this vein was revolutionary literature and the arts. For an early historicist take, see Seymour Menton, *Prose Fiction of the Cuban Revolution* (Austin: University of Texas Press, 1975). For another important, interdisciplinary account, see Rolando E. Bonachea and Nelson P. Valdés, eds., *Cuba in Revolution* (Garden City, NY: Anchor, 1972).

33. Lillian Guerra, "Former Slum Dwellers, the Communist Youth, and the Lewis Project in Cuba, 1969–1971," *Cuban Studies* 43 (2015): 67–89.

34. Louis Morton, "National Security and Area Studies: The Intellectual Response to the Cold War," *Journal of Higher Education* 34, no. 3 (1963): 142–47; Helen Dapar, *Looking South: The Evolution of Latin Americanist Scholarship in the United States* (Tuscaloosa: University of Alabama Press, 2008), 129–83.

35. Enrique Baloyra, "Side Effects: Cubanology and Its Critics," *Latin American Research Review* 22, no. 1 (1987): 265–74; José Luis Rodríguez García, *Crítica a nuestros críticos* (Havana: Editorial Ciencias Sociales, 1988); René Márquez, *Cubanología y Revolución* (Havana: Editorial Ciencias Sociales, 2006).

36. María Cristina Hererra founded the Instituto de Estudios Cubanos in Miami in 1969. The publication in 1970 of the first *Boletín de Estudios sobre Cuba*, which would become the journal *Cuban Studies* in 1974, marked another milestone. *Areíto*, also debuting in 1974, gathered together a cohort of younger Cuban American academics and activists who expressed more open admiration for Cuban socialism and traveled to the island in the 1970s. Meetings and scholarly exchanges between scholars linked to each of these circles (at times overlapping) and colleagues on the island were particularly active during windows of U.S.-Cuba détente, most notably during the Carter administration.

37. For a retrospective look, see Damián Fernández, ed., *Cuban Studies since the Revolution* (Gainesville: University Press of Florida, 1992).

38. Much like Theodore Draper in the United States, British historian Hugh Thomas, author of the iconic 1971 book *Cuba: Or the Pursuit of Freedom*, is a key if complicated point of departure for subsequent work on the Revolution. A small sample of relevant authors, some of them Cuban-born, would include Velia Cecilia Bobes, Karen Dubinsky, Julio César Guanche, Jennifer Ruth Hosek, Menja Holtz, Antoni Kapcia, John M. Kirk, Hal Klepak, Gordon Lewis, Sergio López Rivero, Anthony Maingot, Brian Meeks, Vanni Pettinà, Simon Reid-Henry, Rafael Rojas, Mona Rosendahl, Jean Stubbs, Claudia Wasserman, and Michael Zeuske. The "Memories of the Cuban Revolution" oral history project, directed by Elizabeth Dore at the University of Southampton, represents an important successor to the Oscar Lewis Project.

39. Morris H. Morley, *Imperial State and Revolution: The United States and Cuba, 1952–1986* (Cambridge: Cambridge University Press, 1989); Thomas G. Paterson, *Contesting Castro: The United States and the Triumph of the Cuban Revolution* (New York: Oxford University Press, 1994).

40. Scholars also turned their attention to the formation of the Cuban exile (eventually "Cuban American") community in the United States. In part this was driven by unavoidable evidence of that community's permanence. But for many pioneers of Cuban Studies who were Cuban American themselves, the fraught process of engaging with the island also fueled an inverse desire to come to terms with their own identities and histories. For an influential early text, see Lourdes Casal and Rafael Prohías, *The Cuban Minority in the U.S.: Preliminary Report on Need Identification and Program Evaluation* (Boca Raton: Florida Atlantic University, 1973).

41. For a survey of this literature and its relationship to the Special Period context, see Ricardo Quiza, "Historiografía y Revolución: La 'nueva' oleada de historiadores cubanos," *Millars* 33 (2010): 127–42. Seminal studies in this vein include Louis A. Pérez Jr., *On Becoming Cuban: Identity, Nationality, and Culture* (Chapel Hill: University of North Carolina Press, 1999); Marial Iglesias Utset, *A Cultural History of Cuba during the U.S. Occupation, 1898–1902* (2003), translated by Russ Davidson (Chapel Hill: University of North Carolina Press, 2011). The literature is too vast to fully cite here. See the scholarship of Robert Whitney, Lillian Guerra, Jana K. Lipman, Ricardo Quiza Moreno, K. Lynn Stoner, Alejandra Bronfman, Barry Carr, Robin Moore, Reinaldo Román, Maikel Fariñas Borrego, Melina Pappademos, Rolando Rodríguez, Newton Briones Montoto, Steven Palmer, José Antonio Piqueras, and Amparo Sánchez Cobos. These scholars' work often built on, or existed in tension with, the corpus of Cuba's foremost historian of the Republic, Jorge Ibarra Cuesta; see, for example, *Un análisis psicosocial del cubano, 1898–1925* (Havana: Editorial Ciencias Sociales, 1985).

42. For instance, Gilbert M. Joseph, Catherine C. LeGrand, and Ricardo D. Salvatore, eds., *Close Encounters of Empire: Writing the Cultural History of U.S.–Latin American Relations* (Durham, NC: Duke University Press, 1998).

43. For example, Sujatha Fernandes, *Cuba Represent! Cuban Arts, State Power, and the Making of New Revolutionary Cultures* (Durham, NC: Duke University Press, 2006); Ariana Hernández-Reguant, ed., *Cuba in the Special Period: Culture and Ideology in the 1990s* (New York: Palgrave Macmillan, 2009). On race, gender, sexuality, and inequality in the Special Period and contemporary Cuba, see the scholarship of Nadine Fernández, Jafari Allen, Kenneth Routon, Noelle Stout, Tanya L. Saunders, Megan Daigle, Katrin Hansing, and Marc D. Perry. Much of this anthropological work has emerged from outside Cuba, though sociologists and other academics trained on the island have also taken up similar themes. See, for example, the work of Mayra Espina, Pedro Monreal, Julio Carranza, Roberto Zurbano, Víctor Fowler, Juan Valdés Paz, Haroldo Dilla Alfonso, Sandra Abd'Allah-Alvarez Ramírez, the team of economists at the Centro de Estudios sobre la Economía Cubana (University of Havana), and the collective of journalists behind Periodismo de Barrio. Cuban publications and institutions like the Centro de Estudios sobre las Américas (closed in 1996), *Revista Temas* (supported by the Ministry of Culture since 1995), *Espacio Laical* (published by the Catholic Church since 2005), and *Cuba Posible* (an independent digital outlet founded in 2015) have provided important forums for debates on a range of issues in contemporary Cuban political and social life.

44. Julia E. Sweig, *Inside the Cuban Revolution: Fidel Castro and the Urban Underground* (Cambridge, MA: Harvard University Press, 2002); Samuel Farber, *Origins of the Cuban*

Revolution Reconsidered (Chapel Hill: University of North Carolina Press, 2006); Steve Cushion, *A Hidden History of the Cuban Revolution: How the Working Class Shaped the Guerrilla Victory* (New York: Monthly Review Press, 2016). See also Ricardo Quiza Moreno, "Sujetos olvidados: Los trabajadores en la historiografía cubana," in *La historiografía en la Revolución cubana: Reflexiones a 50 años*, edited by Rolando Julio Rensoli Medina (Havana: Editorial Historia, 2010), 313–47.

45. María del Pilar Díaz Castañón, *Ideologia y Revolución: Cuba, 1959–1962* (Havana: Editorial Ciencias Sociales, 2001), and *Prensa y Revolución: La magia del cambio* (Havana: Editorial Ciencias Sociales, 2010).

46. Alejandro de la Fuente, *A Nation for All: Race, Inequality, and Politics in Twentieth-Century Cuba* (Chapel Hill: University of North Carolina Press, 2001); Lillian Guerra, *Visions of Power in Cuba: Revolution, Redemption, and Resistance, 1959–1971* (Chapel Hill: University of North Carolina Press, 2012).

47. See Abel Sierra Madero, *Del otro lado del espejo: La sexualidad en la construcción de la nación cubana* (Havana: Fondo Editorial Casa de las Américas, 2006); Pedro Marqués de Armas, *Ciencia y poder en Cuba: Racismo, homofobia, nación (1790–1970)* (Madrid: Editorial Verbum, 2014); Michelle Chase, *Revolution within the Revolution: Women and Gender Politics in Cuba, 1952–1962* (Chapel Hill: University of North Carolina Press, 2015); Carrie Hamilton, *Sexual Revolutions in Cuba: Passion, Politics, and Memory* (Chapel Hill: University of North Carolina Press, 2012); Rachel Hynson, "'Count, Capture, and Reeducate': The Campaign to Rehabilitate Cuba's Female Sex Workers, 1959–1966," *Journal of the History of Sexuality* 24, no. 1 (2015): 125–53; Devyn Spence Benson, *Antiracism in Cuba: The Unfinished Revolution* (Chapel Hill: University of North Carolina Press, 2016); Jennifer Lambe, *Madhouse: Psychiatry and Politics in Cuban History* (Chapel Hill: University of North Carolina Press, 2017). See also Marvin Leiner, *Sexual Politics in Cuba: Machismo, Homosexuality, and AIDS* (Boulder, CO: Westview Press, 1994); Lois M. Smith and Alfred Padula, *Sex and Revolution in Socialist Cuba* (New York: Oxford University Press, 1996); Christine Ayorinde, *Afro-Cuban Religiosity, Revolution, and National Identity* (Gainesville: University Press of Florida, 2004).

48. See Ambroso Fornet, "Quinquenio Gris: Revisitando el término," *Revista Casa de las Américas* 246 (January–March 2007): 3–16.

49. For example, Antón Arrufat, *Virgilio Piñera: Entre él y yo* (Havana: Ediciones Unión, 1995); Eliseo Alberto, *Informe contra mi mismo* (Madrid: Alfaguara, 2002); Raúl Martínez, *Yo Publio: Confesiones de Raúl Martínez* (Havana: Artecubano, 2007); Graziella Pogolotti, *Dinosauria soy: Memorias* (Havana: Ediciones Unión, 2011).

50. Carlos Velazco and Elizabeth Mirabal, *Sobre los pasos del cronista: El quehacer intelectual de Guillermo Cabrera Infante en Cuba hasta 1965* (Havana: Ediciones Unión, 2010); Carlos Velazco and Elizabeth Mirabal, *Hablar de Guillermo Rosales* (Miami: Editorial Silueta, 2013); Jorge Fornet, *El 71: Anatomía de una crisis* (Havana: Editorial Letras Cubanas, 2014). Additional scholarship on revolutionary cultural, intellectual, and literary politics is extensive. See the work of Michael Chanan, Robin D. Moore, Ana Serra, Esther Whitfield, Kepa Artaraz, Duanel Díaz, Luciano Castillo, Jacqueline Loss, Jorge Olivares, Alexandra Vázquez, Odette Casamayor Cisneros, Humberto Manduley López,

Guillermina De Ferrari, Pedro Porbén, Rebecca Gordon-Nesbitt, and Juan Antonio García Borrero, among others.

51. See, in particular, Rafael Rojas, *Tumbas sin sosiego: Revolución, disidencia, y exilio del intelectual cubano* (Barcelona: Editorial Anagrama, 2006), and *Fighting over Fidel: The New York Intellectuals and the Cuban Revolution*, translated by Carl Good (Princeton, NJ: Princeton University Press, 2016).

52. For a survey of these developments, see Felipe de J. Pérez Cruz, "Los estudios sobre la Revolución cubana," *Revista Calibán* 16 (May–August 2013), http://www.revistacaliban .cu/articulo.php?article_id=169&numero=16/.

53. See "Díaz Canel por mayor estudio de la historia de la Revolución," *Radio Rebelde*, October 14, 2015, http://www.radiorebelde.cu/noticia/diaz-canel-por-mayor-estudio -historia-revolucion-20151014/.

54. Tania Chappi Docurro, "Escudriñando la historia de la Revolución," *Temas*, February 7, 2014, http://www.temas.cult.cu/ultimo-jueves/escudri-ando-la-historia-de -la-revoluci-n; Tania Chappi Docurro, "Los años 70," *Temas*, August 3, 2015, http://www .temas.cult.cu/ultimo-jueves/los-os-70; *Luneta no. 1*, directed by Rebeca Chávez (Havana: ICAIC, 2012); *Los amagos de Saturno*, directed by Rosario Alfonso Parodi (2014).

55. Fernando Martínez Heredia, "¿Cómo investigar la Revolución cubana?" [two parts], *La Tizza*, March 17 and April 10, 2018, https://medium.com/la-tiza/c%C3%B3mo -investigar-la-revoluci%C3%B3n-cubana-i-2d5a9c18ce7a; https://medium.com/la-tiza /c%C3%B3mo-investigar-la-revoluci%C3%B3n-cubana-ii-7d9b7728346e.

56. See, for example, Michel-Rolph Trouillot, *Haiti: State against Nation: The Origins and Legacy of Duvalierism* (New York: Monthly Review Press, 1990); Richard Turits, *Foundations of Despotism: Peasants, the Trujillo Regime, and Modernity in Dominican History* (Stanford: Stanford University Press, 2003); Mariano Plotkin, *Mañana es San Perón: A Cultural History of Perón's Argentina* (Wilmington, DE: Scholarly Resources, 2003); Robin Derby, *The Dictator's Seduction: Politics and the Popular Imagination in the Era of Trujillo* (Durham, NC: Duke University Press, 2009); Matthew B. Karush and Oscar Chamosa, eds., *The New Cultural History of Peronism: Power and Identity in Mid-Twentieth-Century Argentina* (Durham, NC: Duke University Press, 2010).

57. Scholarship in the former vein is extensive. For a few examples, see Veronique Garros, Thomas Lahusen, and Carol A. Flath, eds., *Intimacy and Terror: Soviet Diaries of the 1930s* (New York: New Press, 1997); Sheila Fitzpatrick, *Everyday Stalinism: Ordinary Life in Extraordinary Times* (New York: Oxford University Press, 2000); Alexei Yurchak, *Everything Was Forever, Until It Was No More: The Last Soviet Generation* (Princeton, NJ: Princeton University Press, 2005); Christina Kiaer and Eric Naiman, eds., *Everyday Life in Early Soviet Russia: Taking the Revolution Inside* (Bloomington: Indiana University Press, 2006); Irina Paperno, *Stories of the Soviet Experience: Memoirs, Diaries, Dreams* (Ithaca, NY: Cornell University Press, 2009). A few historians of the Soviet Union have begun to take up grassroots Cuba-Soviet connections in a serious way; see, for example, Anne Gorsuch, "'Cuba, My Love': The Romance of Revolutionary Cuba in the Soviet Sixties," *American Historical Review* 120, no. 2 (2015): 497–526. In the latter vein, see Laura Engelstein, "Combined Underdevelopment: Discipline and the Law in Imperial and Soviet Russia," in *Foucault and the Writing of History*, edited by Jan Goldstein (Oxford:

Blackwell, 1994); Stephen J. Collier, *Post-Soviet Social: Neoliberalism, Social Modernity, Biopolitics* (Princeton, NJ: Princeton University Press, 2011); Christos Lynteris, *The Spirit of Selflessness in Maoist China: Socialist Medicine and the New Man* (New York: Palgrave Macmillan, 2013); Sergei Prozorov, "Foucault and Soviet Biopolitics," *History of the Human Sciences* 27, no. 5 (2014): 6–25.

58. See Sierra Madero, *Del otro lado del espejo*; Marqués de Armas, *Ciencia y poder*; Lambe, *Madhouse*.

59. For a recent exception, see Emily Kirk, Anna Clayfield, and Isabel Story, eds., *Cuba's Forgotten Decade: How the 1970s Shaped the Revolution* (Lanham, MD: Rowman and Littlefield, 2018).

60. Jon Lee Anderson, *Che Guevara: A Revolutionary Life* (New York: Grove Press, 1997); Fidel Castro and Ignacio Ramonet, *Fidel Castro, My Life: A Spoken Autobiography*, translated by Andrew Hurley (New York: Scribner, 2007); Nancy Stout, *One Day in December: Celia Sánchez and the Cuban Revolution* (New York: Monthly Review Press, 2013); Margaret Randall, *Haydée Santamaría: Cuban Revolutionary* (Durham, NC: Duke University Press, 2015).

61. Exceptions include Ayorinde, *Afro-Cuban Religiosity*; Maya J. Berry, "From 'Ritual' to 'Repertoire': Dancing to the Time of the Nation," *Afro-Hispanic Review* 29, no. 1 (2010): 55–76.

62. Alejandra Bronfman, "'Batista Is Dead': Media, Violence, and Politics in 1950s Cuba," *Caribbean Studies* 40, no. 1 (2012): 37–58; Yeidy Rivero, *Broadcasting Modernity: Cuban Commercial Television, 1950–1960* (Durham, NC: Duke University Press, 2015).

63. José Quiroga, *Cuban Palimpsests* (Minneapolis: University of Minnesota Press, 2005); Guerra, *Visions of Power*.

64. See Lambe, *Madhouse*; Jennifer L. Lambe, "A Century of Work: Reconstructing Mazorra (1857–1959)," *Cuban Studies* 43 (2015): 90–118; Michael Bustamante, "Cuban Counterpoints: Memory Struggles in Revolution and Exile," PhD diss., Yale University, 2016, and "Anti-Communist Anti-Imperialism? Agrupación Abdala and the Shifting Contours of Cuban Exile Politics, 1968–1986," *Journal of American Ethnic History* 35, no. 1 (2015): 71–99.

65. For further insights into this problematic, see Martínez Heredia, "¿Cómo investigar la Revolución cubana?"

2. The New Text of the Revolution

RAFAEL ROJAS

To historicize a revolution, as the French historian François Furet asserts, is to consider how the process inaugurates its own contemporary moment, whether in France or the United States, Russia or Mexico, China or Nicaragua.[1] Few other social phenomena demand that the historian take on the role of both critic and philosopher. In its origins, revolution is an astronomical term, related to accelerated movement in space and time. But it also describes the dynamism of regime change, one in which no realm of social life is left untouched. As such, historical studies of revolutions must treat them as both abstractions and concrete realities. Put another way, it is precisely within revolutions where dreams and terror most clearly converge, or, in the words of Reinhart Koselleck, the "space of experience" and the "horizon of expectations" find themselves in a certain "tension."[2]

Since the romanticist historiography of the mid-nineteenth century, revolutions have been studied as present pasts. Whether for realist and liberal philosophers and thinkers, like Jules Michelet and Alexis de Tocqueville, or their critics, such as Karl Marx and Friedrich Nietzsche, revolution entailed a paradoxical ephemerality and permanence.[3] The irony of the ancien régime's persistence, in Tocqueville, or the idea of history's repetition, first as tragedy and then as farce, in Hegel and Marx, constitute similar ways of understanding the revolutionary event as alternatively past and present, or living and dead time. The revolution's afterlife, following the old regime's destruction and the new one's creation, did not have to do solely with the inner workings of memory but also with institutional operations and the reproduction of the revolution's values, discourses, and practices, more broadly.

Among all of the modern revolutions, Cuba's proposed perhaps the most sustained equivalence between the general concept of revolution and other distinct notions, like the fatherland (*patria*), the nation, or socialism. This resonance has provoked an identification of sorts between the lifespan and everyday realities of the Revolution and those of the state, the Communist Party, and the revolutionary government. The fact that the socialist state has remained in the hands of two leaders of the armed insurgency against the Fulgencio Batista dictatorship, together with the half century of conflict with the United States, has reinforced these semantic linkages, further strengthened by the intense socializing effects of repeated words and symbols over time. This inculcation of a symbolic field did not take place to the same degree in other revolutions, at least not during the twentieth century—in the Bolshevik or Mexican revolutions, for example. In those cases, the term "revolution" itself began to loosen its grip two or three decades after its triumph.

How have past and current interpretations of the Cuban Revolution navigated the fact of this equivalence? As this essay explores, they have done so by revisiting the terms, chronology, and ideological presumptions of official narratives. The new historiography of the Cuban Revolution departs from a homogeneous and changeless image of the period after 1959, while, at the same time, emphasizing the complexity of the old republican regime. In this way, historians have offered a vision of Cuba's revolution that is not timeless but firmly anchored in time, and resolutely plural at that.

"Revolution" Singular or "Revolutions" Plural?

The historiographical debate around the Cuban Revolution has passed through many of the same benchmarks as modern thinking about revolutions since the nineteenth century. During the first three decades of the revolutionary period, from the 1960s through the 1980s, while the new social order was being institutionalized, historical writing on and off the island echoed the ideological and political conflicts produced by the transition to socialism. The government's official documents and authorized historiography instituted a simplistic, binary account that was reproduced in the media as well as in basic and advanced texts for teaching national history. The exile community's propaganda and a good part of the Western, anticommunist historiography articulated, for their part, a countertale, equally black-and-white, that clashed with the official history of the island. These narratives rested on a degree of internal consensus between two political groups that found themselves on opposing sides of the Cold War.

Since the early years following the revolutionary victory in January 1959, distinct historical and theoretical interpretations of the Revolution and its transition to socialism appeared from within the revolutionary government and the island's intellectual and academic communities. Despite their profoundly different approaches to political economy and the Eastern European socialist bloc, Marxist leaders like Carlos Rafael Rodríguez and Ernesto "Che" Guevara coincided on the fact that the Cuban Revolution had gravitated during the insurrection against the Batista dictatorship from a pluralistic movement and politics toward a nationalist revolutionary ideology, neither Marxist-Leninist nor communist. In 1960 both sides converged on the idea of a "transition to socialism," implying either a separation between two phases of one revolution or two distinct revolutions, one that triumphed in January 1959 and another in April 1961, when the arrival of Cuban "socialism" was publicly announced.[4]

Rodríguez would label these two phases of the revolution as, first, "democratic-bourgeois and anti-imperialist" and, then, "socialist." A key turning point between them was reached with the nationalizations of major foreign and domestic business during the summer of 1960.[5] This interpretation, which the Soviet Academy of Sciences would even make official, found ready support among both defenders and opponents of the Cuban Revolution between the 1960s and 1970s. The former celebrated the turning point as the radicalization of the revolutionary process in the context of its confrontation with the United States. Critics denounced it as the "betrayal" of the liberal, democratic values of the fight against the dictator Batista and the result of Soviet expansionism in Latin America and the Caribbean. Critical and heterodox Marxists, including J. P. Morray, Adolfo Gilly, and Marcos Winocur, also subscribed to a theory of two revolutions, while still maintaining some distance from the incorporation of Soviet elements by the revolutionary leadership.[6]

Morray was one of the first from the left to apply the interpretive model of Trotsky's "permanent revolution" to the Cuban case.[7] Precisely because of his familiarity with Trotsky's thesis of the "revolution betrayed" following the Stalinization of the Bolshevik Revolution in the 1930s, Morray protested the liberalist and social-democratic propositions of the Kennedy administration and the first wave of exiles, who interpreted the turn toward Communism as a "betrayal."[8] Gilly would continue this Trotskyist line of thought in his essay *Inside the Cuban Revolution* (1964), though the Argentine Marxist did perceive a Cuban version of Trotsky's "Thermidorian Reaction" in the rising force of a pro-Soviet current that rejected the "skipping of historical stages" (i.e., the idea that Cuba could jump to socialism prior to passing through advanced capitalist development) and policies of agrarian autonomy and corporatism.[9]

Between 1968 and 1975, several reactions to this narrative of two revolutionary phases and socialist transition emerged within the intellectual field and the island's high ideological spheres. These reactions can be understood as corresponding to two different discursive strategies, at times contradictory and at others complementary. On one hand, Fidel Castro's speech "Because in Cuba There Has Been Only One Revolution" (1968) marked the centennial anniversary of the outbreak of the island's first war for independence on October 10, 1868. Castro argued that the socialist model that the Cuban Revolution had adopted was not so much due to an ideological turn toward Marxism-Leninism as it was a natural consequence of the same revolutionary nationalism inaugurated by separatist and antislavery leaders of the nineteenth century: Carlos Manuel de Céspedes, José Martí, Ignacio Agramonte, and Antonio Maceo. Castro's thesis resonated closely with the work of historians like Jorge Ibarra.[10] On the other hand, another Castro speech, delivered on the twentieth anniversary of the storming of the Moncada Barracks in 1973, presented the idea, already developed by Osvaldo Dorticós and other heads of state since the summer of 1961, that the Revolution's leaders were Marxist-Leninists since 1953. This, like the 1968 speech, delegitimized the premise of communist radicalization in 1960, albeit with a different argument.[11]

These moves found echoes in academic historiography. The idea of a totalizing, metahistorical revolution between 1868 and 1968 held a particular appeal for nationalist historians like Ibarra, who were sympathetic to a heterodox Marxism. Meanwhile, the premise of a secretly Marxist-Leninist leadership dating to 1953, forced to conceal its communist leanings in order to dodge the McCarthyism of the Cuban public, found a champion in the work of professional historians like Julio Le Riverend. In his work *La república: Dependencia y revolución* (1966), Le Riverend narrates the fifty-seven years of postcolonial experience in Cuba, from 1902 to 1959, as a prolonged lapse of dependence and underdevelopment that would justify the Revolution's triumph and subsequent socialist legal system. The final pages of his book, dedicated to the revolutionary process, are very careful not to define the 26th of July Movement under a socialist ideology.[12] However, in an essay written in 1975, after the first Congress of the Communist Party, Le Riverend validated the argument that revolutionary leaders had been Marxist-Leninist all along, as previously espoused by Dorticós and Castro. Already this argument had become official in the "Historic Analysis of the Revolution," part of the government's report to the First Congress of the Communist Party of Cuba in 1975. It was even used in the preamble to the socialist Constitution of 1976.[13] In his 1975 essay Le Riverend disputed both liberal and Marxist historians who subscribed to the idea that Castro and the 26th of July Movement's ideology was not originally Marxist and, in passing, also critiqued the opposition and exile communities who brandished the cliché of a "revolution betrayed" by its communist turn:

> Everything came together in Fidel's defense statement [after the Moncada attack], where, in the midst of the armed struggle, he expressed the fundamental concepts that are prerequisites of the socialist conceptions that would develop after 1956. In "History Will Absolve Me" ("La historia me absolverá"), there are specific references to the "Golden calves"—to magnates who claim they will solve the nation's ills when really they were only concerned with their earnings. . . . Without going beyond a brief analysis, justice remains fundamentally rooted in class, given that the courts never indicted rich criminals. Talking heads and so-called "experts" haven't seen that the words of this document coincide with the proper vocabulary of those great creators of scientific socialism, Marx, Engels, Lenin.[14]

It is difficult, in this context, not to read the concluding paragraphs of the essay "Cuba on Its Way to Socialism (1959–1963)," written in 1979 by the vice president of the Council of State and member of the newly minted Political Bureau, Carlos Rafael Rodríguez, as critical of both official theses, that of the "100 years of struggle" and of the original Marxist-Leninist ideology of 26-7-M leaders. Rodríguez was emphatic in his assertion of a radicalization of the revolutionary leaders' ideology between the summer and fall of 1960 as a consequence of the confrontation between the revolutionary government, its internal opponents, and the United States. After detailing the changes introduced as part of the revolutionary government's economic policy of nationalization in 1960, Rodríguez concludes:

> Therefore, though Cuba's formal declaration as a socialist country did not appear in the words of its maximum leader, Fidel Castro, until that dramatic moment on April 16, 1961, when he called out to the workers, who gathered to pay their final homage to the victims of the imperialist bombings that occurred a day earlier, [and told them] to defend the revolution with the cry: "Long live our Socialist Revolution!," the socialist characteristics of the revolutionary process appeared clearly as of October 13, 1960. By our judgment, there is no other way to understand the birth of the socialist revolution in Cuba.[15]

As late as the 1980s, the debate about the ideological identity of the Cuban Revolution still determined a good part of the historiographical production about the period between 1959 and the 1980s. At the same time, it remained hidden in the Cuban public and intellectual spheres and subject to the climate of polarization wrought by the ongoing conflict with the United States and the Miami exile community. Yet after the sequence of events spanning the fall of the Berlin Wall in 1989, the USSR's disintegration and the Fourth Congress of the Communist Party of Cuba in 1991, and the new socialist Constitution of 1992, historiography about the Revolution entered a phase of revisionism and critique. This scholarship has been picking up speed in recent years and has placed in doubt central issues advanced by the opposing narratives of the Cold War.

Books from the decade after the fall of the USSR, like Marifeli Pérez-Stable's *The Cuban Revolution: Origins, Course, and Legacy* (1993), advance a critique of the allegedly eternal and steadfast Revolution as an ideological mystification that essentially superimposed the Revolution on its eminent leaders, the nation itself, or the conflicts between Cuba and the United States, the exile community, or the internal opposition. In addition to suggesting a specific temporal frame for the revolutionary phenomenon—the 1950s to the 1970s—Pérez-Stable endeavored to reconstruct the diverse social and political agents involved in the old regime's destruction and the new regime's establishment. The landmarks of the officialized narrative—the Moncada Barracks, the Sierra Maestra, the *Granma*—remained intact but were now accompanied by other milestones produced by other revolutionary currents. In addition, Pérez-Stable did not shy away from tracing reformist projects or civil and peaceful opposition strategies present in the 1950s and into the beginning of the 1960s.[16]

From an ideological point of view, Pérez-Stable's book explains the transition from radical nationalism to a socialism made up of varied Marxist antecedents. Thus, without entirely abandoning the thesis of the Revolution's two phases, she highlighted a greater diversity of revolutionary and socialist "visions" during the first stages of the new order.[17] She concludes that "institutionalization" in the first half of the 1970s consolidated the construction of the new sociopolitical order and thus put a definitive end to the revolutionary process, strictly speaking. However, she also notes that the bureaucratization of the regime, understood in light of the reforms propagated by Mikhail Gorbachev in the Soviet Union and the beginning of Eastern Europe's transition to market economies and democracy, demanded that the Cuban leadership reintroduce schemes of popular mobilization in order to avoid any movement toward new reformist logics.[18]

As in Pérez-Stable's work, recent academic historiography has taken on the symbolic construction of Cuba's purportedly "continuous" revolution by insisting on more precise chronological demarcations, beginning with the 1950s. In his *Historia mínima de Cuba* (2013), the historian Oscar Zanetti proposes that the decade of the 1950s should be understood as the collision between dictatorship and insurrection, while the concept of "revolution" should be reserved for the big economic, social, and political transformations that took place after 1959, when the revolutionaries came into power.[19] Moreover, Zanetti suggests the terms "socialist experience" and "institutionalization" for the period that commences at the end of the 1960s and the early 1970s, marking a clear endpoint for the Revolution's time frame. Another possible periodization, among many, restricts the revolutionary moment to the years between the 1950s and 1970s—the two decades in which the republican regime was destroyed and the new socialist regime was erected.[20]

Newer scholarship on the Cuban Revolution has also furthered our understanding of the social, political, and ideological plurality of actors in the Cuban past—critical approaches already percolating in the 1990s—while also noticeably focusing on more defined periods of time. Such trends left behind the teleological discourse about the inevitable triumph of the socialist revolution and the adoption of its institutional form in the 1970s. Scholars and historians instead forged new critical space to shed light on specific moments of the last days of the old regime and the first years of the revolutionary experience. Robert Whitney and Charles D. Ameringer, for example, studied the revolutionary change of the 1930s and the Auténtico Party governments of Ramón Grau San Martín and Carlos Prío Socarrás between 1944 and 1952.[21] In his biography of the populist leader Eduardo Chibás, *The Incorrigible Man of Cuban Politics* (2015), Ilan Ehrlich traced the political and electoral emergence of the Orthodoxo Party—the Auténticos' main opposition—and the passionate oratory of its founder.[22] Jorge Ibarra Guitart completed his study on the elite Society of Friends of the Republic and the "Civic Dialogue" talks in the 1950s, which sought and failed to achieve a peaceful resolution to the crisis instigated by Batista's 1952 coup.[23] Julia Sweig focused her analysis on the 26th of July Movement's urban underground between 1956 and 1958.[24] María del Pilar Díaz Castañón reconstructed the intense ideological debate that came along with the socialist transition between 1959 and 1962.[25] Samuel Farber rescued the original ideological diversity of the revolutionary project within those same years, particularly with regard to the weight of the 1930s populist tradition.[26] Sergio López Rivero analyzed the construction of the new hegemonic bloc inside the nascent revolutionary political class.[27]

This new historiography emerged after an explosion of memoirs and testimonials published between the 1970s and 1990s by the Revolution's leading figures, including works by Manuel Urrutia Lleó, Carlos Franqui, Mario Llerena, and Huber Matos, and, more recently, Luis M. Buch, Enrique Oltuski, Julio García Oliveras, and Armando Hart. With archives of primary sources unavailable to most historians on and off the island, these testimonies remedied a material lack of evidence that is still felt in a significant number of studies on the Cuban Revolution. A new historiography thus took advantage of these texts while also narrating and interpreting the past from a more distant and, consequently, more critically sophisticated vantage point—unlike what could be found in the testimonies provided by the protagonists and witnesses of the Revolution themselves.

When Lillian Guerra's *Visions of Power in Cuba* appeared in 2012, the new current of historiography was more than ready to address the transition between the insurrectionary period and the socialist system's construction from a sociopolitical perspective. Beyond the great popular mobilizations and the noteworthy extension of social rights produced by the Revolution, new historians would also describe the resistance and opposition to the new order mobilized by different social sectors, along with the exclusion, repression, exile, or destruction to which these marginalized groups were subjected.[28] Guerra's monograph is, perhaps, the most accomplished example of a new generation of historical studies about the Cuban Revolution. She narrates and interprets the revolutionary process without obscuring its social, ideological, and political plurality. She also elucidates the dialectic of consensus and dissent in which a new revolutionary power structure was forged.

As this edited volume demonstrates, new researchers, both on and off the island, continue to challenge the traditional historiographical presupposition conflating the Cuban populace with its government during processes of social and political change between the 1950s and 1970s. The essays by Guerra, Díaz Castañón, Reinaldo Funes Monzote, Elizabeth Schwall, Christabelle Peters, Michael Bustamante, María A. Cabrera Arús, and Abel Sierra Madero trace a transformation that is more contentious than harmonious. Conflict arises through the construction of the new socialist state as it fractures public opinion and civil society, makes environmental interventions in the name of its developmental and modernizing strategy, and creates a new social choreography by implementing specific cultural policies like the Cuban School of

Ballet. Yet even in the Revolution's more advanced, "institutionalized" years, tensions continue to surface, whether in conflicted attempts to link domestic campaigns against racial discrimination to Pan-Africanism and decolonizing projects in Asia and Africa, the Sovietization of spiritual and material culture in the 1970s, or the propagation of a publicly homophobic morality that subsumes the ideal of the "new man," rejects sexual diversity, and reproduces machismo.

Cabrera Arús's and Sierra Madero's essays, in particular, reconstruct the moments when the island's civil legislation most closely resembled the model propagated in the 1936 Soviet Constitution. In addition to its rigid framing of civil and political rights, the Soviet model penalized habits of consumption, cultural tastes, and other popular customs, while also persecuting "deviant" attitudes or those otherwise excluded from socialist identity. In its civil and penal codes as well as the government's cultural, educational, and ideological policies, the Cuban Constitution of 1976 reproduced an entire mechanism of civil repression that was not solely political in scope. As in the USSR and Eastern Europe, vagrancy, truancy, emigration, rock-n-roll and bohemian lifestyles, homosexuality, Jehovah's Witnesses, and mental illness were subject to political scrutiny.[29]

Funes Monzote's and Schwall's contributions, on the other hand, take up the construction of the Cuban state in the 1960s. The state's modernizing mission aimed to conquer nature, with plans to drain the Zapata Swamp and the Batabanó Gulf in an ambitious geotransformation program. Simultaneously, Cuban authorities aimed to invigorate high culture, such as classical ballet and modern dance, and incorporate forms of popular culture, like the famously spectacular Tropicana cabaret, into state ideology. From nature to culture, there was no facet of life in which the state did not see fit to intervene.

Meanwhile, Peters takes on one of the transnational dimensions of the Cuban revolutionary experiment. Looking to the relationship between Che Guevara and the Tanzanian leader Julius Nyerere, Peters explores the complexities and ambivalences that the ideal "new man" generated in the geopolitics of the anticolonial left in the 1960s. The connection between the Latin Americanist and Pan-African movements during that decade was one of the most creative dialogues among the "Third World" left, but it also produced a series of disagreements given that the nonalignment policy of a government like Tanzania's implied a dialogue, not a rupture, with both the USSR and the United States.

From a distinct perspective, Bustamante tries to deal with the problems presented by an archive as polarized and manipulated as that of the Cuban

Revolution. Bustamante looks to a diverse sampling of literary, filmic, and journalistic documents in order to trace evolving representations of the Revolution's origins and historical development during the era of its institutionalization in the 1970s. During this period, personal memories began to be absorbed, or mediated, by collective memory processes in new ways, while collective narratives of history reached their most distilled, simplified version to date. This was particularly true, as already noted, in the case of official documents from the First Congress of the Communist Party.

If the 1970s saw personal memory collapse more completely into state narrative, the years of insurrection against the Batista dictatorship and the transition between the first and second revolutionary governments (between 1959 and 1960) constitute the moment of the Revolution's first symbolic engineering as myth. Guerra and Díaz Castañón explore this foundational period to locate the genesis of messianic images of and narratives about Castro. Guerra looks to the intervention of the North American press in these origin stories, spotlighting the *New York Times* correspondent Herbert Matthews and, above all, the journalist and photographer Andrew St. George. Díaz Castañón, on the other hand, examines the dialectic between popular demands and revolutionary measures that also reinforced the charismatic link between the Revolution's commanders and the majority of the country.

As one can read in the chapters in this volume, new scholarship on the Cuban Revolution already constitutes a significant historiographical corpus. These works show that a new history of the Cuban Revolution is as much attuned to the mass incorporation of society to the new order as it is to the exclusionary discourses and practices that likewise constituted the socialist state. Besides clearly illuminating power itself, which official histories often confuse with notions of the people or the citizenry, this new work accounts for the birth of subaltern subjectivities under the egalitarian and sovereign Leviathan heading the revolutionary government. The subaltern subject can be seen in surviving sectors of the old regime, but also in new social actors of modest resources who suffered marginalization or who continued to be attached to past mind-sets and traditions.

Indeed, it is odd that subaltern studies, emerging from theories of Orientalism and postcolonial nationalism in India and other Asian, African, and Middle Eastern countries—and already usefully transplanted into Latin American studies—has only rarely been invoked as a frame of analysis for revolutionary Cuba.[30] As studies of subalternity in Eastern Europe suggest, it would be misplaced to understand socialism in Cuba as having overcome the postcolonial condition, let alone eliminated the subaltern subject (allegedly by transforming him or her into the new hegemonic actor). The idea that the formation of a hegemonic power in Cuba during the 1960s and 1970s did not generate its own, new subaltern subjects risks perpetuating the mistaken conflation of revolutionary government and populace, not to mention the belief that conflicts over class, race, and gender disappeared under socialism. These notions can be refuted by applying the tools of subaltern studies to the Cuban case, but also by deploying the theoretical currents of posthegemonic Marxism that are beginning to circulate in Latin American and Caribbean historiography and cultural studies.[31]

In shining a light on conflicts between state and society, the new critical history of revolutionary Cuba forces the historian to take stock of the marginalized, repressed, or exiled during the heroic era of the "new man." Like any modernizing and secularizing process, the Cuban Revolution intervened in the ideas and beliefs, habits and customs of society, shaped, in this case, by an inherited republican order created in 1901 and its reformulation in 1940. Revolutionary, civic strains of Cuban nationalism had also gained momentum since the revolutionary movement of 1933 and were further radicalized by the New Left, especially through Che's platform. At the same time, such values morphed significantly under the growing weight of dogma and orthodoxy characterizing the Soviet-style Marxism-Leninism that gained influence on the island by the end of the 1960s.

The incorporation of Marxism-Leninism as state ideology, starting in the 1960s but especially after the First National Congress of Education and Culture in 1971, had important effects in all spheres of public policy. This indoctrination shaped both economic policy and international relations due to the adoption of a national planning model that resembled those followed by the member countries of the Council for Mutual Economic Assistance, as well as a geopolitical and military alliance with the powers of the Warsaw Pact. Similarly, in elementary, intermediate, and advanced levels of education, culture, the arts, and ethnic, religious, and sexual relations, Cubans contended with the uncritical assimilation of Soviet social scientific models, grounded in atheist, materialist, anthropological, macho, and homophobic references. A great deal of the repression and marginalization suffered in the ideological and cultural fields of those decades clearly had to do with the limits imposed on civil and political liberties; we cannot discount, however, the force of philosophical dogma transplanted from the Soviet bloc.

Both on and off the island, new historians have incorporated the construction of the socialist state into the history of the Revolution. For decades, official narratives only highlighted the epic history of the insurrection against Batista's dictatorship and the great collective undertakings of the 1960s as a means of establishing sovereignty, equality, and social justice as the basic premises of the Cuban consensus. The new historiography insists, however, that the Revolution is not only about the destruction of the old regime but also about the construction of a new social and political order and, as such, of a new hegemonic power. The greater visibility of the Revolution's hegemonic structures, in turn, paradoxically allows historians to depict its constitutive plurality in greater detail. In this way, attention to the delicate balance between popular inclusion and exclusion becomes integral to the Revolution's narration and interpretation.

Such a focus on the dialectic between integration and exclusion in Cuban revolutionary experience breaks with the paradigm of civic homogeneity that accompanied the construction of the socialist state between the 1960s and 1980s. From a Cuban present that, in various ways, maintains its wariness of social heterogeneity and cultural and political diversity, new scholarship fixes its gaze on the resistance exercised by the subaltern against socialist hegemony. Even though it flowed into oppositions and exiles and the antagonistic partisanships of the Cold War, this resistance mobilized around values that were recognized at one time within the pluralistic field of revolutionary ideology. The new history of the Revolution, therefore, is also a history of its dissenters, its oppositions, and its exiles. It keeps steadily in sight the fact that this plurality arose directly out of the intrinsically heterogeneous event of January 1, 1959.

NOTES

Editors' note: The editors thank Ian Russell for his assistance with the translation of this essay.

1. François Furet, *Interpreting the French Revolution* (Cambridge: Cambridge University Press, 1981), 3.

2. Reinhart Koselleck, *Futuro pasado: Para una semántica de los tiempos históricos* (Barcelona: Paidós, 1993), 333–58. Translation drawn from the English edition, Reinhart Koselleck, *Futures Past: On the Semantics of Historical Time*, translated by Keith Tribe (New York: Columbia University Press, 2005), 255–76.

3. Hayden White, *Metahistoria: La imaginación histórica en la Europa del siglo XIX* (Mexico, D.F.: Fondo de Cultura Económica, 1992), 135–60, 212–22, 283–311. See also Ferenc Fehér, *La Revolución congelada: Ensayo sobre el jacobinismo* (Madrid: Siglo Veintiuno, 1989), 1–39.

4. Ernesto Che Guevara, "Algunas reflexiones sobre la transición socialista," in *Apuntes críticos a la economía política* (Havana: Ocean Sur, 2006), 9–20; Carlos Rafael Rodríguez,

"Cuba en el tránsito al socialismo (1959–1963)," in *Letra con filo* (Havana: Editorial de Ciencias Sociales, 1983), 2:386–407.

5. Rodríguez, "Cuba en el tránsito al socialismo," 387–89.

6. Marcos Winocur, *Las clases olvidadas en la Revolución cubana* (Barcelona: Ed. Critica, 1979), 139–70.

7. J. P. Morray, *The Second Revolution in Cuba* (New York: Monthly Review Press, 1962), 4–5.

8. Rafael Rojas, *Fighting over Fidel: The New York Intellectuals and the Cuban Revolution*, translated by Carl Good (Princeton, NJ: Princeton University Press, 2016), 128–29.

9. Adolfo Gilly, *Inside the Cuban Revolution* (New York: Monthly Review Press, 1964), 2–13, 26–33, 83–88.

10. Fidel Castro, *Porque en Cuba sólo ha habido una Revolución* (Havana: Departamento de Orientación Revolucionaria, 1975), 9–37; Jorge Ibarra, *Ideología mambisa* (Havana: Instituto Cubano del Libro, 1972), 21–58, 73–101; Jorge Ibarra, *Nación y cultura nacional* (Havana: Editorial Letras Cubanas, 1981), 7–32.

11. Castro, *Porque en Cuba sólo ha habido una Revolución*, 129–38.

12. Julio Le Riverend, *La República: Dependencia y revolución* (Havana: Editorial de Ciencias Sociales, 1973), 358–73.

13. Fidel Castro, *La unión nos dio la fuerza* (Havana: Departamento de Orientación Revolucionaria, 1976), 40–45.

14. Julio Le Riverend, "Cuba: Del semicolonialismo al socialismo (1933–1975)," in *América Latina: Historia de medio siglo. Centroamérica, México y El Caribe* (Mexico, D.F.: Siglo Veintiuno, 1981), 2:55. In his *Breve historia de Cuba* (1978), Le Riverend reiterated, though with greater caution, this idea of a Moncadista socialism; see Julio Le Riverend, *Breve historia de Cuba* (Havana: Editorial de Ciencias Sociales, 1995), 102.

15. Rodríguez, "Cuba en el tránsito al socialismo," 389.

16. Marifeli Pérez-Stable, *The Cuban Revolution: Origins, Course, Legacy* (New York: Oxford University Press, 1993), 3–13, 61–74.

17. Pérez-Stable, *The Cuban Revolution*, 94–97.

18. Pérez-Stable, *The Cuban Revolution*, 160–73.

19. Oscar Zanetti Lecuona, *Historia mínima de Cuba* (Mexico, D.F.: El Colegio de México, 2013), 255–68.

20. Rafael Rojas, *Historia mínima de la Revolución cubana* (Mexico, D.F: El Colegio de México, 2015), 9–17.

21. Robert Whitney, *State and Revolution in Cuba: Mass Mobilization and Political Change, 1920–1940*, Envisioning Cuba (Chapel Hill: University of North Carolina Press, 2001); Charles D. Ameringer, *The Cuban Democratic Experience: The Auténtico Years, 1944–1952* (Gainesville: University Press of Florida, 2000).

22. Ilan Ehrlich, *Eduardo Chibás: The Incorrigible Man of Cuban Politics* (London: Rowman and Littlefield, 2015).

23. Jorge Renato Ibarra Guitart, *Sociedad de Amigos de La República: Historia de una mediación, 1952–1958* (Havana: Editorial de Ciencias Sociales, 2003); Jorge Renato Ibarra Guitart, *El fracaso de los moderados* (Havana: Editorial de Ciencias Sociales, 2000).

24. Julia E. Sweig, *Inside the Cuban Revolution: Fidel Castro and the Urban Underground* (Cambridge, MA: Harvard University Press, 2002).

25. María del Pilar Díaz Castañón, *Ideología y revolución: Cuba, 1959–1962* (Havana: Ciencias Sociales, 2004).

26. Samuel Farber, *The Origins of the Cuban Revolution Reconsidered* (Chapel Hill: University of North Carolina Press, 2006), 34–68.

27. Sergio López Rivero, *El viejo traje de la revolución: Identidad colectiva, mito y hegemonía política en Cuba* (Valencia: Universitat de València, 2007).

28. Lillian Guerra, *Visions of Power in Cuba: Revolution, Redemption, and Resistance, 1959–1971* (Chapel Hill: University of North Carolina Press, 2012).

29. For more on civil repression and the Soviet constitutional model, see J. V. Stalin, *Constitución de la URSS* (Mexico, D.F.: Editorial Dialéctica, 1937), 70, 169; Leon Trotsky, *La Revolución traicionada* (Mexico, D.F.: Casa Museo de León Trotski, 2014), 217; Arthur Koestler, *El mito sovietico ante la realidad* (Mexico, D.F.: Ediciones Estela, 1946), 84–94.

30. Ranajit Guha and Gayatri Chakravorty Spivak, eds., *Selected Subaltern Studies* (New York: Oxford University Press, 1988), 3–34; Ileana Rodríguez, ed., *The Latin American Subaltern Studies Reader*, Latin America Otherwise (Durham, NC: Duke University Press, 2001), 35–80.

31. Jon Beasley-Murray, *Posthegemonía: Teoría política y América Latina* (Mexico, D.F.: Paidós, 2010), 19–22; Benjamín Arditi, "Post-hegemonía: La política fuera del paradigma," in *Política y cultura*, edited by Heriberto Cairo and Javier Franzé (Madrid: Biblioteca Nueva, 2010), 159–93.

3. Writing the Revolution's History out of Closed Archives?

CUBAN ARCHIVAL LAWS AND ACCESS TO INFORMATION

———

JORGE MACLE CRUZ

Any cursory analysis of the sources cited in most studies of the Cuban Revolution, whether published in Cuba or abroad, would reach a common conclusion. With few exceptions, authors have largely depended on interviews, personal experiences, existing publications, memoirs, speeches, the press, and inferences to render their judgments. In other words, researchers interested in exploring the light and dark sides of Cuba's revolutionary nationalism since 1959 have generally not had access to sources from government archives.[1] To this day most historians remain unable to consult information, documents, or correspondence from within official Cuban institutions.[2]

What have been the intellectual effects of this archival absence and asymmetry over time? How has the closed or otherwise unavailable nature of most Cuban state archives shaped our understanding of the Revolution's past? In the pages that follow, I reflect on the consequences, and the causes, of Cuban documentary paucity for the post-1959 era, as well as the imprint of such source gaps on the scholarship in this volume. Especially in the context of a project that seeks to direct our attention to the Cuban revolutionary process from within, we must consider whether a Cuba-centric history of the Revolution can be conceived without adequate archival sources on the same. Put another way, if the chapters of this book seek to shine new light on the complex interactions between Cuban society and the Cuban state, can such an objective be fulfilled without more state institutions themselves opening their documentary stores?

As the editors to this collection describe, and the contributors prove, it is possible to work around current archival limitations. A substantial, if incomplete historiography on the Revolution—one that has broached sensitive, uncharted, and sometimes forgotten topics—already exists. The scholars in this volume also mine novel sources on and off the island to advance insights and original claims. Nor should we fetishize government sources above all other kinds. Official documents are produced for a specific audience and at a specific time. They are as much "social constructions" as interviews or press accounts; they need to be questioned and dissected, not taken as faithful, factual mirrors of reality.

Still, the evidentiary value that additional archival sources could add to any number of studies on the Cuban Revolution cannot be ignored. One can imagine what internal government materials might add, for example, to many of the essays in this volume. Yet even more germane to the broader concerns of this book, reflecting on existing evidentiary gaps helps us understand the binary traps into which understandings of Cuba's post-1959 history still too often fall. Despite historians' best attempts to avoid official and dissident "grand narratives" of the kind that tend to shape popular representations, the politics of the Revolution's history, as the editors note in their introduction, still invariably loom large. But in a research landscape in which subjective testimony becomes one of the few routes to unearthing grassroots experience, and the "hard truths" of archival fixity continue to elude us, can the specter of "shifting samizdat" (*pace* Lambe and Bustamante) be even partially left behind?

In time Cuba's archival landscape may offer scholars better research options than those available today. As I argue below, drawing on years of experience as an archivist in Cuban institutions, the question is often not so much *whether* government documents exist. Frankly, they do, though evidentiary erasure and disappearance are also realities with which scholars must contend. Rather, we must ask whether sufficient legal norms, organizational practices, and resources are in place in Cuba today to compel regular documentary transfer, processing, and public access. In some cases, the obstacles to access—especially when related to mundane state matters not pertaining to national security—largely stem from bureaucratic, financial, or procedural matters. In others, implicit concerns over the political sensitivity of materials, and the alleged misuses and misrepresentations to which they may be put, create the impression of a conspiracy of government secrecy or neglect.

Thus, this essay traces the landscape of Cuban archival institutions, laws, and practices, past and present, as well as those that still need to take shape, with an eye to elucidating the nature of existing research challenges and future opportunities. My aim is to illuminate both the continued difficulties involved in historicizing the Cuban Revolution and, in so doing, the ingenuity demonstrated by scholars in and out of this volume. More often than not, historians of the Cuban Revolution must find creative ways to navigate a landscape of archival absence, incompleteness, and/or unavailability. But in making adaptations to circumstance, they, together with archivists, must continue to advocate for greater documentary openness on the basis of international principles and standards.

Archival Laws in Cuba: A Primer

Why is access to official archives so important? In the words of one expert, archives "store evidence of activities undertaken and not. They document and verify if the resources of a country are being used adequately, and they give proof to judge those who do not fulfill their responsibilities."[3] Curiously, though, it was Ernesto "Che" Guevara who more pointedly addressed the urgency of the question in a revolutionary context such as Cuba's, where what can be expected to end up in archives is perhaps the first issue one should consider. "A big part of the history of revolutions is underground," Guevara wrote. "It doesn't come to public light. Revolutions are not absolutely pure movements; they are built by men and they are forged in the midst of internal fights, ambitions, and mutual misunderstanding. And all of that gradually becomes silenced and disappears."[4]

What, then, can we say about the state of archives and archival practices in Cuba today? What policies and procedures for the preservation of official records are in place? Do the gaps in available documents confirm the intuitions that Guevara expressed? Or are they the result of more administrative forms of negligence, resource shortages, or legal delays?

A brief history of Cuban archival laws helps put present developments in context. During Cuba's colonial period, from 1559 to 1898, the Spanish Crown promulgated numerous ordinances, royal orders, and royal decrees concerning the protection of documents. Most notably, on January 28, 1840, the Crown ordered the creation of the Archivo General de la Real Hacienda de la Isla de Cuba—later renamed Archivo General de la Isla de Cuba (1857)—to preserve documentation related to Spanish colonial administration. However, access to its holdings remained restricted to specific government officials and intellectuals.[5] By contrast, orders emitted during the short period of the first U.S. occupation (1898–1902) were more interesting from a juridical point of view, as they created the position of director of archives and invested the job with considerable authority in the governing hierarchy. Regulations passed by the occupation government also made it mandatory to archive official documents. This set the stage for the evolution of the prior General Archive toward a new, more accessible modality of a national archive, which opened its doors to the public and researchers for the first time on October 21, 1899.

During the republican period (1902–59), a stronger legal corpus developed. Officially the institution changed its name in 1904 from General Archive of the Island of Cuba to National Archive (with "of Cuba" appended in corresponding documentation).[6] Additional regulations focused on the organization of the institution internally and strengthening the legal protections afforded to documents deposited therein. Documents stored in the National Archive were officially declared part of the national patrimony; as important, any act that jeopardized their integrity and conservation was deemed a crime punishable by law. Finally, after moving locations several times, in 1944 the National Archive moved into a newly constructed building in Old Havana, where it is still housed today.[7]

For a long time after the triumph of the Revolution in 1959, however, only one major law—Law Number 714 from January 22, 1960—concerned archival affairs. In addition to regulating the functioning of the National Archive, this norm endorsed all prior regulations from the republican era. Notably, it also mandated the archival transfer of documents from all state entities after specific periods of time, and it established that only the director of the National Archive could order the purging of documents from the public administration of the state. But rather than set the groundwork for a more comprehensive national system of archives, the law was conceived only for a single National Archive, which could not possibly handle the amount of coordinating, enforcement, or processing work required. Even more damning, the law lacked a series of implementation protocols to make it operational. As a result, state institutions and public organizations never felt obliged to comply. No mechanism forced them to organize their internal documentation according to the standards of archival science or, more specifically, to put in place adequate document management systems. As a result, through the year 2001 the only archives in Cuba that worked together in a coordinated matter were those included in the so-called Network of Historical Archives, which, like the National Archive, generally held processed, accessible materials dating only to 1960.

More than forty years later historiographical needs began to give rise to new demands, and the first steps were taken to begin introducing important modifications to existing archival legislation. On August 8, 2001, the Ministry of Science, Technology, and the Environment promulgated Decree-Law 221, De los Archivos de la República de Cuba (Concerning the Archives of the Republic of Cuba). This legislation created a full National System of Archives, which in turn required that institutional archives be organized in every institution and organ belonging to the central administration of the state, as well as within other government dependencies. Legal foundations, political organizations, and mass organizations were also required by this law to preserve institutional materials. Most important, the law finally outlined the broader institutional architecture to facilitate the obligatory transfer of government documents no longer in use after five years. First, inactive government documents were to be deposited in so-called Central Archives, where they would remain for twenty-five years in a "semi-active" state, still inaccessible to the public. Then, once government documents were deemed to have become fully "inactive," they were to be deposited in the Network of Historical Archives, including the National Archive, for the eventual use of researchers. To assist in these processes, the same law established the National Commission of Expert Control (Comisión Nacional de Control y Peritaje), a collective body charged with overseeing the effective valuation of archival materials and their transfer to archival institutions through local-level commissions. In this way, Decree-Law 221 greatly surpassed prior regulations dating to 1960, which attributed "expert control" functions to a single official.

Archivists successfully proposed further changes to archival legislation in the following years. Most important, Decree-Law 265, from 2009, replaced Decree-Law 221 and established further parameters for the protection of the nation's documentary patrimony, as well as more detailed norms and principles to guide document management. This law also established the National Archive of the Republic of Cuba as the governing methodological organization for *all* archival matters in the country. The National Archive today likewise coordinates the functioning of the full National System of Archives, including the Central Archives of the state and the Network of Historical Archives. By law all institutions in the system function with a significant degree of operational decentralization.

Results: Continuing Challenges in Cuba's Archival Landscape Today

But what, concretely, have been the results of the improved legal framework to date? How can we relate this abbreviated review of archival legal history to the practical question that most interests researchers in this volume: access to information? Unfortunately, a significant gap still exists between legal requirement and archival reality.

First, it is worth noting that a number of post-1959 official documents did come into the National Archive's collections, albeit sporadically, prior to the administrative and legal momentum initiated under the 2001 and 2009 archives laws. These include the archives of the Ministry of Agriculture (processed, covers through 1976); the National Bank of Cuba (processed, covers through 1961); the Havana Stock Exchange (processed, covers through 1970); the National Association of Agronomy and Sugar Engineers (unprocessed, covers through 1963); the National Commission for the Promotion and Defense of Tobacco (unprocessed, covers through 1962); the Regulatory Commission for the Shoe Industry (unprocessed, covers through 1961); the National Customs Office (unprocessed, covers through 1979); the National Exporting and Importing Company for Primary and Secondary Materials (unprocessed, covers through 1965), the National Institute for the Stabilization of Sugar (processed, covers through 1964); the Ministry of Industries (unprocessed, covers through 1967); and the National Treasury (Ministerio de Hacienda, partially processed, covers through 1962). These collections, primarily related to economic affairs, add to the even more important post-1959 files housed at the National Archive before 2001. The latter include the archives of the National Institute of Agrarian Reform (with restrictions, 1959–60), one of the most powerful institutions in the Revolution's early years; the Ministry for the Recovery of Ill-Gotten Goods (with restrictions, 1959–60), responsible for confiscating the property of corrupt pre-1959 families and businesses; the Central Planning Board (unprocessed, covers through 1960), a major economic policy body; and the National Institute of Saving and Housing (unprocessed, 1959–60), responsible for public housing programs. In this sense, the 2001 law served first and foremost to create a strengthened legal framework for the necessary (if slow) processing of those select post-1959 collections that the National Archive and, to a lesser extent, provincial historical archives already had in their possession. It also facilitated, again gradually, the arrival of new, more contemporary material, such as the papers of the state-run CUBALSE Corporation (unprocessed, 1994–2009) and those of the National Office of Free Trade Zones (unprocessed, 1997–2006), despite these files' relatively young age.

But it is also true that these sources constitute only a small portion of those that should, by law or in principle, now make their way to the Network of Historical Archives. For example, archives from the Ministry of Agriculture (after 1976), the Ministry of Finances and Prices, and the Ministries of Foreign

Commerce and Foreign Investment (and their institutional predecessors) remain in state possession and inaccessible to the public. Both the Ministry of Culture and the Ministry of Foreign Relations, meanwhile, maintain proprietary archives of their own. In other cases, legal provisions exempt substantial groups of material from inclusion in the Historical Archives. The Ministry of the Revolutionary Armed Forces, for instance, operates an entirely separate system of generally closed archives. Moreover, Decree-Law 221 (2001) granted the Council of State, the Council of Ministers, and the National Assembly of People's Power authorization to keep documents in their central archives for as long as they deemed necessary, independent of the date of their creation—though this provision is not referenced in the newer Decree-Law 265 from 2009, thus creating a situation of legal uncertainty. Article 50 of this law does mandate that the archives of the leadership of the Cuban Communist Party, the Union of Communist Youth, and other mass organizations be transferred to the Cuban Institute of History. This academic institution, however, answers to the Central Committee of the Cuban Communist Party, not the National System of Archives.

At the very least, then—and leaving aside legislated exceptions—we can say that if current legal requirements for obligatory document disclosure and transfer had been in place all along, historiography produced on the Revolution since the late 1980s could have been strengthened by a much wider corpus of official government sources—particularly on economic and social matters. Instead, even those processes of archival preservation now mandated by law and under way remain hampered by inertia, neglect, a lack of adequate staffing, or a combination of all three. (Witness the thin list of new archival collections donated to the National Archive since 2001.) Many more state institutions and entities still hold onto their files even when they should not. Meanwhile, sources pertaining to the highest echelons of government, no matter how old, or related to military, criminal, and national security matters, generally remain off limits.

Admittedly, the resource problem does play a major role in inhibiting progress. Cuba's National Archive, to take just one example, is already experiencing exponential growth in demand for its services. From just 6,527 users over the course of 2008 (with over 48,316 requests to consult specific documents), the average number of users per year rose to 10,260 between 2011 and 2014 (with 110,587 annual document consultations).[8] This does not include those who use the Archive's library or periodical collection, which would add another 1,000 users and 5,200 consultations of books, newspapers, and magazines annually. Just how high would these statistics rise if all appropriate collections had been transferred from the Central State Archives to the Network of Historical Archives? And would the National Archive, with its current staff, tools, space, budget, and technological deficiencies, have been at all prepared to handle the load?[9]

But as one can infer from the list above, many of the collections of official revolutionary documents that do exist in the National Archive, or in its often underused provincial counterparts, remain either wholly or partially unprocessed. Others are still severely or wholly restricted with regard to public access. For instance, to consult the archive of the National Institute of Agrarian Reform, though now processed and part of a "public" archive, one needs a signature from the minister of agriculture himself or herself. Letters of permission are needed to access other collections as well. Keep in mind, too, that the National Archive continues to process and receive collections from before the 1959 period. This points to the need to improve and clarify the legal and procedural filters through which official documents from the revolutionary period are made available for, rendered useful to, and/or withheld from wide public consultation. The first filter is *legal*; that is, there are administrative rules that legitimately determine the length of time documents remain out of the public eye or that aim to protect the privacy of living individuals named after documents are transferred to the public historical record. The second is that of *conservation*, or the standards by which archives legitimately restrict access to those materials in a poor material condition. A third crucial filter, though, is that of *description*, "the process of capturing, collating, analyzing, and organizing any information that serves to identify, manage, locate, and interpret the holdings of archival institutions."[10] Unfortunately, only starting in 2007 did Cuba begin to widely apply up-to-date, international standards for assigning multilevel descriptors to archival materials—namely, those recommended by the International Council of Archives—and at a fairly slow pace.[11]

The description and cataloguing problem may be most acute in the case of state institutions whose historical materials have not yet been transferred to Cuba's public historical archives. Because even if such documents had been adequately relocated to the required repositories much earlier, the collections to be transferred often do not resemble proper archives at all. Most could be better classified as "warehouses of papers," and the passage of time and new laws have not necessarily remedied the challenge. Document management—including the description of collections—has never been a focus of public administration in revolutionary Cuba. Still, the issue in many cases is best understood not as a lack of documents but rather one of collections spread across the most disparate institutions without any proper organization. I have personally had the privilege of seeing numerous files of documents, belonging to varied institutions and ministries, labeled only with such inscriptions as "Papers from 1961" or "Documents sent by X." It is in these moments that the Cuban archivist grasps the responsibility attached to the profession, as well as how much remains to be done. But the archivist also realizes that a significant part of that which had been presumed to be lost actually exists. It exists, even when, as in all processes of social convulsion, part of the documentation ends up destroyed (as Guevara predicted) and custody falls first on the shoulders of those loyal to the new power, not archivists. It is these disparate traces of historical experience that must be rescued from public ignorance and reclaimed as an integral part of the great puzzle of national memory.

The Historian's Dilemma: Past and Present Strategies

Considering these circumstances, what is the historian to do? How have past scholars inside and outside Cuba gotten around the obstacles enumerated here? And have some scholars found ways, regardless of the rules, to get behind closed archival doors? What are current scholars doing, including those in this volume, to render the internal history of the Revolution more legible? What tasks remain incomplete?

As José Ragas has noted, existing impediments to archival access "have not discouraged researchers from writing about Castro's Cuba."[12] Indeed, given the source types most widely available—the Cuban press, speeches, and published reports and statistics—it has sometimes appeared as easy to write about Cuba's post-1959 history from outside the island as from within it. Referring to his corpus of academic work, the economist Carmelo Mesa-Lago, one of the founders of Cuban studies in the United States, offered the following reflection in a 2012 interview: "All of my work has been written virtually without having been able to undertake proper academic research in Cuba. Between 1967, when I wrote my first book about socialist Cuba, and 2012, when I published my last, I have only been able to visit the island five times: 1978, 1979, 1980, 1990, and 2010. Each one of these visits was limited to six days, and I mostly participated in seminars and meetings with academics and officials."[13] Mesa-Lago alludes to the political effects of strained bilateral relations between Cuba and the United States on possibilities for academic exchange over the years, particularly the awarding of research visas to scholars (Cuban Americans included) who hold critical views of the Cuban government. But notwithstanding these tensions, Mesa-Lago's work has been the subject of praiseworthy and thoughtful critical analysis on the island, of the type that one only receives when one's work is serious.

Yet it is not as if other foreign, let alone Cuban, scholars have fared universally better in gaining access to official materials. Research visas may be relatively forthcoming for others working on the post-1959 period these days—including historians represented in this volume. But open doors to precarious or restricted government archives, including for island-based historians, remain rare. Still, infrequent exceptions tempt us with the possibilities that official archives might offer, in the event that their transfer to public historical archives became more regular. For instance, in the early 2000s the U.S. historian Julia Sweig gained access to the highly restricted collections of the Office of Historical Affairs of the Council of State. This allowed her to write about the internal, contentious history of the 26th of July Movement in the 1950s with an unprecedented degree of detail.[14]

The most extraordinary case of a historian gaining access to classified Cuban government archives, though, may be that of Piero Gleijeses. Before beginning his detailed study of revolutionary Cuba's foreign policy in Africa and participation in the Angolan war, Gleijeses told the Cuban leader Jorge Risquet Valdés that he "believed in the Cubans' word, but it was not the same as if those words were backed up by documents."[15] Cuba then put into Gleijeses's privileged hands fourteen thousand pages of previously classified documents—largely from Cuba's armed forces, but also from the archives of the Council of State and Raúl Castro. Writing in 2013, he recognized the exceptionality of the case: "The Cuban archives for the post-1959 period are closed. I am the only foreign scholar who has been allowed to enter them—after years of effort and failure." "There is no established declassification process in Cuba," he added.[16] In the first instance he refers to the classified status of military documents, which may be similar in any country. But in the second, and in apparent ignorance of the new parameters of Cuban archival law that compel document disclosure in many cases, he references a broader archival reality. This holds because for years there was no effective legal norm that required state institutions to transfer documents to public archives in accordance with their age. In this sense, Gleijeses's experience seems to confirm the impression that Cuba grants exceptional authorizations to consult restricted documentation only to those whom it "trusts." And while select island-based writers have enjoyed access to such materials, anecdotal experience suggests that many Cuban scholars seeking to consult less sensitive files encounter impediments equal to or greater than those their foreign colleagues face.[17]

In many cases, then, it has been left to Cuban libraries to fill the gaps—not by providing access to internal government sources to which they do not have access, but by making available other kinds of materials from which scholars, Cuban and not, can benefit.[18] As recent scholarship and the essays in this volume attest, the revolutionary-era press has proven a particularly rich font of information. Together, surveys of the diverse publications from the earliest years of the Revolution (as María del Pilar Díaz de Castañón shows in her essay) and the recovery of little-known periodicals from later, more restrictive years have permitted historians to dissect discursive frameworks, reconstruct subjectivities, and read between the lines in new ways (see Michael J. Bustamante's essay for an example of the latter). While access to the rarest of these materials, let alone their state of conservation, often remains a challenge, libraries and other academic institutions have also undertaken important, incipient digitization efforts with the help of foreign partners, the results of which sometimes make their way onto flash drives and into scholarly circuits of hand-to-hand exchange. Recently the cultural institute Casa de las Américas compiled a substantial portion of its own internal archive into a searchable database, which is already available for purchase on the academic market abroad.[19] Meanwhile, at the Institute of Cuban History, the José Martí National Library, and ICAIC (Cuba's film institute), a number of important digitization projects involving sources from the revolutionary era are also under way.[20]

At the same time, historians of the Cuban Revolution—particularly those interested in state formation and grassroots experience—also have to be entrepreneurial. Those able, typically foreign scholars, seek out new or unused archival collections abroad (in this volume, see Lillian Guerra's use of the papers of the journalist and photographer Andrew St. George, for instance). Others gather rare documentary materials from private archives, on the island and off, or conduct oral history (in this volume, see Abel Sierra Madero's contribution on Mariel). Most often a combination of these strategies is required, as is the support of a multinational community of committed scholars willing to share materials, advice, and diverse forms of institutional and extra-institutional support. This volume attests to the collaborative possibilities of such academic exchange, even as its contributors acknowledge that Cuban scholars face greater obstacles in obtaining the financing (and visas) to conduct research abroad. But it is worth noting that access to some government materials not in public archives has become possible, if irregular. In this volume, for instance, Elizabeth Schwall makes use of previously untapped sources from the Ministry of Culture—specifically those pertaining to its predecessor, the National Council of Culture (1959–75). Likewise, María A. Cabrera Arús dissects internal government reports on consumption patterns in the 1970s, the product of a multiyear effort to compile her own archive on Cuban material culture under socialism.[21]

Archival deficits notwithstanding, the scholars in this volume show that one can make a significant contribution to recovering popular experience under the Revolution through a combination of creativity, persistence, and analytical skill. As new scholars continue scouting out sources where one might least expect them, the historiography on Cuba's revolutionary period stands to be even further enriched. Meanwhile, demands to see internal government documentation will only increase. Those files constitute the next frontier of research for historians to come.

Inconclusive Conclusions: Guiding Principles for the Future

Clearly, the Cuban archivist's job is far from over. And given the passage of time, not to mention the non-climate-controlled conditions in most Cuban institutions, the dangers of losing untold, disorganized bundles of government documents are real. Where to obtain the resources to undertake such a monumental task is an impossible question to answer at this stage. Still, Cuba's community of archivists is clear on some of the principles that should be followed in the future, whether by way of demanding effective compliance with existing laws or reforms to the same.

First, the freedom of information is legally recognized today by close to one hundred countries,[22] and the International Council of Archives proclaimed it a key principle of the organization in August 2012.[23] In turn, a similar commitment to transparency in Cuba should oblige all institutions to eventually turn over essential documentation to public archival institutions, even that information not yet subjected to proper archival organization. In short, Cuba requires a Freedom of Information Law.[24]

Second, access to most government sources in public archives should be permitted following a reasonable amount of time, facilitated by the work of archivists, and made possible by conservation techniques. That is, the three principal filters that can block documentary access (legal, description, and conservation status)—even after transfer to public facilities—should disappear gradually, as they are not intended to be permanent barriers.

Third, the continued denial of access should be the exception to the rule rather than the norm, and regulated by law. That is, the factors that would justify the prolonged classification of a document—privacy protections, national security concerns, and so forth—should be clearly delimited in archival legislation so that they do not become hidden barriers for the historian.[25] Ideally historians and citizens would have the ability to legally contest classification.[26] According to UN principles, the ethical requirement of "limiting exceptions" to public disclosure means that "the denial cannot be based [solely] on the goal of protecting governments from an embarrassing situation or the revelation of its incorrect acts."[27] Cuba would do well to adopt a similar standard.

Fourth, and as already intimated, Cuba's own archival and information laws require further improvement. Decree-Law 265 (2009) has proven to be insufficient, despite having a section that deals specifically with freedom of information. Even worse, almost a decade after it was approved, its implementing regulations have still not been approved. In response the leadership of the National Archive itself has crafted a new draft law and corresponding rules in an effort to strengthen document management and disclosure requirements. In 2011 the National Archive also compelled the National Assembly to discuss the need for adequate and obligatory document management at all levels of the government. Since then, however, projects for reform have stalled; the new draft archive law does not, at this writing, appear to have advanced much beyond the proposal and discussion stage with relevant government interlocutors. Besides, if Cuba is to clarify the fuzzy line between the principle of free access and the legitimate reasons for which archival documents may still be classified, the creation of a more robust independent entity charged with overseeing the impartial application of an eventual Freedom of Information Law seems equally urgent.[28]

All told, the marginalization of archival science in Cuba, and its delayed implementation in the case of sources from the revolutionary era, has not been the result of any known official directive. But one cannot deny that retellings of Cuba's post-1959 history have thus far been unable to draw from a considerable documentary arsenal. Archivists, as true allies of historians, will always want full access to sources from all official spheres. Yet in order to realize the old aspiration that no document be perpetually secret, a *cultural*, and not just legal, transformation is also required.

Like the historians included in this volume, then, we archivists must be optimistic, putting our faith in the winds of change. Those winds, after all, should not pass by the institutions that can legitimize them in time: archives themselves, which operate something like the "mind" of a society. Documents are akin to anecdotes in our heads, filling and shaping the wider contours of memory. Protecting and preserving them is necessary to break with decades of inertia and remedy a considerable historical debt.

Editors' note: Translated by Michael J. Bustamante.

1. Between 2006 and 2013, for example, the authors José Bell Lara, Delia Luisa López García, and Tania Caram León published a series of seven volumes under the heading *Documentos de la Revolución cubana* (Documents of the Cuban Revolution), corresponding to the years 1959 to 1965. The volumes consisted almost entirely of previously published texts; archival sources appeared only indirectly through the work of Luis M. Buch and Reinaldo Suárez, who had access to the archives of the Office of Historical Affairs of the Council of State and the Executive Committee of the Council of Ministers.

2. By "official Cuban institutions," I do not mean the National Archive of Cuba or institutions in the National Network of Historical Archives, which I describe in more detail below. Rather, I am speaking primarily of the internal archives of government organizations and ministries. While the latter should have ended up in the former after a reasonable amount of time, as I also detail below, currently public archives contain relatively little processed, publicly accessible documentation pertaining to the post-1959 period.

3. Jorge Villagrán (2013), cited by Natalia Torres, "Hacia una política integral de información pública," in *Hacia una política integral de gestión de la información pública: Todo lo que siempre quisimos saber sobre archivos (y nunca nos animamos a preguntarle al acceso a la información)*, edited by Natalia Torres (Buenos Aires: Universidad de Palermo, Facultad de Derecho, Centro de Estudios en Libertad de Expresión y Acceso a la Información, 2014), 155.

4. As cited by Sergio Guerra Vilaboy, *Historia de la Revolución cubana* (Navarra: Txalaparta, 2009), 16.

5. These included luminaries of Cuban and Spanish colonial intellectual life such as Mariano Torrente, Ramón de la Sagra, José Silverio Jorrín, and Antonio-Bachiller y Morales, among others. For example, a supplement to La Sagra's seminal *Historia física, política y natural de la isla de Cuba* (from 1859) drew from materials held in the Archivo General.

6. Later it would also be labeled the National Archive of the Republic of Cuba. It carries this formal name today, as stipulated in Decree-Law 221 from 2001, detailed below.

7. For a good summary of these early developments through the colonial and republican periods, see Martha Ferriol Marchena and Yorlis Delgado López, "El Archivo Nacional de la República de Cuba: Su impronta a 175 años de su Fundación," *Revista de la Biblioteca Nacional de Cuba* 106, no. 1 (2015): 165–76.

8. Users in 2014, for instance, came from thirty-six distinct Cuban institutions; 567 individual users came from foreign institutions, including thirteen U.S. universities.

9. Strict compliance with legal requirements for transferring documents from Central Archives based on their age would quickly overwhelm available space at the National Archive. A number of years ago, in light of this scenario, archive officials recommended that the government support the building of a new edifice to house documentation from the era of "the Revolution in power." I am unaware to what degree this request was seriously contemplated.

10. Victoria Irons Watch, compiler, *Standards for Archival Description: A Handbook*, Society of American Archivists, 1994, http://www.archivists.org/catalog/stds99/chapter1 .html.

11. Recognized multilevel descriptor formats include the *International Standard on Archival Description* (General) (ISAD [G]), 2000, and the *International Standard Archival Authority Record for Corporate Bodies, Persons, and Families*, 1997. As an example of the slow pace, applying multilevel documentary description to one revolutionary-era collection at the National Archive, that of the National Institute of Agrarian Reform, took three years. Cuban archives are simultaneously applying ISAD(G) standards to pre-1959 collections for the first time. (Prior to this, non-multilevel description parameters had been used.) In the first six years, twenty-four collections were processed. In 2014 a record five collections were processed, most entirely concerned with the pre-1959 period.

12. José Ragas, "La Revolución cubana y los archivos: Nuevos documentos disponibles, 1976–1989," *Historia Global Online*, October 19, 2013, http://historiaglobalonline.com /2013/10/19/la-revolucion-cubana-y-los-archivos-nuevos-documentos-disponibles-1976 -1989/.

13. "Mi libro sobre las reformas en Cuba: Entrevista al profesor Carmelo Mesa-Lago," *Revista Espacio Laical* 8, no. 31 (2012): 33–34. Mesa-Lago has since returned to Cuba on other occasions, but for personal visits.

14. Julia E. Sweig, *Inside the Cuban Revolution: Fidel Castro and the Urban Underground* (Cambridge, MA: Harvard University Press, 2002).

15. Pedro de la Hoz, "El internacionalismo cubano es una lección política y moral," *Granma*, June 25, 2015, http://www.granma.cu/cultura/2015-06-25/el-internacionalismo -cubano-es-una-leccion-politica-y-moral.

16. Piero Gleijeses, "Visions of Freedom: New Documents from the Closed Cuban Archives," *Cold War International History Project*, Woodrow Wilson Center for International Scholars, October 16, 2003, https://www.wilsoncenter.org/publication/visions-freedom -new-documents-the-closed-cuban-archives#sthash.DGSYXsDh.dpuf. Studies resulting from Gleijeses's work in Cuban archives include *Conflicting Missions: Havana, Washington, and Africa, 1959–1976* (Chapel Hill: University of North Carolina Press, 2002) and *Visions of Freedom: Havana, Washington, Pretoria, and the Struggle for Southern Africa, 1976–1991* (Chapel Hill: University of North Carolina Press, 2013).

17. In recent years I have been aware of a dozen researchers interested in writing the history of Cuba's Agrarian Reform, using the aforementioned collection of the National Institute of Agrarian Reform at the National Archive. Nevertheless, I can cite only one case in which a scholar received the required authorization from the minister of agriculture to work with the corresponding files: Mayra San Miguel Aguilar, *La reforma agraria en Holguín: 1959–1961* (Holguín: Ediciones Holguín, 2005).

18. The one exception may be the José Martí National Library, which some years ago held the papers of the National Council of Culture (1959–76). This collection has since been transferred to the proprietary archive of the Ministry of Culture.

19. "Brill Partners with Havana-Based Casa de las Américas on Digital Cuban Culture Collection," *Society for Scholarly Publishing*, February 24, 2017, https://www.sspnet.org

/community/news/brill-partners-with-havana-based-casa-de-las-americas-on-digital
-cuban-culture-collection/.

20. On the efforts of the Instituto de Historia, see Manuel Alejandro Hernández Barrios, "La casa de los historiadores cubanos," *Mesaredonda.cubadebate.cu,* May 24, 2017, http://mesaredonda.cubadebate.cu/mesa-redonda/2017/05/24/la-casa-de-los -historiadores-cubanos/. On efforts at the Biblioteca Nacional, see the following Cuban television report from 2013, which refers to efforts to digitize the Cuban press between 1959 and 1970: Cubahora Cuba, "Biblioteca nacional digitalizacion," *YouTube,* October 18, 2013, https://www.youtube.com/watch?v=jMq1igVusAI. The accessibility of these sources to researchers is not entirely clear as of yet. With respect to the ICAIC, in 2012 the Institut National Audiovisuel of France agreed to restore, digitize, and make public *Noticiero ICAIC Latinoamericano,* a newsreel produced on the island between 1960 and 1990. At this writing, 278 episodes, covering the years 1960 to 1973, have been restored and are available online: http://www.ina.fr/evenements/noticiero-icaic-latinoamericano -archives-cubaines/. Restored, digitized copies of these films have been returned to ICAIC as well.

21. See the Cuba Material website: www.cubamaterial.com. Also *Pioneros: Building Cuba's Socialist Childhood,* Exhibition, Sheila C. Johnson Design Center, Arnold and Sheila Aronson Galleries, Parsons School of Design / The New School for Social Research, September 17–October 1, 2015.

22. For example, in Latin America and the Caribbean alone, the following countries have adopted laws concerning access to and freedom of information: Antigua and Barbuda (2004), Belize (1994), Brazil (2011), Colombia (1985), Chile (2008), Dominican Republic (2004), Ecuador (2004), El Salvador (2011), Guatemala (2008), Guyana (2013), Honduras (2006), Jamaica (2002), Mexico (2002), Nicaragua (2007), Panamá (2002), Perú (2002), St. Vincent and the Grenadines (2003), and Trinidad y Tobago (1999). In Argentina a presidential decree concerning the freedom of information was promulgated in 2003. Mexico consecrates this right in Article 6 of its Constitution.

23. International Council of Archives, Committee on Best Practices and Standards, Working Group on Access, "Principles of Access to Archives," August 24, 2012, http:// www.ica.org/sites/default/files/ICA_Access-principles_EN.pdf. Also see the interesting advocacy example of the Spanish association Coalición Pro Acceso, made up of sixty institutions, archival associations, and fifteen hundred individuals: http://www .proacceso.org.

24. I mean freedom of access in the fullest sense. "Freedom" is no longer free if a researcher has to explain for what purposes he or she seeks to consult documents in an archive. The freedom to access information should appear in Cuba's Constitution, in clear language, and with a brief number of articles that are coherent and detail terms, possible situations, and exceptions.

25. *Principles for Archives and Record Legislation* (Paris: International Council of Archives, 2004).

26. In the United States such actions are possible under the Freedom of Information Act (FOIA, 1966, with subsequent modifications in later laws). When requests to declassify documents are denied, individuals and institutions can appeal in court. Since

2007 the Office of Government Information Services, part of the National Archives and Records Administration, is charged with overseeing FOIA policies and implementation, as well as helping to resolve FOIA disputes.

27. Cited in Toby Mendel, *Libertad de información: Comparación juridical*, 2nd ed. (Paris: UNESCO, 2008), 37.

28. For examples, see Perrine Canavaggio, "Archivos y derecho de acceso a la información pública: Una perspectiva internacional," in Torres, *Hacia una política integral*, 158–94.

PART II

Case Studies

The Revolution from Within

4. Searching for the Messiah

STAGING REVOLUTION IN THE SIERRA
MAESTRA, 1956–1959

LILLIAN GUERRA

In August 1959 *Bohemia* magazine revealed how deeply expressions of belief in Fidel Castro's messianism had penetrated the public imagination. According to the journalist Mario Kuchilán, for many Cubans, especially peasants, Fidel was not only "the living incarnation of Jesus Christ" but a new and improved version of him. Recently, Kuchilán continued, Telemundo's broadcast of an artist's fanciful rendition of Fidel had provoked a flood of viewer requests that the television station provide copies of the portrait for display in private homes. With a national circulation of half a million subscribers, *Bohemia* willingly stepped in to satisfy demand. Meant to be clipped out and framed, the sketch revealed Fidel "not as he is physically but as the greater part of the Cuban people see him spiritually. . . . It is, perhaps, a fleeting lightning bolt imprisoned on paper, that extraordinary will of God to cast man in His own image. But it is not Jesus Christ, it is Fidel Castro Ruz."[1]

Until now, historians, myself included, as well as most historical protagonists of these events, have largely focused on the period immediately *after* the flight of Fulgencio Batista in January 1959 to explain Fidel Castro's rise to messianic status.[2] Or they have taken that messianic status for granted without accounting for how it was earned. Giving speeches, chatting with average citizens, and signing autographs in the company of foreign journalists in his eight-day, town-by-town journey from Santiago to the capital, Fidel and his massive convoy parted open the country like a veritable sea in biblical times. Undoubtedly fueled by the euphoria of popular expectations for a new era free of Batista, Fidel's reception among citizens was also highly produced, managed, and choreographed, mostly by Carlos Franqui, a journalist and the national director of propaganda for the 26th of July Movement, and Emilio Guede, an advertising executive and secretary of propaganda for Resistencia Cívica (Civic Resistance).[3] Still, the cultivation of popular and international Fidelismo before these landmark events has been overlooked. By shining a light on forgotten aspects of the anti-Batista insurgency, this essay fills that gap.

Of course, leadership in the 1953 assault on the Moncada Barracks, mass circulation of his eloquent defense "History Will Absolve Me," and a 1955 fundraising tour of the United States had already launched the figure of Fidel Castro as a daring politician.[4] Likewise, in her important *Inside the Cuban Revolution: Fidel Castro and the Urban Underground*, Julia Sweig shows how the 26th of July Movement made strategic alliances with, but ultimately outflanked, other anti-Batista groups. Sweig is also to be credited for making the intrepid, well-documented argument that before 1958 the 26th of July Movement's success owed more to its urban underground than to the rural guerrillas. Yet while pulling the curtain back on intra- and intermovement politics, her sources cannot explain how the myth of the guerrillas' predominance so firmly, and emotionally, took hold.

The military importance of the guerrillas may have been exaggerated, but the image of Fidel as a selfless, Christ-like redeemer, at home and abroad, owed its origins to the Sierra Maestra. There Castro and other 26th of July figures worked to cultivate their reputations as proto-political leaders, responding to, even mimicking strategies of the Batista government already in place. A master of spectacle by design, the dictator Batista crafted a "theatre state" of his own after his March 1952 coup that relied on censorship, violence, and spectacles of mass support to rule.[5] Although Batista created Cuba's first censorship office, euphemistically titled the Ministry of Information, he did not establish blanket censorship until January 1957, when news of rebel victories and violence in the Sierra Maestra broke out.[6] Thereafter, because citizens were constantly called to serve as witnesses to Batista's theatrics through a heavily managed and often explicitly censored press, foreign chroniclers and readers played a central role in reporting the alternative truths of the dictatorship's atrocities and, particularly under the leadership of Fidel's 26th of July Movement after 1956, organized armed resistance. Clandestine newspapers, illicit radio broadcasts from rebel headquarters in the Sierra Maestra, and word of mouth combined to present an entirely different narrative about events, one that arguably required the intervention of citizens' imagination to achieve coherence and completion.

This essay contends that it was precisely on the terrain of citizens' imaginations that Fidel, his initially tiny band of eighteen armed rebels, and hundreds of underground civilian activists managed to project the impossible: their own movement's ultimate moral invincibility vis-à-vis other political forces in Cuban society and anti-Batista groups. That message spread, moreover, both locally in the sierra's growing "liberated zone" and nationally and internationally with the aid of the underground and foreign press. Of course for residents of the sierra themselves, the real effects, and at times the force, of the guerrillas' rule was important to securing loyalty and support. And for many others in Cuba—and in part for progressives abroad, as the historian Van Gosse has explored—the nationalist and anti-imperialist ideals of the 26th of July Movement held an intrinsic, historically rooted appeal.[7] But if Fidel was ultimately able to effortlessly claim the mantle of national leadership in the immediate aftermath of Batista's flight, he did so in large part because of the brilliant public relations campaign that he and his supporters had forged in the Sierra Maestra. This campaign both occluded the role of the urban underground, whose story Sweig has rescued, and had regional, island-wide, and international reach. It wielded real, if selective, evidence of the guerrillas' achievements as well as the affect generated by carefully crafted visual and rhetorical appeals. Rebel leaders achieved this combination through two means: first, by assigning a particularly gifted foreign journalist the role of witness, observer, and chronicler of the guerrillas' exceptional morality to the world; second, by "proving" to those immediately around them, including local peasants and other visitors, that they could replace the state by duplicating its primary functions as a purveyor of justice and defender of citizens from violence. The result, even as the circulation of specific photographic and printed materials remains difficult to document, was a cult of personality and popular faith in and out of the sierra that exploded onto the streets of Cuba in 1959 already quite fully formed.

Fidel's original guerrilla band established a deep, abiding relationship with one foreign journalist: a Hungarian-born, self-taught freelance photographer and former U.S. military intelligence agent in Europe, Andrew St. George.[8] To put it mildly, St. George was Fidel's secret weapon. Far more important in the long run than Herbert Matthews, who spent less than a day with Fidel and his tiny band of survivors for the famous February 1957 cover story printed in the *New York Times*, he nonetheless continues to be less well known.[9] St. George made six trips to the sierra, none of them lasting less than a month, several of them as long as two.

Living, marching, and sacrificing with the guerrillas, St. George produced thousands of unique images of guerrilla life and culture, many of which became central to the clandestine press of Fidel's movement and allied groups like Raúl Roa's Resistencia Cívica. His first portrait of Fidel, taken in April 1957 and titled *Christ and the Cannon*, was published no fewer than 120 times by September 1958.[10] St. George also smuggled a cropped photo taken by his friend and fellow journalist Robert Taber back to New York for use as background on the 26th of July Movement's colorful fundraising *bonos* (bonds) in 1957; the image lives on today, emblazoned on the corner of every daily edition of the Communist Party organ *Granma*.[11] St. George came to see the many Cuban spies, guides, and foot soldiers with whom he lived as friends and even family. When he and his wife, Jean, named their first son Andrew, Fidel Castro offered to serve as godfather and baptize him after the victory, when, he assumed, St. George would naturally move his family to Havana.[12] Alongside one of St. George's most influential articles for *Coronet* magazine, Fidel published "Why We Fight," a manifesto subsequently reprinted in eleven different publications across Latin America.[13]

With the help of St. George's lens and pen, guerrillas consciously imitated the methods of Cuba's nineteenth-century *mambises* in order to claim the fulfillment of a historically frustrated moral mission dear to the Cuban people. They also refuted the legitimacy of Batista's martial rule by creating a real-life alternative state and society in miniature, a simulacrum of the world that Fidel's vision of revolution would make. For peasants in the sierra, the material, lived realities of this mini-state were palpable. Yet in transmitting glimpses of that world into the national and global imagination, the rebels also marketed themselves not as fearsome warriors but as honorable, serious, and likeable living legends. By late 1958 they were decidedly a cause célèbre, receiving dozens of famous visitors to the sierra, not just politicians but prominent figures in the entertainment industry, including Havana's top cabaret stars.

By putting contemporary published accounts in dialogue with largely untouched, "raw" archival sources, this analysis discovers a different, now mostly forgotten story than the one that the mainstream press, and even St. George himself at times, wanted to tell about rebel activities in the sierra. In particular it draws on St. George's dispersed, largely untouched photographic and written archives, a portion of which I helped to catalogue at Yale University Library. Uncatalogued materials also became available to me subsequently thanks to St. George's widow. I am especially grateful to Jean St. George for shipping an enormous box to my home in the summer of 2015; it contained a treasure of "situationers" (highly detailed field notes) and other documents of St. George's work on the island in 1958.[14] In them, and in other related photographic and filmic materials, we discover Fidel, Raúl, and others performing roles derived from national historic myths and the mass culture of television and Hollywood movies for a singular purpose: they wanted to cast their methods of violence, as well as their very *real* plan of economic restructuring (already being enacted in miniature), in an acceptable, civilized, nonthreatening, and often downright entertaining light.

Doing so served the needs and expectations of both a foreign audience and citizens who might otherwise have dismissed the armed rebels as political misfits or untrustworthy radicals. However reluctant Fidel made out his revolutionaries to be in the months he spent with St. George at his side, revolution was revolution, and both of them knew it. Making revolution acceptable for all, Cubans and Americans alike, was a primary, challenging goal.

Andrew St. George and Fidel Castro's Rebels with a Cause

Recalling the conditions that the eighteen surviving members of the *Granma* expedition faced in the winter of 1957, when Herbert Matthews visited the Sierra Maestra, Che Guevara pointedly remarked two years later, "The presence of a foreign journalist, American [by] preference, was more important to us at the time than a military victory."[15] Yet if Matthews's *New York Times* front-page article had humiliated the Batista regime for claiming that Fidel was long dead, St. George fulfilled a far more important and enduring task: he served as an imperial witness to Fidel and his troops' paradoxical self-construction as reluctant altruistic revolutionaries forced to defend a pure people against a barbarous tyrant. As Fidel explained to St. George in handwritten responses in April 1957, the guerrillas faced no real enemy besides Batista and his administration; not even Batista's soldiers were to blame: "The only corrupt thing in Cuba is the tyranny [of Batista]. Because our people are wholesome and highly moral. . . . Unfortunately, before the arms of the dictatorship, one also must have recourse to arms. . . . The army is tired of . . . Batista. . . . The soldiers live under constant surveillance and the terror of the military police. We, in fighting for the freedom of all the people, also fight for the freedom of the soldiers."[16]

According to Fidel, moreover, it was Batista, not his movement, that put Cuba at risk of becoming pro-communist: "[The idea that we are pro-communist] is as absurd as having told the Cuban people more than twenty times that I have died."[17] Not only did businessmen have more to fear from Batista's nationalization plans, remarked Fidel in two recorded interviews (possibly referring to Batista's buyout of the British-American–held United Railways of Havana in 1953), but the best witnesses to the "democratic and nationalist" nature of his movement were foreign reporters like Matthews, CBS's Bob Taber, and, of course, St. George himself.[18] Punctuated with dozens of photos by St. George, Miami's *Sierra Maestra*, the 26th of July's newspaper, seconded this with a two-page spread. It reminded readers of the Communist Party's condemnation of armed protest against the dictator and was titled "Batista: Friend and Protector of the Communists." (Allegations of Batista's "protection" of Cuba's communists stemmed from the alliance between Batista and the Partido Socialista Popular [PSP, Cuba's traditional communist party] during the former's tenure as elected president between 1940 and 1944. Likewise, after Batista's coup in 1952, the PSP had condemned Fidel's 1953 attack on the Moncada Barracks as "putschist" and "bourgeois.")[19]

Fidel's concern with assuaging readers' fears over possible nationalization became one of three consistent themes echoed across St. George's most influential publications.[20] A second was Fidel's repeated denial of any political ambitions. At thirty and then thirty-one, the 26th of July leader argued he was far too young to run for president. Besides, the 1940 Cuban Constitution expressly forbade it, requiring a minimum age of thirty-five.[21] Fidel also insisted he needed a break after the war: "I have never thought of being President of Cuba. After we win, I am going to return to the Sierra Maestra, building roads and hospitals as we have promised."[22]

In addition, Fidel often presented his followers as committed but reluctant, and therefore disinterested, revolutionaries, soldiers who aspired to peace rather than war in the theater of the Sierra Maestra. Explaining this apparent paradox years later, Fidel said, "We had to demonstrate before public opinion, and leave well established, that if there was going to be a war it was not going to be because the revolutionaries wanted one."[23] Thus, in his encounters with St. George, Fidel insisted that the rebels' struggle was not to turn the world upside down in Cuba but to restore the principles of civilization in the face of Batista's culture of barbarism.

For example, Fidel invented, and St. George dutifully echoed, far-fetched, highly fictitious claims as evidence of Batista's savagery. In St. George's first article, Fidel described the now-legendary story of Batista's soldiers torturing Abel Santamaría and providing his sister Haydée proof of his suffering in much more horrifying terms than any post-1959 account. Rather than presenting Abel's extracted eyes on a plate to a horrified Haydée (something that genuinely occurred), St. George quoted Fidel as saying that Batista's soldiers delivered Abel's testicles, not his eyes.[24] In describing the fateful landing of the *Granma*, Fidel similarly explained that eighteen survivors of the voyage "were tortured for the better part of the day and finally put to death by getting their genitals hacked off."[25] A year later St. George echoed Castro, describing the killing at the Moncada Barracks as typical of Batista's forces, "an orgy of sadism and revenge—mostly [relying on death] by castration."[26] However, in meeting *batistiano* fury, Fidel declared that his own forces had and would always turn the other cheek.

Illustrated by photos and a cover shot of Fidel taken by St. George, the 26th of July Movement's official organ greatly promoted this idea. Under the title "Different Ways of Treating War Prisoners," New York's edition of *Sierra Maestra* included a picture of a government *casquito* (helmeted soldier) standing next to a *barbudo* (bearded guerrilla) with the caption, "Batista's soldier captured by rebels, smiles assured that his life and physical integrity will be respected." Immediately below this was a photograph of a man's back, crisscrossed by scars from a severe beating. "Castro's partisan, prisoner of Batista is whipped by the men of the dictator," reads the caption.[27]

According to Manolo Ray, secretary general of the 26th of July Movement's Action and Sabotage units, so successfully did the message of Batista's savagery versus Fidel's chivalry penetrate public consciousness that the movement was able to thwart Batista's censors in Cuba by openly selling postcards with similar images. Buyers then mailed them; no explanatory text was needed. It was the best free publicity the cause had yet to receive, Ray recalled in August 2008: there was no way the censors could stop the mail, even though they tried. "It didn't cost us a single drop of blood."[28] Six years later, I found one such postcard in an archive, featuring a man's back crisscrossed with the marks of an electric prod. Much as Ray described for Cuba during Batista's rule, I knew exactly what that image meant: it needed no introduction.[29] And while it is impossible to verify precisely how many or widely such documents and underground materials circulated, veterans like Ray insist on their cumulative effect.

The idea that Batista's men savagely whipped their rebel counterparts clearly tapped collective memories of Spanish colonial days, when nineteenth-century revolutionaries like José Martí compared the political yoke that white men suffered to the dehumanizing chains of black slaves. In many other ways, however, Fidel and his followers claimed the mantle of mambises, the term used to describe Cuba's revered, often barefoot, and largely black independence fighters. At times the comparison was explicit. Resistencia Cívica, a

Havana-based organization, published a centerfold of portraits by St. George of Fidel's top leaders under the title "The Mambises of the Sierra" in their official, clandestine organ.[30] However, the guerrillas mostly claimed the mambises' heroic legacy through actions glossed as evidence of moral purity and impeccable honor. In recruiting his men, for example, Fidel insisted that the simple habit of cursing, normally a favorite macho pastime in Cuba, was sufficient grounds for exclusion from the rebel army. "I spent many nights watching them," said Castro of new recruits. "It is the way you do little things that really tells. When one of the boys would curse, or shout in anger, fail to obey the quiet word, I sent him home. I wanted a different army, an army of gentlemen. Not the rich or educated kind. I wanted *hidalgos*, natural gentlemen."[31] Through stories and documented scenes like these, Fidel and his willing accomplice St. George ascribed a very different kind of morality and masculinity to the leadership they invited readers and citizens to imagine and thereby endorse. Convincing people that Fidel and his men could one day craft such a revolutionary state, however, took more than mere words and images: it took actions, heroic deeds, and even policies. As the following discussion recounts, the 26th of July Movement managed to carry out such activities through methodical and impressively effective means.

Acting like a State, or How Fidel Forged War without Endorsing War

Photographic evidence from St. George's first month-long stay with Fidel's forces in the sierra documented the methods, culture, and selfless values of the mambises among 26th of July guerrillas in their efforts to not only enact the services of an efficient state but dramatically usurp the moral and political authority of Batista's government in the process. The same photographs, originally published by St. George in a November 1957 edition of *Look* magazine, would be reproduced repeatedly in the United States and Europe during and after the war, publications that likely circulated back to the island as well.[32] The first half of the article focused on the legendary *mambí* method of lighting cane fields on fire, roasting and eating snakes, sleeping on the run, and setting up temporary roadblocks. The other half dealt with a less romantic side to guerrilla life. First, Fidel held oath-taking ceremonies in which his original force of twelve apostles, "Los Doce"—really eighteen in number—asked crowds of local villagers to take pledges of "allegiance, loyalty and support" for the rebels. As St. George noted, *guajiros* (rural peasants) were mostly consigned to involuntary drudgery after taking the oath: growing crops was their "primera consigna," the other bearing cargo. Fleeing the land or refusing to cultivate, Fidel made clear, were punishable acts of betrayal.[33]

Sealing this point, the rebels subsequently created a "jungle judiciary" to try local peasants who refused to take the guerrillas' side and could be accused of "banditry" for this or other offenses.[34] The rebels also held "long talks with *guajiros*" to explain the process, "an essential facet of Castro's strategy."[35] In doing so, the rebels showed themselves to be morally righteous substitutes for government officials and undermined the patron-clientelism of supposedly mutual dependence on which both the local agricultural economy and Cuba's national system of politics under Batista traditionally relied.

Relying on the same term that Batista used to define Fidel's men and the Spanish had used to describe mambises, Fidel defined these peasants as "bandits" for having seized resources left in the wake of a rebel encounter with government soldiers; over such resources only the rebels could claim control, he explained. These outlaw "wolf packs," Fidel claimed, were the rebels' biggest headache. Unpoliced, they pillaged helpless villages for money, weapons, and women. "If we don't keep order in our liberated zone," said Fidel, "the people suffer. Our revolution is tarnished." Prisoners shown were bandit chiefs, captured after a week of relentless tracking by rebels (figure 4.1). The jungle had no prisons. The penalty for extreme crimes was death.[36] Illustrated with photographs of a confessed rapist and leader of a twenty-two-member local gang, the article excused the rebels' "stern jungle justice." Rape was for "mountain people and the puritanical Castro . . . an intolerable crime."[37] Indeed, according to the article, rape was also the *only* crime meriting execution. Privately, however, St. George's notes to editors and unpublished photographs told a much darker tale.

Clearly documented in St. George's many film reels and memos was the dual function of the trials and the executions. On the one hand, the trials themselves served notice to local peasants that by *acting like a state*, the guerrillas were becoming one in *practical* terms, not just in words or in their own minds. Second, initial execution squads, almost always led by Raúl Castro, seemed to include every available armed male member of a troop. Excluded were Fidel and Father Sardiñas, a Catholic priest who offered last sacramental rites to prisoners before they were tied to a tree and shot. Judging from the remarkable, shocked look on many of the executioners' faces after carrying out their first execution in April 1957, the experience of killing such prisoners was meant to harden the rebels in the general absence of encounters with Batista's soldiers, the official enemy.

FIG. 4.1. After the disastrous landing of his expedition on the eastern coast of Cuba in December 1956, Fidel Castro's eighteen-man guerrilla army avoided all military encounters with Batista's forces for several months while attempting to gain the support of subsistence peasant farmers of the Sierra Maestra. Isolated, impoverished, and utterly neglected by the government, the peasants responded positively to the initial "public service" that Fidel offered them: the opportunity to arrest, try, and execute dozens of bandits and rapists who had been preying on the local population with impunity for years. Ably assisted by Humberto Sori Marín, the attorney of the republic-in-arms and former president of the Inter-American Bar Association until Batista targeted him, Fidel presided over the open-air trials of twenty-nine captives in June 1957, when the freelance photographer Andrew St. George first visited. Cuban Revolution Collection, Yale University Manuscripts and Archives, MS 650, Box 1, Folder 20, Book I, Print 19. Full print in the Andrew St. George Papers, also at Yale. Courtesy of Andrew St. George Family.

St. George's first trip to the Sierra Maestra, his subsequent collaboration with the clandestine press of the 26th of July, and his June 15, 1957, story in Mexico City's splashy magazine *Mañana* clearly pleased Fidel. In a handwritten letter delivered by Dr. Miguel Ángel Santos Busch in late June 1957, Fidel personally invited St. George back to the sierra as "the rebel army's 'regular combat correspondent.'"[38] Thus, on October 11, 1957, Celia Sánchez, who used her father's home as a safe house, issued St. George a handwritten safe conduct pass and pink paper flag labeled "Prensa" for him to wear.[39]

Ultimately, the rebels were able to extend the reach of their liberated zone to encompass most of southern Oriente province by the summer of 1958. In that same summer, St. George spent more than two months on a two-hundred-mile guided tour of the impressively expanded rebel zone, especially Raúl Castro's Segundo Frente Frank País. Executions had become a discomforting norm, and Raúl, according to St. George's private notes, the rebels' "heaviest-handed executioner."[40] Fidel and Raúl's forces had also adopted a "peculiar rebel punishment: mock execution. Though none of [the condemned] died, rebels lined them up, fired over their heads, then shouted 'One hasn't been hit!' to make each blindfolded boy think he survived by accident, [and] would get it in the second fusillade."[41] While Raúl had personally tied the boys to trees and directed the scene, St. George witnessed similar tactics on a march toward El Cobre. Intercepted by a rebel platoon, a "suspicious wayfarer" fell in fright when a rifle was fired over his head and Captain Rigoberto Ramírez menaced him with a pistol, "firing past his ear. . . . The threat of summary execution was rebels' only means of coercing information from suspects."[42]

In notes accompanying a "situationer" memo to NBC that describe photographs now preserved at Yale, St. George commented, "Framed in red at bottom is probably the best execution sequence I ever photographed in rebel camp; for technical reasons, it was not published. The victim is a Chinese-Creole half-caste named Henrique (Quiqui) Chang, an apparently depraved sex deviate who invaded the police-less rebel area with a small gang of his own and proceeded to rack up an impressive number of rapes on peasant girls. An open-air rebel court martial convicted him of 21 confessed violations [and the death of one] protesting husband." The same sheet then described St. George's photograph of an official bulletin signed by Raúl Castro, "listing suspected 'government spies' executed at Soledad Sugar Mill in a single day . . . and urging other rebel field commanders to proceed against 'spies' with similar severity." Seconded by classified reports at the U.S. Consulate in Santiago, the list contained thirty-nine names.[43]

Although initially sympathetic, St. George's perspective evolved over several trips: it was not just or even mostly rapists and common criminals whom rebel judges tried and convicted but *chivatos* (government informers and spies), many of whom were women and girls. "Hunting down 'government spies'—i.e. anyone who gives army [the] time of the day—is perhaps top-priority rebel occupation," St. George wrote in an internal memo describing pictures taken during his second trip, in the summer of 1957. The practice was common enough that St. George documented it frequently, often suppressing a rising sense of concern. In notes describing photographs his editors considered too bloody to publish, St. George wrote, "Suspected army spy captured by patrol is threatened with shooting and shot by accident. It's a botched but typical casualty of this family war of accidents and errors."[44]

Accidents and errors, when they affected the lives of alleged "girl spies," could be traumatic. St. George photographed "a chubby girl" as she "[stood] dejectedly between guards" while a rebel leader, Juan Almeida, interrogated her and local witnesses "to determine her degree of guilt" before remanding her to the rebel Judge Advocate's Office for trial and near-certain death.[45] Yet even more disturbing to St. George was the case of Olga Suárez, captured when rebels took the town of Bueycito (population 12,000) and accused of being an informer for Batista's troops. Characterizing Suárez as "a pharmacist, divorced, with three children," St. George was haunted by her distressed visage; he mused in his notes that the "bulk of evidence indicated she would almost certainly be executed."[46] Olga's fate clearly bothered St. George: although he later published her anxiety-ridden portrait in *Der Spiegel*, he refused to witness her killing.[47]

While the vast majority of peasants may have sided with the guerrillas, tracking down and killing the local "bandits" whom St. George described as Fidel's "biggest headache" was bloody business. According to Neill Macaulay, a U.S. citizen-turned-guerrilla, exterminating spies—on flimsy evidence alone—formed a significant part of rebels' regular duties throughout the campaign, one that haunted him for years.[48] Admittedly, Macaulay formed part of a small column in western Pinar del Río province, far removed from central guerrilla activities in the eastern sierra. Yet if the identification of chivatos everywhere was as arbitrary as Macaulay's gruesome account suggests, then the protracted trial and methodical execution to which Fidel subjected the accused when St. George first visited his troops may well have been staged more for the sake of show than routine.

By the summer of 1958, the hardships of war and the creation of a revolutionary state that accepted no neutral side had quickly become facts that

St. George and 26th of July guerrilla leaders neither could nor wanted to deny. The military initiatives of Fidel and Raúl reached new heights of bravado with respect to the United States and local businesses, both foreign and domestic. On the one hand, they continued efforts to recruit imperial witnesses to the rebel cause through Hollywoodesque performances that St. George and others now filmed and did not simply photograph. On the other hand, they steeped those efforts in moral and political righteousness, claiming the mantle of a Christian mission while also establishing with martial fury the sovereignty of the revolutionary state in the Sierra Maestra. Although rebels' use of violence continued to appear defensive in nature, it also became unprecedented in scope.

Performing Power, Projecting Empowerment: Christian Disciples or Bad Boys and Glamour Girls of La Sierra Maestra?

What garnered the rebels their place on the world stage was not simply the romantic image of successful, daring warfare that they forged in the media, but the practical success of their guerrilla methods in 1958, on both a symbolic and an experiential level. At first, the rebels depended on the food and hospitality of the region's impoverished peasants for their very survival. Fairly soon, however, they began a campaign of raids on local ranches and estates from which they exacted "taxes" and other financial contributions to the revolutionary cause (figure 4.2).[49] In exchange, the guerrillas provided receipts and bonds payable upon achieving victory, much as Cuba's historical mambises had once done.[50] As their strength and numbers grew, so did their bravado. Their army drew overt parallels to the kind of world that would result once the revolution against Batista and the Old Republic was won.

Over multiple, two-month-long trips in the summer and fall of 1958, St. George meticulously documented the radical shifts in political control, military power, and organizational effectiveness the rebels now enjoyed. He was clearly impressed.[51] The rebels had opened eight field hospitals that treated injured revolutionaries and local peasants alike: "Extending medical aid to civilian population has always been rebel custom; a humanitarian gesture, it has also proved strongest political lure in an area where the ratio of hospital beds is 8,500 inhabitants for every bed, and where doctors are not seen for decades" (figure 4.3).[52] They founded elementary schools for barefoot, half-naked children. They established toll roads, set up agencies for the taxation and "military protection" of landlords, acquired a government tank, and requisitioned wall phones from United Fruit Company, as well as

FIG. 4.2. By late 1958 the guerrillas controlled much of the rural economy in far-eastern Oriente, including the coffee, rice, and cattle estates of the lowlands. Using revenues generated by taxation and their own power to intimidate through force of arms, guerrillas often enjoyed certain luxuries such as the pig roast seen in this image. According to St. George's field notes, this unit featured a Bolivian recruit whose identity and motivation remain unknown. Andrew St. George Papers, Yale University Manuscripts and Archives, MS 1912, Box 7, Folder 1. Courtesy of Andrew St. George Family.

multiple jeeps from Texaco's nearby refinery.[53] The rebels had also organized roadside *bazukero* teams that, according to the Havana-Santiago Bus Company, destroyed seventy brand new air-conditioned buses in only two months, forcing a suspension of all service.[54] While St. George found Carlos Franqui's founding of Radio Rebelde impressive, he was bowled over by the vast communication network that formerly vulnerable combat patrols now enjoyed. He counted thirty radio transmitters and over a hundred shortwave receivers, some operated by female message decoders such as Magaly Montané.[55]

Most impressive to St. George, however, was the considerable political pull and legitimacy the rebels had achieved. Marching down a two-lane highway with hundreds of rebels, he witnessed their occupation of thirty towns "against half-hearted opposition."[56] Incredibly, thirty-six out of forty-one sugar mills were paying taxes to the rebels by the fall of 1958.[57] Anxious "business-

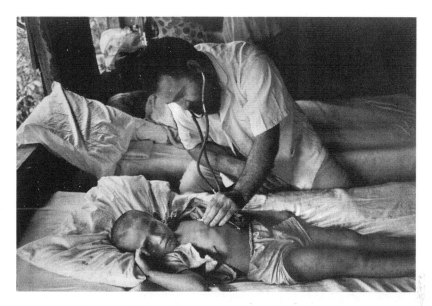

FIG. 4.3. In addition to building one-room schools for the education of long-isolated peasants, Fidel's guerrillas established field hospitals. Because of the infrequency of direct encounters with Batista's troops, doctors treated far more locals than wounded soldiers. Here Dr. Eduardo Ordaz, future legendary head of Cuba's principal psychiatric hospital, Mazorra, tends to a malnourished, listless boy. Cuban Revolution Collection, Yale University Manuscripts and Archives, MS 650, Box 1, Folder 92, Book II, Print 22. Full print in the Andrew St. George Papers, also at Yale. Courtesy of Andrew St. George Family.

men have filled rebel [coffers] but their most significant tribute was running Santiago telephone line directly to rebel outpost," he wrote. "This was the contribution of Cuban Telephone Co. (US-owned), worried sick over getting its plants around Santiago taken out by anti-telephone-company rebels, who have already taken out hundreds of poles, dozens of miles of wiring. This is the first rebel city line since Fidel's landing two years ago and apple of their eye."[58] If the activities of the urban underground before 1958 had achieved more for the movement than those of the sierra, in the final of year of the insurgency, Fidel and growing numbers of 26th of July insurgents had clearly gained control.

Rebel leaders delighted in regularly harassing U.S. companies, often for no other apparent reason than to show their strength and prophesy the future consolidation of Cuba's national sovereignty. The notion that U.S. investors had begun paying "tribute" to Fidel's troops was not lost on U.S. Ambassador Earl Smith, who demanded that they stop. "As Americans," Smith wrote in a private letter to U.S. businessmen, "we [have] no right to pay money to active revolutionaries who are trying to overthrow a friendly government."[59] St. George regularly witnessed rebels taking U.S. company-owned jeeps on joyrides, only to leave them abandoned along roads or in the countryside. They also showed their strength by invading and occupying small towns, none of which they held for more than a few hours.[60] Accompanying a rebel guard to the Texaco refinery near Santiago, St. George watched, dumbfounded, as a 26th of July guerrilla donned a helmet with a covered-up Texaco insignia and then honored Texaco plant managers' request that St. George refrain from taking pictures. Apparently, neither side wanted to heighten tensions with the U.S. government. Pictures of the takeover made relations between rebels and the company seem less than cordial and the guerrilla's occupation of Texaco unwelcome. "These shots escaped confiscation only by lucky accident," St. George explained.[61]

In other words, from all outward appearances, the rebels had successfully recruited Texaco's plant managers, local coffee planters, and assorted foreign and native businessmen into the ranks of the rebel army's enthusiastic supporters. Surely the involuntary nature and pragmatism of their support was not lost on St. George, any more than it was on Fidel himself. For this reason, St. George's careful, sympathetic documentation of the self-sacrifice of individual guerrillas and his unabashed representation of their exploits in a romantic, even glamorous light are significant. However cynically one might interpret guerrilla leaders' reliance on foreign journalists and the craft of image-making, St. George witnessed heroism as well as an abiding sense of the rebels' generosity, and even humor, amid often dehumanizing conditions.

No better example emerges in St. George's private papers and photographic record than that of Luis "El Guajiro" Crespo, one of the rebel forces' premier bomb-makers, to whom St. George dedicated more than a reel of film. A survivor of the *Granma*—the pleasure-yacht that carried Fidel Castro and his original rebel supporters from Mexico to Cuba in 1956, only to be decimated by Batista's forces before a small group escaped to the mountains—the thirty-three-year-old Crespo was a former sugar worker from Camagüey who had been running the rebels' main bomb factory near Fidel's headquarters for over a year. What impressed St. George, however, was the fact that Crespo had adopted a "crippled war orphan as his mascot, whom he has exercised and massaged until the boy is slowly beginning to walk." Admiringly, St. George captured El Guajiro working in his bomb shop and sitting atop a pile of 150-pound unexploded bombs dropped by Batista's air force, while his adopted son played happily nearby.[62] In an image that reversed 1950s-style gender roles, El Guajiro is shown lovingly washing his boy on a large rock next to a stream and dousing him with Johnson's baby powder in the over-the-top way any Cuban would recognize. Importantly, St. George wanted editors to realize that this extraordinarily generous warrior-father was *real*, not just an image. Describing a picture of Crespo massaging the legs of the crippled boy, St. George insisted, in characteristic shorthand, "This is daily routine for rebel ancient known as 'El Guajiro' and not stunt."[63]

Without doubt, however, it was the women in the rebel army who stood out the most. An unpublished series of photographs documenting the lives and routines of these women seemed to ask why anyone, let alone such beautiful creatures, would want to risk their lives fighting a dictatorship in the woods. Examples included mostly forgotten and anonymous "girl guerrillas," such as a "gun-toting rebel mother of four" from Santiago; Anita, the wife of Captain Eusebio Mora, who "marched for fourteen days through the jungle to reach her husband's troop"; Alicia Marín, one of a dozen local girls who worked voluntarily as cooks; and Teresita González, a twenty-four-year-old Havana model and chief of rebel messengers who performed highly dangerous work, crossing back and forth across rebel lines.[64] Cuban women of the Revolution were not only bold but proud to express their feelings and sexuality with the men they loved: "The wives of officers, who get to yearn too hotly for their husband's company, are sometimes permitted to join the jungle army for a few weeks—provided they are hardy enough to put up with the jungle life. Some girls, however, all but outdo the men."[65]

To be sure, many of the comments regarding the role of women that St. George submitted never made it into print. The same is true of many of Fidel's entreaties to U.S. officials, conveyed as statements to the press, which editors entirely ignored. "Let the State Department send up a man here and we'll talk things out. . . . I don't [insist on diplomatic] recognition, don't even want to hear the word, let your man come as a reporter, as a shoe salesman, a company negotiator, I'll keep his presence secret, but let him come," Fidel said.[66] When asked about Raúl's decision to "[put] out an independent, anti-U.S. political line from his command in the Sierra del Norte," Fidel balked and declared his frank disdain. Adding insult to injury, Raúl had also taken to playing the role of trickster, ordering his men to turn the water system on and off at the U.S. Guantánamo Bay Naval Base, thereby demonstrating his power to make the United States anxious and uncomfortable at will.[67] What did Fidel think of Raúl's harassment of U.S. residents and U.S. installations, including the naval base? "Folly."[68]

Still, even if unpublished, these particular remarks revealed rising anxieties about the movement's international and domestic image overall. Dangerous public tensions had emerged between Raúl's new rebel headquarters in the northern range of Sierra Cristal and the U.S. government. In June 1958 guerrillas under Raúl's command took hostage nearly a dozen foreign employees of U.S. oil and mining companies as well as twenty-eight U.S. marines, a story widely reported in U.S. newspapers and forcibly ignored by the Cuban media. Controversy over the official U.S. ban on further weapon sales and Batista's still-obvious reliance on U.S.-manufactured arms had been brewing for months.[69] By early July the number of hostages totaled forty-seven U.S. citizens and three Canadians.[70]

As its intellectual and strategic author, Raúl meant much of this operation—dutifully photographed, filmed, and chronicled in the international press by St. George and others—to appear harmless in its objectives, a mere effort to protest the U.S. military backing of Batista. However, as became clear from Fidel's own negative reaction, Raúl did not just "mug for the camera" in taking foreign executives and U.S. marines hostage; he revealed at least part of the hand of cards that the 26th of July guerrillas had yet to play. As Fidel admitted in a personal note to Celia Sánchez in June 1958, just as Raúl initiated the kidnappings, after the current war against Batista was over a "much wider and bigger war" would commence, one that Fidel secretly called, at the time, his "true destiny." Only openly launched in 1959, that war was with the United States.[71]

Raúl's Wild West and the Great International Hostage Crisis of June–July 1958

According to Military Order No. 30, signed by Raúl Castro, the United States was pulling strings with allied dictatorships of the region to help Batista's armed forces make up for weapons the U.S. government had publicly announced it would no longer provide. Stamped "Made in the USA," bombs shipped from Trujillo's Dominican Republic and tanks supplied by the Somoza dictatorship in Nicaragua testified to the duplicity and "criminal policy" that defined Washington's response to the Cuban war (figure 4.4).[72] For these reasons, announced Raúl, they were "now obliged to expedite Military Order No. 30 which orders all military commanders of the Second Front, as an act of legitimate defense, to detain all American citizens within [the rebels'] reach."[73] According to Mario Llerena, a 26th of July Movement spokesman in New York, the guerrillas decided to take the hostages after receiving credible evidence

FIG. 4.4. Positioned on a lookout post near the national shrine to the Virgin of Charity, this guard worked a twelve-hour shift, watching for Batista's aircraft in the night sky. Desperate to contain peasant support for the guerrillas, Batista's forces began bombing peasant families in the spring of 1958, a strategy continued through the end of the war. Andrew St. George Papers, Yale University Manuscripts and Archives, MS 1912, Box 8, Folder 2. Courtesy of Andrew St. George Family.

that the U.S. government continued to ship weapons to Batista's army through the U.S. Naval Base at Guantánamo, despite its public declaration to the contrary only a few weeks earlier.[74] Called "Operation Anti-Aircraft," the capture of the hostages represented an opportunity for the rebels to fight U.S.-issued bombs with ideas whose moral appeal they hoped would prove contagious.

In his comments to St. George, Fidel characterized the hostage problem as a mere "headache." Similarly light in its assessment, a 26th of July Movement radio broadcast of the Fidel Castro Freedom Network denied any kidnapping had happened at all: "The incident was 'only a tour' to show the devastation caused by Cuban forces using United States arms against the rebels."[75] Yet despite Fidel's dismissals, there is little doubt that for U.S. officials, the kidnapping easily amounted to the greatest hostage crisis in U.S. history until that point. Attesting to this in a recent filmed interview, Robert Weicha—a former CIA agent, vice consul in Santiago, and chief consul Park Wollam's partner in multiple meetings with Raúl to bring an end to the standoff—explained that one key reason for his presence in the negotiations was to better assess conditions for a possible U.S. invasion.[76]

Wollam and Weicha quickly surmised that, regardless of the open hostility and distrust of Raúl's group toward the Americans, the primary goal of the kidnappings was not political provocation, or even diplomatic recognition, but international publicity. Indeed, when Wollam first arrived to meet Raúl, he discovered Jules Dubois was already there. Editor of the *Chicago Tribune* and president of the Inter-American Press Association, Dubois was a longtime ally of the 26th of July underground.[77] Within days St. George and a CBS TV News reporter, Eric Duerschmidt, had arrived; both brought movie cameras.[78]

Before these cameras, Raúl, Vilma Espín, and the guerrillas of Raúl's Segundo Frente provided dramatic evidence that they were not just powerful and in control but extremely relaxed, unhurried, and thoroughly entertained by the American visitors. In a break between meetings, Manuel Piñeiro, or "Barba Roja"—known after 1959 as Fidel's lead international intelligence official—donned tennis whites and showed off his skills to Weicha on an improvised rebel tennis court. Espín played with loaded submachine guns for the camera. Raúl graciously allowed his consular guests to hold the weapons for a group portrait. Yet the rebels did not limit their strategy to intimidating U.S. officials; they illustrated the justice of their cause through the warm and friendly treatment of foreign prisoners before top U.S. reporters. When Duerschmidt and St. George crash-landed an aircraft in Raúl's camp, the rebels brought out U.S. employees of the $100 million U.S. government-owned Cuban Nickel Company.[79] Incredibly, St. George and Duerschmidt even filmed the hostages as they played a lively game of horseshoes while surrounded by smiling peasant boys and amicable armed guards. One is left to wonder whether the rebels or the hostages would have been quite so friendly had the U.S. cameramen, and the respective audiences they represented, not been there. Later Raúl issued an apology in which he admitted the role he assigned to journalists and their readers in the war: "I realize that this was a drastic action. I wanted these [hostages] as international witnesses to see the 26th of July Movement rebel encampment, their cause and [what] they are fighting for—freedom of the people."[80]

St. George's films clearly document a gregarious, mixed-race, and cross-class group of freedom fighters engaged in conversational and cultural exchanges with the representatives of a U.S. corporation. Moreover, the leading protagonists in the films—Espín, wearing a mother-of-pearl button-down blouse; Raúl in his ten-gallon hat; and Fidel, with his nerdy black-rimmed glasses—look as out of place as the U.S. mining company employees, with their linen bowling shirts, sunburns, and fancy pleated pants. Together, they project the idea that only the most unjust of circumstances could have forced otherwise "civilized" and clearly bourgeois people to be there. There is evidence of U.S.-supported bombing raids on civilian populations, yet the relaxed outward countenance of the U.S. citizens seems to confirm their confidence in the ultimate justice and nonthreatening nature of the guerrilla cause. Unfortunately, it remains impossible to track exactly where, or whether, these particular films were seen. Nonetheless, they powerfully speak to the guerrillas' enduring representational strategies to audiences at home and abroad.

Like the photographs shot during St. George's first visits to the Sierra Maestra and later published in the international and Cuban clandestine press, a discourse of total support imbued these films of the hostages to reveal the rebels' total invincibility. Viewed through the lens of St. George's camera, guerrillas' revolutionary reality showed American hostages in a war zone cavorting with their captors as if all were the best of friends and on the same side. In such images, American employees of the U.S.-owned Cuban Nickel Company appear as uninformed victims of their government's hypocrisy, their eyes opened by their captor-rebels to the society suffering around them. In staging these interactions, guerrillas simultaneously sought to authenticate the morality of the cause and the humanity of its leaders through imperial witnesses.

Obviously, guerrilla warfare in the sierra was nothing like how St. George's films—or the earlier, more widely seen CBS documentary *Rebels of the Sierra Maestra*—depicted it.[81] Conflict, tension, and violence—not tranquility, trust, and friendship—had long characterized the region. Until the fall of 1958, rebels restricted the brunt of their verbal attacks, trials, and executions to local peasants rather than confront the more obvious enemy, that is, the local landlords and members of the economic elite who were directly responsible for Batista's power and abuses in Oriente. Indeed, even when they had the chance to do so, they did not kill, hurt, or harm U.S. citizens or the U.S. marines whom the rebels themselves charged with being directly allied to Batista; on the contrary, they courted, charmed, and released them, occasionally before the lens of television cameras. Just as they had done when the CBS film crew visited the sierra earlier that year, the guerrillas made light of resistance among any social class in the fall of 1958, when St. George visited them. Tactically limiting their attacks to the property rather than the persons of the constituted regional order and discursively reducing any opposition to a smattering of confused rural "bandits" allowed the rebels to claim visually what Fidel had stated aloud to CBS reporters a year earlier: "All the people of the Sierra Maestra are with us."[82]

Conclusion

In the Sierra Maestra the 26th of July Movement rehearsed—consciously and unconsciously—the Revolution to come. Through tactics and imagery, the rebels forced protagonists and antagonists onto a visual stage in which *only they* appeared capable of moral action. Symbolic inversions of power and denials of violence flowed through messianic and apostolic images that Fidel and the guerrillas, respectively, presented of themselves. These images spoke loudly and deliberately of a people struggling in reality for liberation against the greatest of odds and the most powerful of imperial states, a society that could be saved only by a great, ideologically impartial moral force embodied in the figure of Fidel Castro and his barbudos. The international and domestic legend that resulted from their collaboration with St. George speaks clearly of the emerging frame of historical and cultural memory within which the Batista regime was supposed to be understood and, through Fidel, finally overturned.

There, in the Sierra Maestra, if actions mattered as much as words to the success of the 26th of July Movement's moral victory over military and political opponents, then elsewhere, outside the spaces rebels controlled, the images that *clandestinos* crafted of the guerrillas and that the guerrillas themselves helped stage combined the power of myth and legend to demoralize foes, convince class adversaries, and garner international support. Arguably, Fidel and other leaders knew that the images St. George crafted could *speak for them* more loudly and more clearly than the rebels could—or perhaps even *wanted*—to speak for themselves.

NOTES

1. Mario Kuchilán Sol, "Historia de un retrato," *Bohemia*, August 30, 1959, 50–51. The author is grateful to Abel Sierra Madero for suggesting this source.

2. Exploring the evolution and deepening of Fidelismo as a form of messianic political religion is one of the key objectives of my book *Visions of Power: Revolution, Redemption, and Resistance, 1959–1971* (Chapel Hill: University of North Carolina Press, 2012). See especially 37–106, 135–69. For additional contemporary accounts, see Ángel del Cerro, "Los panes y los peces," *Bohemia*, August 2, 1959, 56–57, 101, and Fidel Castro's own comparison of his actions with those of Jesus Christ in "Traicionar al pobre es traicionar a Cristo," *Revolución*, August 11, 1960, 1, 6, 12.

3. Emilio Guede, *Cuba: La revolución que no fue* (San Bernadino, CA: Eriginal Books, 2013), 31–44, 69–70, 76–80.

4. An original second edition of the pamphlet, dedicated to St. George by a member of New York's Acción Cívica, claimed that twenty thousand copies were distributed. *La historia me absolverá: Discurso pronunciado por el Dr. Fidel Castro ante el Tribunal de Urgencia*

de Santiago de Cuba el día 16 de octubre de 1953 (New York: Club 26 de Julio de New York, 1957), 1, in Cuban Revolution Collection, Yale University Manuscripts and Archives, New Haven (hereafter CRC, YUMA). Importantly, the first of Fidel's manifestoes, issued in August 1955, declared that his movement held special claim to lead the opposition on the basis of its own past (failed) actions: "the legion of martyrs" that Moncada left in its wake gave them that right. See "Manifesto No. 1 del 26 de Julio al Pueblo de Cuba," August 8, 1955, in CRC, YUMA.

5. Here I follow the lead of Lauren Derby, *The Dictator's Seduction: Politics and the Popular Imagination in the Era of Trujillo* (Durham, NC: Duke University Press, 2009).

6. Kelsey Vidaillet, "Violations of Freedom of the Press in Cuba: 1952–1969," *Association for the Study of the Cuban Economy*, 2006, 285–90; Michael B. Salwen and Richard R. Cole, "The Dark Side of Cuban Journalism: Press Freedom and Corruption before Castro," in *Communication in Latin America: Journalism, Mass Media, and Society* (Wilmington, DE: Scholarly Resources, 1996), 139–43.

7. Van Gosse, *Where the Boys Are: Cuba, Cold War America, and the Making of a New Left* (London: Verso, 1993). Note, however, that Gosse also tracks the appeal of Cuba's revolutionaries to the U.S. New Left on an aesthetic as much as ideological plane. He describes Castro as a "movie-hero come to life" (36), linking his image to that of Latin American heroes in films like *Viva Zapata* and *Where We Were Strangers* (set in Cuba in the 1930s). Moreover, for young people alienated from mainstream post–World War II U.S. culture, Gosse writes, Castro's "revolution appeared to be more than anything a personal, moral decision. . . . At a time of no politics, the 'political' at first could be reclaimed only as the 'personal,' and so, at first, solidarity with the Cuban rebellion could express itself only in the most subjective terms" (36).

8. The best and most accurate mini-bio of St. George before his arrival in the sierra remains the editors' note beginning "Dear Reader" in the February 1958 edition of *Coronet* magazine.

9. Matthews's story was the first to refute the Batista government's assertions that Castro had died in battle following the landing of the yacht *Granma* from Mexico in late 1956. See Herbert L. Matthews, "Cuban Rebel Is Visited in Hideout," *New York Times*, February 24, 1957; Anthony De Palma, *The Man Who Invented Fidel: Castro, Cuba, and Herbert L. Matthews of the New York Times* (New York: Public Affairs, 2007).

10. Andrew St. George, "A Revolution Made Me a Pro," *Popular Photography* 43, no. 3 (1958): 97.

11. See 26th of July Movement bonds in Ernesto Chávez Collection, Special and Area Study Collections, University of Florida, Gainesville. This collection is currently unprocessed but open to researchers.

12. Andrew St. George, "A Revolution Gone Wrong," *Coronet*, July 1960, 112.

13. St. George, "A Revolution Gone Wrong," 113; see also Fidel Castro, "Why We Fight," *Coronet*, February 1958, 80–86.

14. St. George's rigorous publishers (especially at *Life*, *Look*, and Magnum) required him to submit such detailed notes. St. George himself explained, "I had to write 'data sheets' amounting to over 30,000 words. Big magazines are thorough, and without exact caption material compiled *on the spot*, you are done for." See St. George, "A Revolution

Made Me a Pro," 98. Also significant are the many pages of descriptive "captions" that St. George wrote to accompany photographs at the time that Yale University acquired part of his collection in 1969, a rare March 1958 audio recording with Fidel, and filmed outtakes from largely unknown documentaries St. George produced.

15. Carlos Franqui, ed., *Relatos de la Revolución cubana* (Montevideo: Editorial Sandino, 1970), 74.

16. Manuscript notebook of interview by Andrew St. George with Fidel Castro, Box 20, Folder 1, 10–11, 14, CRC, YUMA.

17. Manuscript notebook of interview by St. George with Castro, 18.

18. Fidel wrote, "The only fear that businessmen have in Cuba today, as the U.S. representative Porter stated with regard to Santo Domingo, is that Batista will demand half of the utility payments for himself." See manuscript notebook of interview by St. George with Castro, back of page 18; audio wire recording of Andrew St. George interviewing Fidel Castro, March 1958, CRC, YUMA. The comment can be found between minutes 21:03 and 24:35 of the recording. See similar comments in Andrew St. George, "Exclusive: Inside the Cuban Revolution," *Look*, February 4, 1958, 30. Regarding Batista's buyout of United Railways of Havana, rather than being thrilled, Cubans responded to the public offering of 50 percent of stocks by not buying any. Batista's government owned the other half. See Ruby Hart Phillips, *Cuba: Island of Paradox* (New York: McDowell, Obolensky, 1959), 265.

19. "Batista: Amigo y protector de los Comunistas," *Sierra Maestra*, July 1958, 12–13. See also back-page editorial "Page Dedicated to the American People: Batista and Communism." Edition available in Neill Macaulay Papers, Special Collections, University of Florida. PSP declarations criticizing the Moncada attack appear in "Batista Opens Terror Drive on Unions, CP," *Daily Worker*, August 5, 1953; "Fascist Terror Grips Cuba; Communists Ask U.S. Labor for Aid," *Daily Worker*, August 10, 1953. Not until late 1958 would the PSP consolidate a formal alliance with the 26th of July.

20. Castro, "Why We Fight," 84–85; St. George, "Exclusive," 30; audio wire recording with comments found between minutes 19:50 and 22:00. In St. George's first article, he describes Fidel's economic goals as a plan to bring FDR's New Deal to rural Cuba. See Andrew St. George, "How I Found Castro, the Cuban Guerrilla," *Cavalier: Action and Adventure for Men*, October 1957, 59.

21. Castro, "Why We Fight," 82; St. George, "Exclusive," 30; St. George, "How I Found Castro," 59.

22. Andrew St. George, "Castro on Eve of His Big Bid," *Life*, April 14, 1958, 27.

23. Quoted in Santiago Alvarez, "El mar es un símbolo: Este es un lugar sagrado," *El Caimán Barbudo*, October 1982, 16.

24. Quoted in St. George, "How I Found Castro," 56. Note that in the story, St. George uses the pseudonym María in order to protect Melba from the horror of having her story made public. Jean St. George, interview with author, New Haven, CT, March 6, 2006.

25. St. George, "How I Found Castro," 57.

26. Andrew St. George, "A Visit with a Revolutionary," *Coronet*, February 1958, 77

27. "Different Ways of Treating War Prisoners," *Sierra Maestra*, May 1958, back page. Edition found in Andrew St. George Papers, YUMA.

28. Manuel Ray, interview with author, San Juan, Puerto Rico, August 11, 2008.

29. Unidentified postcard in Elena Kurstin Cuban Memorabilia Collection, Special Collections, Florida International University Libraries, Miami.

30. *Resistencia: Órgano Oficial del Movimiento de Resistencia Cívica* (March 1958), 4–5, Box 20, Folder 4, CRC, YUMA.

31. Quoted in St. George, "How I Found Castro," 56.

32. This series of images was first published in "En la Sierra Maestra: El hombre en quien confía Cuba," *Mañana: La Revista de México*, June 15, 1957, 20–24, and then more extensively with a story by St. George in "Exclusive." The same images can be found in "Dans la jungle, face aux 30,000 hommes de Batista: Un lecteur de Montesquieu," *Jours*, March 8, 1958, 12–17, and "J'ai vécu la victoire de Castro," *Parish Match*, January 10, 1959, 10–19.

33. Andrew St. George, "Photo Identification and Description," Box 1, Folder 1, Folio 2222–4444 in CRC, YUMA. *Mañana's* article published a photograph of the first oath-taking ceremony St. George attended; see "En la Sierra Maestra," 20.

34. St. George, "Photo Identification and Description," Box 1, Folder 1, Folio 2222, and Box 1, Folder 4, Contact Book #1, Print 1 in CRC, YUMA.

35. St. George, "Photo Identification and Description," Box 1, Folder 1, Folio 1515, and Box 1, Folder 4, Contact Book #1, Print 1 in CRC, YUMA.

36. St. George, "Exclusive," 28.

37. St. George, "Exclusive," 29.

38. St. George, "A Revolution Made Me a Pro," 96.

39. Safe conduct pass and flag signed by Celia Sánchez, Box 20, Folder 2, CRC, YUMA.

40. Document titled "Sheet: 7508/G" in Box 20, Folder 2, CRC, YUMA. Note that the handmade "Map Sketch" to which St. George refers in the situationer memo to NBC accompanying these sheets is preserved in CRC, YUMA.

41. Document titled "Sheet: Single clip of four frames, code SG1–69" in Box 20, Folder 2, CRC, YUMA.

42. The photographs of this scene can be found in Box 2, Folder 108, Book II, Print 38, CRC, YUMA. The description given by St. George in Yale's original files is quoted online in the finding aid by Lillian Guerra, *Guide to the Cuban Revolution Collection*, MS 650, http://drs.library.yale.edu/HLTransformer/HLTransServlet?stylename=yul .ead2002.xhtml.xsl&pid=mssa:ms.0650&query=Cuban Revolution Collection&clear -stylesheet-cache=yes&hlon=yes&big=&adv=&filter=fgs.collection:"Manuscripts and Archives"&hitPageSht.

43. This document forms part of a thick folio of sheets related to a documentary called "Behind Rebel Lines" that St. George hoped to produce. This document is titled "Sheet: c-7230/c4." Park Wollam, U.S. Consul in Santiago, confirms the circulation of this list of those executed at Ingenio Soledad in his unpublished memoir, page 73, private collection of the author.

44. Document titled "St. George—Behind Cuban Rebel Lines—OA 35611, Sheet c-42" in Andrew St. George's personal archive, private collection of the author.

45. Document titled "St. George—Behind Rebel Lines—OA 35611, Sheet c-35" in Andrew St. George's personal archive, private collection of the author. For the photographs

here described, see Box 1, Folder 89, Book II, Print 19: Cdte. Juan Almeida Bosque and rebel radio and administrative staff in CRC, YUMA.

46. Document titled "St. George—Behind Rebel Lines—OA 35611, Sheet C-41" in private collection of author.

47. Andrew St. George, "Cuba in Oproer," *Der Spiegel*, January 17, 1959, 26.

48. Thomas G. Paterson, *Contesting Castro: The United States and the Triumph of the Cuban Revolution* (New York: Oxford University Press, 1995), 86; Neill Macaulay, *A Rebel in Cuba* (New York: Quadrangle Books, 1970), 10–11.

49. Group 650, "Photo Identification and Description," Box 1, Folder 1, folio 2222–3333, CRC, YUMA.

50. Raúl Castro, "En la Universidad Popular," *Obra Revolucionaria* 2 (May 17, 1960): 24.

51. See images in Box 1, Folder 12, Contact Book #1, Print 12, CRC, YUMA; see also St. George, "Photo Identification and Description," Box 1, Folder 1, folio 1212–1313, section titled "Sheet Y-12."

52. Document titled "St. George—Behind Rebel Lines—OA 35611, Sheet C-16" in private collection of author. St. George continues, "Here Dr. Luis [sic; should be Eduardo Bernabé] Ordaz examines six-year-old boy suffering from parasitism, an ubiquitous disease."

53. St. George describes photographs of the tank and telephones in a document titled "St. George—Behind Cuban Rebel Lines—OA 35611, Sheet C-57, p. 2" and the capture of an entire "motor pool of Texaco" in a document titled "St. George—Behind Rebel Lines—OA 35611, Sheet C-6" in private collection of the author.

54. St. George first reported on the destruction of buses after his summer trip in a document titled "St. George—Behind Cuban Rebel Lines—OA 35611, Sheet C-30," and then again in a "General Situationer" memo dated December 4, 1958, 2, in private collection of the author.

55. Document titled "St. George—Behind Rebel Lines—OA 35611, Sheet C-4" in private collection of the author.

56. Document titled "St. George—Behind Rebel Lines—OA 35611, Sheet C-31" in private collection of the author.

57. "General Situationer" memo dated December 4, 1958, 3, in private collection of the author.

58. Document titled "St. George—Behind Rebel Lines—OA 35611, Sheet C-2" in private collection of the author.

59. Earl E. T. Smith, *The Fourth Floor: An Account of the Castro Communist Revolution* (New York: Random House, 1962), 148.

60. Sound recording of Andrew St. George narrating Reel #3 and #5 of his films, 1969, Box 21 in CRC, YUMA.

61. Document titled "St. George—Behind Rebel Lines—OA 35611, Sheet C-51" in private collection of the author.

62. Portraits of Crespo and the boy in Box 7, Folder 1, Andrew St. George Papers, YUMA.

63. Descriptions from document titled "St. George—Behind Rebel Lines—OA 35611, Sheet C-21" and "St. George—Behind Rebel Lines—OA 35611, Sheet C-18" in private collection of author.

64. Document titled "St. George—Behind Rebel Lines—OA 35611, Sheet C-53" in private collection of author.

65. Documents titled "Sheet C-2, pg. 2," "The Girls with the Guerrillas: II," and "St. George—Behind Rebel Lines—OA 35611, Sheet C-53" in private collection of the author.

66. Document titled "St. George—Behind Cuban Rebel Lines—OA 35611, Sheets C-23, C-33, C-30, C-45, C-12," p. 2 of 3, in private collection of the author. The document begins, "These are, with exception of frames listed below, head shots of Fidel Castro. In my notebook and on tape, I have some salty Fidelisms to go with them."

67. Mario Llerena, *The Unsuspected Revolution: The Birth and Rise of Castroism* (Ithaca, NY: Cornell University Press, 1978), 247.

68. Document titled "St. George—Behind Cuban Rebel Lines—OA 35611, Sheets C-23, C-33, C-30, C-45, C-12," 1.

69. Paterson, *Contesting Castro*, 160–78; Smith, *The Fourth Floor*, 140–41. See also Cuban accounts of the kidnappings such as Efigenio Ameijeiras Delgado, *Más allá de nosotros: Columna 6 "Juan Manuel Ameijerias" II Frente Oriental "Frank País"* (Santiago de Cuba: Editorial Oriente, 1984); Olga Miranda Bravo, *Vecinos indeseables: La base yanqui en Guantánamo* (Havana: Editorial de Ciencias Sociales, 1998), esp. 122–23.

70. Manuel Fajardo, quoted in Carlos Franqui, *Cuba: El libro de los doce* (Mexico, D.F.: Ediciones Era, 1966), 76; Smith, *The Fourth Floor*, 141. Fajardo claims they captured thirty-six marines, while Ambassador Smith and Paterson claim the lower figure of twenty-eight. In all, Smith admitted that forty-seven U.S. citizens and three Canadians were captured that summer.

71. Nancy Stout, *One Day in December: Celia Sánchez and the Cuban Revolution* (New York: Monthly Review Press, 2013), 277–78. A mimeographed copy of the note with Fidel's signature was later printed as a large-size revolutionary poster commonly found in Cuba from the 1970s through the 1980s.

72. Circular issued by Raúl Castro titled *Denuncia del Comandante Raúl Castro ante la Juventud del Mundo. Contiene La Verdad sobre la detención de los Americanos. La denuncia de la ayuda militar yanqui a Batista. La Orden Militar Num. 30*, June 27, 1958, 4, in CRC, YUMA.

73. *Denuncia del Comandante Raúl Castro*, 5. An original copy of Orden Militar No. 30 is contained in the same collection.

74. Llerena, *The Unsuspected Revolution*, 244–45.

75. Peter Kihiss, "US Aide in Cuba Plans New Talks," *New York Times*, July 5, 1958.

76. Filmed interview with Robert Chapman (alias Weicha) by Glenn Gebhard, Edenton, North Carolina, January 12, 2010.

77. Wollam noted this in his unpublished memoir, private collection of the author, 84–85. The untitled typescript of Wollam's memoir was apparently completed in the early 1970s upon his retirement from public service. I obtained the manuscript through Glenn Gebhard, who interviewed Wollam's widow, Jean Wollam, in Carlsbad, California, on December 14, 2009.

78. Jean St. George, email communication with author, February 9, 2006.

79. Smith, *The Fourth Floor*, 149, provides this estimate of the mine's value; for name and circumstances of the invitation, see Andrew St. George, Sound recording, Group

650, Box 21 in CRC, YUMA. With the help of Yale's information technology specialist Pam Patterson, I layered this recording of St. George speaking over the appropriate images that he described in 1970 as they were being projected. The *Chicago Tribune* reported, "The mine was built by the U.S. government on a concession granted in 1942 to provide nickel for high-grade steel production in the United States." Clay Gowman, "Cuba Steps Up Pressure on Big U.S. Plant," *Chicago Tribune*, December 5, 1959.

80. Peter Kihiss, "Brother of Castro Said to Apologize," *New York Times* July 4, 1958.

81. Yeidy Rivero, *Broadcasting Modernity: Cuban Commercial Television, 1950–1960* (Durham, NC: Duke University Press, 2015), 116–20.

82. Quoted in Rivero, *Broadcasting Modernity*, 85.

5. "We Demand, We Demand . . ."

CUBA, 1959: THE PARADOXES OF YEAR 1

MARÍA DEL PILAR DÍAZ CASTAÑÓN

What's past is prologue—it usually repeats itself. The future closes in, though, like an impending storm, quickly opening up from above. Many voices have characterized the *before*, and myriad more the *after*, of Cuba's elusive first revolutionary year. But almost every analysis a posteriori—whether focusing on the Revolution's imaginary and its manipulation, the occasionally infantile attempts to transform the environment, or the terrible cultural battles of the 1970s—overlooks a curious, quick, and decisive metamorphosis during the first months of 1959.[1] This change marked the contemporary of the revolutionary moment, the person who received the Revolution's subversions of the previous order.

This chapter sets out to explore the transition from a rhetoric of "we demand"—constitutive of any change of government over the course of the island's history—to one of "we give." The contemporary of the revolution, in other words, evolved in 1959 from the person who takes to the person who provides, becoming the protagonist of generous "offerings" that would characterize the first revolutionary decade. I trace this transition by examining the language employed in advertisements welcoming the Revolution's triumph as well as the nature of Cubans' sustained participation—across all social classes—in the fundraising campaign for agrarian reform that *Bohemia* magazine announced in March 1959.

Of course, the greatest difficulty in evaluating the nuances of this change stems from the diverse voices that described the island's panorama during the 1950s. Arguably none was more precise in illustrating the Cuba that would soon generate revolutionary change than that of the writer Jorge Mañach.

Mañach enjoys a reputation that the passing of time has not tarnished. The absence of his texts from the island's bookstores has not prevented a great number of potential readers from coming to know him, by reference, as the author of *Indagación del choteo* or, perhaps, *Martí, el Apóstol*. Still, the fact that these texts are no longer widely read only serves to confirm their importance. His theses on high culture and its crisis continue to be talked about by specialists.

Mañach the columnist, by contrast, enjoys less renown today. "Our Jorge," as the intellectual Rubén Martínez Villena elegantly satirized him, acquired a deserved seat in Cuban letters, not only for the grace of his pen but also for the sheer range of its deployment: as an essayist, a journalist at *Bohemia* and the *Diario de La Marina*, a professor of the history of philosophy at the University of Havana, a commentator at CMQ Radio-Television, a narrator, and always a distant observer of the political climate.[2] During his time his opinions garnered a respect in which even archenemies could share, comparable only to the esteem in which Herminio Portell Vilá's or Gastón Baquero's writings were held.[3]

Mañach's voice, though, would be heard most clearly from that monument that Miguel Ángel Quevedo would baptize the "Bohemia de la Libertad" (Bohemia Liberty Edition), outlining what he called "El drama de Cuba" (The Cuban Drama). Written originally in 1958 for the Parisian magazine *Cuadernos*, with the intention of exposing the singularity of Cuba's misfortune, this lengthy essay essentially offered two theses.[4] First, Mañach argued that it was the people's apathy that permitted "The Cuban Drama" to take place. Second, he contended that Cuba's drama was the consequence of a malady summed up in the solemn sentence: "Throughout its fifty odd years of Republic, Cuba has never been a democracy satisfied with itself."[5] In other words, it had never been a democracy at all.

As such, it might seem logical to assume that the country would look to the dawn of 1959 with the clear expectation of finally becoming a democracy. Politics—or, more precisely, political disorder—demanded a radical change, though for some any change would have sufficed. How Cuba attempted to achieve such a feat with the passive citizenry so well described by Mañach has been the subject of other reflections.[6] Very few, however, would have

Enrique Núñez Rodríguez's courage to publicly and forthrightly claim the fear involved. "I have the courage to be an honest man," he wrote, "who did not have the courage to rise to the occasion."[7]

It is worth remembering that some insistent, albeit scarce voices in Cuban political life (Andrés Valdespino, Ángel del Cerro, Mario Llerena, Father Ignacio Biaín) did refer to the necessity of deep change as an inevitable task of the triumphant revolution.[8] But for everyone else, the time of asking—of presenting demands—had arrived.

Thus, after the mix of elation and uncertainty of those first days of January passed, the *ahora sí* (now it's finally time) moment had arrived.[9] A wave of patriotic advertisements—inset text boxes or vignettes that replaced the usual copy describing a product's benefits with a welcome to the victors—elucidated the reception afforded by businesses, property owners, and associations to the changes being inaugurated.[10] They simultaneously laid out some of their initial expectations: the achievement of liberty and gratitude to those who made it possible, the hoped-for creation of new sources of employment, faith in Cuba's future, and, of course, recognition of the Revolution's leading figures.[11]

In an amusing mix of the bygone and that which was still to be born, some advertisements welcomed Dr. Manuel Urrutia Lleó as "Honorable Señor Presidente Provisional" (Honorable Mister Provisional President), but also as "Ciudadano Presidente" (Citizen President), "Primer Magistrado" (First Magistrate), "Intachable Magistrado" (Impeccable Magistrate), or simply "Sr. Presidente de la República" (Mr. President of the Republic).[12] This is the case of the sober text that the Parke-Davis Laboratory inserted in *Diario de La Marina*, in which Fidel Castro very clearly figured in second place.[13] Greetings given to the president did extend to Castro as well.

The majority of the well wishes expressed by businesses and associations in January would not follow this model, however. For Polar Brewery, Fidel Castro was "the maximum inspiration of the Cuban Revolution and the first soldier of true liberty."[14] For the Wholesalers and Textile Importers, he served as the "paladín de la libertad" (guardian of Liberty).[15] According to Antillana Steel, Fidel supplied the "brawn and brain behind the revolution giving faith back to the people."[16] And for "Baby's Home" and the Bay of Havana Association of Commerce and Industry, he was, matter-of-factly, the "líder máximo" (maximum leader).[17] The title *jefe supremo* (supreme chief), offered by the Rex and Duplex cinemas, seems to be an exception but nonetheless fits a pattern of exalting the combatants and offering general expressions of hope for liberty, justice, and progress.[18] For the London City store, Fidel Castro was simply "Fidel Castro," and the revolutionary government, the "Revolutionary Government."[19]

Granted, the more cautious stuck to saluting mothers or quoting a line by José Martí.[20] There were those who welcomed the outset of the year with the *mambí* cry "¡Viva Cuba Libre!" (Long live Free Cuba!), comfortable in the safe territory that earlier historical referents provided.[21] But the desire to make a good impression became inseparable from the expectation of real change, catalyzed by the idea that "ahora sí." *Now* anything seemed possible. Though, of course, what was possible for some was not possible for others.

The "ahora sí" impulse has a storied history for Cubans. The inverted conscience of the nation—that "most beautiful land" where nothing other than beauty existed—had forged a myth of subjunctive possibility: "If they only let us . . . If they only cut taxes . . . If the market . . . If . . ." This belief held true independent of the particular characteristics of product and market. Any Cuban businessman had complete faith that his business could flourish, if only *they*, those in charge, got rid of the biggest hindrances from above.

This certainty, together with the complex notion formed over centuries that Cuba "could be"—that it had potential but had not been allowed to flourish—was as typical in the mentality of a powerful sugar trader like Julio Lobo as it was in the mind of a humble rice farmer. One of the constants of Cuba's divided bourgeoisie, which Alfred L. Padula characterized with such skill, was the repeated hope that "what may come" would benefit *them*.[22] If it is a detriment to others, well, *that's business*. The complex matrimonial alliances that linked different sectors of the Cuban bourgeoisie did not prevent any individual from pursuing self-interest. Naturally, each investor saw the world only through his own two eyes.

In this way, for the *hacendados*, landowners of the Cuba over which Her Sweet Majesty Sugar reigned, the oft-announced Agrarian Reform—one of the few laws that unavoidably was coming down the pike—did not at all seem like it should be cause for consternation.[23] It was the cattle ranchers who owned the most land in Cuba, extending across the island. The hacendados had only sugar refineries. Quite different from the tendency of revolutionary rhetoric to identify as *latifundista* any owner of private agricultural property, the hacendados did not possess huge extents of land. Thus, the iconic photo of the revolutionary leader Antonio Núñez Jiménez—Cuban flag in hand, leading a small troop on horseback about to take over a farm—marks his entry onto King Ranch, the biggest and most elite of North American commercial *cattle* interests.[24]

Consequently, it seems entirely logical that the all-powerful Asociación Nacional de Hacedados de Cuba (ANDHEC, National Association of Cuban Hacendados), known for skillfully lobbying the state since its inception, publicized its contribution to the Agrarian Reform very explicitly and very early on with a huge inset, on two facing pages, in the widely read magazine *Bohemia*. It is worth citing the entire text, which calls to mind the *Arabian Nights* in its attempt to change out new lamps for old:

> Today, February 24, we, Cuba's hacendados, men of the sugar harvest, call on the leaders of the Revolution, the men of the 26th of July: We need to achieve Agrarian Reform and the Industrialization of Cuba! And if to achieve them we need to address the basic structural troubles of the sugar industry, then there is no problem. Because together with you, we—working hard and studying together—very soon, among all of us, will find a solution. And these are not mere words. For our part, this is already an accord, a call to action, and a firm decision.
>
> (Signed) NATIONAL ASSOCIATION OF CUBAN HACENDADOS[25]

As seen here, the hacendados not only supported the Agrarian Reform and Cuba's industrialization, neither of which affected them; in a style formerly deployed during their Republican trajectory, they envisioned (1) heading the Reform themselves and (2) telling the revolutionary government how it should proceed.

Note, too, that February 24, the anniversary of the beginning of Cuba's second war of independence, was the date chosen for the assembly to reach the above accord. The use of history as a source of legitimation could not be clearer. Neither can we ignore the commanding tone with which they asserted the necessity of what were already, as far back as the skirmishes of the Sierra Maestra, two of the Revolution's most obvious, public goals.

The hacendados also made their demands. Elegantly, yes. But their petition showed support for the Agrarian Reform as a way to resolve the interferences and problems that they, the "men of the sugar harvest" (as they called themselves) faced.

And to accomplish their goals—how could it be otherwise?—they named a commission that would reach corresponding accords.[26] This was the tenor of Year 1: commissions proliferated because, now, associations of every type wanted to be heard—and they made their demands known.

With the skill that made them masters of the country's economic destiny, the hacendados' accords reflected a simple idea: We will collaborate with our experience, and we will support you with our resources, but be so kind as to understand that you, the Revolution, need us.[27] Keep us in mind. Without sugar, as the old expression goes, there is no country.

Indeed, hidden behind the melodic phrase "the basic structural troubles of the sugar industry," what the hacendados were really asking was that things basically return to how they were—or, as they say in Cuba: *que el relajo tenga algún orden*, that there be order to the chaos. Troubles, though, continued to multiply. Sugar workers made more demands. Time spent attending various committee meetings was production time lost. Demands to reinstate workers fired during the Batista regime created even more serious problems. The hacendados also complained that the workers' "snail's pace" was endangering the harvest, a veiled threat that in the past would have made the country tremble.[28]

But not anymore. The ever irate union leader Conrado Bécquer declared that "this [would] be the last harvest" in which the hacendados did as they pleased and "[tried] to avoid the differential," a bonus payment due to sugar workers.[29] But in truth, this had nothing to do with the problems at hand, nor did it respond to what was, in fact, a logical request of ANDHEC to address delays in the pace of work. Let's be honest: it was all very well that the Revolution wanted to end unemployment as promised, but not by arbitrarily placing three workers in the same job with at least two more salaries to pay.

These all stand as clear signals of one world being phased out and another still struggling to find, or create, its place. This is the foundational paradox of Year 1. The Revolution's men had clearly defined ideas of what needed to get done. Each was premised, though, on the only world they knew, the very world that those same men were demolishing. Who could expect the interregnum to involve much more than enthusiasm and the acceptance of unavoidable change?

In this context, the hacendados, like everyone else (or almost everyone else), presented an image of collaboration with the new government and the new strongman.[30] In contrast to the more nationalist sector of the Cuban middle classes, however, they did not need to struggle for control of the domestic market. They had the quota—a fixed portion of the import market, by treaty, in the United States.[31] In short, they enjoyed the guaranteed backing of the North American political system and the protection of the Cuban state.

By contrast, albeit with serious internal differences regarding capital, competition, and state protection, the non-sugar-affiliated industrial class was the most nationalist sector of Cuba's complex bourgeoisie. This class—dedicated to industrial sugar cane processing, construction material supply, and scarce food and textile plants—suffered from competition with North American products in Cuba's internal market. Generally, U.S. commercial imports benefited from customs exemptions and other fiscal protections.

So for the non-sugar industrialists, the Revolution and its industrial diversification project looked like the fulfillment of an old dream. Their "ahora sí" was the "ahora sí" of the entire nation. They had spent decades fighting to obtain state protections already given to the sugar industry. Their most lucid minds— Pazos, Boti, López Fresquet, Cepero Bonilla—advocated for them time and again.[32] According to the commonsense reasoning of two of these professionals, reflected in the "Economic Theses of the 26th of July Movement," developing national industry went hand in hand with eliminating unemployment.[33] Citizen support would be vital, too, in bringing about the inevitable end to sugar's leading economic position.[34]

During Year 1, therefore, Cuba's industrialists did not have to make demands. They had been doing so since the 1920s. Now they felt fully within their rights to head a movement taking as its economic banner their old desire: the industrial diversification of the country. In fact, the revolutionary government was executing the industrialists' plans. Operación Honestidad (Operation Honesty), a campaign to get citizens and businesses to pay their back taxes, was already under way and national industry enjoyed total state support. Additionally, the intention to exhaustively exploit the country's natural resources and protect profitable industries was evident. Already the exploitation of sugar cane and sugar by-products for industrial purposes was being eagerly considered.[35]

For these reasons Cuba's industrialists saw fit to remind the Comisión de Ministros designada para la orientación y planificación de la economía nacional (Commission of Ministers Designated for the Orientation and Planning of the National Economy)—*the* commission par excellence—that, unlike others, they were not bandwagon "January 2" revolutionaries as far as the diversification project was concerned. Their "continuous efforts," they argued, had contributed to fostering national awareness around the issue.[36] And did they ever succeed. In April, Operación Industria Cubana (Operation Cuban Industry) showed off the principal achievements of this sector at the University of Havana's Medical School with the objective of proving that it was entirely unnecessary to turn to foreign markets. "Consumir lo que el país produce" (Consuming what the country produces)—the Cuban industrialists' old slogan—was now complemented with the legitimizing corollary for all: "es hacer patria" (is to be patriotic).

But being patriotic also required settling an old moral debt. The most neglected class, those who most contributed to the country's independence, the peasants, could not be forgotten.

The precarious conditions in which the peasantry lived and the repeated abuses they suffered under republican governments had been a constant refrain in the press. On January 8 Havana was able to see them in the flesh. The majority of the *barbudos* (the bearded revolutionaries) were obviously peasants. They arrived smiling, beaming with the aura of triumph. However, on the 22nd of the same month, CMQ Radio-Television broadcast the peasants' faces to the whole country, "sad, gaunt, scored with hardship," "each one marked by the backwardness, abandonment, and misery through which 'our' rural families have lived for centuries."[37] These were the countrymen and -women who came to testify at the trial of the ex-Batista military leader Jesús Sosa Blanco.

The trial, besides being public, took place in the sports complex Palacio de los Deportes, today the Ciudad Deportiva.[38] By way of comparison, the *Bohemia* news column "En Cuba" (In Cuba) recalled the impact of the 1950–51 Kefauver Commission hearings on organized crime in the United States, whose broadcast had paralyzed the country from coast to coast.[39] The photo-story in *Bohemia* captured the witnesses at the very moment they testified. They were numerous, accusing Sosa Blanco of committing 108 murders. The terror was encapsulated in the well-known phrase: "¿Qué pasa si Sosa pasa?" or "What might come to pass, if Sosa passes by?"

The trial "was a cruel, harsh, and bitter spectacle, but illuminating and necessary," noted the column "En Cuba."[40] And as the direct sequel to "Operación Verdad" (Operation Truth)—a campaign, culminating just days before, in which foreign journalists were invited to the island to witness the trials of other Batista-regime criminals—the prolonged proceedings built on ongoing efforts to secure support for revolutionary justice.[41] But the trial also allowed Cuba's urban public to see the peasant *not* as stereotype—spotless *guayabera*, boots, smiling ear to ear under a palm-frond sombrero—but in the flesh: skinny, toothless, poorly dressed, and with limited vocabulary. The invitation of half a million peasants to the capital (in July 1959) was still in the future. The astonished students of the "Ana Betancourt" schools for rural women had not yet flooded Havana's streets. Yet already by the end of February, the notion of a debt owed to the peasant was being repeated all over the press.

Considered a "debt of honor," the Agrarian Reform was thus seen not only as part of the project to diversify the economy but as the ideal way to pay penance for the nation's secular sins.[42] February 24, the anniversary of the launching of Cuba's final war for independence in 1895, marked the beginning of the effort.[43]

From there, initiatives multiplied. The idea of founding a "Fidel Castro Agrarian Column" would not materialize, but the tractors gathered soon thereafter in Havana's "La Tropical" Stadium were quite tangible.[44] At the same stadium, donated "agricultural implements" of all kinds, ranging from machetes to hoes and metal files, piled up.

Then *Bohemia* issued a surprising call to participate in "La Colecta de la Libertad" (The Collection for Freedom).[45] Those alive at the time have forgotten this particular fundraising campaign, since "there were so many."[46] But for the researcher, it is a gift—and not because it was the first of its kind.

The Colecta represented a call "to the Cuban people" that Miguel Ángel Quevedo launched during a "moment of genuine civic miracle."[47] Not only were citizens asked to donate a day's worth of their salary to the Revolution, as is typically remembered. In addition, Quevedo called on the totality of Cuban society, beyond the boundaries of haves and have-nots, to contribute whatever they could.[48] Hacendados, industrialists, laymen, and professionals were all asked to collaborate by underwriting the financing of the Agrarian Reform. But the campaign also appealed to citizens, teachers, house servants and nannies, even children, who were asked to donate their snack money.[49] For the sake of integrity, checks were to be made out to "Fidel Castro. *Bohemia* Magazine, Havana."

In an accompanying two-page photo-story illustrating the peasant's real-life conditions, the inset text informed the reader of dedicated telephone lines for the project and *Bohemia*'s address. But last and most important, the text advised the public, "Weekly until April 30 we will publish the roster of organizations and people who mail their financial support."[50]

Mail? People showed up. *Bohemia*'s offices were immediately flooded by a mass of citizens eager to contribute and make their donation count. The human tide that invaded the magazine's headquarters forced a quick expansion of space, telephone lines, and staff specially assigned to the task. Moreover, it obliged the magazine to print page after page filled with participants' names and their corresponding donations.

Here the researcher is left dumbfounded by the results. Even with the magazine closing at 12:00 p.m. on Tuesday, March 3, it took only three days to gather $260,739.81.[51] Believe it or not, and to Quevedo's own surprise, children did contribute their modest snack money, and they even showed up with piggy banks.[52] The request that citizens donate a full day's pay for the industrialization project was also favorably received.[53]

The first to show up were the employees of the celebrated Casa de los Uno, Dos y Tres Centavos (House of the One, Two, and Three Cents)—popularly known as the Casa de los Tres Kilos—with the sum of $256.50, after which the owners, obviously, had to contribute as well.[54] Reading the "First Roster" ("Primera Relación") reveals donations of $3 given by three people. Many gave only $1, and someone even donated forty cents.[55] The old servants of the deceased former president Mario García Menocal donated $11.[56] There were eleven of them. Contributions were also sent via post. One of the letters is especially interesting because it reveals how sure the donor was that Fidel Castro himself had convened the Colecta de la Libertad.[57]

This qualifies, perhaps, as the first sign of what would later become a general tendency: the attribution of all revolutionary initiatives to Fidel. In a letter written to the magazine, though, Castro explicitly thanked Quevedo for his brilliant idea and contributed to the Colecta himself, a donation that was duly registered on a second page as part of the "Second Roster" of contributors.[58] The lengthy name that Quevedo gave the project—Movimiento Patriótico de Apoyo Económico a la Reforma Agraria y el Desarrollo Industrial (Patriotic Movement of Economic Support for the Agrarian Reform and Industrial Development), which Castro mentioned in his letter—became a way to legitimate the contributions of important donors, who posed for History by handing over donations in front of an enormous banner boasting the ostentatious title.[59] Of course, the movement became an association with corresponding members and identified by the complex initials MPAERA. Even con artists pretended to gather donations on behalf of the association.[60]

And yet *Bohemia* itself, with its characteristic journalistic talent, called each of its weekly features about the campaign a "Report to the People," in white letters on a black band. Underneath was the boldface heading "COLECTA DE LA LIBERTAD," followed by the quantity collected and, in parentheses, an indication of whether the list of donors was the Second, Third, or Fifth Roster. The complete name of this "Movement"—echoing that other "Movement," the 26th of July—would have filled the entire page.

All told, Quevedo's call to action was a success. The extensive list of the Second Roster brings to light another interesting fact: Cubans in New York and Tampa, Florida, also sent in contributions to the Agrarian Reform.[61] Additionally, for the first but not the last time, an anonymous donor was listed.[62] This was the final roster in which names of donors appeared in one column, with the amount of their contribution beside them. By the third publication, the names and donations were referenced one after the other, separated by a simple semicolon, a clear indicator that the magazine needed to save space to include every participant.

A complete study of the Colecta and its repercussions would require a book. For now, the most crucial aspect to highlight is that its very existence and continued success marked the first incorporation into the revolutionary arena of that citizen who "did not know how to fight," as Núñez Rodríguez had written, but who could now collaborate.[63] The campaign's call to action allowed each citizen to claim a role in the essential tasks of the nation.

By contrast, in mass audiences at public speeches, or in the dialogues and sometimes interrogations that Fidel Castro engaged in with the crowd, the individual citizen remains invisible. It is always the people (plural), the multitude, that dominates our interpretations. This holds true even for the first massive response to a political mobilization, what would later be known as the beginning of Operación Verdad.[64] It was not in vain that such acts were immediately called *concentraciones*, or concentrations. Individual wills were condensed; individualities were lost.

The Colecta, on the other hand, named the individual citizen: José Vidal, Lucila F. Machín, Vivian Fernández García, or Enrique de la Osa, who donated $25.[65] The participation of associations constrained individuality only as far as groups limited their self-definition: workers and employees from the España sugar mill, employees from Arenal Cinema, Juan Cañizares Youth Lodge, and teachers and staff from the Escuela de Hogar (Home Economics School) of Manzanillo.[66] One of the more curious cases is that of the workers of Leslie Pantin and Sons, who apparently made contributions in three different groups on the same day, each identified, simply, as "employees of Leslie Pantin and Sons."[67] The repeated appearance of anonymous donors indicates that not everyone was proud to see their name appear in *Bohemia*, clearly an indication of the residual caution displayed by citizens unwilling to risk causing trouble. But though they collaborated without being named, they collaborated all the same.

The Colecta de la Libertad thus illustrates one of the most significant paradoxes of Year 1. Far from listing demands, as both big and small associations had insistently done since January, the individual citizen in this instance *gave* the little that he or she had, knowing that the name and contribution amount would appear in Cuba's—and Latin America's—most widely read magazine. In a society where worrying about "What will they say?" still dominated social mores, the fact that one might reveal the state of one's finances by going all the way to *Bohemia* just to hand over forty cents sent a powerful message.

Gossip, for once, seemingly did not matter to the contemporary of the Revolution. Originally slated to conclude in March, the end date for the Colecta was pushed back over and over again due to the surge of donations and individual donors from all directions. For instance, the Havana Port Workers' Union sent in its contribution, but not to *Bohemia*. For whatever reason, they gave their check to Commander Juan Almeida, who deposited it at the magazine with a huge grin across his face.[68] Every type of association, from rural schools all over the country to Masonic lodges and the famous Havana Business Association, sent their contributions.[69] Several participants, moreover, noted that their donation was made possible by reductions in rent costs, the result of another government measure.[70] The absenteeism of the citizenry, the main culprit in Mañach's "Drama of Cuba," seemingly had begun to disappear.

Of course, big businesses and organizations donated, too. To this end, the roster recorded $250,000 from the Rice Harvester's Association, $70,528.22 from the workers of the Cuban Electric Company, a measly $25,000 from the staff of the Trust Company of Cuba, and, last but not least, $250,000 from Shell, the first big foreign firm that signed onto the Colecta.[71] In fact, big businesses donated so much that, once their contribution was removed, the Colecta's total dropped from a grand $13 million to a little over $1 million, almost reaching $2 million.[72] So, what happened?

What happened was the Agrarian Reform itself. Foolishly, yesterday's men held onto an unwavering belief that the world they had so long dominated was still the same. This was a grave error.[73]

Though everyone knew that the Agrarian Reform was coming, that did not prevent many from wishing that it would occur at their convenience. We should recall that already starting in February the hacendados had offered to design the Agrarian Reform themselves, yet they were paid no mind.[74] In March they announced to *Bohemia*, as a result of a General Assembly of their members (Junta General de Asociados), a contribution to the Colecta *not* from ANDHEC but from the sugar industry as a whole, which the magazine calculated at $8 million.[75] That same month the hacendados communicated to *Bohemia* their contribution as a class, still insistent on participating in the Reform's design. They announced "a $2,500,000 fund destined for study and execution of the early phases of Agrarian Reform and the industrialization of the country."[76] Quevedo incorporated the donation into the fifth roster.[77] (The supposed studies have disappeared without a trace.)

Meanwhile, the all-important cattle ranchers—who, as noted, had the most to lose in terms of land—also proposed making their own large donation in kind to the Colecta, quite apart from the efforts of other sectors. And they reportedly had assurances that the actual measures of the Agrarian Reform would be moderate. A firsthand witness and longtime fighter in the struggle against the Batista tyranny, as well as a member of the most elite Cuban–North American bourgeoisie, commented years later, "Everyone knew that the cattle ranchers sat down time and again with [the revolutionary leader] Sorí Marín asking him to moderate the law. . . . It was being said that the day before [the signing of the Agrarian Reform Law in La Plata] Sorí had assured everyone that the law would not be radical. . . . Sorí was the one taken by surprise."[78]

But in the end the reaction of today's men astonished the powerful of yesterday. In a televised appearance, Fidel Castro refused to accept the contributions of the cattle ranchers, considering them bribery and extortion.[79] With this same attitude, he rejected every one of the big businesses' contributions as well.[80] In a forgotten chart that has not been seen in fifty years, Quevedo explained the consequences of this decision. The numbers reveal a reality that the subject of the Revolution did not then appreciate but is now evident. And as no one has taken a look at them in half a century, here they are:

Former Balance $13,572,178.91

MINUS:

National Association of Cattle Ranchers' Contribution
of 10,000 pregnant heifers with an approximate value of $1,250,000.00

Sugar Industry Contribution. Approximate value of
100,000 tons of sugar. $8,000.000.00

Cuban Hacendados Association's new contribution $2,500,000.00

Total to deduct after Dr. Fidel Castro
renounced those contributions $11,750,000.00

Collection's Total after Deduction $1,822,178.00

Ground Transport Retirees and Workers. $20,000.00

Members of the Union for Encomenderos and Mataderos. $10,000.00

Contribution of the town of Yagüajay, Las Villas,
given to citizen president Dr. Urrutia $20,060.02

Rest of Roster: $73,424.86

General Total . . . . $1,945,663.79[81]

Fidel Castro believed that he had refused $5 million. No. Looking at the hard figures, we can see he rebuffed a much more significant sum. But he also rejected much more. By taking this action, without realizing it Fidel refused to conserve the myth of popular hegemony that the Colecta had originally produced. His gesture showed the contemporary of the Revolution that, after everything, the famous $13 million hadn't come from their own efforts—no matter how hard they had worked. It was the same characters as always, the rich and the powerful, who had made the Colecta grow.

Here, though, the foundational paradox of Year 1 reveals itself again. The absentee citizen of the Republic had become a participatory subject in the Colecta. But the myth of popular decision-making power held strong. People would firmly believe, from this moment on, that their participation was decisive. And in more than one sense, it was. The Colecta was the first time in the young Revolution's history that the individual citizen appeared with a first and last name. So no matter the actual balance between individual donations and those of traditional interests, Cubans would still be eager to take part in any of the period's many other demands.

The Colecta's fizzling out did not mean that attention to the Agrarian Reform ended. In fact, Operación Reforma Agraria was just getting under way.[82] Strategy, however, turned from collecting money to gathering signatures. During debates around the law, an army of women took to the streets of the capital asking for "signatures for the Agrarian Reform." Likewise, the Agricultural and Livestock Exposition at Quinta de los Molinos and the Agricultural Festival of la Rampa were said to "enjoy public approval."[83] These events served as a precursor to an avalanche of attention to agrarian issues that would take place in July. In the same television appearance in which he rejected big business's contributions, Castro invited half a million peasants to Havana, a mass gathering that would take place a month later.

The "we demand" of January 1959 transformed from March through June into "we give." The revolutionary dynamic, however, soon de-emphasized the value of the individual citizen's offerings, relegating him or her again to anonymity.

But what could not be taken away was the conviction that effort could decidedly influence the country's course. La Colecta de la Libertad did not appear in the exhaustive "Panorama de la Libertad" at the end of 1959, in which *Bohemia* included the year's most noteworthy events. Nor did the magazine say anything in that issue about the participatory citizen and his or her short-lived individuality. Starting in 1960 the masses would already be that: an anonymous multitude. Yet they would remain convinced, as in the Colecta, that their individual participation was decisive, even as they sacrificed civic individuality in accordance with the vicissitudes of political life. The fleeting civil society that was redesigned during the Revolution's Year 1 would cede its place to politics, and, eventually, the citizen became a militiaman. But that, as Kipling liked to say, is another story.

NOTES

Editors' note: The editors thank Ian Russell for his assistance with the translation of this essay.

The quote in the chapter title is from Arroyito, "Las demandas después del 1ro de enero" (cartoon), in "En Cuba," *Bohemia*, February 15, 1959, 86.

1. See Lillian Guerra, *Visions of Power: Revolution, Redemption, and Resistance, 1959–1971* (Chapel Hill: University of North Carolina Press, 2012); Funes Monzote, this volume; Jorge Fornet, *El 71: Anatomía de una crisis* (Havana: Letras Cubanas, 2013).

2. Mañach's frequent changes in allegiance—member of the Grupo Minorista of intellectuals in the 1920s, founder of the ABC secret organization in the 1930s, along with almost every other possible flip—were the butt of jokes among other members of his generation. With his typical *criollo* humor, the anti-Machado activist and intellectual Pablo de la Torriente-Brau, writing from prison, asked Mañach to send his picture, since in jail they allowed anything "not political" to enter. He added that he and his jail mates would know exactly where to hang it. Zoe de la Torriente-Brau, interview with author and Katia Pradere, Havana, 1988.

3. Herminio Portell Vilá (1901–1992) was a historian, essayist, journalist, and university professor. He was very influential in Cuban intellectual life during the 1940s and 1950s. Among his most important historical texts, *Céspedes, el padre de la patria cubana* and *Narciso López y su época* stand out. In his 1959 column in *Bohemia*, he harshly criticized what he perceived as errors of the revolutionary process. He emigrated from Cuba in 1960. His papers are conserved at the Cuban Heritage Collection of the University of Miami Libraries. Gastón Baquero (1916–1997) was a poet, essayist, journalist, and editor of *Diario de la Marina* in its final era. His article "Words of Farewell and New Beginning" ("Palabras de despedida y recomienzo"), *Diario de La Marina*, April 19, 1959, marked his public dissent from the revolutionary process. He emigrated to Spain in 1959, where he continued his literary career.

4. For more on the essay, see María del Pilar Díaz Castañón, "Jorge Mañach, la sociedad civil y Bohemia," in *Éditos inéditos: Documentos olvidados de la historia de Cuba*, edited by María del Pilar Díaz Castañón (Havana: Editorial Ciencias Sociales, 2005), 83–87.

5. Jorge Mañach, "El Drama de Cuba," *Bohemia*, January 11, 1959, 6.

6. María del Pilar Díaz Castañón, *Ideología y revolución: Cuba, 1959–1962* (Havana: Editorial Ciencias Sociales, 2001). See chapter 4, "Vivir la Revolución," in particular.

7. Enrique Núñez Rodríguez, "Poema del padre que no supo pelear," *Carteles*, January 25, 1959, 43.

8. Andrés Valdespino (?–1974), doctor of philosophy and letters, was an essayist, journalist, and influential Catholic layman during the 1950s. As demonstrated in an interview with *La Quincena*, he enthusiastically defended the first measures of the revolutionary government, arguing for their compatibility with the Christian search for social

justice. His articles in *Bohemia* revealed fissures between the Catholic hierarchy and the laity. He left for the USA in 1960. In exile he wrote the book *Cuba como pasión* (Cuba as Passion) and collaborated in an interesting anthology about Latin American theater. Ángel del Cerro (1928–2013), a graduate of philosophy and letters at the University of Havana, was an important director of Catholic Youth at the end of the 1940s and, above all, during the 1950s. Like Valdespino, he criticized social injustices and the Catholic hierarchy's restrictions on the evangelizing activities of young people. His articles in *Bohemia* in 1959 showed allegiance to the revolutionary government and his belief in the compatibility between revolutionary measures and Christian doctrine. In 1960 he left Cuba for Miami, where he became one of the leaders of the Cuban Revolutionary Council, an anti-Castro organization financed by the CIA. He stayed only briefly in the United States before settling in Venezuela, where he achieved renown as a television screenwriter and telenovela author. He presided over the Christian Democratic Party of Cuba (in exile) between 1995 and 1997. Mario Llerena (1913–2006) was an influential lawyer and Catholic essayist. He collaborated with the 26th of July Movement in Mexico. His break with Castro became explicit in the first months of 1959 and was publicized in articles in *Bohemia* in which he criticized central aspects of revolutionary governance. He emigrated to the United States. Ignacio Biaín Moyúa (1909–1963), OFM, was a Basque priest who exercised notable influence over the Catholic youth of the 1940s and 1950s. He was the general director of the Federation of Cuban Catholic Youth, from which he led resistance against social injustice at every level, no matter the risk. He dabbled in film criticism and radio programs with similar objectives. He maintained this attitude in the excellent magazine that he would found, *La Quincena* (1955–59), whose editorials denounced the social injustices of the 1950s and the horrors of the Batista regime. His pamphlet *Orientaciones cristianas para la reforma agraria* (Christian Approaches to Agrarian Reform) promoted the need to undertake such a process before it had fully materialized. He adhered to the Revolution with both enthusiasm and his always critical eye, which ended up making him the target of criticism from the faithful and his superiors. He was replaced by the Church hierarchy as magazine director and, eventually, banned from participating in public life. The Church hierarchy was also responsible for the closure of *La Quincena*, the best publication of Cuban Catholic thought during the twentieth century. Biaín did not emigrate. He died in Cuba.

9. "'Ahora Sí!,' Electro-Sales," *Diario de La Marina*, January 11, 1959.

10. See numerous examples from *Diario de La Marina*, January 9, 1959. For example, "Nuestro Saludo," advertisement placed by the Almacenistas e Importadores de Tejidos de la Cámara de Comercio de la República de Cuba (Shop Owners and Textile Importers from the Chamber of Commerce of the Republic of Cuba); "La Asociación de Comercio e Industria de la Bahía de la Habana"; "Saludamos al Dr. Fidel Castro y a sus valerosos combatientes," advertisement from the Asociación Nacional de Fabricantes de Fósforos (National Association of Match Makers); advertisement by the Asociación Nacional de Importadores de Maquinaria (National Association of Machinery Importers); "El gallo canta a la Libertad y Saluda a los nuevos héroes de la patria," Porbén y Hnos.

11. Again, from *Diario de La Marina*, January 9, 1959: "Un abrazo sincero al pueblo de Cuba," Cía Empacadora La Unión, Fabricante de productos "Catedral"; Baby's Home;

Cía Cubana de Electricidad; "Glorioso Renacer," Óptica El Almendares; Cía Importadora González del Real, January 9, 1959; "Patria Feliz," inset text placed by the Cía Cubana de Óptica, exclusive distributors of Bausch & Lomb, January 9, 1959, and in the same issue: Julio C. Granda, "Invierta ahora, tenga fe en el futuro de Cuba."

12. "Nuestra Bienvenida!," Supermercado Delmónico; "Al Pueblo de Cuba," Asociación Nacional de Productores de Leche (National Association of Milk Producers); also, "El Gallo canta a la Libertad y saluda a los nuevos héroes de la Patria"; "Nuestro Saludo"; "Unión de Comerciantes e Industriales de la Calle de la Muralla y Anexas," all from *Diario de La Marina*, January 9, 1959.

13. "El Laboratorio Parke-Davis de Cuba, S.A.," *Diario de La Marina*, January 9, 1959.

14. "Nuestro Saludo . . . Nuestra Bienvenida. . . . Nuestro Agradecimiento . . . Nuestra Satisfacción," *Diario de La Marina*, January 9, 1959.

15. "Nuestro Saludo."

16. "Compañía Antillana de Acero, S.A." and "Cabillas Cubanas, S.A.," *Diario de La Marina*, January 9, 1959.

17. "Asociación de Comercio e Industria de la Bahía de la Habana."

18. "Honor y Gloria a los Soldados, Clases, Oficiales y Jefes, que inspirados y dirigidos por el Jefe Supremo Dr. Fidel Castro Ruz han liberado a Cuba y han logrado que renazcan vigorosos los anhelos de libertad, justicia y progreso y la confianza en nuestro destino, Rex Cinema, S.A.," *Diario de La Marina*, January 9, 1959.

19. "London City," *Diario de La Marina*, January 9, 1959.

20. "Embotelladora Ironbeer" and "General Electric Cubana, S.A.," *Diario de La Marina*, January 9, 1959.

21. "Cía Importadora González del Real," *Diario de La Marina*, January 9, 1959.

22. Alfred L. Padula Jr. "The Fall of the Bourgeoisie: Cuba, 1959–1961," PhD diss., University of New Mexico, 1974.

23. Roland T. Ely, *Cuando reinaba su majestad el azúcar: Estudio histórico-sociológico de una tragedia latinoamericana* (Buenos Aires: Universidad Sudamericana, 1963). The Agrarian Reform was one of the most anticipated of the revolutionary government's initiatives, already foretold in Castro's speech "La historia me absolverá" (History Will Absolve Me), after his failed attack on the Moncada Barracks in 1953. It was reiterated as a goal in all of the 26th of July Movement's programs (not to mention those of other reform groups) from that moment forward, including in the so-called Law No. 3 of the Sierra Maestra during the insurrection. The Agrarian Reform was promulgated at a national level on May 17, 1959. It outlawed, among other things, *latifundium* (defined for individual landowners as a property with more than 402 hectares) as well as land possession by foreign citizens or businesses (except in the cases of small farms). A second and more intense Agrarian Reform would be issued in October 1963.

24. It is worth noting that the cattle ranchers did not worry very much about the Agrarian Reform either. Business was booming in 1958, and exports to Latin America were more than profitable. Consequently, many hacendados were investing in the flourishing cattle industry.

25. "Un mensaje de los hombres de la zafra a los gobernantes de la Revolución," *Bohemia*, March 1, 1959, n.p.

26. "FIRST: Name a special commission to study Agrarian Reform plans for Cuba in relation to the Sugar Industry and, through the Industrial Commission, intensify the work being done to put into immediate activation specific measures to avoid unemployment." "Acuerdos tomados por la Asociación Nacional de Hacendados de Cuba con respecto al problema de la Reforma Agraria y la Industrialización de Cuba," *Bohemia*, March 1, 1959, n.p.

27. "SECOND: Offer the revolutionary government all means at our disposal and those that could be available to this Association and its members so that, in collaboration with the technical organizations and the people the revolutionary government designates, agrarian reform and industrial achievement can become realities, thus achieving Cuba's economic progress." "Acuerdos tomados."

28. "En Cuba," *Bohemia*, March 8, 1959, 86.

29. "En Cuba," 86. Conrado Bécquer Díaz (1920–1998) was an important leader of sugar workers and their representative in the National Federation of Sugar Workers. Though he joined the 26th of July Movement late, he contributed to the success of the general strike called by Castro in early January 1959 by declaring that the sugar workers from Las Villas to Oriente provinces were on strike. In 1959 he also sparked conflict with industry management by demanding the payment of the sugar cane differential that was already included in salaries. He also contributed to securing control of the unions.

30. The third and final accord keeps with the spirit of the times: "THIRD: Pledges allegiance to the pronouncements of the maximum leader of the Revolution, Dr. Fidel Castro Ruz; understands the reach of his aims; and only aspires to their fulfillment, so as to best benefit our fatherland." "Acuerdo tomados."

31. Passed by the U.S. Congress in 1934, the Jones-Costigan Act established a system of quotas, by country, for the importation of sugar into the United States. In Cuba this system would lead to the Ley de Coordinación Azucarera (Law of Sugar Coordination, 1937) and then the foundation of the Instituto de Coordinación y Establilización Azucarera (Institute for Sugar Coordination and Stabiliziation), with the objective of distributing the U.S. quota among the 161 refineries that were members of the ANDHEC. In line with the logical dependence that this secure arrangement promoted, the mechanism of the quota provoked internal adjustments that dispossessed small sugar producers in favor of large operations. See Raúl Cepero Bonilla, *Política azucarera: 1952–1958* (Mexico, D.F.: Editora Futuro, 1958), 19. The fear of losing the quota would go on to be a determining factor in the attitude that the hacendados assumed toward the young revolution. See Díaz Castañón, *Ideología y revolución*, chapter 4.

32. Felipe Pazos Roque (1912–2001) was a brilliant Cuban economist and president of Cuba's National Bank (1950–52), which he helped to found. He renounced the position due to his disagreement with Fulgencio Batista's policies. He collaborated in drafting the "Manifesto No. 1 of the 26th of July to the Cuban People," known as "The Economic Manifesto of the 26th of July," which outlined the organization's economic objectives. The revolutionary government named him president of the National Bank, a position that he held from January to November 1959, when he resigned. Together with Rufo López Fresquet and Raúl Cepero Bonilla, he helped shape economic policy in the first revolutionary year and helped increase his government's credibility. He moved to

Venezuela, where he worked as an advisor to diverse international organizations. Regino Boti León (1923–1999) studied economics at Harvard University and the University of Havana. He was a founding member of the Economic Commission for Latin America and the Caribbean at the United Nations. He collaborated with Pazos in the composition of "The Economic Manifesto of the 26th of July." In 1959 he was named director of the National Economics Council. In this role, and in the name of the revolutionary government, he took over the Institute of Sugar Coordination and Stabilization with Pazos. He acted for twenty years as vice president, and then advisor, of an important Cuban state company, Corporation CIMEX. He received the National Prize of Economics in 1998. Rufo López Fresquet (1911–1983) was a brilliant Cuban economist. Named secretary of finance in January 1959, his tax policies succeeded in filling the coffers of the young revolutionary state. Like Pazos, his singular presence in the cabinet initially aided in building trust and credibility for the revolutionary government with the middle and upper classes. The text of "Law 40" ("Operación Honestidad") is a revealing portrait of how the greed protected by Batista impeded the businesses of the Cuban middle class. He resigned in March 1960. He emigrated to the United States and wrote *My Fourteen Months with Castro*, an important testimony of the period. Raúl Cepero Bonilla (1921–1962) was a lawyer, brilliant economist, essayist, journalist, and author of books on the Cuban economy that earned him great prestige among all of the island's sectors, such as the influential *Política azucarera* and *Azúcar y abolición*. He was the revolutionary government's first commerce secretary (1959–60) and then minister-president of the National Bank of Cuba (1961–62). Cepero was the third—and very respected—member of the "magic troika" (Pazos, Rufo, Cepero). He was also the only one who remained aligned with the Revolution. He had to deal with the petty ambitions of small producers and their failure to understand policy in the first months of 1959. His economic policy, like López Fresquet's, promoted industrial diversification. He died in an airplane accident in November 1962 when returning from the Congress of the Food and Agricultural Organization.

33. Regino Boti and Felipe Pazos, "Algunos aspectos del desarrollo económico de Cuba (Tesis del Movimiento Revolucionario 26 de Julio)," *Revista Bimestre Cubana* 75 (July–December 1958): 249–82.

34. "The correct path is to establish a rational plan of economic growth, with strong citizen backing, that increases national production, develops the Cuban economy, creates fruitful employment and, finally, elevates per capita income, without excluding any measure that social justice demands. . . . If the sugar industry cannot facilitate a progressive economic growth for us in accordance with the new increases in the population or cannot obtain enough dollars and foreign currency to buy machinery and consumer goods, Cuba should immediately increase its internal production, as much in national consumer products as in export goods." Boti and Pazos, "Algunos aspectos."

35. Among others, these are the principal aspects that the National Association of Cuban Industrialists (ANIC) considered indispensable for the full realization of the diversification project. See *Boletín de la ANIC*, February 1959, 6.

36. "We firmly believe that we have managed to create a national conscience in favor of the patriotic work that already constitutes a demand, more than a wish, of all the

Cuban people." See "Memorándum enviado a la Comisión de Ministros designada para la orientación y planificación de la economía nacional, 11 de febrero de 1959," *Boletín de la* ANIC, February 1959, 6.

37. "Hay que redimir a los pobres del campo," *Bohemia*, February 1, 1959, 60–61.

38. The trial began on Thursday, January 22, at 5:30 p.m. Humberto Sorí Marín presided, with Raúl Chibás and Universo Sánchez also serving as judges. The trial lasted until the early morning of January 23. See "En Cuba," *Bohemia*, February 1, 1959, 97, 102.

39. "Juicio: Un criminal de guerra," in "En Cuba," *Bohemia*, February 1, 1959, 96.

40. "Juicio," 97.

41. A mass rally in support of Operation Truth took place on January 21, in front of the Presidential Palace, the day before Sosa Blanco's trial started. "Más de un millón de ciudadanos reiteró una vez más su apoyo al Gobierno Revolucionario," *Bohemia*, February 1, 1959, 122–25.

42. "Those who sacrificed it all for our political freedom have more than earned our effort and, even, our sacrifice for their economic freedom. . . . And the debt is not only current. The peasants were, in their majority, those who, in 1868, carried out the first Liberation Invasion with Gómez and Maceo." "La Reforma Agraria: Una deuda de honor," inset text placed by Cervecería La Tropical ("La Tropical" Brewery), *Bohemia*, March 1, 1959, 79.

43. "Let us commemorate this 24th of February to promote the success of the Agrarian Reform, to begin to pay back our Debt of Honor with the Cuban countryman." "La Reforma Agraria," 79.

44. The first ones were donated by "La Tropical" Brewery. "Haciendo buenas sus palabras, La Tropical dona los primeros tractores y los primeros implementos agrícolas," *Bohemia*, March 1, 1959, 79.

45. "La Colecta de la Libertad (Pueblo de Cuba, responde)," *Bohemia*, March 1, 1959, 70–71.

46. Pedro Pablo Aguilera Patton, interview with author, Havana, February 18, 2001.

47. "La Colecta de la Libertad," 70–71.

48. "Cubans, we must contribute! The task at hand belongs to all: rich and poor, black and white, children and elders, men and women. The Revolution does not make distinctions; it united us all to destroy tyranny, it needs us all now to fortify victory. No one can withhold their contribution—no matter how small. No one can hide their right hand; we must offer it to give, to serve, to save Cuba."

49. "La Colecta de la Libertad," 70–71.

50. "Cubano: Esperamos tu contribución," *Bohemia*, March 1, 1959, 72–73.

51. The $ in this case, and throughout this essay, refers to Cuban pesos. $ is the symbol used to designate peso-denominated currencies throughout Latin America. In 1959, one Cuban peso was also in fact equivalent to one U.S. dollar.—Eds.

52. The first person to contribute was Alina Dávila, who gave ten cents of her snack money. Siblings Alicia and Felipe Varela brought their piggy banks, which contained $4.42. The girls Onelia and Grisela Socarrás brought a contribution from their savings, which amounted to $10.33. See "Informe al Pueblo: Primera Relación: $260,739.81," *Bohemia*, March 8, 1959, 74–76.

53. The first were workers from the Nazábal sugar refinery. The labor leader Conrado Bécquer appears with them in their photo. See "Informe al Pueblo: Primera Relación," 75.

54. They sent $500. See "Informe al Pueblo: Primera Relación," 74.

55. Such is the case of Cristina Forrest. See "Informe al Pueblo: Primera Relación," 74.

56. See "Informe al Pueblo: Primera Relación," 74. Mario García Menocal (1866–1941) was an engineer who graduated from Cornell and served as a general during the last Cuban war of independence. He was the third president of the Republic (1913–21). His contested reelection in 1916 led to the so-called War of the Chambelona.

57. "Fidel: I recently heard your call to the people through *Bohemia*," wrote Julio Hernández Martín. See "Cartas interesantes," *Bohemia*, March 8, 1959, 75.

58. "EL DR. FIDEL CASTRO CONTRIBUYE CON SU SUELDO DE PRIMER MINISTRO A LA REFORMA AGRARIA," *Bohemia*, March 15, 1959, 87. The magazine published a photograph of the mailed letter, dated March 3, 1959, and its transcription, as well as photos of the sent checks, corresponding to the first wages—$392.80—and $211.77 received for expenses.

59. Such was the case of William Gálvez, who donated his salary as inspector general of the army. See photo and caption, *Bohemia*, March 15, 1959, 85. Likewise, we can point to the example of Paulino Marrero, representative of the Peasant Association of the San Leandro neighborhood in Palma Soriano. See photo and caption, *Bohemia*, March 15, 1959, 86. Fidel Castro wrote, "Dear Miguel: With strong emotion, I read the *Bohemia* editorial about the Patriotic Movement of Support for the Agrarian Reform and Industrial Development." From letter transcribed in *Bohemia*, March 15, 1959, 87.

60. "In particular neighborhoods of Havana, unscrupulous persons are carrying around collection boxes, claiming that these funds are for the Agrarian Reform. . . . Those people are not authorized to carry out collections of any kind. . . . The only authorized people to receive these donations are those that work in the offices situated in the *Bohemia* building." "No se deje sorprender!," *Bohemia*, April 19, 1959, 77.

61. "Informe al Pueblo: Segunda Relación," *Bohemia*, March 15, 1959, 84.

62. "Informe al Pueblo: Segunda Relación," 85.

63. Núñez Rodríguez, "Poema."

64. "En un acto sin precedentes, más de un millón de cubanos ratifican todo el apoyo de la Patria al gobierno de la Revolución," *Bohemia*, February 1, 1959, 3.

65. "Informe al Pueblo: Segunda Relación," 85, 86.

66. "Informe al Pueblo: Segunda Relación," 86, 85.

67. "Informe al Pueblo: Segunda Relación," 85.

68. "Informe al Pueblo. Colecta de la Libertad. $13,168,247.36 (Décima Relación)," *Bohemia*, May 10, 1959, 78.

69. For example, "Students and Superintendent, rural school 47, Ciego de Ávila, 6.30; . . . Teacher and students, rural school 34, Las Caobas, 4.70." "Informe al Pueblo. Colecta de la Libertad. $13,168,247.36," 86. One social club that contributed was the well-known "Sociedad Gran Maceo," from Limonar, Matanzas, which sent $60.19 (86, 79).

70. For instance, "José Antonio Gómez (2 months' rent reduction), 42.50." Also, "Alejandrina Franco de González (rent reduction), 27." Informe al Pueblo. Colecta de la Libertad. $13,168,247.36," 77, 79.

71. "Informe al Pueblo: Colecta de la Libertad $12,962,893.19 (Séptima Relación)," *Bohemia*, April 19, 1959, 76–79, 97, 100; "Informe al Pueblo: Primera Relación," 74; "Informe al Pueblo. Colecta de la Libertad: $10,046,469.42," *Bohemia*, March 29, 1959, 76, 77.

72. "Informe al Pueblo. Colecta de la Libertad: $1,945,663.79 (Décimoquinta Relación)," *Bohemia*, June 21, 1959, 85.

73. *Bohemia* reflected this idea in March, in a curious vignette that mentions the applause received in the ANDHEC by "the unsinkable Arturo Mañas": "In Cuba there are still people that haven't learned that the country has experienced a huge social and moral transformation since the 1st of the year. Evidence of this could be seen last week at the Hacendados' Association, when the arrival of Arturo Mañas—a surprise for those looking to reform the institution, updating it for the new era—was greeted with applause. . . . The unsinkable Arturo Mañas, despite the applause of his peers, cannot figure in any way as a guiding light in sugar-industry circles, unless intrigues against the security of the country and social justice are allowed to prosper under the Revolution's tolerance." "El Insumergible Mañas," in "En Cuba," *Bohemia*, May 31, 1959, 87.

74. See note 25 above.

75. In a formal letter addressed to Quevedo and dated March 11, 1959, Amado Aréchaga and Gregorio Escagedo Jr., ANDHEC president and secretary, respectively, summarized the accords discussed the day before. The second one should be highlighted: "2. Support the initiative that the Sugar Industry, as a whole, donates 100,000 tons of sugar from the most recent harvest to the Colecta, distributed in installments, and with the collaboration of workers, *colonos* [small to medium-size growers who sold their sugar cane crop to a refinery], and hacendados." See "Contribución de la Asociación Nacional de Hacendados a la Reforma Agraria," *Bohemia*, March 22, 1959, 77.

76. Also signed by Aréchaga and Escagedo on March 25, the message lays out the accords of the General Assembly of the 23rd. The third accord references the cited figure. See "Nueva contribución de la Asociación Nacional de Hacendados de Cuba y periódico *El Mundo*," *Bohemia*, April 5, 1959, 73.

77. See "Informe al Pueblo. Colecta de la Libertad: $12,605,803.74 (Quinta Relación)," *Bohemia*, April 5, 1959, 72–75.

78. Pedro Pablo Aguilera Patton, interview with author.

79. "Fidel Castro. Defendiendo al pueblo," in "En Cuba," *Bohemia*, June 21, 1959, 91, 92.

80. "I wish to say here that we will renounce the contribution of two million pesos that the *colonos* offered. Just as we will renounce the 10,000 pregnant heifers from the cattle ranchers, and the Hacendados' 2.5 million. Which is to say, we will be renouncing 5.5 million pesos for different reasons. . . . We only accept individual donations. We do not want to make the revolution with the same money being used to organize counter-revolutionary campaigns." "Fidel Castro. Defendiendo al pueblo," 91.

81. "Informe al Pueblo. Colecta de la Libertad: $1,945,663.79," 91.

82. "Panorama. En la Barricada," in "En Cuba," *Bohemia*, June 28, 1959, 79.

83. "En Cuba," *Bohemia*, June 28, 1959, 79. Convened through the Provincial Leadership of the 26th of July Movement, the campaign aimed to collect a million signatures, illustrating the majority support that, according to a *Bohemia* survey, the Agrarian Reform enjoyed.

6. *Geotransformación*

GEOGRAPHY AND REVOLUTION IN CUBA
FROM THE 1950S TO THE 1960S

———

REINALDO FUNES MONZOTE

On June 29, 1967, in a meeting with the Directorate of the Cuban Academy of Sciences, Antonio Núñez Jiménez, its founding president, addressed how the Academy could contribute to the transformation of Cuba's natural environment.[1] He made reference to a conversation with Fidel Castro a month earlier, in which the two had discussed creating a freshwater reservoir in the Ensenada de la Broa (La Broa Inlet), as suggested by the director of the Institute of Oceanology.[2] The revolutionary leader showed an interest in the idea, remarking that it cohered well with other projects in development, such as the draining of the Gulf of Batabanó and the building of a road to the Isle of Pines.[3] As a result, a meeting with specialists from various institutions was called for the next day at the University of Havana. There, it was agreed that no project that seemed unrealistic would be disclosed to the public for the time being, even if it might be "feasible [once Cuba arrived at] a higher phase of social development."[4]

Núñez Jiménez's interest in the topic nonetheless remained keen. He went on to recall that when discussing the potential of the new man and of a socialist and communist revolution to transform the natural environment, the prime minister (Castro) had jokingly remarked, "After all, the Soviets, the Americans, aren't they trying to reach the moon? Well, this project is our voyage to the moon." On the basis of this notion, Núñez Jiménez argued that "Cuba's voyage to the moon would be the large-scale transformation of the country's natural environment."[5] He was quick to clarify, though, that at least ten years of research would be required before any project could be seriously undertaken, except in the case of small-scale experimental endeavors. In his view, the conversion of the Ensenada de la Broa into a freshwater reservoir was the true priority, as the rapid growth of and numerous advancements in Cuban agriculture could soon lead to a dearth of arable land, creating the need for "revolutionary methods" to increase productivity within a shorter span of time.

All reservations aside, in 1968 Núñez Jiménez published his seminal work, *Geotransformación de Cuba*, as a series through the Academy of Sciences. The work was also publicized that very same year in *Granma*.[6] It is difficult to say whether this represented a shift in communication strategies or an attempt to highlight the potential and promise of science and technology to improve living conditions in Cuba, by then already immersed in the so-called revolutionary offensive, a campaign to radicalize the Revolution's social model, including via the nationalization of remaining private businesses.[7] Of course, it could also be attributed to the author's sole initiative, as he had previously proposed preparing a book highlighting current ideas on the relationship between nature and development.[8]

This chapter explores the concept of "geotransformation" used by Núñez Jiménez to characterize plans, great and small, to transform Cuba's natural landscape after 1959. There are numerous and varied factors to consider, and it is impossible to cover them all in their full complexity. Ultimately, geotransformation drew upon loaded ideas such as "progress," "civilization," and "development," which imply an anthropocentric stance on the relationship between humans and the rest of the natural world. The pages that follow focus on the context of the 1950s and 1960s in order to illustrate links between the evolution of geographical thinking and the revolutionary movement that rose to power in January 1959.[9] This perspective, one that traces connections across the republican and revolutionary periods—and specifically in the realm of scientific or economic endeavors—tends to be absent from explanations of the origins and dynamics that led to the proclamation of a socialist revolution.

The few studies that make reference to environmental and geographical themes in revolutionary Cuba have placed greater emphasis on the notion of "the conquest of nature" within communist ideology and the resulting environmental effects of its implementation.[10] However, it would be inaccurate to assert that only those states that adopted so-called real socialism pursued this objective.[11] Within Cuba itself, a review of the prerevolutionary press offers ample evidence of the excitement aroused by numerous chimerical projects around the globe. An article by a French scientist reprinted in the magazine *Carteles* in 1959, for example, highlighted such projects as the creation of an inland sea in the heart of Africa from the waters of the Mediterranean and a train that would travel from London to New York, crossing the Bering Strait.[12]

In order to analyze Cuba's plans for transforming the natural environment in the first decade of the socialist revolution, this essay takes geographical ideas from the era preceding 1959 as its point of departure. In particular, I will trace Núñez Jiménez's trajectory, from his professional training as a geographer to his work and involvement in the upper echelons of the Cuban Revolution and, above all, his central role in the consolidation of a new scientific and political culture.

Before this, however, it is necessary to briefly review the career of Salvador Massip, considered the father of modern geography in Cuba, and that of his wife, Sarah Ysalgué, who had a decisive influence on the professional formation of Núñez Jiménez. Several of their works published before 1959 attempted to affirm and secure geography's relevance as a profession, while also rejecting environmental or geographical determinism as frameworks for contemplating and, ultimately, solving the nation's problems. The predominance of this same theoretical inclination during the subsequent post-1959 phase does not mean that other geographical ideas were wholly absent at the outset of the Revolution, but these cannot be addressed here for lack of space.

Together, the work of Massip and Núñez Jiménez illustrates the ways revolutionary ideas left their mark on "geography" as both space/territory and academic discipline over time. The convergence of these representatives of two distinct generations is evident in their shared rejection of geographical determinism and the presumed incompatibility of tropical zones with "civilization." Both likewise believed in the central role of geographical science in economic planning, as well as the possibility of achieving development by changing humans' relationship with the natural environment.[13] In parallel, this essay also takes up issues that can contribute to understanding the particular influence of geographic thinking after 1959, such as the renewed official emphasis on the sugar and agricultural industries after 1963 (after prior efforts at industrialization fizzled) and the impact of the Cold War on the competition between capitalist and communist countries in the realms of science and technology.

The decade of the 1950s would see a number of significant changes to major geographical theories and concepts. These built on the evolution of industrial society, the rise of social revolutions and economic crises, and accelerated advancements in science and technology facilitated by the age of oil. After the end of World War II, new ideas about economic development, coupled with the struggle for decolonization in Asia and Africa, began to crack the monolithic hegemony of "Western civilization" and social Darwinism. These changes directly influenced the transition from a deterministic vision of geography to new tendencies that sought to define the human as an active agent in relation to the natural world. An example that can be cited in this respect is "Man's Role in Changing the Face of the Earth," a colloquium held at Princeton University in 1955.[14]

Most of the geographical literature on Cuba written through the 1940s, produced by nationals and foreigners alike, was suffused with deterministic presumptions. This can be observed in articles by geographers from the United States, such as Ray H. Whitbeck and Derwent S. Whittlesey.[15] Likewise, Cuban geographers were influenced by the environmental and geographical determinism of authors such as Ellen Churchill Semple and Ellsworth Huntington, who argued that the optimal climate for civilization was the temperate zone, seen as more stimulating of human achievement.[16]

The professional trajectory of Salvador Massip Valdés (1891–1978) epitomizes the evolution of geographical concepts then permeating debates about Cuban society. Over the course of his long career as a geographer, spanning the period from the 1920s to the 1970s, new ideas about the role of geography in national socioeconomic and sociopolitical processes gained influence in Cuban academic discussions and public life. After completing his studies at the University of Havana in 1909 and working as a professor of geography and history at the Instituto de Segunda Enseñanza in Matanzas, Massip left for the United States to study geography and graduated with a master's degree from the Department of Natural Sciences at Columbia University in 1922. Starting in 1924, after returning to Cuba, he worked as a professor of geography at the University of Havana for over four decades. By then he could already be considered the father of human geography on the island.[17]

Massip and his wife, Sarah Ysalgué (1894–1989), whom he married in 1924, played a decisive role in the institutionalization of geography in higher education through the establishment of professorships dedicated to the discipline, first at the University of Havana's School of Education (Facultad Pedagógica) in

1927, and then at its School of Philosophy and Letters (Filosofía y Letras) in 1933. A native of Guantánamo, Ysalgué graduated with a degree in teaching and pedagogy from the University of Havana in 1919, while teaching geography and history at the Escuela Normal of Matanzas. Between 1920 and 1921 she completed studies in geomorphology at Columbia University Teacher's College, where she also received a master's degree in 1942. As university professors of geography, both she and Massip introduced field research and field excursions into all of their courses. Their professional influence was decisive in young students like Núñez Jiménez, who was mentored by Ysalgué as he completed his graduate thesis about Cuba's "Bellamar" caves.

One could say, with some caveats, that Massip, who identified as a follower of Semple's social geography, was greatly influenced by deterministic ideas and discourses through the 1940s. *Factores geográficos de la historia de Cuba* (1931) and *Factores geográficos de la cubanidad* (1941), which grappled with the role of insularity, uniformity, and "tropicality" (*tropicalidad*) in the formation of Cuban culture, are two works that exemplify this trend.[18] Still, despite the weight he afforded to "geographical factors," Massip's early adoption of anti-imperialist stances on the role of European powers and the United States in Latin America was a central characteristic of his work. This can be observed in his translation of and commentary on an article written by John E. Pomfret, "Human Geography and Culture," published in Havana in 1938.

Pomfret rejected deterministic geographers, to whose "limited vision" he attributed the "gross exaggerations" that exposed them to the "greatest ridicule." In contrast with the deterministic view, he saw man as capable of overcoming the limitations of his environment. He felt that this had already occurred in the nations of Western Europe and the United States that had managed to subdue and control the natural environment "to such a point that they have molded it, almost willfully, to their own benefit." Regarding the United States in particular, he wrote, "The conquest of the environment is representative of Euro-American Culture. All around the globe it appears in search of raw materials for its industry. All environments are forced to pay it tribute."[19]

Although he broadly agreed with the author, Massip included an endnote distancing himself from what he called the "physical transformation of the face of the Earth." In his view, this had another name: "quite clear and significant, that of imperialism." The so-called New World had entered a new era of this phenomenon, and the United States, "with its massive riches and enormous industrial development, [had] made its influence felt within the weaker nations of the rest of America." U.S. methods, according to Massip, consisted in attracting a president (Porfirio Díaz in Mexico, Juan Vicente Gómez in Venezuela, Augusto Leguía in Peru, and Gerardo Machado in Cuba) and securing his position in power in exchange for relegating the country to the status of financial and economic colony. When these tactics proved ineffective, the United States provoked revolutions, or otherwise made governments fall. In this regard, "what the government in Washington, Wall Street capitalism, and its many allies call 'communism' is little more than the awakening of the survival instincts of Hispanic-American groups, whose existence is compromised by the threat of being completely absorbed or reduced to servility by Anglo-Saxon groups."[20]

While Massip maintained these political leanings, in the 1950s his work turned toward a more pragmatic vision of geography, one geared toward solving practical problems. In various writings he defended the need for planning in Cuba, which could have been influenced by his knowledge of Puerto Rico's progress on this front, which he experienced firsthand when he was a visiting professor at the University of Río Piedras between 1946 and 1947. A good example of this can be found in the inaugural address he gave for the 1951–52 academic year at the University of Havana, titled "Geography and Its Importance for Resolving the Problems of the Cuban Nation."

Among other aspects, Massip highlighted the influence of geographical factors on the Cuban economy, the risks associated with the depletion of the country's riches and resources at the hands of an extractive economy that was favorable to very few, and the need to study the relationship between environmental and social factors. The artificial distortion caused by the hoarding of lands, on one hand, and Cuba's scarce population, on the other, imposed "a typically colonial regime [on the nation], where the rewards of capitalism were enjoyed by a handful of millionaires who traveled outside the country that produced it, while the masses suffered unspeakable misery." According to Massip, "Few countries in the world [had] such a large quantity of resources . . . in such a relatively small space; but also in few areas of the world was there such a brutal contrast between the extreme wealth of a few and the extreme poverty of the majority."[21]

Massip emphasized the urgent need for a politics of planning, in accordance with the recommendations of the Truslow Mission of the International Bank for Reconstruction and Development in 1950.[22] He also made reference to the five-year plans of the Soviet Union, planning efforts in countries with a democratic state—such as the United States and England—and even the Marshall Plan to rebuild Europe. But he insisted above all on the case of Puerto Rico, pushing for the establishment of a *junta de planes* (planning board), as was the case in that neighboring island. Although such a body would involve numerous specialists, it would be a geographer's job to coordinate their efforts, for which a map already created by Cuban and U.S. cartographers might serve as a useful tool. The central characteristics of the plan, which reflected nationalistic goals, would be (1) the moral and physical rehabilitation of the populace, an intensification of health and hygiene, and a new educational direction; (2) agrarian reform, consisting in dividing idle *latifundios* (large estates) into parcels, granting lands to the *campesinos* (Cuban farmers), and providing them with the necessary means of production; (3) the diversification of agricultural production and the achievement of self-sufficiency; and (4) the gradual industrialization of the country.

Thus, at the First National Conference on Planning in Havana (1956), Massip and Ysalgué presented a conference paper titled "Geography and Planning," which reiterated these same ideas.[23] They began by making reference to the classic experience of the Tennessee Valley Authority, where geographers, including the project's director, Donald Hudson, as well as engineers, architects, economists, medical doctors, and other professionals, had played a central role. They also cited various irrigation works that had been carried out since 1933 by Zionist settlers in Palestine—draining swamps and building canals until they made the desert bloom. A final reference point was the case of Belgium, where planning, they argued, had reached the utmost perfection with the distinguished and significant involvement of expert geographers.

In Massip and Ysalgué's view, the existing work of Cuban engineers and architects (who had been working on these issues for some time), suggestions made by foreigners, and papers presented previously by Rafael Picó in 1953 at the Cuban Society of Engineers all pointed to the need for a great national planning initiative. This project, they insisted, would have to prioritize regional needs and would require numerous technical experts, such as geographers, geologists, engineers, architects, economists, sociologists, medical doctors, and hygienists. Some could be hired from within the country itself, as had been the case in Puerto Rico's planning process. But if necessary, Massip and Ysalgué were not opposed to hiring qualified candidates from abroad, as the USSR had done during its first five-year plan.

These ideas about planning in Cuba—adapted, as we have seen, from such diverse reference points as Western Europe, the United States, the USSR, and even a colonial site such as Puerto Rico—also built on significant, ongoing changes within geography as an academic discipline and geographical ideas at large. We might cite, for example, reformulations within the field of tropical geography and its gradual replacement by the so-called geography of development.[24] Also relevant was the emergence of subfields such as active geography and constructive geography, dedicated to not only caring for but multiplying natural resources available for human betterment.[25] Massip and Ysalgué's trajectories are emblematic of these transitions and transformations, as well as of a growing social commitment and political consciousness within the discipline. Their work signaled a departure from the field's previous status as mere intellectual curiosity or, at best, a curricular requirement. Moreover, both Massip and Ysalgué were not only critical of the dictatorship of Fulgencio Batista that began in Cuba on March 10, 1952; they openly opposed it and subsequently took part in the revolutionary social processes that began in 1959.

Núñez Jiménez and Ideas for Transforming Cuba's Natural Environment

The influence of Massip and Ysalgué, as mentioned earlier, was decisive for Núñez Jiménez's training as a geographer. Born in Alquízar, Cuba, in 1923, Núñez Jiménez became the founder of the Cuban Speleological Society in 1940 at the age of seventeen. From that point, he would prove a diligent explorer of the country's many regions, thus becoming deeply acquainted with the social, economic, and environmental realities of the Cuban countryside.[26] Between 1946 and 1951 he studied at the School of Philosophy and Letters at the University of Havana, specializing in geography. Aside from his professional training, he also took part in various revolutionary struggles during this period, joining the Socialist Youth chapter at the university and becoming a member of the Popular Socialist (or Communist) Party.[27] As such, in 1951 he headed the Cuban delegation to the Third World Youth and Students for Peace Festival, held in East Berlin, and in 1952 he presided over the organizing committee for the "Month of Soviet-Cuban Friendship." Because of these political affiliations, starting in 1946 Núñez Jiménez was frequently accused of "communist activities" and was arrested on various occasions.

Both as a university student and later as a professor of geography and history at the Instituto de Segunda Enseñanza of Vedado, Núñez Jiménez continued his explorations of Cuba, organized by the Speleological Society. As a result of more than fifteen years of expeditions across the Cuban archipelago, including reconnaissance flights, in 1954 he published *Geografía de Cuba* (Geography of Cuba).[28] Because of the book's critical perspective on socioeconomic problems, above all in rural zones, as well as its denunciation of the effects of U.S. imperialism, Batista himself ordered that it be withdrawn from circulation, labeling it communist propaganda. Between January 16 and 17, 1955, copies of the book in bookstores, as well as printed copies at the Lex publishing house and the original printing plates, were confiscated. Its author, moreover, was interrogated by the Military Intelligence Services, and on March 30 the Ministry of Education prohibited the use of the book as a source, reference work, or reading material in public primary, middle, and secondary schools, or private educational institutions subject to the Ministry's oversight.

Regardless, the geographical thinking that imbued this work proved influential. Of note is Núñez Jiménez's rejection of the environmental determinism of authors as diverse as Angel Ganivet (Spain), Baron de Montesquieu (France), Ellsworth Huntington (United States), and Francisco Bulnes (Mexico). To this end, he lamented the work of those intellectuals who contended that Latin Americans were inferior, whether because of racial mixture, the physical environment of the region, or many other factors. In Núñez Jiménez's opinion, these types of theories only tended to justify "international abuse or paralyze the creative work of our peoples." On the contrary, he believed, it was social and economic regimes that bore responsibility for those evils "some try to blame on climate, topography, or the transparency of the sky." The physical environment could have influenced primitive humanity, but that relationship had already been inverted: "Today man influences his geographic surroundings. He is capable of dominating a flood, merging two wide rivers like the Volga and the Don, making Antarctica habitable, turning the most arid deserts into gardens, transforming dry climates into humid ones, lowering the temperature in warm places, and producing heat in cold environments. Not only does modern man change natural conditions. He is also capable of modifying the characteristics of man himself, and he is capable of correcting factors of inheritance."[29]

Núñez Jimenez's *Geography of Cuba* was also unique in its concrete proposals, such as the need for an agrarian reform "that to be true needs to involve the expropriation of all latifundia and the free distribution of land among farmers." By the same token, the author also suggested various ideas for transforming Cuban nature. These included protecting forests that covered the course of rivers and easily erodible soils; constructing dams, hydroelectric plants, irrigation channels, and aqueducts; and preparing the Cuban people for projects of reforestation.[30]

Núñez Jiménez had already disseminated these ideas in major press outlets such as the magazines *Carteles* and *Bohemia*, where he described his travels through the country and discussed changes that Cuba's geography required. In 1951, for instance, he argued that, when ready, the country needed to confront the problem of deforestation, improve its soils, and undertake projects to take better advantage of surface and subterranean waters—all with the collaboration of scientists and technicians from disciplines such as geography, geology, botany, and zoology. Small, individual geographical transformations, he contended, "would enrich small geographic areas, together amounting to a grand and positive transformation of Cuba."[31]

Likewise, on the occasion of an expedition down the Toa River in 1948, Núñez Jiménez outlined his belief that the river could truly transform the island. On one hand, the river offered a great potential resource for providing electricity to Oriente province, an opinion supported by the U.S. hydroelectric engineer Erkin Birch. But more important, he argued that the untapped mineral wealth of the area, when supplied by said hydroelectric plants located along the Toa, could convert Oriente province into a powerful industrial zone. There was also, in his view, great potential for growing coffee and bananas. Nevertheless, much of the territory along the river remained totally idle. Núñez Jiménez thus concluded, "We have within our reach, as a gift from mother nature, the means to make our country the garden of the Americas. But, sadly, if we do not react against our own apathy we will turn Cuba into a wasteland of famished settlers who will have to wait for everything to come to them from across the seas."[32]

Two frequent themes in his articles were water and the ongoing devastation of Cuba's forests. On the first topic, Núñez Jiménez warned that the island was in danger of running out of the liquid vital to the progress of the country.[33] On the second, he highlighted the impact of deforestation on erosion and rivers, while also arguing that it was necessary to prohibit the destruction of coastal mangroves. With respect to man's capacity to become the master of nature, he mentioned examples from the United States, such as the transformation of the Tennessee Valley; China, with its great dikes and forests planted to dominate the wide River Huai; the Soviet Union, where the Don and the Volga had been merged into one river and enormous bordering forestlands had also been created; and Mexico, where various efforts were also under way to win the battle over the land. But in Cuba, "if such a battle was also undertaken [in the past], it was only to mistreat and impoverish the land, not to protect it. Thus, all energy should be channeled to curing these ills."[34]

After the scandal surrounding *Geografía de Cuba*, Núñez Jiménez moved to Marta Abreu University in Santa Clara, where he obtained the position of professor of geography and geomorphology in November 1955. From there he presided over the Junta of Patriotic Unity (Junta Patriótica de Unidad) between 1957 and 1958, which brought together militants from the 26th of July Movement and the Revolutionary Directorate—leading anti-Batista insurgent organizations—and those of the Popular Socialist Party. Finally, after the failed general strike of April 1958, a crucial turning point in the evolution of the anti-Batista struggle, Núñez Jiménez joined the rebel troops commanded by Ernesto "Che" Guevara following the latter's arrival in the province of Las Villas. At that point he was designated chief of Topographical Services and of Military Contacts (Enlaces Militares, i.e., with other insurgent factions) for the rebel army, earning the rank of captain. With his cartographic knowledge, he contributed to the pivotal takeover of Santa Clara by the rebels.

The triumph of the Revolution in 1959 opened unprecedented possibilities for putting into practice Núñez Jiménez's ideas for transforming Cuban nature. The relationship between revolutions and the environment in Cuban history is a complicated theme, whose full analysis exceeds the scope of this essay. By way of precedent, though, it is enough to note here that Cuba's Revolution of 1933 also generated interest in regenerating nature, as can be seen in the creation of the Conde de Pozos Dulces National Forestry School that same year. Likewise, the goal of adequately using Cuba's natural resources was present from the beginning of 1959, and Núñez Jiménez played a decisive role in this respect. No longer was he just one of a small group of professional geographers. From his high position in the new government, he was able to begin implementing ideas that, until that point, had circulated only on a theoretical plane.

Notably, on October 20 of that same year, a new edition of his *Geografía de Cuba* was published. It was presented in the halls of Lex publishing house by the guerrilla commanders Raúl Castro and Camilo Cienfuegos, together with the intellectual Jorge Mañach—who had denounced the confiscation of the work in 1955—and the former Guatemalan president Juan José Arévalo, the author of influential anti-imperialist works such as *The Fable of the Shark and the Sardines: Latin America Strangled* (1956).[35] By that point Núñez Jiménez was already a close collaborator of Fidel Castro, with whom he had been involved in student battles at the University of Havana. He would later recall, "The 30th of January, Fidel returned to visit us at La Cabaña [fortress]. From that day forward, I started to work more assiduously with the Commander in Chief. After a long conversation with Che, I headed to Havana one night with Fidel. Along the way, we talked about the necessary transformation of Cuba's natural environment. Fidel showed himself to be passionate about the theme. 'But first it is necessary to transform man,' he told me."[36]

Subsequently, Núñez Jiménez's knowledge of geography influenced his being named the first executive director of the National Institute of Agrarian Reform, a position he held until 1962. In fact he was one of the authors of the first law of agrarian reform promulgated on May 17, 1959. In parallel, he became a guide of sorts to Castro, with whom he explored Cuba's landscape. Castro recognized as much in a speech on January 15, 1960, at the Academy of Medical, Physical, and Natural Sciences of Havana, on the occasion of the twentieth anniversary of Cuba's Speleological Society. With regard to this organization's work, Castro stated that it had been useful not only for scientific purposes but for the national economy as well. Many early initiatives had been inspired by spelunkers' knowledge of caves and other geographical features of the island. These included tourist developments in Cayo Largo and, especially, efforts to transform the largest "swamp" of the country: "Thanks to the insistence of comrade Núñez Jiménez, we went to the Zapata Swamplands [Ciénaga de Zapata], and thanks to his interest in that region of Cuba, thanks to his knowledge of that region, an interest arose in all of us for the Zapata Swamplands, and today, in just a few months' time, the Zapata Swamplands is becoming not only one of the most beautiful tourist centers of Cuba, but also one of the richest regions of the country."[37]

Fidel described Núñez Jiménez as the best companion with whom to travel throughout the island. He was a tireless explorer, "a true encyclopedia of knowledge about Cuba." Through him, Fidel claimed, he had been educated "in a pleasant and enjoyable way with knowledge of the nation and recoup[ed] time wasted while a student, instead of dedicated to the study of geography." At another moment he argued that the nation's destiny depended on Cubans' identification with its land and soil. The goal, he said, was to forge "a people who yearn to work and enjoy the setting and the wealth of the land where they live." For this reason it was necessary to awaken in youth an interest in scientific activity, to that point limited to a small circle of researchers. The future of the country belonged, Fidel claimed, to the "men of science."[38]

A New Science for the Transformation of Nature

As an expression of this growing interest in promoting scientific research, the revolutionary government proposed, via Law 1011 of February 20, 1962, to establish the National Commission of the Cuban Academy of Sciences, charged with replacing the hundred-year-old Havana Academy of Sciences founded in 1861. Its first president and founder would be Núñez Jiménez, with a counsel of recognized researchers from the natural and social sciences.[39] The new organization's purpose was, above all, to accompany projects for economic and social development initiated by the government and study Cuba's natural resources through various institutes established to this end. According to one of the protagonists of these efforts, on April 24, 1964, during a meeting of the Directorate of the Academy with Che Guevara in attendance, the Academy's potential role in new agricultural plans was discussed, thus marking the first application of its scientific activities to the concrete needs of the country.[40]

The concept of "geotransformation," announced by Núñez Jiménez soon thereafter, fit within this growing emphasis on the role of science in the intensification of agriculture. By that point the revolutionary leadership saw the need for a "technical revolution" to complement Cuba's social revolution, echoing the terms of the Cold War competition between the great powers to prevail in science and technology. Examples of some of the projects undertaken therein include hydraulic megadams; the use of atomic energy; the growing use of chemical fertilizers, herbicides, and agricultural mechanization; and efforts to control the climate—all of which generated interest in Cuba. According to the historian John McNeill, the imperative for economic growth, together with the preoccupation with national security, shaped the basic socio-ecological trajectory of the twentieth century, independently of the ideas, programs, or political structures that governed particular scientific endeavors.[41] So too on the island, though at no time more so than during the Cuban Revolution.

Not surprisingly, the new Cuban Academy of Sciences ultimately established its most solid links with its peer organizations in countries from the socialist bloc. Still, collaboration with scientists from other countries and international organizations, such as the Food and Agriculture Organization of the United Nations and UNESCO, was not absent. Indeed, the push to develop science and technology in Cuba was directed above all to the battle to dominate nature, an objective very much in line with broad development schemes embraced by the West in the wake of World War II. Moreover, the idea of "dominating nature" could also trace its origins to schemes for the "conquest of the tropics" by the "white man" that were influential in the transition from the nineteenth to the twentieth century. This latter vision appears in numerous texts of the era and, of course, was not restricted to the conquest of the Latin American tropics alone.[42]

Nonetheless, more and more, Western development frameworks would share the spotlight—around the world and in Cuban eyes—with the idea of the "conquest of nature," which acquired great prestige in the Soviet Union, perhaps because that country did not possess tropical territories as such.[43] In particular, in 1948 the Soviet government initiated an ambitious program called the Stalinist Plan for the Transformation of Nature. Some even identify it as Stalin's version of the Marshall Plan.[44] Key elements included reforestation to protect the soil, the growth of more food crops, and the construction of reservoirs to assure stable harvests in regions of the so-called Steppe of Hunger. In line with the gigantic scale of Soviet agrarian policies, it was said that these plans were without parallel anywhere in the world.[45] Similarly, in the communist revolution in China led by Mao Zedong, socio-environmental transformations were undertaken. Controlling nature was seen as a symbol of the awakening of the nation, helping to "move the mountains of apathy that were the great obstacle to developing countries."[46]

In his articles from the 1950s, as we have seen, Núñez Jiménez showed he was up to speed with these kinds of projects in diverse parts of the world, particularly in the socialist countries. His interest in the latter, coincidentally, was facilitated by a goodwill visit in July 1959 to the United States at the same time that the Soviet Exposition of Science, Technology, and Culture was on view in New York. He took advantage of an extra-official exchange with the exhibition's organizers to inquire about the possibility of bringing it to Cuba. Months later a formal invitation to this end was extended to the vice president of the Soviet Council of Ministers, Anastas Mikoyan, during the latter's visit to Mexico in November. On February 4, 1960, the Soviet leader himself arrived in Havana to inaugurate the Exhibition of the USSR's Advancements in Science, Technology, and Culture at the National Museum of Fine Arts the next day.[47]

In June of that same year, Núñez Jiménez led Cuba's first official delegation to the USSR. Upon his return, in a television appearance on July 15, he told viewers that it had been a lifelong dream to visit that country, since he belonged to a generation for whom "everything Soviet was vetoed, [and] getting to know the Soviet Union was impeded. Those [Cubans] who did get to know the country and returned were jailed by the tyranny [the Batista government]."[48] Among the subjects that he discussed were the USSR's great efforts to transform nature, which he had been able to witness during some of his travels and in several exhibitions. Despite having some previous knowledge of these initiatives, he confessed to being surprised by the technology involved. One example cited was an ongoing effort to modify on a grand scale the USSR's desert areas, converting them into "true gardens for agriculture." He also mentioned the unification of enormous rivers and their channeling toward the oceans of the North, the Baltic Sea, and territories neighboring the Mediterranean. Núñez Jiménez assured the Cuban public that, as a professor of geography, he had been impressed by everything he had seen.[49]

He also described in special detail his visit to the Soviet Union's Academy of Sciences, as well as that institution's projects to create the material bases for a future communist society. Among others, he mentioned plans to redirect all rivers in Siberia, which flowed from South to North, so they would flow from East to West, with the objective of creating a "Sea of Siberia." From there the waters of this man-made sea would be directed via special channels toward the deserts of central Asia to create lands useful for agriculture. Another Soviet plan under study involved building a large dam north of the Kamchatka peninsula and Alaska and placing enormous atomic energy motors there to direct the warm currents of the Pacific Ocean toward the Arctic. The goal was "to defrost the northern part of the entire Asian and European continent, thus achieving one of the most extraordinary conquests of man over nature."[50]

In 1962 Cuba's National Council of Culture (Consejo Nacional de Cultura) published a book that shared Soviet ideas about the conquest of nature with the Cuban public. At one point it read, "When man works according to a unitary plan, with one objective, society will be able to do anything that it proposes. It will have thousands of arms and a giant brain at its disposal: world science united. All of nature will be its enormous economy, sensibly organized and planned."[51]

As this quote attests, at the time officials and citizens placed great faith in the power of science to transform human society and solve grave problems faced by a good number of formerly colonized countries or, as in the case of Cuba, those highly dependent on external powers. The attractiveness of this conviction for practitioners in the field of geography was also undeniable, and in large part this explains the evolution of professionals like Massip and Ysalgué toward ever more radical positions, in spite of their advanced age. Massip, after taking part in several diplomatic missions for the revolutionary government, was named a member of the National Commission of the Cuban Academy of Sciences and the first director of its Institute of Geography and Geology, founded in 1962. Ysalgué held various positions at the same institution between 1962 and 1967, such as chief of the Department of Physical Geography.

In 1965 Massip recalled how university graduates in geography before 1959 were presented with few career options other than teaching.[52] After that date, in contrast, the possibilities had widened considerably due to the applications of the field in the discovery and management of natural resources for the benefit of the masses. As an example, Massip cited the Soviet geographer Innokentii Gerasimov's ideas with respect to the problems presented by Soviet geography at the time. Scientific research in the USSR, Gerasimov proudly boasted, had become oriented toward the transformation of the physical environment and the utilization of natural resources to grow the socialist economy. Massip felt Cuba could achieve the same.[53]

In Massip's view, the creation of the School of Geography as the result of Cuba's university reform in 1962, and the subsequent increase in the number of students in the discipline, made it possible to envision a moment in which Cuban geographers could perform the same services for their country that geographers in the USSR and other socialist nations were already performing in theirs. Nonetheless, in a 1968 summary of the evolution of geographic thinking about Cuba over the previous hundred years, he listed a considerable number of challenges still facing the field:

> First, the exploration of the national territory, in order to discover new natural resources and develop [the island's] productive forces; second, better knowledge of the physical environment, to increase the yield of the land and combat the havoc caused by droughts, floods, deforestation, erosion, and hurricanes; third, a better distribution between agricultural areas (by crop type) and industrial areas; fourth, the study of the physical environment to design communication networks and achieve better use of the means of transportation; fifth, the division of the national territory into economic regions to establish distinct companies for industrial, agricultural, and cattle production; sixth, the study of the insular platform and the waters that cover it, to make better of use of fishing and other sea-born resources.[54]

To fulfill these objectives, Cuban geographers would soon have at their disposal a new *National Atlas of Cuba* (1970), a crucial resource that the Institute of Geography of the National Academy of Sciences was developing with the collaboration of Soviet geographers. With respect to the atlas, Massip—who worked with Núñez Jiménez, Ysalgué, and others to prepare it—believed it would give proof of Cuba's capacity for collective work and its revolutionary advances. With this work behind them, he insisted, "high-level national planning [could] now be facilitated, and Cuba now [had] a solid base for developing further geographical and other types of research."[55]

The Geotransformation of Cuba

It was in this context that Núñez Jiménez's seminal text on geotransformation in Cuba was published. But importantly, that concept, and efforts toward its implementation, also coincided with a crucial period of radicalization within the Cuban revolutionary process. The year was 1968, a time when various controversial projects related to the transformation of nature converged. Among others, one could mention the Invading Brigade of Agricultural Machinery (Brigada Invasora de Maquinaria Agrícola, later named after Che Guevara); the Havana "Greenbelt" (Cordón de la Habana), a pilot project to grow coffee on the outskirts of the capital; the founding of the National Botanical Garden and the National Zoo, together with the building of Lenin Park, thus creating an extensive green zone on the capital's periphery; and, finally, the birth of the "Schools in the Countryside" (Escuelas en el Campo), a system of boarding schools throughout the rural countryside where students would combine academic study with agricultural work. Of course one also has to mention the preparations for the Ten-Million-Ton Harvest between 1969 and 1970, an ambitious plan to achieve a historic sugar crop whose returns would purportedly help Cuba "leap" to a higher stage of development.

Yet if such events marked a significant turning point in the Revolution's evolution, Núñez Jiménez's text stuck to a more familiar chronological framework. After offering a brief historical and philosophical preamble, he divided his analysis of the history of Cuban geotransformation into two periods: a negative one, running from colonization through 1959, and a positive phase since that year. From the first era, he highlighted harmful impacts such as the salinization of the Laguna de la Leche (Cuba's largest freshwater lake), as well as the groundwater of the coastal plains; the deforestation of upper river basins; the destruction of other forests; and erosion. He also recognized positive changes to the environment, such as irrigation channels in the zone of the Mayabeque River and the construction of the Roque Canal to control flooding on the plains of Colón.

But only in the new revolutionary era, in his view, did a true path toward positive geotransformation open, thanks to scientific development. For Núñez Jiménez—as for Massip before him—science and technology allowed Cubans to begin studying the changes that needed to be made to the geography of their entire archipelago, with the geographer playing a central role as a new kind of engineer, alongside specialists from fields such as geology, geophysics, and geochemistry. Geography, as he put it, was the science of dominating nature, and its role, together with other sciences, was to aid Cubans in constructing socialism and communism. It would do so by restoring devastated forests and creating new ones; detaining erosion and forming new soils; constructing dikes to create new, workable lands and building reservoirs to bring water to where it was necessary; diverting the flow of rivers for productive ends; and cultivating the depths of the seas. Núñez Jiménez also highlighted the need to take advantage of the sun, the internal heat of the planet Earth, the wind, ocean currents, atomic energy, and even the enormous power of hurricanes to generate energy for human development. Waters contaminated by industry would be purified and reutilized. In short, Núñez Jiménez's ambitions were all-encompassing and, for his time, could even seem fantastical: "We will control our highly variable climate by taking the heat energy from the sun to transform it into a temperate environment; we will create clouds and make them rain, in accordance with agricultural needs."[56]

In line with these objectives, the president of the Academy of Sciences suggested that "the greatest undertaking of the future man of communist society [would] be the great, bloodless battle to transform nature." To achieve this, together with the development of new technology and science, "[Cubans] would have to embark on the most difficult task of constructing the man of the twenty-first century."[57] Here Núñez Jiménez obviously drew on the formulation of Guevara, for whom the construction of a new society depended on "the formation of the new man and the development of technology."[58] But for Núñez Jiménez, that new man, as a communist, also needed to have an "equally developed" consciousness about "how evolved new machines will be that, under his command, will transform seas into land, or will begin to harvest the moon."[59]

In contrast to these theoretical imaginings, plans actually put into place mostly had to do with the effective management of water, almost always in close relation with efforts to intensify agricultural production or expand lands dedicated to it. One of the highest priorities was better controlling rivers by building large reservoirs and canals to help manage floods and irrigation. Advances in this respect took place in Oriente and a few other provinces following the devastation of Hurricane Flora (1963). In parallel, environmental and agricultural authorities oversaw the building of agricultural terraces and forested areas to control erosion in zones such as the Sierra del Rosario (mountains in Pinar del Río province), the Sierra Maestra (the island's largest mountain range in the east), the Isle of Pines, and the hills on the outskirts of Havana.

Still, more ambitious, concrete projects were also envisioned. One of the most important involved draining the Zapata swamp, in parallel with initiatives to promote tourism in the area and protect native species (such as crocodiles and manatees).[60] In essence, authorities hoped to reclaim large swaths of swampland and make them suitable for agricultural production, especially the harvesting of rice. In truth, similar ideas had circulated among Cuban scientists before 1959. But in contrast to those efforts, Núñez Jiménez argued, "only the Revolution in power began to transform all of Zapata region, building highways through the swamps and dogtooth limestone coasts, building towns, schools, dikes, opening canals, and cleaning up the zone."[61] He also referenced the work of technicians from the Dutch company NEDECO who, at the beginning of 1959, helped build a pilot polder in the area—a parcel of land reclaimed from the sea—dedicated to growing grass for grazing.[62] These specialists also undertook studies to the same end at the mouth of the Cauto River, the island's longest, running through an extensive area in eastern Cuba.[63]

Geographers studied other wetlands to see if they could be similarly reclaimed. One idea, for example, was to convert into dry land the 190 kilometers between the northern coast of Camaguey province and the set of large island keys offshore. This territory, it was thought, could be useful for agriculture or mariculture—via the planting of edible algae—or even industrial purposes. Added to this was the already referenced study for draining the Gulf of Batabanó between the Cuban mainland and the Isle of Pines. If accomplished, such a grand endeavor could increase the size of agricultural lands in the country by an amount equivalent to the territory of Oriente province, the island's largest.

Among those projects focused on the better management and use of existing waters, the idea of diverting the flow of the Toa River in the northeast of Oriente province was among the most developed. Specialists hoped to redirect the river southward to supply the driest portion of the province, then carry its waters to Guantánamo Bay via an artificial canal. Utilizing the slogan "Not one drop of water to the sea," Núñez Jiménez also recommended constructing a canal that circled the entire Cuban coastline to retain groundwater.[64] Likewise, he suggested blocking the currents of subterranean rivers at points close to the coastline and diverting the flow for purposes of irrigation. At the time, a canal was already being constructed at the mouth of the Cauto to capture runoff from the river basin.

More ambitious proposals involved forming large reservoirs of freshwater out of the Ensenada de la Broa, off the southern coast of Havana and Matanzas provinces, and Nipe Bay, off the northern coast of Oriente. Núñez Jiménez attributed the Nipe Bay idea, in particular, to the leader of the Revolution, who proposed blocking the entrance of salt water to the narrow bay and transforming it into an internal lagoon into which freshwater rivers would continue to flow, thus naturally desalinating the water. Studies conducted by the National Institute of Hydraulic Resources indicated that this project could be completed in three years. The successfully desalinated water would then be used for irrigation.

Yet another idea to which Núñez Jiménez and other interested scientists paid serious attention was that of generating artificial rain. As an alternative to drying out the Gulf of Batabanó, scientists proposed creating a kind of natural cloud machine in its deep waters. By growing dark algae, those waters would, in theory, absorb more solar radiation, become warmer, and thus contribute to extending the rainy season in the southern area of the island between Pinar del Río and Las Villas provinces. Likewise, at the Experimental Department for Cloud Physics of the Academy of Sciences, located south of Havana, a group of Cuban, Soviet, Czech, and French specialists worked on techniques to "'milk' the necessary water from clouds." With this goal in mind, fifty large petroleum-burning machines—called Meteotron engines—were installed to create gigantic dark clouds for testing whether intensified rains could be generated.[65]

Perhaps the last geotransformation project worthy of mention is the "communist hectare" (*hectárea comunista*)—a plan, as mentioned in a speech by Castro, for marking off hectares of dogtooth limestone, covering them with soil brought in by truck, and dedicating the land to harvest. This would demonstrate that "with the help of machines, human work multiplies many times over and anything is possible."[66] Such a conviction was also fueled by ongoing efforts to convert the outskirts of Cuba's capital into a "greenbelt" for agricultural production.[67]

In the end, a great number of these projects never came to fruition. This demonstrates that what may have been feasible from the standpoint of geoengineering was not always workable from other points of view—the economic, or the organizational, for example. These projects thus stand mostly as testaments to an era of great optimism in man's capacity to dominate nature. More work needs to be done to determine whether subsequent scientific research or the evolution of environmentalism helped to persuade those in charge that many of these projects would in fact be difficult to execute. One has to keep in mind, however, that events such as the preparation for the Ten-Million-Ton Harvest, and the failure to achieve this goal, may have redirected attention away from such projects and caused authorities to question their viability.

Geographers in Cuba nonetheless kept discussing these themes and proposals in subsequent years. Some Cuban ideas even became reference points for Soviet and other international authors.[68] At the First International Workshop on Transforming the Geographic Environment in Cuba, organized by the University of Havana in 1988, a paper presented by Luisa Iñiguez defined "transformation" as a way to optimize the geographic setting, using "a series of measures for the rational utilization of natural resources and their protection, improvement, and enrichment." Grander schemes in this direction may not have materialized—some thankfully so, given the environmental devastation they would have caused. But Cuba had, she noted, made notable strides toward restoring vegetation and forest cover, improving hydraulic management through irrigation, creating layers of cultivable soil in areas where there previously was none, experimenting with climate control via artificial rain, and fighting off erosion through the creation of terraces, the use of fertilizers, and the desalination of the soil.[69]

A Brief Assessment

Evaluations of Cuba's potential for economic and social development before 1959 generally reflected scarce knowledge of the island's natural resources and their inefficient use. One 1953 study, for example, concluded that information available about these issues was relatively scarce, irregular, and uncentralized. It also lamented the absence of scientific centers and researchers dedicated to exploring Cuba's natural environment.[70] Some steps were made toward changing this situation in the 1950s, such as the celebration of the First Symposium on Cuban Natural Resources, held February 3–14, 1958. But the deficiencies in the field remained notable.[71]

In the socialist era the Cuban Academy of Science dedicated its efforts to filling this gap. The Mexican economist Juan F. Noyola, who first arrived in Cuba as an expert for the United Nation's Economic Commission for Latin America and the Caribbean and subsequently joined the revolutionary project, noted in 1963 that one of the island's priorities should be the promotion of scientific, technological, and natural resources research. The limited available material and the lack of trained scientists made it difficult to study Cuba's natural resources and their more rational use. But in his opinion Cuba enjoyed some clear advantages, such as the quality of its soil, its mineral resources, its geographic position, and, in particular, its tropical climate. After emphasizing the need for agricultural, livestock, and forestry research, he concluded, "It can be affirmed that Cuba is today the best equipped country in the world to guide other people in the tropical regions toward a path for the conquest and better use of nature."[72]

Holding similar views, Núñez Jiménez gave great importance to the fact that Cuba hosted the only socialist Academy of Sciences in the intertropical zone. Among the Academy's first affiliated institutes was the Cuban Institute of Tropical Research, whose objective was to "rapidly employ the techniques obtained in more temperate climates for the study and better use of the resources of our environment."[73] To this end, he recalled the great contribution of the pioneering nineteenth-century Cuban physician Carlos J. Finlay, "who with his discovery [in the 1880s of the fact that yellow fever was transmitted by mosquitos] made the tropics habitable, without greater dangers for the life of man than in more temperate climates." For all these reasons, Cuba's preeminent geographer affirmed:

> We believe that Cuba, as the most developed country in all of the tropical areas of the world, should be the guiding light for scientific research on the same, thus contributing, with an internationalist spirit, to the development of all tropical zones. Imperialist nations like Holland, for example, created great research centers of this type, like the Institute of Tropical Research in Amsterdam (the most complete in the world); but, naturally, these institutions were established with the purpose of exploiting the natural and human resources of the tropics. Our socialist homeland is in the position, with the fraternal assistance of the socialist nations, to create an Institute of Tropical Research where we do not only develop our own resources, but also collaborate to develop better management strategies for natural resources in all tropical countries around the world.[74]

This line of thinking concerning the tropical condition was very different from old deterministic concepts that presented tropical regions as incapable of self-government. In this way, the Cuban Revolution inspired hope that a tropical country could achieve development through socialism. In 1982, upon receiving the title of professor emeritus at the Central University of Las Villas, Núñez Jiménez wrote the following about his *Geografía de Cuba* from 1954: "In that work, I advocated for the disappearance of the myth of geographic fatalism, I demanded an agrarian reform, I supported the 'Cubanization' of our industries, and, among other evils, I directly attacked Yankee imperialism and its meddling in Cuba."[75]

As this essay has argued, and Núñez Jiménez's 1954 text proves, this opinion was not entirely a product of the Revolution itself. To a significant degree it coincided with a strain of geographic thinking in Cuban academia that before 1959 also contested the deterministic visions that had dominated the profession historically. After World War II decolonizing nations rejected theories that condemned the tropical world to backwardness and a position of tutelage vis-à-vis Western powers. At the same time, this turn also intersected with the promotion of development policies that continued to adapt ideas from the old metropolises.

It is difficult to say precisely to what degree these geographic ideas influenced other leaders of the Cuban Revolution. But at least in the case of Núñez Jiménez, we can say that his work reflected a deep familiarity with old debates between determinist and "possibilist" positions. Already by the 1950s experiences of economic planning around the world—from the New Deal in the United States to the Five Year Plans of the USSR, and even the proximate case of Puerto Rico—were cited as models to demand a transformation of the Cuban reality. And not all prerevolutionary Cuban governments were indifferent to these calls for change.

Still, with the radical changes initiated in 1959, and in step with the consolidation of a strategic alliance with the Soviet Union after 1960, ideas about the transformation of nature came to occupy a privileged position among the objectives of a new socialist society. All the same, historians must study more deeply the implications of the concept of geotransformation in academic debates of the time. In particular we must look more closely at the transition between the 1950s and 1960s toward new tendencies in Soviet geography that questioned the dualism between physical geography and human or economic geography, or the presumed preeminence of the former.[76]

And yet, despite all the excitement, despite the development of considerable, novel research agendas, most of the more ambitious projects never came to fruition. The most notable changes had to do with the intensification of agriculture and the control of water. One visible inheritance from this period are the reservoirs constructed to expand Cuba's water reserves. Together they boast a storage capacity 150 to 180 times larger than that available before 1959. At the same time, thanks to the fact that large projects like the reclaiming of the Zapata Swamplands were never completed, Cuba today has been able to preserve a unique ecosystem, considered the largest wetlands in the Caribbean. Indeed, in later years Núñez Jiménez distanced himself from various geotransformation projects from the 1960s. As early as the fortieth anniversary of the Speleological Society of Cuba (in 1980), he launched the campaign "Towards a Culture of Nature" to contribute to greater public consciousness about socio-environmental problems. A year later, his work was crucial to the drafting of Cuba's 1981 Law for the Environment and the Rational Use of Natural Resources.

After the first discussions at the National Assembly about this law, Núñez Jiménez wrote an article on the subject for *Granma*, the Communist Party daily, at the request of Fidel Castro.[77] He argued that the economic development of the country had led, on occasion, to damaging tracts of soil. It was a pity, he suggested, that Cuba could not develop a greater "consciousness about protecting nature in general and the soils in particular, planting trees wherever doing so was not an obstacle to the functioning of modern machines." According to the author's later testimony, however, Castro told him that the best part was that which affirmed, "The battle to protect the integral Cuban landscape is a long battle without rest, because it has many enemies—the largest of which is our own lack of knowledge of the laws governing the equilibrium of nature."[78]

NOTES

Editors' note: Translation by Michael J. Bustamante, with assistance from José A. Villar-Portela.

1. "Words of Antonio Núñez Jiménez at the meeting of the directors and administrators of the Cuban Academy of Sciences, June 29, 1967," in *Discursos ante los Directores de la Academia*, vol. LXVII, Havana, 1967, 22–26, Fundación Antonio Núñez Jiménez (henceforth ANJ).

2. The man referenced is Dr. Dario Guitart. See Ingvar Emilsson, *Investigaciones sobre la hidrología de la ensenada de la Broa con vista a su posible transformación en un embalse de aguadulce*, Serie Transformación de la Naturaleza 5 (Havana: Academia de Ciencias de Cuba, Instituto de Oceanología, 1968).

3. The idea for a road to the Isle of Pines was promoted years before by public figures such as the historian Herminio Portell Vilá. See, for example, "El caso de la isla de Pinos," *Bohemia*, June 21, 1959, 74, 93. We can trace discussions about draining the Gulf of Batabanó to an article by Waldo Medina: "Dos Islas: Un Continente," *El Mundo*, February 8, 1947.

4. "Words of Antonio Núñez Jiménez," 25.

5. "Words of Antonio Núñez Jiménez," 26.

6. Antonio Núñez Jiménez, *Geotransformación de Cuba*, Serie Transformación de la Naturaleza 6 (Havana: Academia de Ciencias de Cuba, 1968). The articles appeared with the following subtitles: 1. "Geotransformación de Cuba" (day 16); 2. "Dominar ríos y ciénagas" (day 17); "Rescatar territorios al mar" (day 19); and "La batalla por el agua y la tierra, perspectivas" (day 22).

7. Rafael Hernández, "El año rojo: Política, sociedad y cultura en 1968," *Revista de Estudios Sociales* (Bogotá) 33 (August 2009): 44–54.

8. See "Palabras del capitán Antonio Núñez Jiménez el día 1 de Junio de 1967 en la Academia de Ciencias de Cuba, con los Directores de Institutos sobre su entrevista con el compañero Fidel Castro," in *Discursos 1967* 46, no. 39, Academia de Ciencias de Cuba, ANJ.

9. For more on the links between geography and revolutions in history, see David N. Livingstone and Charles W. J. Withers, eds., *Geography and Revolution* (Chicago: University of Chicago Press, 2005).

10. The most extensive study is Sergio Díaz-Briquets and Jorge Pérez-López, *Conquering Nature: The Environmental Legacy of Socialism in Cuba* (Pittsburgh: University of Pittsburgh Press, 2000). This book offers a more balanced critique than other studies of the effects of the socialist system on the natural environment. Compare to Carlos Wotzkow's *Naturaleza cubana* (Miami: Ediciones Universal, 1998).

11. John McNeill, *Something New under the Sun: An Environmental History of the Twentieth-Century World* (London: Penguin Books, 2001), 325–56.

12. Lucien Bernier, "El Nuevo rostro de la tierra," *Carteles*, June 7, 1959, 92–95, 97.

13. The bibliography on geographical determinism and cultural identity in the tropics is extensive. See, for example, Harold M. Elliot, "Mental Maps and Ethnocentrism: Geographic Characterization of the Past," *Journal of Geography* 78, no. 7 (1979): 250–65; Richard Peet, "The Social Origins of Environmental Determinism," *Annals of the Association of American Geographers* 75, no. 3 (1985): 309–33.

14. William L. Thomas, ed., *Man's Role in Changing the Face of the Earth* (Chicago: University of Chicago Press, 1956). Academics such as Carl O. Sauer, Lewis Munford, and Marston Bates played a central role.

15. Ray H. Whitbeck, "Geographical Relations in the Development of Cuban Agriculture," *Geographical Review* 12, no. 2 (1922): 223–40; Derwent S. Whittlesey, "Geographic Factors in the Relations of the United States and Cuba," *Geographical Review* 12, no. 2 (1922): 241–56.

16. Ellen Churchill Semple, *Influences of the Geographic Environment* (New York: Henry Holt, 1911); Ellsworth Huntington, *Civilization and Climate* (New Haven: Yale University Press, 1922) and *Mainsprings of Civilization* (New York: John Wiley & Sons, 1945). See, for example, Mercedes García Tuduri de Coya, "Influencia del medio en el carácter cubano," *Revista Bimestre Cubana* 40 (1937): 5–25.

17. Salvador Massip, *Introducción a la geografía humana* (Havana: Imprenta El Siglo XX, 1918).

18. Salvador Massip, *Factores geográficos en la historia de Cuba* (Havana: Imprenta Avisador Comercial, 1931) and *Factores geográficos de la cubanidad* (Havana: Cultural S.A., 1941).

19. John E. Pomfret, *La geografía humana y la cultura* (Havana: Molina y Cía, 1938), 14. [Translator's note: Quote is a translation from the Spanish version of text, not the English original.]

20. Pomfret, *La geografía*, 15–16.

21. Salvador Massip, "La geografía y su importancia en la resolución de los problemas planteados a la nación cubana," *Revista de la Sociedad Geográfica de Cuba* 24, nos. 1–4 (1951): 34, 31.

22. Francis Truslow et al., *Report on Cuba* (Baltimore: Johns Hopkins University Press, 1951), 14–32.

23. Salvador Massip and Sarah Ysalgué, "Geografía y Planificación," in *Memoria del Primer Congreso Nacional de Planificación, diciembre 12 al 17 de 1956* (Havana: Úcar, García, S.A., 1958), 211–19.

24. Marcus Power and James D. Sidaway, "The Degeneration of Tropical Geography," *Annals of the Association of American Geographers* 94, no. 3 (2004): 585–601.

25. See, for example, Pierre George et al., *Geografía activa* (Barcelona: Ediciones Ariel, 1966); I. P. Gerasimov, *La geografía constructiva soviética: Tareas, enfoques y resultados* (Moscow: Ed. Nauka, 1976).

26. For information on the explorations he undertook in these years, see *Veinte años explorando a Cuba: Historia documentada de la Sociedad Espeleológica de Cuba* (Havana: n.p., 1961); Antonio Núñez Jiménez, *Medio siglo explorando a Cuba: Historia documentada de la Sociedad Espeleológica de Cuba*, vol. 1 (Havana: Imprenta Central de las FAR, 1990).

27. For example, as a representative of the Federation of University Students, he participated on November 3, 1947, in the receiving of the historic Demajagua bell at Havana's railway station. Originally rung to launch Cuba's first War for Independence in 1868, the bell was stolen from where it was preserved in Manzanillo by Castro to protest the government of Ramón Grau de San Martín. See "Recordarán acción de Fidel con la campana de la Demajagua," *Granma*, November 1, 2007, http://www.granma.cu/granmad /2007/11/01/nacional/artic10.html.

28. Antonio Núñez Jiménez, *Geografía de Cuba* (Havana: Editorial Lex, 1954).

29. Núñez Jiménez, *Geografía de Cuba*, 15.

30. Núñez Jiménez, *Geografía de Cuba*, 196, 206–14.

31. Antonio Núñez, "Transformemos la naturaleza de Cuba en beneficio de sus ciudadanos. Algunas ideas para una futuro transformación de la naturaleza en Cuba," in *Con la mochila al hombro* (Havana: Ediciones Unión, 1963), 351 (originally published in *Carteles*, June 17, 1951).

32. Antonio Núñez, "Expedición al Toa, el río que puede transformar a Cuba," in *Con la mochila al hombro*, 192 (originally published in *Revista Orto* [Manzanillo], January–February 1948).

33. "¿Porqué Cuba se puede quedar sin agua?," *Carteles*, January 4, 1948, 15; "Un problema de vida o muerte: La isla sin agua," *Bohemia*, September 30, 1956, 20–23, 129; "¿Qué cantidad de agua tenemos para el progreso de Cuba?," *Bohemia*, October 14, 1956, 36–38, 110–11.

34. "La Tierra que se nos va," *Bohemia*, February 24, 1957, 116.

35. Juan José Arévalo was president of Guatemala from 1945 to 1951. A social reformer, he was succeeded by Jacobo Arbenz. See Juan José Arévalo, *Fabula del tiburón y las sardinas: América Latina estragulada* (Buenos Aires: Ediciones Meridion, 1956).

36. Antonio Núñez Jiménez, *En marcha con Fidel, 1959* (1982; Havana: LetrasCubanas, 1998), 57.

37. "Palabras de Fidel Castro, Primer Ministro del Gobierno Revolucionario de Cuba, en el acto por el vigésimo aniversario de la Fundación de la Sociedad Espeleológica de Cuba," in Núñez Jiménez, *Medio siglo explorando a Cuba*, 388. Núñez Jiménez's first position in 1959 was as executive director of the Rehabilitation Plan for the Zapata Swamplands.

38. "Palabras de Fidel Castro," 395.

39. From the social sciences: Fernando Ortiz, Julio Le Riverend, Emilio Roig de Leuchsenring, Juan Marinello, and Salvador Massip; from the natural, medical, and exact sciences: José López Sánchez, Abelardo Moreno Bonilla, José Altshuler, and Gilberto Silva.

40. Rolando Álvarez, "De la Academia de Ciencias de Cuba: A los 90 años del nacimiento de Antonio Núñez Jiménez," *Revista Anales de la Academia de Ciencias de Cuba* 3, no. 1 (2013): 2.

41. McNeill, *Something New under the Sun*, 325–56.

42. Richard P. Tucker, *Insatiable Appetite: The United States and the Ecological Degradation of the Tropical World* (Berkeley: University of California Press, 2000).

43. Influential works of Soviet scientific literature in this vein include M. Ilin (Ilya Marshak), *El hombre y la naturaleza* (Buenos Aires: Editorial Futuro, 1955) and *La conquista de la naturaleza* (Buenos Aires: Editorial Futuro, 1960).

44. Stephen Brain, "The Great Stalin Plan for the Transformation of Nature," *Environmental History* 15 (October 2010): 670–700.

45. Douglas R. Weiner, "The Predatory Tribute-Taking State: A Framework for Understanding Russian Environmental History," in *The Environment and World History*, edited by Edmund Burke and Kenneth Pomeranz (Berkeley: University of California Press, 2009), 276–315.

46. Rhoads Murphey, "Man and Nature in China," *Modern Asian Studies* 1, no. 4 (1967): 313–33. At the time of the triumph of the Cuban Revolution, China was in the midst of the Great Leap Forward (1958–60). See William A. Joseph, "A Tragedy of Good Intentions: Post-Mao Views of the Great Leap Forward," *Modern China* 12, no. 2 (1986): 419–57; Judith Shapiro, "Mao's War against Nature: Legacy and Lessons," *Journal of East Asian Studies* 1, no. 2 (2001): 93–119.

47. On the Soviet exhibition in Havana and reopening of relations between both countries, see Luis M. Buch and R. Suárez, *Gobierno revolucionario: Primeros pasos* (Havana: Ciencias Sociales, 2009), 400–412; Núñez Jiménez, *En marcha con Fidel*, 317–20; Nikolai S. Leonov, *Raúl Castro: Un hombre en revolución* (Havana: Editorial Capitán San Luis, 2015), 28–30.

48. "Informe sobre la URSS. Comparecencia del capitán Antonio Núñez Jiménez, director ejecutivo del INRA, por el canal 2, 'Televisión revolucionaria,' al regreso de su viaje a la Unión Soviética. 15 de julio de 1960," *Obra revolucionaria*, Cuaderno 15 (Havana: Imprenta Nacional de Cuba, 1960), 5.

49. Denis J. B. Shaw, "Mastering Nature through Science: Soviet Geographers and the Great Stalin Plan for the Transformation of Nature, 1948–1953," *Slavonic and East European Review* 93 (January 2015): 120–46.

50. "Informe sobre la URSS," 10.

51. O. N. Pisarshevsky, *La conquista de la naturaleza* (Havana: Editorial Nacional de Cuba, 1962), 178.

52. Salvador Massip, *La geografía en la Unión Soviética* (Havana: Universidad de La Habana, Escuela de Geografía, 1965).

53. Innokentii P. Gerasimov was director of the Institute of Geography at the Soviet Academy of Sciences. He was one of the vice presidents for the *Atlas Nacional de Cuba* project finished in 1970.

54. Salvador Massip, *La evolución de las ideas geográficas en Cuba*, Serie Geográfica 3 (Havana: Academia de Ciencias de Cuba, 1974), 19.

55. Massip, *La evolución*, 19.

56. Núñez Jiménez, *Geotransformación de Cuba*, 6.

57. Núñez Jiménez, *Geotransformación de Cuba*, 7.

58. Ernesto "Che" Guevara, *El socialismo y el hombre en Cuba* (Havana: Ediciones R, 1965), 41.

59. Núñez Jiménez, *Geotransformación de Cuba*, 7.

60. Claudia Martínez, "Protección de la naturaleza y turismo en la revolución cubana de 1959: El caso de la Ciénaga de Zapata," HALAC 1, no. 2 (2012): 193–217.

61. Núñez Jiménez, *Geotransformación de Cuba*, 9.

62. The National Development Commission (La Comisión de Fomento Nacional) issued an invitation to NEDECO (Netherlands Engineering Consultants) in 1959 to study the "cleansing" of the Zapata Swamplands and those of the Cauto River delta. The studies were undertaken from March 21 through April 17 of that year. The resulting report, *El Saneamiento de la Ciénaga de Zapata*, La Haya-Países Bajos, 1959, is housed in the archives of the Antonio Núñez Jiménez foundation in Havana.

63. Cuba's interest in reclaiming swamps remained alive until the international community began to change its appraisal of swamp ecosystems at the Ramsar Convention (1971). The Zapata Swamplands (Ciénaga de Zapata) was declared a Biosphere Reserve in 2000 and a Ramsar Site in 2001.

64. Núñez Jiménez, *Geotransformación de Cuba*, 12.

65. Experiments to create artificial rain were conducted in Camaguey by the U.S. firm Howel Associates in 1954. After the triumph of the Revolution, new Cuban efforts were begun in 1962 but gained momentum only in 1965 through the Institute of Cloud Physics, part of the Institute of Meteorology. The series Transformación de la Naturaleza, published by the Cuban Academy of Sciences, dedicated its first four publications to this theme.

66. Núñez Jiménez, *Geotransformación de Cuba*, 15.

67. A brief description of this project can be found in José Álvarez, *Cuba's Agricultural Sector* (Gainesville: University Press of Florida, 2004), 236. Also see *Gran siembra de primavera: 1968, año del guerrillero heroico* (Havana: Instituto Cubano del Libro, 1968).

68. K. Paskang and N. Rodsievich, *Protección y transformación de la naturaleza* (Havana: Editorial Pueblo y Educación, 1983).

69. Luisa Iñiguez, "La protección de la naturaleza en Cuba," in *Transformación del mediogeográfico en Cuba: Primer Taller Internacional*, edited by Amparo Avella and Eduardo Salinas (Havana: Universidad de La Habana, 1988), 198–233. Her presentation summarized her doctoral thesis, directed by Núñez Jiménez and José Mateo as codirector. See Luisa Iñiguez, "Aspectos geográficos de la protección de la naturaleza de Cuba," PhD diss., Universidad de La Habana, 1983.

70. Antonio Chávez, *Reporte sobre la información disponible de los recursos naturales de Cuba*, Proyecto 29 (Havana: Instituto Panamericano de Geografía e Historia, 1953), mimeograph copy.

71. *I Simposio sobre Recursos Naturales de Cuba* (Havana: Sociedad Colombista Panamericana, 1958).

72. Juan F. Noyola, "La orientación de la investigación científica, tecnológica y de recursos naturales: Una gran tarea revolucionaria," *La economía cubana en los primeros años de la revolución y otros ensayos* (Mexico City: Siglo XXI, 1978), 270–79.

73. Antonio Núñez, "La naciente Academia de Ciencias de Cuba," *Cuba Socialista* 4, no. 32 (1964): 30. The Institute was first established in 1966 as the Alejandro de Humboldt Institute of Tropical Agriculture.

74. Núñez, "La naciente Academia," 31.

75. "Palabras de Antonio Núñez Jiménez al recibir el título de Profesor de Mérito de la Universidad Central de las Villas," November 29, 1982, *Cuadernos de Trabajo*, 934, ANJ.

76. J. M. Hooson, "La Unión Soviética," in *La geografía actual: Geógrafos y tendencias*, edited by R. J. Johnston and P. Claval (Barcelona: Ariel, 1986), 92–98; John E. Chappell Jr., "The Ecological Dimension: Russian and American Views," *Annals of the Association of American Geographers* 65, no. 2 (1975): 144–62.

77. Antonio Núñez Jiménez, "Defensa de la Naturaleza en la Asamblea Nacional," *Granma*, July 4, 1980, 4.

78. Antonio Núñez Jiménez, *Hacia una cultura de la naturaleza* (Havana: Letras Cubanas, 1998), 466.

7. Between *Espíritu* and *Conciencia*

CABARET AND BALLET DEVELOPMENTS IN 1960S CUBA

ELIZABETH SCHWALL

In 1968 two visitors to Cuba considered the fraught place of cabaret and ballet in a socialist society. The Jamaican intellectual Andrew Salkey spent New Year's Eve at the famous Tropicana Club. As bedazzled "chorus girls highkicked," Salkey's travel companions, fellow foreign visitors, took issue with the perceived foreignness and commercialism of the show, apparent "handme-down left-overs from Broadway and Batista." Salkey, though, saw "native Cuban contributions to the vulgarity," leading him to accept the performance "on its own terms."[1] A few weeks later, the British critic Arnold Haskell delivered a lecture on ballet appreciation sponsored by Cuba's National Ballet. One might have expected him to equivocate too, wondering about the role of an elite dance form in a society preoccupied with radical transformation. Haskell nonetheless lauded Cuban ballet dancers as "hard workers . . . with a truly revolutionary fervor." Cubans, he contended, had built a national ballet aesthetic thanks to a "talented and artistic people with a tradition of popular dances and a rich folklore."[2]

In many ways, both cabaret and ballet represented holdovers from the Cuban Republic. Before 1959 cabarets served as hubs for entertainment and illicit activities, especially after Fulgencio Batista came to power by military coup in 1952. Starting in the 1940s, Cuba also boasted an impressive ballet establishment, thanks to civic associations like the Sociedad Pro-Arte Musical and the Cuban ballet pioneers Alicia Alonso, her husband Fernando Alonso, and her brother-in-law Alberto Alonso. When the 26th of July Movement overthrew Batista in 1959, cabarets bore associations with vice, exploitation, and the deposed ruler. Ballet, on the other hand, represented an elite dance originally formed in European and Russian courts and enjoyed mostly by the Cuban bourgeoisie.

Ironically, the dance forms also resonated with divergent ideals of the new political order. On the surface, dances in cabarets, venues associated with freedom of movement and indulgence, mirrored the spirited insouciance of the Revolution's jubilant first years. Ballet, by contrast, depended upon controlled choreography and ascetic dedication, characteristics that dovetailed with the stricter ideological landscape that prevailed in Cuba as the 1960s continued. In other words, cabaret embodied a liberated revolutionary spirit, while ballet represented a disciplined revolutionary consciousness. In 1967 an unnamed Cuban student interviewed by U.S.-based Chicana writer and activist Elizabeth Sutherland, described revolutionary spirit and consciousness as defining attributes of 1960s politics. While not originally used to discuss dance, these categories also encapsulated parallel ideological tensions in the Cuban dance world. According to the Cuban teen, "'Our generation has a perfect balance of Revolutionary spirit'—enthusiasm, spontaneity—'and Revolutionary conscience'—discipline, selflessness. 'I think the next generation will have more conscience and less spirit.'"[3] Although the original Spanish does not appear in the text, the youth likely invoked the common terms *espíritu revolucionario* (revolutionary spirit) and *conciencia revolucionaria* (revolutionary conscience in Sutherland's translation, but here I suggest the more precisely political term, "consciousness").[4] Revolutionary spirit pointed to unbridled excitement for the future, like when Fidel Castro attributed his tireless late nights not to wakeful drugs, but to *"pastillas del espíritu revolucionario"* (pills of revolutionary spirit).[5] Revolutionary consciousness suggested a model political militancy, such as when writer Juan Marinello described *"conciencia revolucionaria"* inspiring socially engaged art.[6] According to the Cuban youth's prediction of revolutionary change, the unbridled euphoria of initial revolutionary triumph would fade, and the imperative of more rigid organization and discipline would gain steam. In kind, the fates of cabaret and ballet in post-1959 Cuba might be expected to track an ascendant conformism in society broadly.

This chapter, however, shows important similarities in how cabaret and ballet changed over time as innovators in both forms improvised to navigate sociopolitical shifts. Improvisation, according to Danielle Goldman, involves "giving shape to oneself by deciding how to move in relation to an unsteady landscape"; indeed, Cuban cabaret and ballet dancers improvised to reframe their art and accentuate its relevance to a protean political project.[7] This meant that cabaret and ballet choreographies at times reflected ideas about spirited rebellion and at others militant sacrifice. As a result, I argue that revolutionary spirit and consciousness coexisted in Cuban cabaret and ballet and, by extension, Cuban society at large. While ballet's increasing public profile might seem to reaffirm a growing conservatism and less tolerance of mass cultural expressions, both forms adapted, persisted, and in some instances tested the limits of state power. As a result, Cuban cabaret and ballet dancers moved actively between *espíritu* and *conciencia* throughout the 1960s.

Tracing the fates of "lowbrow," popular cabaret and "highbrow," elite ballet revises existing understandings of dance in revolutionary society and cultural politics in 1960s Cuba. Scholars have described the post-1959 government's support for concert dance forms (above all, ballet, but also modern and folkloric dance) as well as dancers' reciprocal political backing of the new government in power.[8] Existing analysis, however, has not considered resonant dynamics in cabarets, the role of dancers in advocating for their art, conspicuous and inconspicuous dissent, and the messiness of improvised changes alongside institutional and cultural inertias. Dance also provides a vivid, underutilized lens for examining the reach and limits of state power in 1960s Cuba.[9] As an art of motion, dance eludes fixity and lacks the precision of verbal language, making it more open to interpretation than other discursive forms. Dance thus provided a powerfully ambiguous medium for promoting revolutionary ideals, especially as political intentions passed from choreographers to dancers to audiences. While operating within nationalized dance establishments, cabaret and ballet dancers individually interpreted the complicated revolutionary project and modified the scope of revolutionary culture. In doing so, they inhabited subjectivities in the interstices of narrowing political paradigms.

Revolutionizing Revelry: From Sensual Liberation to Combatant Happiness

In a 1984 memoir, Carlos Franqui, a 26th of July Movement intellectual and later critic of Fidel Castro, described how Cubans initially created a "*pachanga* revolution . . . of freedom and joy." This meant approaching the serious business of revolution with a festive air. "We Cubans try to have fun with everything," Franqui claimed, bordering on stereotype: "cyclones, demonstrations, hunger, even war." The Revolution thereby entailed "a Cuban way of changing life: voluntary labor, militia duty, rumba, all at the same time."[10]

Although this "Cuban" ebullience pervaded the island immediately following 1959, such levity eventually dissipated and a defensive moralism took hold. In this context, sensual dances, particularly those performed in cabarets, seemed in many ways antithetical to revolutionary norms. As this section details, however, dance makers creatively appropriated discourses of revolutionary spirit and consciousness, reasserting the social value of their performances. The result in the cabaret world was a fascinating, if vexed, blending of old and new.

In the first days of 1959 Cubans clashed over the revolutionary appropriateness of leisure places and pastimes, especially those associated with tourism. On January 1 mobs attacked hotels where Batista's followers congregated. The new leadership initially closed all casinos and several cabarets and hotels.[11] Yet while some heralded the move, employees protested, since casino revenues sustained the tourism industry.[12] The new regime conceded and recognized the benefits of tourism: jobs for Cubans, money for national coffers, and international goodwill. To reconcile such activities with the Revolution, the government rewrote gaming laws to ensure central controls over gambling.[13] Resolving these immediate issues, the new government then launched "Operation Tourism" with a reconstituted Instituto Nacional de Industria Turística (National Institute of Tourist Industries, or INIT) aiming to make tourism a "second national *zafra*" (sugar harvest).[14] Despite government initiatives, however, tourism floundered as a result of political instabilities. According to figures issued by INIT, Havana received 258,789 tourists in 1957; 197,789 in 1958; and only 168,621 in 1959.[15] Reacting to the decline, the Cuban government seized large hotels operated by U.S. entrepreneurs, such as the Hotel Nacional and the Habana Hilton, along with other residential hotels and the Tropicana Club, in June 1960.[16] Casinos closed and gambling eventually became illegal.[17] The hotel takeovers coincided with contemporaneous nationalization efforts, such as the government seizure of the U.S. oil companies Texaco and Standard Oil for refusing to refine Soviet crude petroleum. On October 13, 1960, authorities nationalized 382 private enterprises, including eleven of the country's most luxurious hotels.[18]

These political and economic developments also affected cabarets, some of which were attached to major hotels. According to famed dancer Sonia Calero, the 1959 Revolution brought immediate pay cuts for the highest-paid performers, equalizing an industry that had considerable hierarchies of salary and fame.[19] Moreover, distinctions in the entertainment and audiences of different clubs reportedly lessened. Before 1959 the most opulent cabarets, such as the Tropicana and Sans Souci, catered to tourists and local elites.[20]

Middle- and lower-class Cubans, meanwhile, went to places like the Ali Bar, Sierra, Alloy, and Night and Day.[21] Top-tier clubs featured big-name artists and extravagant productions, while second- and third-tier establishments offered more modest shows. State interventions after 1959 challenged these demographics; lower entry costs helped to diversify the clientele. The 1960 show *Pachanga en Tropicana*, for instance, advertised tickets at "revolutionary prices, so that all of Cuba can enjoy it."[22] New, smaller clubs also opened as INIT worked to employ the large number of performers.[23] For the moment, old, if now more broadly accessible, forms of entertainment remained perfectly compatible with revolutionary praxis.

While the regime change affected audience composition and pay structure behind the scenes, changes manifested more slowly under the spotlights. Shows resembled spectacles of the previous decades, drawing heavily on erotic exoticism, particularly through the display of the female body. According to a description in the entertainment magazine *Show*, Club 66 in August 1959 demonstrated through music, dance, and menu offerings the "existence of a piece of Africa in the capital." The star dancer Eva Torres impressed audiences as her "graceful body, undulating and sensual, carrie[d] the rhythm of the drums with feverish passion."[24] In *Bienvenido, amigo* (Welcome, friend) at Club Parisien in the spring of 1960, dancers performed "Polynesian rituals" with elaborate costumes and mesmerizing ribbon dances.[25] Along similar lines, the Habana Riviera debuted a show in January 1961 featuring performers portraying Hawaiians dancing in and out of their canoes while traversing the Pacific seas.[26]

Slowly, however, signs of revolutionary times began to appear on stage. For example, in May 1959 the Capri Casino premiered a show choreographed by Alberto Alonso, *Consumiendo productos cubanos* (Consuming Cuban Products), which aligned with contemporary efforts to encourage citizens to buy domestic goods.[27] An announcement described the spectacle as "100% Cuban," in both content and production, thereby complying with government mandates to maintain a mostly Cuban workforce.[28] Tributes to the eastern city Santiago de Cuba were also common and carried clear political valences. On June 6, 1959, *Canto a Oriente* (A Song for Oriente) at the Tropicana paid tribute to the historic "birthplace of heroic *mambises* and rebels."[29] In April and May 1961 shows at the Habana Libre (former Habana Hilton) included numbers celebrating current agricultural efforts such as "A tumbar la caña," wherein smiling performers held machetes and sang about cutting sugar cane.[30] Whether the result of top-down content directives, an opportunistic catering to the political moment, or autonomous personal convictions, the industry was "revolutionizing" revelry. Unfortunately, available sources do not record the negotiations, bureaucratic chains of influence, and compromises that undoubtedly took place among cabaret operators, midlevel managers, directors, choreographers, and political leaders.

What we do know is that a significant turning point for the politicization of dance—albeit outside of the cabaret milieu—came with the confiscation of the film P.M. in late April 1961. This short, now infamous "free cinema" documentary lacked a single spoken word and instead featured the late-night choreographies of lower-class, mostly mixed-race Cubans carousing in bars near Havana's port during the winter holiday of 1960–61.[31] Released soon after Cuba repelled the Bay of Pigs invasion, the film offered, in the eyes of officials, "a biased image of Havana nightlife that, far from giving the spectator a correct impression of the Cuban people in this revolutionary stage, impoverishes, disfigures, and distorts."[32] Following P.M.'s controversial censorship, artists, intellectuals, and government officials met in June 1961 to discuss the parameters of cultural production. During the final meeting, Fidel Castro delivered a speech known thereafter as "Palabras a los intelectuales" (Words to the Intellectuals), asserting that only art that furthered the Revolution had a right to exist.[33] The film's portrayal of dance and indulgence ostensibly failed in this respect. The censorship of P.M. hinted at the transgressive power of sensual liberation, and it foreshadowed developments on the cabaret stage.

Following the P.M. affair, moralizing in cabaret performance became more common, though no direct causal link can be established. Starting in December 1961, the Tropicana show choreographed by Armando Suez, *Leyenda Antillana*, featured performers in Chinese and Russian costumes, interpreting national dances as well as numbers about the literacy campaign.[34] This likely reflected and responded to the audience, which a U.S. report from March 1962 described as mostly "middle-class Cubans, Communist bloc technicians, and a few out-of-town farmers who often turn up with their children." The same author lamented that, contrary to the "propaganda" at the Tropicana, the Habana Riviera had the "only girlie act in all of Cuba." Yet even that show was tame by comparison to those of the past, featuring "girls wander[ing] around in briefs, tossing confetti at the audience, and trying to appear enticing, yet moral."[35] In Carlos Franqui's estimation, the growing puritanical ethos resurrected "all the punishments [Fidel] suffered as a boy in his Jesuit school . . . separation of the sexes, discipline. . . . All sensuality, of course, is anathema to him."[36] According to this admittedly retrospective and imaginative view, growing signs of social conservatism may have represented the continuation and intensification of bourgeois scruples in a revolutionary key.

But even though such entertainment seemed incompatible with an increasingly austere revolution, these activities had political importance, according to period observers. An October 1961 article claimed that widely patronized "cabarets and nightclubs of a first, second, and third order" signaled an increase in the average citizen's purchasing power and evidenced government efforts to keep entry "prices affordable to all."[37] Further, a March 1962 article asserted that, in contrast to "lying reports" about social disarray in the international press, Cubans enjoyed a vibrant club scene. Though no longer featuring "trashy striptease," the five large cabarets in Havana still boasted shows with budgets as high as $26,000, and a hundred or so smaller clubs operated at full capacity nightly.[38] Another, more sanctimonious piece described how the Revolution offered an alternative, equally inspiring nightlife of pupils studying by candlelight, government employees working late into the night, and militants guarding against "imperialist sabotage."[39] All the same, cabaret performance continued, and a 1964 commentator summed up the recent changes to the Tropicana by describing a refreshing lack of "gross sensuality." Dance, the observer found, now filled evenings with "alegría combatiente," a combatant happiness, indicative of Cuban revolutionary resiliency and good taste.[40]

The 1964 film *Nosotros, la música* (We, the Music) captured the cheerful image of a lively, celebratory Cuba that such articles promoted.[41] The film goes through various manifestations of popular culture, including a scene with the dancer Ana Gloria performing in the cabaret Johnny's Dream. Ana Gloria was a fixture on cabaret circuits before and after 1959, well-known for her performances of the mambo, cha-cha-cha, *guaracha*, *son*, and rumba. In the film she wears a black leotard and saunters with swaying hips through the audience to enter the small, intimate stage. Upon arrival, she drops to a low, grounded stance. With arms and knees bent, her feet move rhythmically and constantly as she dances with command and abandon. Nothing about this performance signaled revolutionary change; the scene easily could have occurred in 1958. Yet in a wider context, the dancers in the film embodied the healthy (and sometimes titillating) combatant happiness described by the Cuban press of the period. In director Rogelio París's estimation, the *pachanga* of the early years remained alive and well.

As supporters in the mass media reformulated revelry as a symbol of revolutionary spirit and cultural vitality, dancers also defended the social value of their performances by pointing to their professionalism and audiences. In 1964 a foreign reporter, identified only as "Lisa," interviewed two female cabaret dancers for a Canadian Broadcasting Corporation special on

Cuba. The interview followed a cabaret performance that resembled pre-1959 productions—complete with women in extravagant attire, Ana Gloria, and couples performing acrobatic versions of popular Cuban dances.[42] Speaking with "Lisa" immediately following their routine, the dancers remained in their skimpy costumes, still perspiring from the performance. Through a translator, the reporter asked the first woman if she missed U.S. audiences. The dancer carefully deflected the question while promoting her status as an artist. For the dancer, performing for small audiences posed no problem since, in the translator's words, "she likes her art and she works with pleasure even . . . when there is [sic] a few people around." Using the term "art" instead of "entertainment," the dancer cast her performances as meaningful revolutionary work. Later, the reporter asked the dancers about the differences between pre- and post-1959 working conditions. The first responded that before 1959, she performed mainly for foreigners and elites. In the post-1959 moment, "she now works for the people. . . . This working place belongs to them," the translator asserted. A second dancer largely concurred: "The main difference is in the public. . . . Now we find all kinds of people, intellectuals, workers, professionals, all kinds of people that compose the Cuban society of this day."[43] In these responses the dancers used populist values to reframe their art as an important contribution to the Cuban nation.

Still, while the performers adopted elements of prevailing political rhetoric, they were also strategic in their invocation of patriotic tropes. When the interviewer asked the first dancer if she was a communist, she smiled slyly and responded, "I am Cuban." "Not communist?" the reporter pressed. "Cuban and nothing more," came the reply. Later, her colleague expressed admiration for the Revolution and Fidel, but she underscored revolutionary nationalism rather than Marxist–Leninist belief. As the translator put it, "She only knows that she's Cuban. . . . And she fights for her country and does anything she has to do." When asked if she hoped "someday to become a good Marxist Leninist," the dancer laughed: "It's too dull to become a good Marxist Leninist." In these ways, while complimenting Fidel as an "important man," the performers indicated their suspicions of dry communist doctrines.[44] In these exchanges, individualist revolutionary spirit and tactical expressions of collective consciousness comingled, suggesting the dancers' complicated professional and political standing.

Despite cabaret dancers' assertions of their cultural and revolutionary value, cabaret venues continued to hold an uncertain place in revolutionary society, prompting a careful defense published in 1967. Entitled "El Cabaret, ¿También Cultura?" (Cabaret, Also Culture?), the article reflected on the dark history of such establishments: exploitative impresarios, demeaning displays of women's bodies, and unthinking audiences in a drunken stupor. Mediocre performances had wasted the talents of Cuban women, the author argued. Such productions had no place "in a society that . . . tries to elevate not only the economic but also the moral and cultural level of its members . . . like ours today." Nonetheless, the article insisted that "the cabaret also can be an instrument of culture." In particular, the text praised *Labana* in the Capri Cabaret, "a show that manages to entertain and amuse, within the framework of cabaret, by means of culture and not against it." Without providing any indication of the show's content, the author assured readers that the "Capri has not been converted into a dusty and silent library. There are bottles. There is music, dances, scenery, jokes, swaying. There are also female thighs, always very delightful." The Capri managed to achieve a delicate balance, according to the writer: "without abandoning the drink," the cabaret contributed to a "cultured and happy society."[45]

In late 1967 and early 1968, however, Salkey had trouble reconciling well-worn conventions and novel content on and off similar stages. One night, in search of a club, a Cuban acquaintance informed Salkey's group that none of them "would be allowed into the cabaret at Hotel Capri without a jacket." This astounded the visitors. Not dressed according to old bourgeois codes, they instead went to a more casual club where they watched an opulently dressed performer sing a jazzy, sentimental song about Vietnam for a "proletarian audience." The venue mixed U.S. influences with revolutionary messaging and publics. The extravagance of larger clubs, meanwhile—like the Tropicana during the New Year's Eve show mentioned earlier—continued to surprise. "Three full orchestras . . . magnificent luminous costumes, fire-work displays and gushing tinted smoke screens dazzled the large audience," Salkey recalled. Two nights later Salkey and his friends went to the Caribe, where they watched a satire about Batista-era prostitution and U.S. exploitation. "As in the Tropicana cabaret," he concluded, "we saw the old, tried format . . . being used here for a somewhat new purpose." While appreciating Cuban inventiveness, Salkey wondered at the "staleness" of the genre and how it related to the political present. Cubans that he spoke with "agreed that there was a 'gap' between the new life in Cuba and the many forms of popular entertainment."[46]

Perhaps unsurprisingly, then, the cabaret sector did enter a crisis a few months after Salkey's visit. In March 1968, Castro declared the beginning of a revolutionary offensive to address ideological lapses and economic stagnation. In addition to nationalizing all remaining Cuban-owned private businesses, Castro forced cabarets, along with bars and places selling alcohol—even state-owned establishments—to close their doors.[47] The radicalization also sought to remove distractions; citizens were to focus on the utopian goal of harvesting 10 million tons of sugar in 1970.

After the sugar campaign concluded unsuccessfully, INIT reopened cabaret doors. For the Tropicana's grand return to operations, its director Joaquín M. Condall staged *Así eran los romanos* (The Romans Were This Way), complete with stately images from antiquity.[48] Perhaps the choreographer aimed to promote the "culture" of an institution previously dedicated to gratuitous glitz, or perhaps he alluded to the heroism of a regime persevering through crisis. Either way, the piece provided a strange performative comment on a moment of austerity, one that may have entertained but also inspired audiences to reflect on the sometimes surreal juxtapositions of the revolutionary here and now.

Revolutionary Ballet: Gestures of Support and Discontent

While Cubans worked to "revolutionize" revelry in cabarets, dancers and government officials described ballet as inherently revolutionary starting in 1959. This designation, however, necessitated reframing aspects of ballet history and aesthetics at odds with the populism, masculinist ethos, and radicalism of Cuban nationalist, and eventually socialist, politics. Toward this end, ballet leaders embraced the Cuban revolutionary state's promotion of traditional gender roles and ideals of corporeal discipline.[49] Yet while ballet mirrored state policies and cultural discourses in this way, the prominence of the dance form also challenged narrow notions of revolutionary masculinity by exalting a nontraditional male figure, the ballet-dancing man. Furthermore, though some ballet dancers supported the cultural and political status quo, others challenged aesthetic and political boundaries. Conceptual maneuvers to accommodate ballet to revolutionary culture paralleled those found in cabaret. Also like cabaret, ballet was not monolithic and dancers differentially prioritized conscientious discipline and spirited innovation. Thus a form closely associated with the Revolution harbored ideological multiplicities that signaled fissures in the political unity sought by the state.

Ballet and revolution may appear to make strange bedfellows, yet this affiliation built upon more than a decade of Cuban ballet leaders working to establish a relationship with various Cuban governments. In 1948 Alberto, Fernando, and Alicia Alonso founded the first professional ballet company in Cuba, the Ballet Alicia Alonso, which soon enjoyed an annual subsidy of $43,000 from President Carlos Prío Socarrás. After Batista's 1952 coup, the company and supporters campaigned in performance programs and the press to augment this sum, contending, "The Ballet Alicia Alonso needs urgently an annual subsidy of no less than $200,000."[50] Along with these appeals, Ballet Alicia Alonso performed for Batista's 1955 "inauguration" and adopted the name Ballet de Cuba in anticipation of greater official support.[51] Yet the Ballet de Cuba's relationship with Batista deteriorated in 1956. That year the government eliminated the existing subsidy and instead promised Alicia $500 a month for her "artistic merits" and service to the country.[52] This set off a firestorm after Alicia publicly rejected the offer. The Ballet de Cuba staged a nationwide protest tour and then suspended activities until early 1959.[53] Despite vacillating political alliances, ballet leaders remained steadfast in their determination to secure state funding for a world-class ballet establishment.

Early in 1959 Fernando and Alicia joined forces with the new leadership. On February 3 the Ballet de Cuba performed for the first time since 1956, and on February 15 the company mounted the same program in tribute to the new government.[54] On September 17 a performance program declared the company's alliance "with the Revolution."[55] Besides these proclamations, Fernando and Alicia had deep ties to members of the 26th of July Movement, such as the geographer Antonio Núñez Jiménez. Fernando and Alicia befriended Núñez Jiménez in the 1940s and participated in excursions with his spelunkers society, the Sociedad Espeleológica de Cuba.[56] In 1952 Núñez Jiménez married Lupe Velis, a ballerina in Fernando and Alicia's company. He began to actively support ballet soon thereafter. Company documents, correspondence, and performance programs listed him as being in charge of "administration" in the early 1950s.[57] Additionally Núñez Jiménez served as first vice secretary of the Institución Ballet Alicia Alonso, a civic association founded in 1952 to support the company.[58] Perhaps unsurprisingly, Núñez Jiménez facilitated a partnership between the 26th of July Movement and ballet in the spring of 1959. Late one night, he visited Fernando at home, accompanied by Fidel Castro. After hours of conversation, Fidel famously asked the company director how much money he needed.[59] Fernando supposedly told him $100,000, to which Fidel replied, "Take $200,000 and make it good."[60] This often-repeated legend celebrates Fidel's beneficence but ignores the fact that Alicia and Fernando had pushed for $200,000 in public support since the early 1950s.[61] The gentlemen's agreement became Law 812, passed on May 20, 1960.[62] Explosive evidence of the partnership between ballet and the new government came in August 1960, when counterrevolutionaries planted a bomb at the Ballet de Cuba studios.[63]

In the meantime, Alicia had emerged as a paragon of revolutionary citizenship because of her tenacity, talent, unswerving political support, and embrace of a carefully gendered role.[64] According to a 1960 article, Alicia achieved her stardom through hard work and bravery in the face of long-standing vision problems: "Alicia has had to overcome her deficient eyes. . . . Hers is a triumph of will. . . . Alicia is a great ballerina because she wants to be."[65] In the realm of Cuban politics, Alicia participated in mass organizations, including the Federación de Mujeres Cubanas (Federation of Cuban Women, founded in August 1960). She also led the Ballet de Cuba in forming its own Comité de Defensa de la Revolución (Committee for the Defense of the Revolution), declaring institutional commitment to "revolutionary vigilance."[66] Most important, Alicia became an archetype of revolutionary femininity. As one article declared, she had broken a "myth" by demonstrating "her indisputable supremacy in the world of ballet," while also being a "complete woman, mother of Laurita, grandmother of Iván."[67] Alicia ostensibly contributed to social advance through professional success, political participation, and fulfilling traditional familial obligations. These discourses on discipline and gendered tropes suggest the partial persistence of bourgeois norms and their incorporation into the lived experience of the Revolution's early years.

Contrary to the cult of Alicia and ballerinas in general, male ballet dancers combated preconceptions in Cuba before and immediately after 1959. Existing Cuban ballet figures such as Fernando and Alberto Alonso taught and choreographed. Alicia partnered with foreign-born male dancers from New York and Latin America initially and then the Soviet Union in the 1960s. Yet despite these examples, widespread homophobia and assumptions about dance as an effeminate art deterred families from allowing their sons to dance. As a 1961 article put it, the "erroneous prejudice of some families" impeded the development of Cuban male dancers.[68] Soon after 1959, ballet leaders worked to address this problem by revising the means and methods of ballet training.

The Academia Municipal de Ballet de la Habana (Municipal Academy of Ballet of Havana) played an important role in achieving this end. Cuban teachers Josefina Elósegui, Fernando Alonso, and Russian émigré Anna Leontieva spearheaded efforts to reorganize the school after 1959. The original Academia Municipal was founded in 1948 with Elósegui as a ballet teacher, school subdirector, and advisor to a civic association founded by parents to support the school.[69] After 1959 she continued to administer the Academia Municipal de Ballet, and in August 1960 the municipal government appointed her director of the school. At that time, the Academia Municipal occupied studios in Central Havana (at the streets Rastro and Belascoaín) and Miramar (at the school Leontieva founded in the 1950s). The Academia Municipal consolidated and began relocating in 1961 to a new building at L and 19 streets in the Vedado district, where it continues to operate today.[70] Simultaneously, Leontieva and Fernando designed a detailed curriculum for ballet students, complete with milestones for nine years of instruction.[71] The government made official its support for ballet education in the March 1961 Law 742.[72] In July 1961 over nine hundred children auditioned for 250 state-funded scholarships to study at the academy.[73]

While the government supported dance education, dance leaders focused on addressing "the lack of male dancers," according to a document produced by the Academia Municipal.[74] Dance leaders implemented curricular changes to counter prejudices against dancing boys and men. Article 10 of the Academia Municipal de Ballet bylaws asserted that boys and girls would train separately starting in the second year of study, and boys would have a male teacher. This ensured that boys did not "imitate" girls' gestures, as clarified in a note following the stipulation.[75] In a 1960 document on future plans for dance pedagogy, Fernando and Leontieva wrote, "To promote in Cuba the cultivation of ballet . . . among men in order to solve the current shortage of [male] dancers . . . [we need] a lot of propaganda and a curriculum that, in terms of men, presents dance as what it is and should be, besides an art, a way to achieve the totality of masculine physicality, the development of strength as well as grace and elegance, and a supreme aesthetic expression of *virility*" (emphasis in the original).[76] A summary reiterated that propaganda needed to insist on male dancers' "hygienic, virile and even . . . sporting aspects."[77] Fernando promoted the image of a masculine dance maker through words and actions. A photograph accompanying an article on ballet training shows him teaching class armed and wearing fatigues (figure 7.1). He projects a masculine martial discipline and symbolic battle readiness. As ballet leaders tried to promote male dancers as virile revolutionaries, they reaffirmed prevailing pre- and post-1959 heteronormative frameworks.

Along with reworking ballet instruction, ballet leaders promoted a more muscular image of Cuban ballet dancers choreographically. An early, illustrative example is *Avanzada* (1963), a "ballet inspired by a heroic event in the battle of Stalingrad," choreographed by the Soviet dancer Azari Plisetski.[78] In the ballet, dancers in fatigues performed strong movements of aggression. The ballet establishment not only staged the work in Havana theaters for familiar publics, but also traveled to reach new audiences and proselytize the notion of ballet, like revolutionary defense, as a calling for patriotic men and women. In 1964, ballet dancers presented *Avanzada* to Cuban soldiers in Guantánamo,

FIG. 7.1. "The dynamic Fernando Alonso, militant, director general of the Ballet, doing a dance step in the center of the salon." *INRA*, August 1961, 93.

foregrounding the similarities between the dancers on stage and the servicemen in the audience given their shared costuming, physical exertion, and devotion to the cause (figure 7.2). In 1966 the connection between dancers and armed fighters became a staged reality. In June sixty-six members of the Batallón de Ceremonias de la Defensa Popular (Ceremonial Battalion of Popular Defense) joined six ballet dancers in a special performance of *Avanzada*. Ballet dancers performed the original choreography and the battalion danced moves inspired by "throwing grenades, various exercises, all based on choreographic designs," the newspaper reported.[79] In this event, soldiers of art and actual soldiers danced together, performing their militant, equally masculine support for the Revolution in tandem.

And yet, despite these efforts, the ballet establishment could not avoid the repressive suspicions, practices, and attitudes toward the culturally and politically "marginal" taking hold in society at large. Starting in the mid-1960s, reigning political discourse labeled homosexuals, Jehovah's Witnesses, Seventh Day Adventists, Catholic priests, Protestant preachers, some artists and intellectuals, and young peasants who resisted collectivization "antisocials."

FIG. 7.2. A 1964 performance of *Avanzada* in Guantánamo. Courtesy of the Museo Nacional de la Danza, Havana, Cuba.

As scholars have shown, between 1965 and 1968 the government "reeducated" many in forced labor camps.[80] Several male ballet dancers were detained and interrogated, but Alicia intervened on their behalf.[81] Male dancers who suffered discrimination became increasingly dissatisfied with political developments. When the Ballet Nacional de Cuba (formerly Ballet de Cuba, renamed in 1962) traveled to Paris for an international ballet competition in 1966, ten male dancers defected. The defectors explained, "We are not opposed to the revolutionary action of the present regime. But we deplore the arbitrary persecution . . . which affects anybody showing the least sign of nonconformity either in his way of life, his religious opinions, or simply his clothes. It has become impossible for us to work as artists in such a climate of threats and incertitude."[82] In their statement the dancers suggested that the current regime had betrayed the Revolution through its repressive cultural policies.

Along with explicit defections and protests, other ballet practitioners subtly subverted genre and political conventions through their work. The choreographer Alberto Alonso was one important case. He built on a previous history of creative independence. After cofounding Ballet Alicia Alonso with Fernando and Alicia, he branched off to form his own ballet company in 1950 and to choreograph for cabaret and television. After 1959 he directed a new company, eventually named the Conjunto Experimental de Danza de la Habana (Experimental Dance Ensemble of Havana), which performed works featuring a mix of ballet and popular dance styles, such as the production *El Solar*. Alberto created a ten-minute version of *El Solar* for television and nightclub audiences in 1951, and he revived and reworked the piece in 1963. The new version ran forty-five minutes and was set in the early 1960s. As his co-collaborator, writer Lisandro Otero described in a performance program, Alberto choreographed "a national dance, popular and cultured," that depicted the experiences of everyday citizens.[83] The ballet thrilled Cuban audiences, inspiring a musical, *Mi Solar* (1964), and a film, *Un día en el solar* (1965).[84] Moreover, when the Conjunto Experimental toured abroad from late 1965 through early 1966, the ballet so impressed the Bolshoi ballerina Maya Plisetskaya that she asked Alberto to choreograph a ballet for her.[85]

In spite of these achievements, however, the Conjunto Experimental abruptly dissolved in 1966. Alberto told the story of this dissolution and its aftermath after leaving Cuba in the early 1990s. In a 1994 interview with the Cuban dance historian Célida Parera Villalón, Alberto confided that, upon returning to Cuba in 1966, he discovered that the government had appointed a new director of his company.[86] In a speech to audiences in Gainesville, Florida, in the 2000s, he elaborated: "The new director, a party member, of course, knew nothing about art, much less about dancing. He was a tailor."[87] Alberto thus left the company in protest and traveled to the Soviet Union to collaborate with Plisetskaya, the composer Rodion Shchedrin (Plisetskaya's husband), and the stage designer Boris Messerer (Plisetskaya's maternal cousin). All three of Alberto's collaborators had firsthand experience with the strictures and violence of the Soviet state.[88] *Carmen* (1967), the resulting work inspired by the classic Bizet opera, depicted what Alberto described in an elliptical 1983 interview from Havana as a clash between a rebellious gypsy woman and the authoritarian monarchy of nineteenth-century Spain.[89] In the 1990s and 2000s, by that point in exile, Alberto alleged the piece contained another layer of meaning: it was a metaphorical critique of the Cuban state.

Whether this subversive intent existed from the beginning remains difficult to corroborate given the retrospective nature of Alberto's testimony. The setting, story line, and characters of the ballet nonetheless did conceivably leave room for critical interpretations. *Carmen* is set in the middle of a bullfighting ring. Spectators represent supporters of a dictatorial government. They sit around the arena, coldly judging the action, "much like an inquisition."[90] Carmen, by contrast, is a nonconformist "antisocial." She fights against her oppressive antagonist Zúñiga, a swaggering Spanish overlord.[91] Although Carmen must submit to Zúñiga's rules, he "fears most what she represents—freedom," Alberto stated in the 2000s.[92] Don José, a tragic character, falls in love with Carmen and her ideals, but he ultimately defends the status quo. Escamillo, the bullfighter, seeks to conquer Carmen while also dancing with a bull (or fate) performed by a woman in black. Although bulls typically symbolize virility, Alberto made the bull a woman to link her to Carmen, who stubbornly defends her independence. In the final scene, Carmen dances with Don José and the bull with Escamillo, until both women collapse. Although Carmen dies, Alberto contended that she triumphed by never giving up her principles.[93]

It is therefore possible to see the ballet as a metaphor for the relationship between the nation and state in 1960s Cuba. In this reading, Carmen symbolizes liberty and the Cuban people, while the male characters personify agents of an overbearing political authority. Zúñiga might represent authoritarian control (or even Castro); Don José, empty ideologies; and Escamillo, performative bravura. The choreography seems to reinforce these associations, as Carmen performs stylized movements, such as flourishes of the arms, hands, and hips, referencing her Spanish nationality, while representatives of the state perform choreographies of inertia. In the opening scene, Carmen cuts through the air with high kicks, sweeping jumps, and deep lunges. This contrasts with the masked onlookers sitting heavily in oversized wooden chairs above the bullring. Later, when Zúñiga, Don José, and Escamillo perform movements similar to Carmen's, they appear robotic and constricted.[94] In the final scene Carmen and the female bull fly into wielded knives, consummating their sacrifice in pursuit of a repressed ideal.

Cryptic program notes from *Carmen*'s Cuban premiere in August 1967—just a few months after its April showing in Moscow—provide little help in discerning Alberto's true intentions. An impressionistic sentence appears next to the performance credits: "Love, hate, passion and conflict, forces that in the arena of life, the bullfighting ring, oscillate ominously among each other, driven by the impetuous temperament of one woman: Carmen."[95] Though not an obvious political denunciation, the line avoids absolute narration, encouraging audiences to meditate on broader themes like "passion and conflict" that may have resonated with Cuba's recent past. In a detached insert to the performance program from August 2, 1967, Alberto alludes to these possible connections: "I wanted to identify the theme of 'Carmen' with the character of our times. . . . The struggle between the cold, dry, inhuman, and mechanical, and the passionate fight for what one wants . . . for the right to be free. . . . 'Carmen' does not give up. . . . 'Carmen' dies without surrender."[96] Perhaps, then, this statement did gesture to veiled critical commentary about the increasingly "cold, dry . . . mechanical" postures of the Cuban state. Here, Alberto wrote the word "Carmen" in quotation marks, referring ambiguously to the female protagonist, the ballet, or both. In this way, he arguably implied that the ballet itself, and not only its protagonist, defied an oppressive order.

Yet even if Alberto intended a broader critique, contemporary audiences in Cuba and abroad missed or remained silent about such interpretations. They instead focused on the ballet's talented performers and its significance for international relations. One review praised the Cuban and Soviet collaborators, describing the ballet as a "living symbol" of Cuban-Soviet cooperation.[97] Mexican and Cuban critics, moreover, marveled over Alicia's portrayal of the sensual, fiery gypsy.[98] Ironically, *Carmen* became one of her favorite roles. As Alicia, a staunch supporter of Castro, performed the ballet, she undermined a critical reading of its contents. Abstract indirectness may have allowed Alberto to air otherwise unacceptable opinions. Yet nonverbal, ephemeral dance also made it possible for such statements to go unnoticed.

If no one understood or mentioned veiled meanings, one might wonder if Alberto's inscrutable critique mattered. But at the very least, the transgressive message ostensibly embedded in the ballet mattered to Alberto. The choreographer later disclosed that he never expected *Carmen* to spark citizen or government action: "Carmen was just my opinion, a small drop in a vast ocean, but it made me feel good and somehow at peace with myself."[99] This history challenges assumptions that the Cuban ballet establishment uniformly supported the state. Moreover, for considering the potential of political critiques through dance, *Carmen* provides a unique source.

Conclusion

In the 1960s, revolutionary spirit morphed from a symbol of youthful rebellion to endurance in the face of adversity. At the same time, manifestations of revolutionary consciousness took on increasing complexity as individual interpretations of Cuba's political project went in different directions—dovetailing, clashing, or coexisting tensely with state prescriptions. Choreographers and dancers reconfigured cabaret festivities into gestures of "combatant happiness." Ballet practitioners, in turn, portrayed their art as a metaphor for the more restrained values of revolutionary dedication and order. Yet even as the political environment hardened, subjecting more commercial forms of entertainment to critique, late-night cabaret celebrations persisted. Acts of ballet agency likewise stretched the supposed political conservatism of that form. These varied performances became physical manifestations of ingenuity and perseverance. As Orlando Jiménez Leal, one of the creators of the controversial documentary P.M., commented decades later in exile, "The revolutionary triumph of 1959 brought the country a great party. However, already in 1961 there existed an enormous political tension in the atmosphere; in some ways, the lights had been turned off at the party, but people continued dancing."[100] Even in fraught times, choreographic innovations across genres continued, and Cubans kept dancing with, and in spite of, state mandates.

Juxtaposing traditional and nontraditional sources—historical texts as well as dancing bodies—this chapter has examined how Cubans expressed rebellious liberation, ordered devotion, and combinations of the two in the context of a revolutionary society still finding its political bearings. With each performance, cabaret and ballet forged a place in Cuban society despite surface incongruities with socialist times. Not unlike the geographers and fashion designers discussed by Reinaldo Funes Monzote and María A. Cabrera Arús in this volume, Cuban dancers, choreographers, and teachers broadly interpreted the Revolution on their own terms, navigating its tantalizing possibilities and pressing limitations. Performers expanded the parameters of revolutionary culture (to incorporate "low" and "high" forms), revised standing definitions of masculinity (to include the male ballet dancer), and even articulated subtle forms of political critique (decrying authoritarianism). The state invested in and to a certain extent controlled dance venues, but dancers and choreographers alone inhabited the stage and directly dialogued with audiences. In doing so Cuban dance professionals did not march in lockstep behind the Revolution but interacted with the political project as one would a dancing partner: constantly improvising and negotiating for agency within generalized routines. Through such maneuvers, dancers moved between *espíritu* and *conciencia*, inserting flexibility and motion into their political present and future.

NOTES

1. Andrew Salkey, *Havana Journal* (Harmondsworth, UK: Penguin, 1971), 52–53.

2. Arnold Haskell, "La Clausura del Seminario sobre crítica y apreciación del ballet" (March 15, 1968), Sala de Arte, Biblioteca Nacional José Martí, Havana, Cuba (hereafter SA-BNJM).

3. Elizabeth Sutherland, *Cuba Now* (New York: Dial Press, 1968), 65.

4. See, for instance, consciousness as discussed in Karl Marx and Friedrich Engels, "The Communist Manifesto," in *The Communist Manifesto*, ed. Jeffrey Isaac (New Haven: Yale University Press, 2012), 90; see also Marifeli Pérez-Stable, *The Cuban Revolution: Origins, Course, and Legacy*, 2nd ed. (New York: Oxford University Press, 1999), 102–20.

5. Fidel Castro, April 2, 1959, reprinted in *La Revolución Cubana*, ed. Gregorio Selser (Buenos Aires: Editorial Palestra, 1960), 288.

6. Juan Marinello, "El Congreso Cultural de la Habana marca una fecha histórica en la construcción de una sociedad y un hombre nuevos," *Bohemia*, January 12, 1968, 44.

7. Danielle Goldman, *I Want to Be Ready: Improvised Dance as a Practice of Freedom* (Ann Arbor: University of Michigan Press, 2010), 5.

8. Lester Tomé, "Swans in Sugarcane Fields: Proletarian Ballet Dancers and the Cuban Revolution's Industrious New Man," *Dance Research Journal* 49, no. 2 (2017): 4–25; Miguel Cabrera, *El ballet en Cuba: Apuntes históricos* (Havana: Cúpulas, 2011); Suki John, *Contemporary Dance in Cuba: Técnica Cubana as Revolutionary Movement* (Jefferson, NC: McFarland, 2012); Yvonne Daniel, *Rumba: Dance and Social Change in Contemporary Cuba* (Bloomington: Indiana University Press, 1996).

9. I build on studies that have made excellent use of different media in examining state power; for instance, music in Robin D. Moore, *Music and Revolution: Cultural Change in Socialist Cuba* (Berkeley: University of California Press, 2006); film in Lillian Guerra, *Visions of Power in Cuba: Revolution, Redemption, and Resistance, 1959–1971* (Chapel Hill: University of North Carolina Press, 2014); and visual images in Devyn Spence Benson, *Antiracism in Cuba: The Unfinished Revolution* (Chapel Hill: University of North Carolina Press, 2016).

10. Carlos Franqui, *Family Portrait with Fidel: A Memoir*, translated by Alfred MacAdam (New York: Vintage Books, 1984), 91, 68.

11. Moore, *Music and Revolution*, 61–63.

12. R. Hart Phillips, "Cuba May Have a Tourist Season," *New York Times*, January 11, 1959.

13. "Cuba to Restore Gambling Friday," *New York Times*, February 17, 1959.

14. Mario G. del Cueto, "El Fomento Turístico: Gran Fuente de Riqueza Pública," *Bohemia*, May 31, 1959, 88, 90; Rosalie Schwartz, *Pleasure Island: Tourism and Temptation in Cuba* (Lincoln: University of Nebraska Press, 1997), 200.

15. R. Hart Phillips, "Cuba Cuts Rates to Spur Tourism," *New York Times*, January 31, 1960.

16. "Cuba Takes Over 2 American-Operated Tourist Hotels," *Washington Post*, June 12, 1960.

17. Castro spoke out against gambling as a vice allowed only for foreign visitors. As the numbers of tourists waned, casinos became an unnecessary evil. In 1962 reports asserted that gambling had halted, though scholars have noted that betting on sports and cockfighting persisted. Roy Shields, "Cuba Casinos, Brothels Vanish with Tourists," *L.A. Times*, March 22, 1962; John Andrew Gustavsen, "Tension under the Sun: Tourism and Identity in Cuba, 1945–2007," PhD diss., University of Miami, 2009, 177–79.

18. Louis A. Pérez, *Cuba: Between Reform and Revolution*, 3rd ed. (New York: Oxford University Press, 2006), 248; Adriana Orejuela Martínez, *El son no se fue de Cuba: Claves para una historia, 1959–1973* (Caracas: Fundación Celarg, 2013), 158.

19. Sonia Calero, interview with author, December 5, 2013, Miami.

20. Other elite cabarets included Montmartre, Hotel Habana Riviera's Copa Room, Hotel Nacional's Club "Parisien," Hotel Habana Hilton's (later renamed Habana Libre) El Caribe, and Hotel Capri's Casino Capri.

21. Other midlevel clubs included Las Vegas, Rumba Palace, St. John's, Club 66, Pennsylvania, Autopista, among many others. Orejuela Martínez, *El son*, 129.

22. Orejuela Martínez, *El son*, 159; Rosa Lowinger and Ofelia Fox, *Tropicana Nights: The Life and Times of the Legendary Cuban Nightclub* (New York: Harcourt, 2005), 391.

23. Orejuela Martínez, *El son*, 185, 239.

24. "Rincón de sabor africano en la carretera de Santa Fe," *Show*, August 1959, 48–49.

25. "Carlos Sandor amenaza en el Club 'Parisién' con la revista del año," *Show*, March 1960, 46–49.

26. "La producción del Habana Riviera proclamada como la mejor del año," *Show*, January 1961, 47.

27. "La gran producción del Casino de Capri," *Show*, August 1959, 38–39; Guerra, *Visions of Power*, 96–98.

28. The revolutionary support that Alonso staged at the Capri resonated with his choreography for other venues in the early 1960s. For instance, *Cimarrón* on April 21, 1960, according to the program, was "representative of the efforts made by the Revolutionary Government in its proposal to recuperate and dignify our music and our folklore, long subject to foreign influences." *Cimarrón*, performance program, April 21, 1960, SA-BNJM; Orejuela Martínez, *El son*, 97.

29. Lowinger and Fox, *Tropicana Nights*, 391.

30. "Fiesta de ritmo y sabor, la producción del 'Habana Libre,'" *Show*, April–May 1961, 44–45.

31. *P.M.*, directed by Sabá Cabrera Infante and Orlando Jiménez Leal (Havana, 1961).

32. William Luis, *Lunes de Revolución: Literatura y cultura en los primeros años de la Revolución cubana*, Verbum Ensayo (Madrid: Editorial Verbum, 2003), 50–51, 224.

33. Franqui, *Family Portrait*, 132–33; Luis, *Lunes de Revolución*, 49; Guerra, *Visions of Power*, 164.

34. "Estrena 'Tropicana' nueva y fastuosa revista titulada 'Leyenda Antillana,'" *Show*, January 1962, 60–61.

35. Shields, "Cuba Casinos," 18.

36. Franqui, *Family Portrait*, 170.

37. Orlando Quiroga, "La Habana noche tras noche," *Bohemia*, October 1, 1961, 36.

38. Orlando Quiroga, "De Viernes a Viernes," *Bohemia*, March 2, 1962, 84.

39. José Gil de Lamadrid, "La Habana, Cuba Territorio Libre de América," *Bohemia*, August 10, 1962, 30–31, 34.

40. "El pueblo cautivo se divierte," *Bohemia*, July 3, 1964, 38.

41. *Nosotros, la música*, directed by Rogelio París (Havana: ICAIC, 1964).

42. "Images of Havana and Fidel Castro's Personal Interactions with the Public," DVD, CBC Films, Box 75U, Cuban Revolution Collection, Yale University Manuscripts and Archives, New Haven (hereafter CRC, YUMA).

43. "Entrevista a artistas de cabaret," DVD, CBC Films, Box 70U, CRC, YUMA.

44. "Entrevista a artistas de cabaret."

45. Muñoz-Unsain, "El cabaret, ¿También cultura?," *Bohemia*, February 3, 1967, 34.

46. Salkey, *Havana Journal*, 40, 52, 75, 76.

47. Rafael Lam, *Tropicana: Un paraíso bajo las estrellas* (Havana: Editorial José Martí, 1997), 65; Guerra, *Visions of Power*, 301.

48. Lam, *Tropicana*, 65–66.

49. Tomé discusses ballet dancers' discipline as part of what he calls the "proletarianization of ballet," that is, the promotion of ballet dancers as ultimate revolutionary workers ("Swans in Sugarcane Fields," 7–16). Whereas Tomé posits that ballet dancers projected a singular, heroic image in 1960s Cuba, I examine the ideological diversity within the ballet establishment, so often portrayed as a monolithic entity of revolutionary support.

50. Ballet Alicia Alonso, performance program, August 25 and 29, 1952, SA-BNJM; Oscar Abela, "El Ballet de Cuba en la Encrucijada," *Carteles*, September 23, 1956, 36–37, 80.

51. "Toma de Posesión del Presidente Mayor General Fulgencio Batista, Función de Gala por el Ballet Alicia Alonso," February 25, 1955, Folder Ballet-Danza 1955, Centro de Documentación y Archivo Teatral, Teatro Nacional de Cuba, Havana, Cuba (hereafter CDAT-TNC).

52. "Suplemento al numero 13 de la Revista 'Nuestro Tiempo,'" *Nuestro Tiempo* 13 (September 1956), n.p.

53. Toba Singer, *Fernando Alonso: The Father of Cuban Ballet* (Gainesville: University Press of Florida, 2013), 76.

54. Singer, *Fernando Alonso*, 85.

55. Folder Ballet-Danza 1959, CDAT-TNC.

56. Antonio Núñez Jiménez, *La Gran Caverna de Santo Tomás: Monumento nacional* (Havana: Ediciones Plaza Vieja, 1990), 84–87.

57. "Ballet Alicia Alonso: Sur América y Cuba," Fundación Antonio Núñez Jiménez de la Naturaleza y el Hombre, Havana, Cuba.

58. Legajo: 175, Expediente: 3503, Fondo: Registro de Asociaciones, Archivo Nacional de Cuba, Havana, Cuba (hereafter ANC).

59. Singer, *Fernando Alonso*, 85.

60. Al Burt, "Cuba Ballet Cast in Soviet Mold," *Washington Post*, March 28, 1965.

61. Elizabeth Schwall, "Dancing with the Revolution: Cuban Dance, State, and Nation, 1930–1990," PhD diss., Columbia University, 2016, 65–78.

62. Cabrera, *El Ballet en Cuba*, 339–42.

63. "Dos protestas de *Lunes*," *Lunes de Revolución*, August 29, 1960, 2.

64. Deirdre Brill calls her the ultimate "new man." Deidre Brill, "La Escuela Cubana: Dance Education and Performance in Revolutionary Cuba," PhD diss., University of Pennsylvania, 2007, 176–218.

65. "Un perfil de Alicia," *Lunes de Revolución*, April 4, 1960, 13.

66. Rpt. in Cabrera, *El Ballet en Cuba*, 342.

67. Orlando Quiroga, "Alicia en el 66," *Bohemia*, February 18, 1966, 18–19.

68. Ana Pardo, "Inicia Cuba una nueva escuela de ballet," *INRA*, October 1961, 64.

69. Exp. 3358, Leg. 172, Fondo: Registro de Asociaciones, ANC.

70. Josefina Elósegui, letter to Rolando López del Amo, November 30, 1961, Folder Municipio de la Habana, Academia Municipal de Ballet, Ballet de Cámara, 1960–1961,

Fondo: Ministerio de Educación (1940–1961), Sección de Fondo: Dirección General de Cultura, Archivo General del Ministerio de Cultura, Biblioteca Juan Marinello, Havana, Cuba (hereafter ME-DGC, AGMC-BJM).

71. Folder Municipio de la Habana, Academia Municipal de Ballet, Ballet de Cámara, 1960–1961, ME-DGC, AGMC-BJM.

72. Copy of "Resolución Ministerial No. 742 de 1961," *La Gaceta Oficial de la Republica*, March 13, 1961, Folder Municipio de la Habana, Academia Municipal de Ballet, Ballet de Cámara, 1960–1961, ME-DGC, AGMC-BJM.

73. Ana Pardo, "Inicia Cuba una nueva escuela de ballet," *INRA*, October 1961, 61.

74. "Proyecto para la escuela de ballet del municipio de la Habana," Folder Municipio de la Habana, Academia Municipal de Ballet, Ballet de Cámara, 1960–1961, ME-DGC, AGMC-BJM.

75. "Escuela Ballet de Habana, Reglamento," Folder Municipio de la Habana, Academia Municipal de Ballet, Ballet de Cámara, 1960–1961, ME-DGC, AGMC-BJM.

76. Anna Leontieva and Fernando Alonso, "Proyecto Para la Escuela de Ballet del Municipio de la Habana," October 8, 1960, Folder Municipio de la Habana, Academia Municipal de Ballet, Ballet de Cámara, 1960–1961, ME-DGC, AGMC-BJM.

77. "Proyecto para la escuela de ballet del municipio de la Habana, resumen de sus ideas centrales," Folder Municipio de la Habana, Academia Municipal de Ballet, Ballet de Cámara, 1960–1961, ME-DGC, AGMC-BJM.

78. Ballet Nacional de Cuba, performance program, November 9, 1967, Folder Ballet-Danza 1967, CDAT-TNC.

79. Pedro Abreu, "Actuarán en un ballet 66 reservistas y 6 bailarinas," *El Mundo*, May 20, 1966.

80. Guerra, *Visions of Power*, 227–31.

81. The actual number of dancers remains unclear. Julio Medina recounts his own experience being detained and saved by Alicia, and Jorge Riverón only says "many dancers . . . had been persecuted." Néstor Almendros and Orlando Jiménez-Leal, *Conducta impropia* (Madrid: Editorial Playor, 1984), 123–25, 129.

82. Kathryn Kenyon, "Cuban Ballet's 'Giselle' Is Success Despite Defections," *L.A. Times*, November 17, 1966.

83. Conjunto Experimental de Danza de la Habana, performance program, *El Solar*, SA-BNJM.

84. *Mi Solar*, performance program, March 25, 1964, personal archive of Sonia Calero, Miami; *Un día en el solar*, directed by Eduardo Manet (Havana: ICAIC, 1965).

85. "Así vino 'El Solar' la critica Francesa," *Bohemia*, January 14, 1966, 28–29; Maya Plisetskaya, *I, Maya Plisetskaya*, translated by Antonina W. Bouis (New Haven: Yale University Press, 2001), 271.

86. "Alberto Alonso," video recording, September 20, 1994, *MGZIA 4–2078, New York Public Library for the Performing Arts, Jerome Robbins Dance Division.

87. Alberto Alonso, untitled, undated speech, personal archive of Sonia Calero.

88. See Plisetskaya, *I, Maya Plisetskaya*, 32–39, 156–58, 192–97, 268–81.

89. Pedro Simón, "*Carmen* en su aniversario cuarenta," *Cuba en el Ballet* 114 (May–August 2007): 13–15.

90. Alberto Alonso, untitled, personal archive of Sonia Calero.

91. Simón, "*Carmen* en su aniversario cuarenta," 13–15.

92. Alberto Alonso, untitled, personal archive of Sonia Calero.

93. Simón, "*Carmen* en su aniversario cuarenta," 14–17.

94. *Carmen* (Havana: ICAIC, 1968). Although my analysis is based on the filmed version of the ballet created in 1968, a video of the staged performance from 1982 may be found at the New York Public Library for the Performing Arts, Jerome Robbins Dance Division, *MGZIC 9–357, *Carmen* (1982).

95. Ballet Nacional de Cuba, performance program, August 1, 3, 4, 1967, Folder Ballet-Danza 1967, CDAT-TNC.

96. Folder Ballet-Danza 1967, CDAT-TNC.

97. Anna Ilupina, "Carmen opta por la libertad," *Bohemia*, June 9, 1967, 10–11.

98. Juan Vicente Melo, "Alicia Alonso," *Bohemia*, May 31, 1968, 80–81; Orlando Quiroga, "Alicia en el país de la ciencia-ficción," *Bohemia*, April 3, 1970, 34–35.

99. Alberto Alonso, untitled, personal archive of Sonia Calero.

100. "Un baile de fantasmas: Entrevista a Orlando Jiménez Leal por Manuel Zayas," *Encuentro de la cultura cubana* 50 (2008): 191.

8. When the "New Man" Met the "Old Man"

GUEVARA, NYERERE, AND THE ROOTS
OF LATIN-AFRICANISM

———

CHRISTABELLE PETERS

Among the "great men" whose stories have come to dominate grand historical narratives of post-1959 Cuba, Ernesto "Che" Guevara remains a standout, even stand-alone, figure. At the same time, however, even a hero of his stature may be considered a victim of the fragmentation and underdevelopment that—as Michael Bustamante and Jennifer Lambe write in the introduction to this volume—beset "our knowledge of the social, cultural, and political history of revolutionary Cuba." The challenge, then, becomes one of forging new pathways to understanding that connect across the multiple gaps and divides that characterize the Cuban historical experience. Put more succinctly, it is a matter of finding the missing links. Thus can a historian, faced with a lack of so-called hard evidence in the quest to solve a particularly compelling mystery, be inspired to act like a detective when confronted with a cold trail, which means piecing together a case by tracing back from an action (effect) to its likely inspiration (cause). Above and beyond the capacity to understand human psychology, this type of investigation calls for imagination. And this essay will probe the potentialities that lie within imagination as a research method in order to investigate one of the unexplained conundrums in the history of Cuban foreign relations, namely Guevara's fateful decision to fight with rebel forces in the Congo when it appeared as though he had elected to do exactly the opposite.

On the one hand, imagination may be seen as bridging the gap between research in the arts and the sciences, to the extent that it highlights the intersection between qualitative techniques and scientific research principles. Many of the greatest advances in science have imagination at their core. And it is generally accepted that we cannot discover what we do not know, or explain what we do not understand, without the creativity of envisioning what we cannot see. On the other hand, it is possible to see imagination as a natural progression from the affective turn in social and humanities research, in which the consideration of feelings and emotions in human actions has taken on increasing importance over the course of the past decade.[1] The focus on affect and the emotional life-world has extended discussions about culture, subjectivity, identity, and bodies that were begun in critical theory and cultural criticism, particularly by poststructuralists and deconstructionists. What particularly interests me is how this process has opened up the hypothetical dimensions of lived experience in a way that allows a natural flow of understanding to emerge from imaginative inquiry as a method of doing history and, specifically in this study, how it elucidates Cuba's role in the global history of decolonization.

Aside from his exploits and achievements as a physician, guerrilla fighter, military strategist, and political thinker, Che Guevara is remembered for being one of revolutionary Cuba's and the global left's greatest dreamers. It was his "African dream," culminating in the ill-fated covert operation in the Congo, that exercised perhaps the most decisive influence on later Cuban policy for that continent, at the same time that the experience almost destroyed him. As Rafael Rojas indicates in this volume, revolutions are the moments when dream and terror (or hope and horror) collide, and in that regard it can be argued that Guevara has come to symbolically embody the hair-raising "point of collision" between all that is terrifying and what is sublime about transformations of all kinds (be they political, social, or even personal), as well as those specifically connected to his adopted homeland after 1959. My intention is to draw attention to the cultural reverberations inherent in political revolutions by discussing how the problematic of race and national identity in Cuba intersected with the revolution's policy for Africa, as can be seen in the cultural discourse of Latin-Africa that first emerged at the time of "Operation Carlota," the Cuban military engagement in the Angolan Civil War in November 1975.

For the investigative experiment at hand, I propose that we imagine a conversation that might or might not have taken place between Che Guevara and Julius Nyerere, the first president of independent Tanzania, in the capital city of Dar es Salaam during the course of the Argentine's stay there in February 1965. After sketching out a background to Guevara's visit, I will make the case for the imaginary dialogue by moving back and forth between its possible contents and the "evidence" of subsequent events, with a focus on Cuban policy for Africa. The aim of this task is to discover the dynamic qualities of self-consciousness that are present in action: those points of significance that are interwoven into the ongoing meaning and unfolding of personal life, and which, I would like to suggest, may finally guide, shape, and influence political events.

Finally, since so much of African diaspora history is made up of "shadow" lives—discourses and journeys that fall outside of the confines of "official" channels, a history of intimacies and personal ties—this imagined conversation between Guevara and Nyerere may additionally be conceived as my attempt to theorize aspects of postrevolutionary Cuban diplomatic history within an Africanist frame of reference. Doing so, moreover, decenters Cuban revolutionary history from its own insular exceptionality, staging an exchange in which a representative of Havana's government (in this case an Argentine) takes *in* lessons rather than spreading the island's "superior" example.

Chronicles of a Death Foretold

Often in this type of phenomenological inquiry we find that meaning appears in a type of narrative form as a theme permeating the experience in question. The theme that appeared in the process of my research for this essay was "the journey," in particular, the journey as a transformational experience. We know that Guevara undertook a number of important, life-transforming journeys before his death in Bolivia in 1967. He was also an avid chronicler, and so we have been able to read his journals and diaries from some of the most important stages of his journey through life. We recall, for example, *Notas de Viaje*, a record of the great tour of Latin America that he undertook in 1952 with his friend Alberto Granado, which was published in English as *The Motorcycle Diaries* (1995). This travel diary is as important for its testimony of Che's political enlightenment as for the spectacular geographical scenes described within its pages. Of even greater significance for our study, however, was Guevara's recognition that the journey had changed him. Following his return to Argentina, he observed, "The person who wrote these notes died upon stepping once again onto Argentine soil, he who edits and polishes them, 'I,' am not I; at least I am not the same I was before. That vagabonding through our 'America' has changed me more than I thought."[2]

Another important chronicle of adventure was Guevara's diary of guerrilla warfare in Cuba between 1956 and 1958, *Episodes of the Cuban Revolutionary War* (1963), in the wake of his fateful meeting with Fidel Castro. In his personal journal of the time, he wrote, "A political occurrence is having met Fidel Castro, the Cuban revolutionary, a young man, intelligent, very sure of himself and of extraordinary audacity; I think there is a mutual sympathy between us." And it would be this same Fidel who ensured that Cuba was first to publish the diary written during twelve months of the guerrilla campaign in Bolivia, adopting the title *The Secret Papers of a Revolutionary: The Diary of Che Guevara* (1968).

Given this lifetime habit of keeping a diary or journal, it goes without saying that Guevara's first visit to sub-Saharan Africa between December 1964 and March 1965 was carefully recorded, and his thoughts about the leaders of the newly independent states that he visited inscribed in his notes.[3] This is especially so given the importance attached to the tour at both the personal and political level. Consequently, it is a tragedy for those of us who study African themes that his impressions of the continent that has glorified him over generations as a symbol, martyr, and even father of liberation have not been publicly available. Without question the tour formed the cornerstone of Cuban policy for Africa, inciting the internationalist missions that took place in a dozen or more countries (including Algeria, Guinea, Sierra Leone, South Yemen, Syria, and Somalia) in the ensuing years, culminating in the epic military and humanitarian operations by Cuban soldiers, military advisors, doctors, teachers, engineers, and others in the Angolan Civil War.[4] But traveling through Africa also captivated Guevara's romantic spirit. On the way back to Cuba from his Africa tour, he held a conversation with the intellectual and writer Roberto Fernández Retamar in which he confessed that Paris had held a strong attraction for him as a young man, but that that was before Africa.[5]

Representing the Revolution abroad in its first year, Guevara embarked on a whistle-stop tour of countries of major and minor interest (whether economically or politically), including the North African nations of Egypt and Morocco, as well as Sudan. However, the odyssey that interests us here took place between December 1964 and March 1965, involved multiple cities on the African continent, and seemed to have been, at least initially, inspired by a strong impulse to counter attempts by the new and old colonial powers to regain control of the Belgian Congo, including via the execution of independence leader Patrice Lumumba. In later years the tour would hold particular importance for establishing the blueprint of Havana's grandiose strategy of engagement on the African continent, since it was then that the first contact between a high-level representative of the Cuban government and numerous African liberation movements (including the Popular Movement for the Liberation of Angola [MPLA]) took place.[6]

During this era the most radical leaders in the Organization of African Unity (OAU), known as the "Group of Six," were Gamal Abdel Nasser of Egypt, Ahmed Ben Bella of Algeria, Kwame Nkrumah of Ghana, Sékou Touré of Guinea, Modibo Keïta of Mali, and Julius Nyerere of Tanzania.[7] Within this circle Algeria, Guinea, and Tanzania were founding members of the OAU's Liberation Committee, which was established in Addis Ababa in May 1963 with the purpose of coordinating and assisting the continent's diverse array of independence movements. For a variety of reasons, including political stability and the existence of well-established links between the communist countries and the liberation movements, which all had offices in the Tanzanian capital, Dar es Salaam was chosen as the Liberation Committee headquarters.

During his initial three-month tour, Guevara visited and consulted with all six of these "revolutionary" states, and were we to attempt to single out one particular nation or friendship for its influence upon his thinking at the time, our first instinct would perhaps be to indicate Algeria.[8] Altogether he spent over a month on an extensive tour of that country, developing a firm bond with the former revolutionary fighter and first president Ben Bella and thus hatching the major initiative in international politics that would become the foundation of Cuba's policy for Africa. It was in Algiers that Che planned the remainder of his tour, and he later returned there to share his observations on the situation in Africa with Ben Bella, including his nascent plans to support the armed struggle in the Congo. We know that the Algerian president was set against Guevara's plans for the Congo, and he was supported in this view by Nasser. Ben Bella recalled, "The situation in black Africa was not comparable to that prevailing in our countries; Nasser and I, we warned Che of what might happen."[9] Sources close to Guevara hold different opinions about the impact of Ben Bella's counsel. For instance, some claim that his resolve to go to the Congo had already started to wane toward the final days of his time in Algiers. However, all appear to agree that the week he spent in Tanzania was when the final, fateful decision was taken.[10] This leads us to wonder what might have happened during the time he spent there. What significant event could have eclipsed the advice of his most trusted foreign ally?

We can search for clues to the mystery in Che's writings, this time in *The Diaries of the Revolutionary War in the Congo*, set down in Tanzania between December 1965 and January 1966, which starts with the somber and foreboding words, "This is the history of a failure."[11] Guevara recounts the visit he had made in the previous year thus:

> In a story of this kind, it is difficult to locate the first act. For narrative convenience, I shall take this to be a trip I made in Africa which gave me the opportunity to rub shoulders with many leaders of the various Liberation Movements. Particularly instructive was my visit to Dar es Salaam, where a considerable number of Freedom Fighters had taken up residence. Most of them lived comfortably in hotels and had made a veritable profession out of their situation, sometimes lucrative and nearly always agreeable. This was the setting for the interviews, in which they generally asked for military training in Cuba and financial assistance. It was nearly everyone's leitmotif.[12]

We can just picture the ascetic revolutionary sneering as he penned this damning portrait, and certainly the text that follows provides no evidence of an enlightening encounter or event taking place that could account for the hardening of purpose that witnesses agree took place during this period. Yet some important experience must have occurred. Outside of the "interviews" that Guevara describes in this passage, there was another meeting that appears only fleetingly in the records but that I suspect had a far greater impact than we have been able to ascertain.[13] This was the meeting that took place between the Argentine revolutionary and the Tanzanian leader, Julius Nyerere, who was known as "Mwalimu" (the teacher), in reference to his former profession but also to his ability to impart deep learning. We know that Nyerere greeted Guevara at a reception held by Foreign Affairs Minister Oscar Kambona to welcome him to the country and that the two men spoke.[14] But what they talked about has not been reported. Still, I imagine that Che's observations were duly noted that night before sleep or perhaps on the following morning before his talks at the hotels began in earnest. What would he have recorded?

Notes on a Native Son

One of the things that would have struck and impressed Che was Mwalimu's self-sacrificing disposition. He fasted on a regular basis and dressed modestly in a Mao tunic, eschewing the more flamboyant styles adopted by other African heads of state and thus matching the Argentine's preference for simple forms of attire. Also, unlike many of his contemporaries, Nyerere did not siphon off his nation's wealth for personal gain. He was considered by many to possess a nobility of spirit that Che would have admired. Finally, like Guevara, Nyerere was drawn toward policies of collectivization and guerrilla warfare influenced by the People's Republic of China under Mao Zedong.[15] In the 1970s he would introduce a policy of collectivization in the country's agricultural system known as *ujamaa* (translated as "unity," "oneness," or "familyhood").

The two men also shared a similar social philosophy. Although it was not until 1967 that Nyerere issued the Arusha Declaration, which outlined in detail the concept of ujamaa that came to dominate his policies, he had already started publishing ideas on traditional African socialism that would certainly have struck a chord with the architect of Cuba's "New Man," who wrote poetic verse in his military fatigues.[16] Indeed, it was from Tanzania that Guevara filed his article "El socialismo y el hombre en Cuba" for the Uruguayan newspaper *Marcha*, which published it on March 12, 1965, and evokes for the first time the concept of "el hombre nuevo."[17]

In a 1962 pamphlet with the title *Ujamaa: The Basis of African Socialism*, Nyerere writes the following:

> Socialism—like democracy—is an attitude of mind. In a socialist society it is the socialist attitude of mind, and not the rigid adherence to a standard political pattern, which is needed to ensure that the people care for each other's welfare. . . . In traditional African society *everybody* was a worker. There was no other way of earning a living for the community. Even the Elder, who appeared to be enjoying himself without doing any work and for whom everybody else appeared to be working, had, in fact, worked hard all his younger days. The wealth he now appeared to possess was not *his* personally; it was only "his" as the Elder of the group which had produced it. He was its guardian. . . . When I say that in traditional African society everybody was a worker, I do not use the word "worker" simply as opposed to "employer" but also as opposed to "loiterer" or "idler." One of the most socialistic achievements of our society was the sense of security it gave to its members, and the universal hospitality on which they could rely. But it is too often forgotten, nowadays, that the basis of this great socialistic achievement was this: that it was taken for granted that every member of society—barring only the children and the infirm—contributed his fair share of effort towards the production of wealth.[18]

Imagine for one moment the impact of those sentiments on the moralistic revolutionary who in a series of speeches and essays—including the above-mentioned "Socialism and Man"—would try to build a logical case for a new work ethic:

> In order for it to develop in culture, work must acquire a new condition; man as commodity ceases to exist and a system is established that grants a quota for the fulfillment of social duty. . . . Man begins to free his thought from the bothersome fact that presupposed the need to satisfy his animal needs by working. He begins to see himself portrayed in his work and to understand its human magnitude through the created object, through the work carried out. . . . [This] signifies an emanation from himself, a contribution to the life of society in which he is reflected, the fulfillment of his social duty.[19]

Then perhaps later on, over cigars, the two men might have talked over the opinions that Nyerere had summarized toward the end of his pamphlet:

> We in Africa, have no more need of being "converted" to socialism than we have of being "taught" democracy. Both are rooted in our own past— in the traditional society which produced us. Modern African socialism can draw from its traditional heritage the recognition of "society" as an extension of the basic family unit. But it can no longer confine the idea of the social family within the limits of the tribe, nor, indeed, of the nation. For no true African socialist can look at a line drawn on a map and say, "The people on this side of that line are my brothers, but those who happen to live on the other side of it can have no claim on me": every individual on this continent is his brother.[20]

It is possible that Guevara, his eyes shining with the excitement that came from encountering a kindred spirit at the end of his long journey, began shortly afterward to sketch out what is considered to be one of the most important speeches in his career, which he delivered on February 24, 1965, at the Second Economic Seminar of the Organization of Afro-Asian Solidarity held in Algiers. In it he maintained, "Socialism cannot exist without a change in consciousness resulting in a new fraternal attitude toward humanity, both at an individual level, within the societies where socialism is being built or has been built, and on a world scale, with regard to all peoples suffering from imperialist oppression. We believe the responsibility of aiding dependent countries must be approached in such a spirit."[21]

The difference in language before and after the African journey cannot be overlooked. In his speech before the United Nations on December 11, 1964, prior to embarking on the Africa tour, we find such phrases as "we express our solidarity with," "the maintenance of internal unity, faith in one's own destiny," and so on.[22] Similarly, in an interview with the widow of Frantz Fanon, Josie Fanon, which appeared in the December 26, 1964, issue of *Révolution Africaine*, at no time do we find expressions related to spirituality or emotional or familial ties. First of all, Guevara explained that one of the reasons for his visit was to discuss African problems with the "compañeros" of the Algerian government. He then went on to present his analysis of the African situation in impersonal, strategic terms, pointing out the possibilities for and dangers of the fight against imperialism. Without direct experience of living among the African peoples that he was discussing, the conversation appeared clinical and completely impersonal. This contrasted with his response to a question about revolution in Latin America. He answered, "You know, that is something close to my heart; it's my keenest interest."[23] The language seems to reflect a sense of (be)longing or identity.

With this view in mind, let us consider Algiers a couple of months later, on his way back from Tanzania, and the way he began his speech to the Organization of Afro-Asian Solidarity: "Dear brothers." Then, continuing on, "It is not by accident that our delegation is permitted to give its opinion here, in the circle of the peoples of Asia and Africa."[24] Surely the overlap with Nyerere's thinking could not have been accidental either. The meeting appears to have reignited a transcendental line of thinking that Che had shown after his first official overseas tour, as previously mentioned in an article published in the September–October 1960 issue of *Humanismo* with the title "America from the Afro-Asian Balcony." "Might it not be," he asked, "that our fraternity can defy the breadth of the seas, the rigors of language and the lack of cultural ties, to lose ourselves in the embrace of a fellow struggler?" He went on, "I must say . . . to all the millions of Afro-Asians that . . . I am one brother more, one more among the multitudes of brothers in this part of the world that awaits with infinite anxiety the moment [when we can] consolidate the bloc that will destroy, once and for all, the anachronistic presence of colonial domination."[25] Such expressions became muted as time went on, but they carry the seeds of the Latin-African identity that Fidel Castro famously formulated over a decade later to explain the Cuban military mission in Angola.[26]

It was in this same speech in Algiers that Guevara gave voice to the opinions that appeared to indicate a political rift between himself and Fidel.[27] It turned out also to be a farewell of sorts because it was his final appearance before disappearing from public view—prior to secretly entering the Congo. In Algiers he accused the Soviet Union of not doing enough for the developing nations, Cuba in particular, and (even worse) of colluding with imperialism:

"The socialist countries have the moral duty to end their tacit complicity with the Western exploiting countries."[28] To be sure, an inherent moralism had always prevailed in Guevara's political thinking, but what is significant is how pronounced it became following his stay in Tanzania. The conclusion must be drawn that a change had taken place. Soon after the speech Guevara was denounced as "the apple of discord in the socialist front" in the Havana daily newspaper *Hoy*.[29]

Aside from Nyerere, no other African leader of the time was devising the affective principles of revolutionary socialism. Likewise, it was only Guevara who openly declared that the true revolutionary was guided by strong feelings of love. In fact, he said, "It is impossible to think of an authentic revolutionary without this quality."[30] Therefore, we can imagine that the idea that Africans possessed a predisposition toward the social consciousness that he espoused as a condition of correct ideological development, and which permitted them to make sacrifices and take political action "naturally" out of feelings of solidarity, carried immense psychic power for an idealistic and romantic dreamer such as Che.[31] We can imagine that immersion in this dream of natural African socialism, however brief, may have been just the transformative experience required to make everything that happened subsequently predictable. He resigned from his post as Minister of Industries several months after returning from his African tour, in the famous letter of farewell addressed to his great friend Fidel, which included the declaration: "I renounce formally my positions in the leadership of the party, my post as minister, my rank as *Comandante*, my status as Cuban citizen."[32]

The historian Azaria Mbughuni claims that Guevara actually visited Tanzania three times, once openly and twice in secret, between February and November 1965, spending, in total, over four months in the East African nation.[33] Although, for the purpose of the present exposition, I have chosen to circumscribe the time frame for the imagined conversation to the period of the official visit, the potential for multiple conversations between Guevara and Nyerere to have been held over an extended period further expands the possibility for the latter's influence upon the former.

Awakenings

In the case of both Nyerere and Guevara, however, the dream proved to be nothing more than a dream. First, the Congo mission culminated in disaster, and Guevara laid some of the blame on the Tanzanian government, which, because of the agreements reached at a meeting of African presidents in Accra, decided to end its assistance to the Congolese National Liberation Army, the guerrilla front Guevara had endeavored to assist. Moreover, although Nyerere had sought for his nation both self-reliance and financial independence from Western creditors, while he was president Tanzania went from being Africa's largest exporter of food to its biggest importer. However, he made the decision to step down in 1985 rather than cling to power in the face of defeat. Certainly his economic development policies inflicted hardship and distress on his countrymen, but few doubt his integrity and good intentions. And amid the ruins of Nyerere's economic reforms, other policies, such as in literacy and health care, are acknowledged to have flourished and even proved exemplary among African nations.[34] Even after the failure of his socialist experiment, he retained, according to a *Guardian* obituary from 1999, his "worldwide moral authority."[35]

In a similar vein, not a single one of the economic goals that Guevara elaborated was achieved by Cuba. As Daniel James damningly reported a few years after Guevara's death, while he was Minister of Industries the country had registered declines in every sector forecast to increase, and by the end of his term the Cuban economy was actually less productive than under Batista.[36] However, like his political and spiritual ally Nyerere, he did not seek to hold on to power when his plans failed.

Che was an international revolutionary before he arrived in Cuba to fight in the 26th of July Movement. He expanded his horizons from the Americas until they encompassed the entire developing world through his Tricontinental strategy—the attempt to organize a covert network of guerrilla operations linking La Paz, Havana, Algiers, Brazzaville, Dar es Salaam, Prague, Moscow, and Beijing. But the odds were stacked heavily against this idealized vision. What I have tried to show in this essay is that, during his African travels, the "sleeping" internationalist had been reawakened from his ministerial slumber by the impossible dream of revolutionary ujamaa. If, as Richard Bjornson has written, the estrangement and alienation that come from overseas travel inspire a reconstitution of identity "in light of new knowledge and expanding horizons," then Nyerere's utopian dreams helped Guevara to recover values and perspectives that affirmed his sense of self and gave meaning to his life narrative.[37] "And let us develop a true proletarian internationalism," Che urged the Tricontinental Congress from Bolivia in 1967. "The flag under which we fight would be the sacred cause of redeeming humanity. To die under the flag of Vietnam, of Venezuela, of Guatemala, of Laos, of Guinea, of Colombia, of Bolivia—to name only a few scenes of today's armed struggle—would be equally glorious and desirable for an American, an Asian, an African, even a European."[38]

The cultural politics that I refer to as Latin-Africanism can be considered a uniquely Cuban form of the Pan-Africanism that had drawn dreamers of a new African reality to Tanzania in the 1960s. It combined the political principles of anti-imperialism, antiracism, and social revolution with an added cultural imperative that gained moral sustenance from the historical ties between the Caribbean nation and the peoples of sub-Saharan Africa. Within the framework of the Latin-African identity that Fidel claimed for his nation in November 1975, the decision to send thousands of Cuban soldiers to fight in defense of the government of Agostinho Neto against the allied enemy forces of the National Union for the Total Independence of Angola (UNITA), the National Liberation Front of Angola (FNLA), American mercenaries, and apartheid South Africa sprang not only from preexisting political ties with the ruling Marxist MPLA but also from blood ties inherited from a slaving past. According to this narrative, ingrained in a country that had been built upon the bodily sacrifice of enslaved Africans was the moral responsibility to come to the defense of an African nation being threatened by racist and imperialist forces—particularly when the arrayed enemies put into equal peril a nascent socialist revolution.

However, as I have explained elsewhere, due to the continuation of racial inequalities in Cuba after the promises of the Revolution (including a predominantly white political administration), Latin-Africanism performed a double duty, standing in this sense inside the Freudian model of the dream as catharsis.[39] In other words, it represented a strategy to purge history to redeem the present social reality. In an incongruous twist to the revolutionary state's earlier project to eradicate African-derived religions as vestiges of the nation's colonial past, to which Alejandro de la Fuente refers in his contribution to this volume, these same spiritual practices (Palo Monte, Santería, Abakuá, and so on) now constituted the bedrock of *africanía* upon which Cuba's Latin-African cultural identity was purportedly to be built.

Nevertheless, even in its potential contradictions—and keeping in mind the framing of the present collection of essays around culture as a central axis of interpretation—I would suggest that Cuba's Latin-African identity can be understood as an offshoot of the major Pan-African sensibility that was forged among black intellectuals in the years after World War II, manifested most saliently in the Paris-based cultural institution, magazine, and publishing house *Présence Africaine*. The First Congress of Black Writers and Artists was held in Paris at the Sorbonne in 1956, a historic meeting that was organized and sponsored jointly by *Présence Africaine* and its newly created affiliate, the Société Africaine de Culture.

In his incisive essay on the study of identity in cultural studies, Lawrence Grossberg writes, "The modern is not merely defined by the logics of difference and individuality; it is also built upon a logic of temporality." Not only that, but, continues Grossberg, "at the heart of modern thought and power lie two assumptions: that space and time are separable, and that time is more fundamental than space." The natural consequence of this privileging of time over space was the conceptualizing of identity as "entirely an historical construction."[40] This understanding is clearly recognizable in the strong historical focus of the Paris meeting. In his opening remarks, the Senegalese writer and cofounder of *Présence Africaine*, Alioune Diop, contextualized the conference as an interruption and contestation of History "with a capital h" that had been the exclusive preserve of the Western world. It was, he suggested, a first assault by the "peoples without history" against imperialist and racist interpretations of their pasts and, above all, a revalorization of their original cultures and ancient civilizations: "Thus, we, colonized peoples, are prevented from exulting in our classics, from revalorizing them for the purpose of our present situation, and denied the freedom to imagine a future in proportion to our love of the world. Under such conditions, the present is reduced to an uncertain period beset by the most ridiculous states of confusion and distress."[41]

The first thing we note is that the call for a return to the classics did not arise out of some vainglorious exercise in nostalgia but was tied up with the urgent and compelling need to respond to the modern age's current "crisis of identity." What place existed for those denied any form of subjectivity (whether individual or collective) and, by extension, any possibility of agency, in a world of change, splintering, and fragmentation? Without the sustenance of the past, Diop and the other advocates of negritude claimed, the future held nothing but annihilation. The seeds of this annihilation had been sown in the past by the transatlantic slave trade, which at the same time was the historical antecedent binding together the diverse group of delegates from Africa, Europe, and the Americas who had assembled in Paris: "Over centuries, the dominant event in our history was the slave trade. This is the first link between us, delegates, which justifies our meeting here. Black people from the United States, the Caribbean, and the African continent, whatever the distance that sometimes separates our spiritual worlds, we have this undeniably in common, that we are descended from the same ancestors."[42] We recognize this discourse of the common ancestor as one of the principal logics of temporality involved in the construction of identity, not only in the *Présence*

Africaine project but also in the later framing of Latin-Africa at a crisis point in Cuban history.[43] In this way, slaving history became a resource "in the process of becoming rather than being"—so that we might regard Latin-Africanism, in its essence, as a dream.[44]

The problem for many of the delegates to the Paris conference hailing from the Americas, however, was that the institution and administration of African enslavement in their nations had rested upon a color-caste system that subsumed both ethnicity and culture under race, with the consequence that black history could not be separated from slave culture. Not only that, but for others, such as the Cuban intellectual and historian Walterio Carbonell, the Pan-Africanist link between subjectivity (culture) and agency (politics) was obstructed by the dominant (and historical) belief system of *mestizaje* (mixedness), which tied racial awareness to racial discrimination. For black Cubans especially, organizing on the basis of race had historically drawn charges of *promoting* racial division rather than seeking redress.[45]

Nor did the 1959 Revolution succeed in dislodging a nationalist ideology of "racelessness" that can be traced back to the writings of the Cuban apostle José Martí during the independence movement of the late 1800s, such as "Mi raza" (My Race). ("Cuban is more than black, more than white, more than mulatto," he famously wrote.)[46] Instead, Martí's ideas were revalorized to promote national unity in the face of real and perceived threats to the new society from forces within and outside of the country in the 1960s and 1970s.[47] Thus, one consequence of the contradictory policy of inhibiting political organization around the experience of racism internally while encouraging cultural identification with Africa was a projection of the postrevolutionary phenomenon of *la doble cara* (two-facedness) into the international arena.[48] This left the government open to charges of hypocrisy and duplicity, particularly in view of Havana's open and vociferous support for black liberationists in the United States, at the same time that possibilities for similar forms of activism were restricted at home.[49] It is a sad but telling irony that Cuba's preeminent Africanist, Armando Entralgo, was himself a victim of this conflict between internal racism and external Afrocentrism when his marriage to a black Angolan, Olga Lima, whom he had met during his tour of duty as ambassador to Ghana, became the subject of consternation upon returning to his homeland after the military coup against Nkrumah in 1966. According to his widow, Leonor Amaro, Olga returned to Angola following that country's independence and became active in the Angolan Women's Union (Unión das Mulheres Angolanas).[50] In light, moreover, of Cuba's intensified ties to the Soviet bloc in the 1970s (see Cabrera Arús and Bustamante, in this volume), Latin-Africanism projected externally may have had the ancillary effect of counterbalancing (or even obscuring) the simultaneous cultural, political, and economic "Sovietizations" of Cuban society within.

But such criticism overlooks the duality intrinsic to Pan-Africanism and that is manifest in the foundational rationale for the OAU itself, involving an external part that asserted an "African personality" and anticolonialism, and an internal element that stressed cooperation, (re)conciliation, and cohesiveness.[51] More than politicians, it was poets, artists, and writers (and, as we know, some revolutionary leaders were both) who were able to galvanize these dual directives most effectively—that is to say, those who, like Che Guevara, dreamed with the dawn.[52]

Tangem sinos na madrugada
vai nascer o sol.

[The bells toll as day breaks
The sun is on the rise.]

—Agostinho Neto (first president
of the Republic of Angola)

NOTES

1. Foundational works include Jonathan H. Turner and Jan E. Stets, eds., *The Sociology of Emotions* (Cambridge: Cambridge University Press, 2005); Patricia Ticineto Clough and Jean Halley, eds., *The Affective Turn: Theorizing the Social* (Durham, NC: Duke University Press, 2007); Joan Davidson, Liz Bondi, and Mike Smith, eds., *Emotional Geographies* (Aldershot, UK: Ashgate, 2007); Jennifer Harding and E. Deidre Pribram, eds., *Emotions: A Cultural Studies Reader* (London: Routledge, 2009); Sara Ahmed, *The Cultural Politics of Emotion* (London: Routledge, 2014); Ian Burkitt, *Emotions and Social Relations* (London: Sage, 2014); Margaret Wetherell, *Affect and Emotion* (London: Sage, 2012). In addition this period has witnessed the appearance of subject-related academic journals, for example, *Emotion, Space and Society* (from 2008), *Emotion Review* (2009), and *Subjectivity* (2008).

2. Jon Lee Anderson, *Che Guevara: A Revolutionary Life* (London: Bantam Books, 1997), 95–96.

3. Guevara's first visit to the African continent was to newly independent Algeria in July 1963.

4. Cuban involvement in Angola before and after independence has been well-documented in a number of works published inside and outside of the island, including Edward George, *The Cuban Intervention in Angola, 1965–1991: From Che Guevara to Cuito Cuanavale* (London: Frank Cass, 2004); Piero Gleijeses, *Conflicting Missions: Havana, Washington, and Africa, 1959–1976* (Chapel Hill: University of North Carolina Press, 2002); César Gómez Chacón, *Cuito Cuanavale: Viaje al centro de los héroes* (Havana:

Editorial Letras Cubanas, 1989); Christine Hatzky, *Cubans in Angola: South-South Coop-eration and Transfer of Knowledge, 1976–1991* (Madison: University of Wisconsin Press, 2015); José Ortiz, *Angola: Un abril como Girón* (Havana: Editora Política, 1979); Christabelle Peters, *Cuban Identity and the Angolan Experience* (New York: Palgrave Macmillan, 2014); Nelson Valdés, "Revolutionary Solidarity in Angola," in *Cuba in the World*, edited by Cole Blasier and Carmelo Mesa-Lago (Pittsburgh: University of Pittsburgh Press, 1979), 90–95.

5. Simon Reid-Henry, *Fidel and Che: A Revolutionary Friendship* (London: Bloomsbury, 2011), 322.

6. There is photographic evidence of Guevara's meeting with leaders of the MPLA at their exile headquarters in Brazzaville in December 1964 in Gleijeses, *Conflicting Missions*, 83. The author reports that Cuban military instructors were dispatched to the Congo to train MPLA guerrilla fighters shortly thereafter.

7. It must be remembered that nonalignment formed one of the founding principles of the OAU. This position, in turn, informed one of its primary objectives, which was the unification of all freedom fighters. Ben Bella and Nyerere famously held divergent views on the subject of unity, the latter insisting that unification or a merger of nationalist parties necessarily leads to a more powerful liberation movement, while the former argued that unity was not a prerequisite. See Emmanuel M. Dube, "Relations between Liberation Movements and the O.A.U.," in *Essays on the Liberation of Southern Africa*, edited by N. M. Shamuyarira (Dar es Salaam: Tanzania Publishing House, 1971), 43. In the case of Angola, Ben Bella asserted that insisting on a united front would be harmful to the struggle. Also, according to Dube (45), the clash was likely influenced by differences in their personal experiences; this suggestion seems very feasible. After all, liberation in Tanzania was achieved through constitutional means; meanwhile, Algeria's two liberation movements endured a long and bitter war fought against the French.

8. By the time of Guevara's visit, Algeria had distinguished itself among the OAU states as a major supporter of African liberation movements. Indeed, Van Walraven asserts that Algerian "militancy on colonialism was accepted by, and provided the turning-point of" the OAU's founding conference. Klaas Van Walraven, *Dreams of Power: The Role of the Organization of African Unity in the Politics of Africa, 1963–1993* (Aldershot, UK: Ashgate, 1999), 151.

9. Jorge G. Castañeda, *Compañero: The Life and Death of Che Guevara* (London: Bloomsbury, 1997), 283.

10. This conclusion is apparent in a number of biographical accounts, including in Anderson, *Che Guevara*; Castañeda, *Compañero*; Paul J. Dosal, *Comandante Che: Guerilla, Soldier, Commander, and Strategist, 1956–1967* (University Park: Pennsylvania State University Press, 2003); Daniel James, *Che Guevara: A Biography* (London: George Allen and Unwin, 1970).

11. Ernesto Guevara, *The African Dream: The Diaries of the Revolutionary War in the Congo* (London: Harvill Press, 2001), 1.

12. Guevara, *The African Dream*, 1.

13. Examples include Azaria Mbughuni, "Why Did Che Guevara Come to Tanzania Secretly? Part One," *Business Times*, September 19, 2014; Richard L. Harris, *Che Guevara:*

A Biography (Santa Barbara, CA: ABC-CLIO, 2011), 122; Roberto Occhi, *Che Guevara: La Piú Completa Biografía* (Baiso, Reggio Emilia: Verdechiaro Edizioni, 2007), 209.

14. See Godfrey Mwakikagile, *Congo in the Sixties* (Dar es Salaam: New Africa Press, 2014), 188; Mbughuni, "Why Did Che Guevara."

15. Beijing had helped to build a railroad from Tanzania to the Atlantic coast, and Premier Zhou Enlai visited Dar es Salaam in October 1965.

16. In addition to Nyerere, the African independence leaders most associated with the concept of African socialism were Léopold Senghor of Senegal, Kwame Nkrumah of Ghana, and Sékou Touré of Guinea. The participation of Senghor, whose political viewpoint and economic strategies differed quite widely from the others, highlights the cultural vision of African socialism as an antidote to corrosive Western or European values, which resonated with prevailing and influential ideas of "negritude." As a guiding influence to policy, the term has been defined differently according to local conditions and the subjective interpretation of those in power; however, in the main, it is understood as a collection of practices rooted in traditional African principles of the extended family system. *Ujamaa* is the Swahili word for "extended family." In its starkest terms, it promotes collectivism, sharing, and the community over (Western or European) individualism, self-interest, and greed.

Since Nkrumah was the first of the four leaders to declare independence, he is often assumed to be the chief architect of African socialism and the others as following in his footsteps; however, it is perhaps more useful to think in terms of an Afro-centric zeitgeist that influenced the heads of some of the first sub-Saharan African countries to be liberated.

17. Ernesto Guevara, "El socialismo y el hombre Nuevo en Cuba," in *El socialismo y el hombre Nuevo en Cuba* (Mexico, D.F.: Siglo Veintiuno, 1979), 7.

18. Julius Nyerere, *Ujamaa: The Basis of African Socialism* (1962; Oxford: Oxford University Press, 1973), 3.

19. Ernesto Guevara, *Socialism and Man in Cuba and Other Works* (London: Stage 1, 1968), 13.

20. Nyerere, *Ujamaa*, 9.

21. Ernesto Guevara, *Che Guevara Speaks: Selected Speeches and Writings* (Charlottesville, VA: Merit, 1967), 127.

22. Ernesto Guevara, *Che: The Diaries of Ernesto Che Guevara* (Melbourne: Ocean Press, 2009), 102, 100.

23. Guevara, *Che Guevara Speaks*, 105.

24. Guevara, *Che Guevara Speaks*, 106.

25. Anderson, *Che Guevara*, 457–58.

26. Prior to Fidel's December 22, 1975, speech, discourses of cultural identity in Cuba had always been framed within a broader Latin American (but Eurocentric) context that highlighted linguistic ties, a Spanish cultural heritage, and a shared history of independence wars against Imperial Spain. However, on that day, for the first time outside of a folkloric or anthropological framework, the Cuban leader made the striking claim, "Nosotros no sólo somos un país latinoamericano, sino que somos también un país latinoafricano" (We are not only a Latin American country but also a Latin African country).

27. It is hard to ascertain the extent or even the existence of any disagreement between Fidel and Guevara. If, on the one hand, Fidel's public attitude toward the Soviet Union was guided by pragmatism and a necessary restraint in the face of a complicated relationship, then it is possible that Guevara was simply giving voice to prevailing but closely guarded opinions. However, the same outspokenness could be viewed as condemnation of his old friend if their divergent reactions are taken at face value. Readers might find much of interest regarding the complex political and personal relationship between the two men in Reid-Henry's engaging study *Fidel and Che*.

28. James, *Che Guevara*, 132. At the time of the speech, Moscow was at the height of its "peaceful coexistence" phase of its international politics, which included signing trade agreements with several anticommunist Latin American nations. At his UN speech on December 11, 1964, Guevara made clear, "As Marxists we have maintained that peaceful coexistence among nations does not encompass coexistence between the exploiters and the exploited, between the oppressors and the oppressed" (*Che: The Diaries*, 102).

29. James, *Che Guevara*, 132.

30. Guevara, *Socialism and Man*, 19–20.

31. Although since its early stages the essentialism inherent in negritude has been debated and criticized by Richard Wright and others, we cannot ignore the lyrically persuasive elements in this pro-African (if not anti-Western) and anticolonial cultural politics.

32. James, *Che Guevara*, 154.

33. Mbughuni, "Why Did Che Guevara."

34. Julius Nyerere, "Mwalimu Julius Kambarage Nyerere—Biography," 2015, http://www.juliusnyerere.org/about/category/biography.

35. "Julius Nyerere," *Guardian*, October 14, 1999, https://www.theguardian.com/news/1999/oct/15/guardianobituaries.

36. James, *Che Guevara*, 139.

37. Richard Bjornson, "Alienation and Disalienation: Themes of Yesterday, Promises of Tomorrow," in *The Surreptitious Speech: Présence Africaine and the Politics of Otherness, 1947–1987*, edited by V. Y. Mudimbe (Chicago: University of Chicago Press, 1992), 148.

38. Ernesto Guevara, *The Secret Papers of a Revolutionary: The Diary of Che Guevara* (Mattituck, NY: American Reprint Company, 1975), 15.

39. Peters, *Cuban Identity*.

40. Lawrence Grossberg, "Identity and Cultural Studies—Is That All There Is?," in *Questions of Cultural Identity*, edited by Stuart Hall and Paul du Gay (London: Sage, 1996), 100.

41. "Ainsi donc le culte de nos classiques, leur revalorisation en fonction de notre situation présente, sont refusés aux peuples colonisés, en meme temps que la liberté de penser un avenir à la mesure de leur amour du monde. Dans ces conditions, le présent se réduit à une période informe caractérisée par le désarroi, la détresse absurdes." Alioune Diop, "Discours d'ouverture," *Présence Africaine: Revue Culturelle du Monde Noir* 8–9 (1956): 13–14.

42. "Pendant des siècles, l'événement dominant de notre histoire a été la traite des esclaves. C'est le premier lien entre nous, Congressistes, qui justifie notre réunion ici.

Noirs des Etats-Unis, des Antilles et du continent Africain, quelle que soit la distance qui sépare parfois nos univers spirituels, nous avons ceci d'incontestablement commun que nous descendons des mêmes ancêtres." Diop, "Discours d'ouverture," 9.

43. See Peters, *Cuban Identity*, for an in-depth analysis of the cultural politics at play during the first five years of the Cuban mission in the Angolan War.

44. Stuart Hall, "Introduction: Who Needs Identity?," in *Questions of Cultural Identity*, edited by Stuart Hall and Paul du Gay (London: Sage, 1996), 4. It is important to highlight that Latin-Africa comprised the *cultural* side of the Cuban mission in Angola, which I trace back to Guevara coming under the influence of Pan-African ideas. However, Operation Carlota demonstrated the major shift in the *political* strategy of Havana's policy for Africa, in other words a rejection of the guerrilla cell (*foco*) for conventional, large-scale military engagement.

45. The fate of the Independent Party of Color in 1912 offers the most extreme example of the consequences of race-based political organization in prerevolutionary Cuba. See Aline Helg, *Our Rightful Share: The Afro-Cuban Struggle for Equality, 1886–1912* (Chapel Hill: University of North Carolina Press, 1995).

46. José Martí, "Mi Raza," *Patria*, April 16, 1893. See Ada Ferrer, *Insurgent Cuba: Race, Nation, and Revolution, 1868–1898* (Chapel Hill: University of North Carolina Press, 1999).

47. See Alejandro de la Fuente, *A Nation for All: Race, Inequality, and Politics in Twentieth-Century Cuba* (Chapel Hill: University of North Carolina Press, 2001), 259–316; Lillian Guerra, *Visions of Power in Cuba: Revolution, Redemption, and Resistance, 1959–1971* (Chapel Hill: University of North Carolina Press, 2012), 151–57, 265–78.

48. The term refers to the practice of maintaining an outer compliance with the tenets of revolution while privately maintaining oppositional or alternative opinions.

49. Perhaps the best-known example of this kind of indictment is Carlos Moore in *Castro, the Blacks, and Africa* (Berkeley: Center for Afro-American Studies, University of California, 1988). On early connections between African American political movements and Cuba, see Devyn Spence Benson, "Cuba Calls: African American Tourism, Race, and the Cuban Revolution," *Hispanic American Historical Review* 93, no. 2 (2013): 239–71.

50. I learned this information from a 191-page unpublished memoir of Entralgo written by Amaro as an introduction to a future collected volume of his writings. Leonor Amaro, "Entralgo en el recuerdo," 62. Unpublished manuscript held in private collection of author. Readers are welcome to contact me to request further details.

51. It is a matter of some relevance to our affective analysis that in his comprehensive study of the OAU, the political scientist Klaas van Walraven explicitly defines pan-Africanism as "a collection of ideas and emotions" (*Dreams of Power*, 85).

52. The Congolese historian Jean-Michel Mabeko Tali has written that Pan-Africanism's greatest influence on the future leaders of the independent Portuguese African nations (Amilcar Cabral, Lucio Lara, Mario Pinto de Andrade, Marcelino dos Santos, etc.) was intellectual since it expounded a unifying theory of a shared civilization. See Jean-Michel Mabeko Tali, "Um Olhar sobre O 'Outro' Lúcio," *Tchiweka: 80 anos—Testemunhos*, 2008, https://sites.google.com/site/tchiweka/Home/livros-editados-1/tchi80-testemunhos/um-olhar-sobre-o-outro-lucio.

9. The Material Promise of Socialist Modernity
FASHION AND DOMESTIC SPACE IN THE 1970S

MARÍA A. CABRERA ARÚS

By the time it approached its second decade, the Cuban revolutionary government had ushered in deep changes in the island's material and political environment. Imported consumer goods from the United States had disappeared from store shelves; gone, too, were private shops, brands, and advertised sales associated with the capitalist past. This new existence was mostly born of scarcity, prompting Cubans to devise ever more inventive uses for items, garments, and machines left over from prerevolutionary times. Radical economic policies of the 1960s, though, also introduced new objects into Cubans' everyday realities, whether olive-green militia uniforms in their wardrobes or new political icons displayed in their homes.[1]

With the turn of the decade, increased Soviet influence in Cuban society brought new changes to the island's material culture. Two years after the failure of 1970's "Ten Million Ton Sugar Harvest," Cuba became a full-fledged member of COMECON (the Eastern bloc's principal trade organization), receiving products and financial investments in ever greater amounts from the Soviet Union and Eastern Europe. A shift to more pragmatic patterns of central economic planning and higher sugar prices in the world market contributed to notable GDP growth.[2] The resulting period of economic recovery not only impacted national economic development; it also modified popular consumption practices established during the 1960s, introducing modern mass consumer goods and alternative channels for their commercialization. Economic reform helped to legitimize and institutionalize the revolutionary state in new ways, even as it raised questions about the radical equality government authorities had promoted in the previous decade.

This essay traces how these new realities manifested in domestic spaces and fashion in the 1970s and early 1980s, a period frequently overlooked in the historiography of the Cuban Revolution. If anything, the 1970s tend to be remembered for other reasons, namely, intensified intellectual repression under Sovietizing cultural norms (the so-called *quinquenio gris* or *decenio amargo*).[3] How can we reconcile these two faces of Soviet influence— economic pragmatism and consumption, on the one hand, and cultural narrowing, on the other? Changes in material culture, I argue, accompanied and in fact contributed to the consolidation of a state socialist bureaucracy. New economic policies thereby reversed and responded to the exhaustion of early revolutionary programs shaped by voluntaristic mobilization schemes as well as confrontations with the Revolution's enemies (internal and external).[4] As Michael Bustamante explores in this volume, reflections on the recent past in public space and cultural production also staged this transition from the ideal of ascetic revolutionary commitment to a reality of socialist stability.

And yet, as much as the 1970s bore witness to verifiable material shifts, this essay seeks to understand how those changes were represented, promoted, and sometimes overstated by diverse state actors. Early in the decade, official publications framed new modalities of consumption as a sign of Cuban economic progress, modernization, and the comfort that individual Cubans enjoyed under socialism. In the process, representatives of the state began to make novel claims for the Revolution's legitimacy, based less on a dignified battle against historic "underdevelopment" than in new, if still imperfect (or fictional) socialist achievements. To some degree, these claims were grounded in a context of obvious improvement: despite narrowing ideological parameters in the realm of culture, many Cubans experienced the late 1970s and especially the early 1980s as a period in which material security seemed to be more attainable than during the preceding years.

Nonetheless, there was no simple or direct relationship between the new material utopias celebrated in the state press and the consumer realities of ordinary Cubans. At times products appeared more often in print than they did in stores; brand names advertised an abundant, even technologically sophisticated future to which the government still aspired, as opposed to one it had fully achieved. For the Soviet Union, the historian Djurdja Bartlett has used the term "representational fashion" to describe a kind of virtual material universe, composed of objects (clothing in her case) that were symbolically potent but materially inaccessible. Representational fashion, as she describes it, was "exclusively produced as a unique prototype, presented at domestic and international fairs and socialist fashion congresses, and published in the magazines," all while remaining unavailable to consumers.[5] In Cuba during the 1970s and early 1980s the real and "representational" material orders blurred, with obvious material improvements coexisting, sometimes uncomfortably, with visions of plenty far exceeding what most Cubans could acquire. Meanwhile, both of these frameworks—and their implicit endorsement of stratified consumption—sat uneasily with a lingering emphasis on radical egalitarianism and unity.

From store displays to design aesthetics, state actors in the fashion and consumer sectors strategically parsed and navigated such tensions. This essay thus foregrounds the discursive frameworks through which goods, real and imagined, circulated in the island's popular culture. At times mutually reinforcing, at times contradictory, discourses on Cuba's material reality grew out of the uneven interaction of socialist institutions and officials—not a uniform conspiracy. They thus drew on multiple, often incongruous conceptions of consumption and material objects: valorizing Cuba's traditional cultural heritage on the one hand and celebrating its modern socialist future on the other, or touting egalitarianism while also sanctioning new kinds of individual material distinction previously seen as taboo.

Though we cannot precisely identify those responsible for developing these discourses, or direct evidence of citizen responses to them, there is much we can gain from reading Cuba's state-run consumer landscape in the 1970s as a multivalent "text." To do so puts us in the position of Cuban purchasers, ration-card holders, and state company managers, intuiting the unique possibilities and contradictions of Cuba's Sovietizing moment, as well as the differences between "represented" material progress and a more continuous material reality still characterized by intermittent shortages and unfulfilled wants.[6] Discourses emanating from diverse state actors offer us a unique, if incomplete lens onto the rich middle ground of interactions between the state and the populace, thus reframing our understanding of Cuba's incorporation into the Soviet bloc. For while popular experiences of this transition remain difficult to access, state discourses around consumption reveal a still unformed official position on Soviet rapprochement. State actors struggled to "sell" a cohesive material reality to everyday citizens that, for most of them, did not yet fully exist.

Decades often denote chronological divisions of convenience, a change in digits more than historical substance. Not so for socialist Cuba, where the inability to produce 10 million tons of sugar during the 1970 harvest brought an abrupt end to a period of radical experimentation and social change. Economic policies of the previous decade had appealed to moral incentives, personal sacrifice, and autonomy from Soviet norms. In the mid-1960s Cuba's leadership began directing these ideals to an increasingly single purpose: mobilizing large sectors of workers to achieve a massive sugar crop. Under Fidel Castro's guidance, the state deprioritized other industries, believing that one big sugar haul could propel the island's leap to development. When the economy failed to reach that target (despite producing the largest sugar harvest in Cuba's history), the resulting political and economic crisis weakened the popular "legitimacy of communism and, by extension, Fidel's right to rule," as Lillian Guerra has written.[7] In response, the Cuban government turned to increased material and symbolic support from the Soviet Union and Eastern European governments. In time, the formalization of a state socialist regime of Soviet type, together with the implementation of Soviet-style material incentives for workers, helped improve national economic performance while promoting new forms of political socialization.[8]

Indeed, economic changes altered the relationship between revolutionary authority and citizen mobilization. Most important, individual charisma took a backseat to more institutional means for shoring up revolutionary legitimacy.[9] Castro remained a dominant figure, of course; his public persona and influence over government policy continued to be preponderant. Still, the intensely personalistic style of governance that had characterized the 1960s now merged with the operations of a more rational bureaucracy that reproduced many of the features of the Soviet Union's government.[10] Carmelo Mesa-Lago pointedly notes that Cuba's Constitution of 1976—approved after the First Congress of the Cuban Communist Party the year before—more or less recognized Soviet tutelage: "32 percent of the articles . . . come from the Soviet constitution of 1936, 36 percent [come] from Cuba's constitution of 1940, 18 percent are influenced by both sources but with Soviet predominance, and only 13 percent of articles are at least partially innovative. The U.S.S.R. is mentioned by name in the preamble of the Cuban constitution—perhaps the only instance in recent history where a foreign country appears in the constitution of another."[11]

Yet the notable changes associated with the 1970s did not spring from solely foreign sources; the previous decade's education policies also began to bear fruit. As the number of agricultural workers decreased, those employed in industrial sectors grew considerably. The size of the professional labor force likewise expanded, reaching levels similar to those in the period preceding the exodus of the anti-Castro middle class in the early 1960s. These dynamics gave rise to a "revolutionary intelligentsia" composed of new professionals educated under socialism. Paradoxically, though, a deceleration of upward mobility accompanied these transformations after many professional and administrative positions were filled.[12] Regardless, members of this cohort, and those aiming to join it, also harbored expectations for material advancement and well-being that state planning bodies felt pressure to fulfill.

The government thus mobilized to satisfy new material needs and desires. Imported products from the socialist bloc (radios, televisions, canned foods) filled gaps in Cuba's own domestic economy. Meanwhile, state investments in light industry and infrastructure, coupled with later commercial policies like the legalization of free peasant and artisans markets in the early 1980s, aimed to elevate living standards through personal consumption and local production.[13] To respond to and help advance this conjuncture, in 1971 the Cuban government created the Cuban Institute of Research and Orientation of Internal Demand (ICIODI) under the supervision of the Council of Ministers. Born of Soviet inspiration, the ICIODI mostly focused on market research, though it also promoted fashion and industrial design in a more limited capacity (designing new school and work uniforms, for example). Ironically, the study of consumption and consumer taste had once been denounced as a frivolous capitalist tool for maximizing profits.[14] Now, this field had fallen under the direct jurisdiction of the socialist government's highest executive and administrative body.

The Cuban state in these ways embraced material comfort as an economic value—something that would have been anathema only years earlier. This shift manifested in ways great and small, from the promotion of material incentives—the awarding of goods and appliances to exemplary workers—to the creation of new opportunities for individual consumption. In 1971, for instance, the state opened so-called *casas de regalos* (gift stores) in every provincial capital, where consumers could buy nonrationed goods at higher prices than in the rationed market.[15] That same year, officials implemented Plan CTC-CI, which regulated the sale of durable mass consumer goods—specifically electronics and domestic appliances—through Cuba's national labor umbrella organization. According to the sociologist Susan Eckstein, between 1975 and 1980, "for every hundred homes with electricity, the percentage with television sets . . . rose from 33 to 74, with refrigerators from 15 to 38 percent, with washing machines from 6 to 34 percent, and with radios from 42 to 105 percent."[16] Even bigger changes were to come after 1980, with an auspicious reduction in the consumption of rationed goods, the establishment of previously referenced peasant markets, and the opening of a wider nonrationed "parallel market" in 1983.[17]

Beyond personal consumption, high-profile infrastructure projects also advanced and symbolized government efforts to translate economic growth into individual material well-being. Following on an idea first proposed by Fidel Castro in 1970, in 1971 revolutionary authorities and the Ministry of Construction launched a new national housing program based on the labor of ad hoc "micro-brigades" of workers.[18] Additional modernizing initiatives followed, such as the 1973 reintroduction of color TV broadcasting and the 1974 creation of the vaguely named Empresa de Producciones Varias (EMPROVA, Multiple Productions Company), which assembled the first TV sets made in Cuba, largely with Soviet parts.[19] In 1975 Castro inaugurated the first twenty-five-kilometer section of a reconstructed central railroad that would link Havana and Santiago de Cuba via express train.[20] In 1978 he opened the thermoelectric plant of Cienfuegos, quintupling the island's capacity for electric generation compared to the prerevolutionary period.[21] Finally, in 1979, Cuba's leader personally attended the opening of the Santa Clara textile complex, the biggest in the country, with a capacity to produce 60 million square meters of fabric a year.[22] Building on such enhanced production facilities, the Ministry of Light Industry (MINIL) also created new clothing and fashion companies such as CONTEX, which would soon begin manufacturing jeans and other fashionable garments for state-owned Cuban stores, though in limited quantities.[23]

In short, increased opportunities for consumption, coupled with significant investments in infrastructure, were devised to convey the idea that Cuba was on a path to definitive stability and progress. Cubans, officials suggested, could finally look forward to a modern and efficient industrial society, comparable to contemporary capitalist economies but more inclusive and just. So bullish did Cuban leaders become—and after such a quick turnaround following the failed sugar harvest of 1970—that in 1975 they predicted Cuba would soon be able to end the rationing of most goods. The memoirs of the First Congress of the Cuban Communist Party gloated that the economic "success" achieved after 1971 would allow "gradually limiting the distribution area in which rationing is still necessary [to] those essential items whose sales are still insufficient to meet the growing needs of the population through a market freed from rationing and at prices all can afford."[24] The document celebrated the commercialization of appliances and other consumer durables as a particular success in this regard.

And yet the hypothetical premise of the quoted statement suggests that Cubans had not yet fully achieved the material utopia to which they aspired. As the island's leaders admitted at the Party Congress, Cuba still remained in the first stage of the development of socialism according to Marxist-Leninist theory.[25] The Soviet Union, by contrast, had reached the third, with the attainment of full communism expected by the 1980s.[26] Many Cubans held up Soviet superiority as positive; Soviet-made Aurika washing machines, Minsk refrigerators, and Lada and Moskvitch automobiles (among countless other mass consumer goods circulating on the island) provided hints of the kind of development still to come. As the Soviet foreign policy analyst Yuri Pavlov later reflected, "Two generations of Cubans [were] brought up in the belief that the U.S.S.R. represented today what Cuba would become tomorrow."[27] The report of the first Party Congress, indeed, presented the Soviet Union as a "bastion of world progress,"[28] and many Cubans evidently shared in this belief. The writer Eliseo Alberto, for instance, recalled during the 1990s that the USSR had seemed to Cubans "the center of the world, the promised land, the new Mecca, almost like New York."[29] But whereas Castro had predicted in 1959 that Cuba would surpass the socioeconomic development of both the Soviet Union and the United States, in the 1970s Cuba's material progress continued to be, to a considerable degree, imported and mortgaged (requiring generous trade subsidies, donations, and loans) rather than autonomously produced.[30]

The "representational" world of material symbolism helped to bridge this gap between present and future circumstances. The fashion brochure *Moda '75, Edición Especial*, for instance, features sketches of modern clothes never sold in Cuban stores. Also included are cropped images from foreign (probably Eastern European) magazines, featuring such nontropical garments as scarves, gloves, and hats made of fabrics like corduroy, polyester, and wool (figures 9.1 and 9.2).[31] The vicarious tone of these promotional materials hints at Cuban aspirations to consumption possibilities not yet fully their own. Admittedly, these types of images served "representational" purposes in the Soviet Union as well.[32] Yet the Cuban investment in Soviet *kulturnost*—"tasteful" acquisition as a sign of "culturedness" and dignified material

También para el traje de la novia se impone el bordado. En telas de un solo color, el bordado en varios tonos, de termina la alegría del vestuario.

FIGS. 9.1 AND 9.2. Fashion illustrations published in *Modas '75, Edición Especial*. Fig. 9.1, from page 4, appears cropped from a foreign magazine. Fig. 9.2, from page 22, is simply a sketch of an outfit never produced. Cuba Material Collection, New York, NY.

satisfaction—spoke to a new, but unfulfilled, ideal of socialist modernity at home.[33]

Cuban material culture in the 1970s was thus caught in a web of contradictions. The legitimation of selective consumption of Soviet technology and goods invested both *actual* and *representational* objects with notable importance. Yet it would have been impossible for even the island's integrated government to seamlessly align this new material context with a previous emphasis on nationalism, sovereignty, and radical equality. The outcome was a consumer landscape characterized by ambiguity as much as cohesion. Whether in the state press they read, new brand names they created, or work-issued coupons they carried, Cuban designers, economic planners, and shoppers alike negotiated the ideological compromises attending Cuba's turn toward the Soviet bloc.

The expression of Cuban nationalism through material culture can be traced back as far as the nineteenth century. Creole elites supporting independence from Spain painted their estates with the colors of the Cuban flag; other nationalists attached ribbons and accessories to clothes in the colors or shapes of patriotic emblems.[34] Nationalist "looks" and styles later gained momentum in fashion, design, and architecture in the 1950s, as a way to counter the predominant U.S. influences in Cuban culture during that period. As the historian Louis A. Pérez Jr. has shown, some private producers, merchants, and consumers at mid-century demonstrated a preference for goods and styles adapted to the conditions of life in the country rather than uncritically copying North American models. These expanding "calls to buy national products and protect home industries" played no small part in feeding the Cuban Revolution's initial appeal.[35]

Only after the Revolution's triumph, however, did the Cuban state begin taking an active interest in promoting a nationalistic material culture. In 1959 "Operation Cuban Industry" organized an exhibition of Cuban-made goods that toured the country in train coaches, part of a wider state campaign called "Consume Cuban Products" targeting both private producers and individual consumers.[36] Then, as the government began nationalizing economic activity, state enterprises themselves took up the production of goods representative of nationalistic ideals and ideologies, especially through the use of rural aesthetics, local materials, or forms representative of Cuba's aboriginal cultures.

Designs reflecting a rural or rustic component played a particularly important role in dramatizing the government's patriotic, increasingly agrarian and anti-elitist politics over the 1960s. The countryside, arguably less "contaminated" by foreign influences than cosmopolitan Havana, was especially salient in sartorial representations of nationalism. Garments like the traditional guayabera shirt and the peasant hat, together with materials and colors associated with the Cuban climate and its flora and fauna, gave shape to a "nationalistic-revolutionary" narrative in which, as Pérez argues, "Cuba became the dominant fashion motif."[37] These goods implicitly reversed the previous cultural sway of the United States, stressing after 1961 the originality and authenticity of Cuban socialism vis-à-vis Soviet paradigms. Yet in a climate of rising scarcity and mass mobilization, designs for frequently donned work clothes and ubiquitous military and militia uniforms visibly emphasized utilitarian function as much as form.

Moving into the 1970s, one might expect such nationalistic approaches to material culture to have receded due to the increased Sovietization of the country. As the island sought greater advice and resources from the Eastern bloc, economic solutions arguably drew less on a culture of stoic asceticism, self-reliance, and local tradition than imported know-how. Yet a closer examination of objects, clothes, and even imported appliances of the era reveals that references to nationalist idioms increased rather than disappeared under Soviet influence. In fact, materials, crafts, logos, and brand names explicitly connoting and naming Cubanness acquired new symbolic significance as avatars of local values and lore. Such gestures arguably served a "representational" or at least euphemistic function, shoring up an imaginary of national exceptionalism against a new reality of Soviet economic tutelage.

This trend is particularly evident in adaptations made to the guayabera, the most culturally iconic article of Cuban clothing. Long considered dress or (in short-sleeve variety) casual attire for landowners and wealthy peasants and, by midcentury, professional and upper-class men (generally white), this classic Cuban shirt was valorized for its nationalist symbolism in the Revolution's first years. Yet as the political process radicalized, the garment fell out of fashion, harkening back too closely to the style of corrupt politicians from the defunct prerevolutionary republic.[38] Regardless of this association, the guayabera experienced a definite revival in the 1970s, when designers employed by state enterprises produced cheaper versions of this shirt, and some even transformed it into a feminine dress. By the end of the decade, CONTEX women's and children's clothing collections incorporated outfits inspired by the design (figure 9.3) and would soon successfully commercialize them in "parallel market" retail stores.[39]

The guayabera, though, was hardly the only item in otherwise Sovietizing times invested with resilient nationalist symbolism. From the 1970s through the 1980s, Cubaforma, a workshop producing mostly handcrafted goods made with local materials, created modern fashion accessories with seashells, coconut, tortoiseshell, antlers, wood, and copper. Other state enterprises attached to MINIL, such as CONTEX, or to the Ministry of Culture, such as the Cuban Fund of Cultural Goods, manufactured clothing and accessories with domestic inputs and nationally produced cotton.

To be sure, most of what these companies produced was intended for export or foreign consumption. Visitors to the island seeking mementos of "authentic" local culture not only generated hard currency revenues but also indirectly promoted a kind of Cuban revolutionary "soft power" abroad.[40] "Representational" nationalist fashion, in this way, could take on an external- rather than internal-facing guise. Yet nationalist goods also found a domestic market, though on a limited scale. For instance, CONTEX and the ICIODI

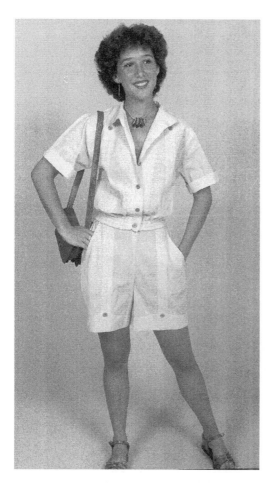

FIG. 9.3. Casual feminine outfit inspired by the guayabera shirt, commissioned by Cachita Abrantes and produced by CONTEX. Photograph from the late 1970s, courtesy of Cachita Abrantes.

opened small retail spaces in 1980s Havana catering to local professional elites. Likewise, the furniture maker EMPROVA sold small batches of furniture sets made with leather, rattan, and wickerwork in parallel-market stores.[41]

Yet the aesthetic influence of nationalism reached beyond the niche artisanal market. Nods to local objects, traditions, and terms could also be found in the brand names tacked onto newly mass-manufactured goods. The production of these items unmistakably depended on Cuba's access to socialist trading partners in the Eastern bloc. Nonetheless clothing brands like Agro (a reference to agriculture), Payito (the nickname for a villager), and Yarey (the fiber from a palm-like plant that Cuban peasants use to make straw hats) referenced an implicitly rural world, long a vector for (and vesicle of) Cuban nationalist mythologies. Other clothing brands, such as Jiquí (referencing the

FIG. 9.4. Recreo brand name and logo. From the Oficina Cubana de Propiedad Industrial.

aboriginal name of a Cuban tree), Criolla (creole, the name for an island-born woman of Spanish descent), and Caimán (alligator, whose shape arguably resembles that of the island as a whole), drew upon aboriginal words and elements from Cuba's natural environment. Finally, the brand Rumba took its name from the well-known Cuban rhythm and dance, while the insignia for the clothing brands Recreo (translated as "break" or "escape") and Diana, produced in the central provinces of Camagüey and Ciego de Ávila, respectively, included a large clay pot typical in those regions (figure 9.4).[42]

Even more obvious technological artifacts of Soviet design—produced in Cuba but with foreign machinery and parts—received "creolizing" local monikers. Thus, the first buses manufactured in Cuba were dubbed Girón, after the beach where Cuban exile forces landed in 1961 at the Bay of Pigs. Taíno and Montuno, respectively, became the names for locally produced trucks and jeeps.[43] The royal palm tree adorned the logo of both Caribe brand TV sets, otherwise similar to the Soviet Electron, as well as Siboney radios, similar to the Soviet Vef. ("Siboney" referred to an indigenous group in pre-Columbian Cuba.) Last but not least, the logo of the Taíno portable radio, closely resembling the Soviet Radiotehnika RT, featured an image of the wooden *dujo* chair, used by the island's pre-Columbian Taíno indigenous chiefs.

In sum, the combination of local and Soviet aesthetics in objects produced on the island and imported from the socialist camp produced uncanny pastiches across Cuba's evolving consumer landscape. The evident effect, nonetheless, was to domesticate—at least discursively—Soviet influence and thereby reconcile new goods with Cuba's national culture and "revolutionary" ethos.[44] Overall the expression of nationalistic discourses in material culture and fashion seems to have added up to aesthetic success, at least abroad: Cuban-made consumer goods won prizes in international festivals and fairs. As gifts to foreign dignitaries, politicians, and celebrity guests—in addition to the ubiquitous cigars and rum—they also offered state officials a convenient way to highlight Cuban distinctiveness.[45]

Determining who was behind this nationalist "defense," though, can be challenging. In some cases, it seems to have been centrally directed. EMPROVA, for instance, answered directly to the Council of State, as it was founded by Celia Sánchez. Fidel Castro's personal assistant and close collaborator, she commissioned and championed many of these projects.[46] Likewise, Cachita Abrantes—the sister of General José Abrantes, minister of the interior between 1985 and 1989 and Castro's former bodyguard—founded and directed both CONTEX and La Maison fashion houses. Even in these cases, however, it is difficult to distinguish between high-placed personal connections and official policy. Assessing the genuine centrality of nationalistic concerns to individual actors or whether they merely served to advance the personal and professional interests of those involved remains an interpretative problem.

It is also hard to know the extent to which many of these goods were actually available to the public. Outside of testimonial evidence, official sales volumes for particular goods or aggregate figures per region are unavailable. We can nonetheless speculate about "nationalist" consumption's symbolic effects. Did efforts to "Cubanize" Brezhnev-era "real socialism" convince island buyers? We have tantalizing, if limited evidence of popular reception in the area of fashion.

In a recent interview, Caridad Abrantes noted that throughout the 1980s sales of CONTEX products on the upper floor of Roseland, the state-owned department store in Havana, were higher than in any other area of the store where clothes imported from socialist countries were sold. In 1983, for example, CONTEX brought in 5 million pesos on the "parallel market" alone.[47] This would suggest that some state companies did succeed in translating local and national designs into real consumer appeal. The popular acceptance of nationalistic discourses can be deduced too from the popularity of the artisans markets, legalized in the early 1980s and celebrated in popular recollections of the period. There, consumers expressed a clear preference for high-quality, nationally made goods.[48]

On the other hand, Jesús Frías, former director of a fashion atelier in Havana affiliated with the Higher Institute of Industrial Design, insists that it was not until well into the 1980s that "what consumers hoped for" began coinciding with "what they could effectively buy amidst national proposals" overall.[49] In 1974 delegates to the Third Congress of the Union of Young

Communists acknowledged that the "search for foreign-made products" constituted a "serious ideological weakness" among the young—a likely consequence of "representational" nationalist fictions not matching everyday experience and aspirations.[50] As of 1985 ICIODI studies showed that young people were *still* dissatisfied with the outdated aesthetics and coarse finishing of most clothing available for purchase, not to mention the perceived politicization of consumption through nationalistic appeals.[51] A decade of economic developments had done little to remedy this "vice."

To some degree, then, popular nonconformity may have stemmed from not only disappointment with *what* was actually on offer but also contradictions in the *way* consumption was represented. As representations of not just nationalist feeling but modernity and progress, new goods and clothing items betokened expanded personal acquisition. But a continued emphasis on egalitarian values—that is, the assumption that a socialist material culture based on modern living standards should be equally available to all—chafed against the new social distinctions greater consumption made possible. It was the political and rhetorical incongruity between the egalitarian narrative of parity and the modernizing discourse of progress and consumer distinction of the Sovietized 1970s and early 1980s that perhaps proved most difficult to square.

A Revolution for All? Equality and Socialist Distinction

One of the principal political tenets of the Cuban Revolution was the eradication of social inequalities separating economic elites from the urban and rural poor. Dating even to their insurgent days before 1959, revolutionary leaders had demonstrated commitment to these goals through redistributive policy proposals and symbolic strategies marshaling "spectacles" of popular empowerment and class erasure (see Guerra in this volume).[52] Often, this antimaterialist ethos was conveyed—somewhat paradoxically—through material objects. These included the olive-green fatigues of soldiers and militiamen or the straw hats and machetes wielded by the revolutionary *pueblo* gathered at early mass rallies and distributed by state organizations and, in some cases, the organizers of such rallies.[53] The modernist architect Nicolás Quintana recalls an early meeting with Che Guevara, in which the toes of the guerrilla leader turned economic administrator could be seen sticking out of worn socks.[54] By 1968 a beauty pageant during the Festival of the Havana Green Belt, which in that year replaced Havana's legendary carnival, highlighted androgynous work clothes as "fashionable" choices when volunteering in experimental agricultural projects on the city's outskirts.[55]

Significantly, after a hiatus due to the "Ten Million Ton Sugar Harvest," carnival returned in 1970. And in this and subsequent editions, beauty contestants were more likely to dress "in maxi skirts and hot fingerless gloves," parading through Havana "on a carriage of shiny, false mirrors towed by a Soviet tractor," as one observer recalled of celebrations in 1971.[56] But if such over-the-top displays foreshadowed the decade's "representational" abundance, authorities continued to promulgate the Revolution's egalitarian themes. If in the 1960s populist celebrations of workers' clothing had echoed early Bolshevik efforts to shed Russia's monarchical accouterments and distance the revolutionary present from a prerevolutionary past, mechanisms for distributing new consumer goods in the 1970s would mirror Brezhnev-era economic schemes and practices under "real" socialism.[57] Recently debuted clothing brands and the creation of a state "parallel market" (e.g., via the *casas de regalos*) made possible newly selective shopping and indicators of social distinction. But to a significant degree, many of the material perks of Cuba's Soviet era continued to be accessible only through centralized, ostensibly equitable means.

Take, for example, the case of (mostly imported) household appliances, which the state began to commercialize and distribute in 1971. The historian Jorge Fornet recalls the significance of these handy 1971 arrivals, appearing shortly after the resounding failure of the 1970 sugar harvest, when the ten-million-ton target was not achieved and economic collapse followed: "*Granma* announced a plan for the distribution of 'electrical and domestic appliances' in workplaces. Workers could choose among refrigerators, television sets, bicycles, mixers, pressure cookers, and even wrist- and pocket watches. It was undoubtedly a pleasing piece of news, coming as it did at the tail end of a year of privation and monumental efforts."[58]

The mechanisms of distribution of these material rewards were strict, but in theory clear and fair to everyone. In public assemblies celebrated at workplaces all over the country, administrators, union leaders, and employees discussed the assignment of televisions, pressure cookers, automobiles, and even homes and vacations resorts to overachieving workers. The determination of political merit and the awarding of material goods went hand in hand. Performance assessments were grounded in indicators of productivity, such as the fulfillment of production quotas, but also the accumulation of awards, diplomas, and certificates for political participation.[59] Workers also performed their virtue by attending public rallies, participating in voluntary work projects on weekends, and, by 1980, partaking in the so-called *actos de repudio* carried out against those leaving the island via the port of Mariel.[60]

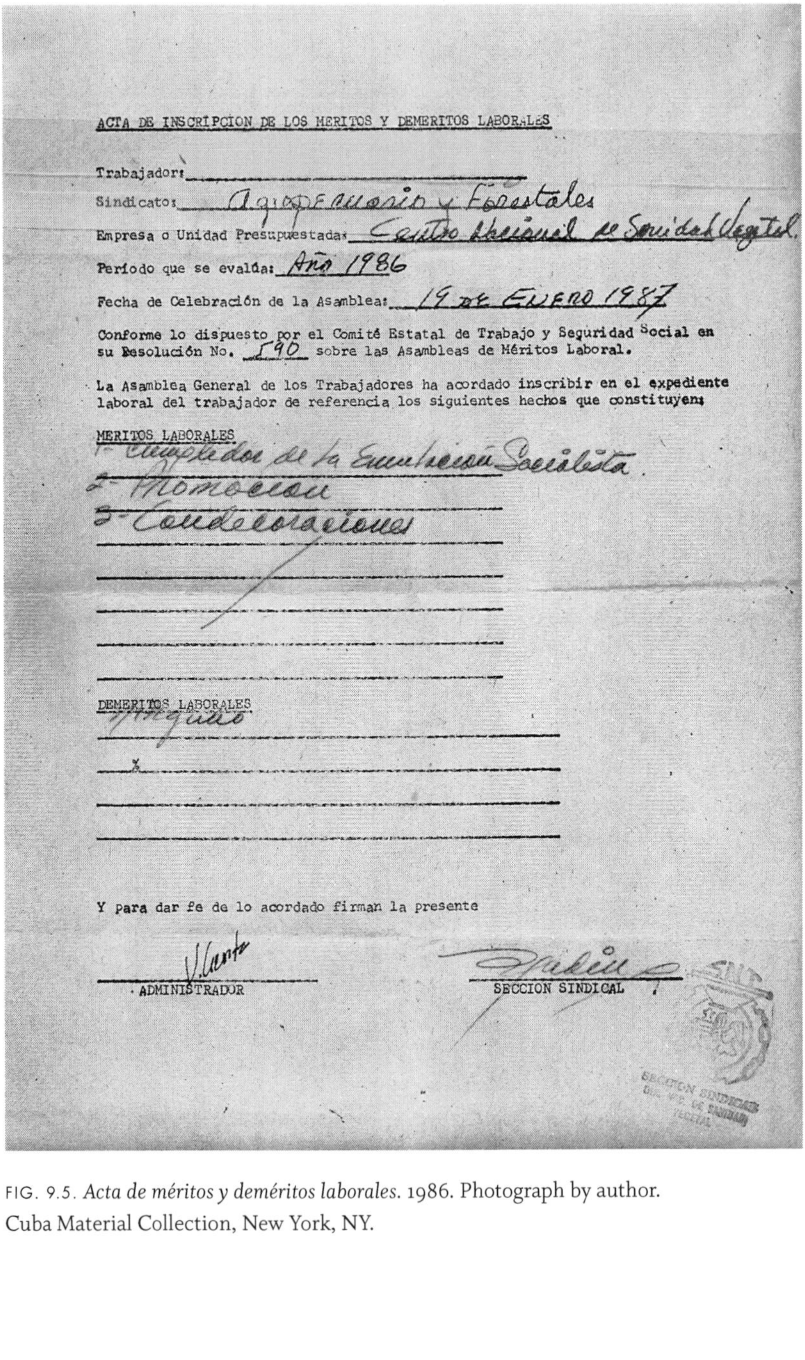

ACTA DE INSCRIPCIÓN DE LOS MERITOS Y DEMERITOS LABORALES

Trabajador:_____

Sindicato:_____ *Agropecuario y Forestales*

Empresa o Unidad Presupuestada: *Centro Nacional de Sanidad Vegetal.*

Período que se evalúa: *Año 1986*

Fecha de Celebración de la Asamblea: *19 DE ENERO 1987*

Conforme lo dispuesto por el Comité Estatal de Trabajo y Seguridad Social en su Resolución No. *190* sobre las Asambleas de Méritos Laboral.

La Asamblea General de los Trabajadores ha acordado inscribir en el expediente laboral del trabajador de referencia los siguientes hechos que constituyen:

MERITOS LABORALES

1- Cumplidos de la Emulación Socialista.
2- Promoción
3- Condecoraciones

_____
_____
_____
_____
_____
_____

DEMERITOS LABORALES
Ninguno

X
_____
_____
_____

Y para dar fe de lo acordado firman la presente

_____   _____
· ADMINISTRADOR   SECCION SINDICAL

FIG. 9.5. *Acta de méritos y deméritos laborales.* 1986. Photograph by author.
Cuba Material Collection, New York, NY.

Employers recorded these "achievements" in a document called the "Certificate of Workplace Merits and Demerits," archived in each workers' personnel file (figure 9.5). In Cuba's socialist meritocracy, mostly individuals with the best economic and political records obtained material rewards, although "need" was sometimes also taken into account.[61]

In more ways than one, work thus offered a principal gateway to increased consumption. In Havana, for example, the state rationing system had since 1969 divided residents into different groups to better organize the distribution and purchasing of goods. Each group (A, B, C, etc.) was assigned a Thursday-to-Wednesday "buying period," so that people would not try to shop at the same time.[62] The Ministry of Domestic Commerce also reserved by decree the first day of each period for state employees, providing workers access to a wider array of goods, as deliveries normally arrived early that day, as well as a less crowded shopping experience.[63] To benefit from this plan, workers had to show store personnel their CTC-CI identification card (figures 9.6 and 9.7), thus providing their employer's name, work shift, and good standing within the island's sole, state-run labor union. On the one hand, this bureaucratic contrivance incentivized long-term workplace participation, as the ID cards had to be updated every three months. But, on the other, it communicated that, even in a time of material incentives and meritocracy, the state remained committed to covering the needs of the working masses.

Official investment in egalitarian, anticapitalist principles also reverberated elsewhere, especially in the emergence of brand names associated with the working class, popular culture, and grassroots solidarity. This was the case, for example, with the clothing lines Montero and Cazador, both words for "hunter" or a person who hunts to make a living; Unión; and Festival, the word for popular celebrations. Likewise, Pionero portable radios referenced members of the Soviet-inspired mass organization in which schoolchildren enrolled between the first and ninth grades. In the most radical expression of anti-elitist values, brand names were erased altogether. In the case of clothing, for instance, shoppers might find a detachable cardboard or textile tag, identifying little more than size and inventory information for vendors. As for appliances, generic names and technical information at times simply informed buyers of the nature and expected performance of the article for sale. Calling an iron La Plancha (The Iron) stripped the product of any nonutilitarian connotations (figure 9.8).

But references to the technical capacity of material objects were not always so concrete or mundane. Just as often they denoted an imagined future of socialist progress and modernization, theoretically available to all. With

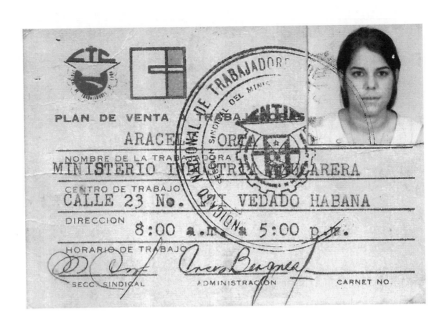

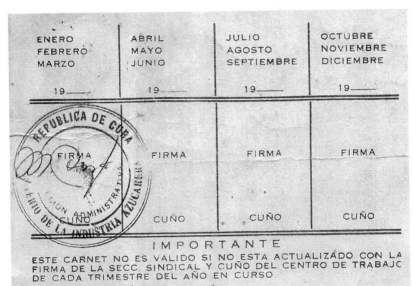

FIGS. 9.6 AND 9.7. CTC-CI ID card. Photograph by author. Card courtesy of Janet Vega Espinosa.

FIG. 9.8. Packaging of La Plancha iron. Made in the USSR. Photograph by author. Cuba Material Collection, New York, NY.

its logo featuring an atom, the clothing brand Futura, for example, conjured up a future characterized by applied science and technology. Similarly, Órbita (orbit), Cometa (comet), Horizonte (horizon), and Ilusión (hope) brand clothes referenced space-age terms and goals, or even the much-celebrated Soviet space program itself. In truth, most of these garments were rather plain and coarsely designed. They lacked much in consumer appeal. Yet they were still the clearest material expression of a revolutionary project that, despite having reached supposedly unprecedented indicators of achievement, remained preoccupied with the obligation and challenge of providing Cubans with universal basic goods.

Over time, however, the persistent disconnect between universal material fulfillment in theory and the quality of available goods in practice became an acute problem. Here we have another manifestation of the contrast between the "representational" and the real in Cuba's consumer life. By the late 1970s economic losses from unsold goods reached more than 800 million pesos, resulting in costly surpluses.[64] In 1986 Carlos Rafael Rodríguez, Cuba's chief economic tsar, admitted that "for people willing to die for the Revolution, it was challenging to live within the Revolution" because of its deficient material order.[65]

Even more troubling was the fact that these lingering egalitarian commitments persisted alongside emergent avenues of distinction *within* workplace distribution and new forms of nonrationed sales. By promoting competition among workers for desirable consumer goods, Cuban institutions stimulated productivity and political participation, as the political scientist Eloise Linger has noted.[66] Yet they simultaneously revised and recapitulated the logic of a capitalist class system. Purchasing power was no longer tied to capital accumulation, but there was still plenty of room for material differentiation in this ostensibly merit-based order. Material incentives could vary greatly depending on *where* one worked or at what level. Members of the political and professional elite—doctors, teachers, state enterprise administrators, military officers, and other priority groups—were generally granted preferential access to housing, automobiles, and vacations at state resorts and villas. Average workers, by contrast, tended to receive more unremarkable prizes, such as watches and radio receivers.[67]

Meanwhile, over time, new opportunities to buy goods outside of rationed or otherwise regulated distribution systems did significantly undermine centralized mechanisms. Describing the slowly emerging operations of the "parallel market," the economist Carmelo Mesa-Lago notes that, beginning in 1971, certain industrial goods appeared intermittently for "liberated" or "freed" (*liberada*) sale: "silver wedding rings . . . plastic shoes and slippers . . . and some cosmetics and perfumes (including brands with such exotic names as 'Red Moscow' and 'Bulgarian Rose')." Workers who received trips to hotels and vacation resorts also found "convenient, freed goods such as swimsuits, lifesavers, sunglasses, [and] cosmetics" on offer at the hotel shops.[68] Alongside modest disparities in public salaries, the outcome of such practices was a reality of disparate consumption possibilities, one that grew particularly noticeable in the 1980s.

All told, despite continued insistence on universal access and equitable rewards for work and participation, the material landscape of Cuban "real socialism" was characterized by considerable material differentiation. Over time class differences became increasingly and uncomfortably visible, if still notably different from those of the prerevolutionary past.[69] Newer Soviet automobiles distinguished the political and professional elite from both the owners of aging North American cars and the carless majority; working-class residential districts built with prefabricated Soviet technology were largely segregated from the euphemistically termed *zonas congeladas* (frozen zones) of former middle- and upper-class homes generally occupied by those in strategic government positions.[70] According to ICIODI, "liberated" goods appealing to higher-income urban dwellers, professionals, and state administrators were commercialized in quantities falling far short of demand.[71] But compared with the meager quota of clothing offered by the rationing system, these items represented virtual "luxuries" that visibly broke from the government's egalitarian narrative.[72]

Even when dressed up in egalitarian principles, labels, and brands, systems of material reward and selective consumption ushered in real and lasting change. The historian Muriel Nazzari maintains that "from a commitment to carry[ing] out as much distribution as possible according to need," a new socialist praxis tied distribution "principally . . . to the wage."[73] This new material logic may in turn have promoted new forms of political opportunism. As Karen Kettering would say of Soviet Russia, to gain selective access to "some of the trappings of bourgeois life," perhaps some Cubans were willing to pay with loyalty to the socialist state.[74] In this sense, material culture may offer an important realm within which to explore popular political attitudes. In the Sovietizing 1970s Cuban citizens likely learned to measure their government's evolving claims to legitimacy in the previously verboten territory of desirable consumer goods.

Conclusion: Grassroots Reinventions and Reappraisals

In the 1970s the Cuban government portrayed socialist institutionalization and the accompanying rapprochement with the Soviet Union as a process of renovation, represented in part by the commercialization of modern mass consumer goods. The new material landscape heralded a more affluent future while also looking to nationalist and egalitarian values of the previous decade. These strategies created small but visible spaces for ostensibly incongruous social distinction, reconciling (if not always comfortably) the pragmatic teleology and ethos of "real existing socialism" with the revolutionary narrative of redemption. In their convergences and contradictions, the revised material practices of the 1970s birthed an ecumenical symbolic repertoire, with room for both regime officials and ordinary citizens to strategically activate distinct discourses at different times. Overall, socialist practices of the 1970s largely resisted ideological purity, both in principle and in practice.

The sociologist Samuel Farber argues that Cubans have largely experienced their history as objects rather than determinative subjects.[75] The material dynamics discussed in this essay might seem to support this notion, insofar as popular appraisals of consumer options remain difficult to access. Nonetheless, even in this largely state-directed realm, evidence suggests Cubans exercised agency in shaping their context. Persistent popular demand, after all, led the state to open alternative spaces for consumption such as artisans free markets and the parallel state market in the early 1980s.[76] Ordinary citizens also accommodated the material consequences of socialist policies by devising ingenious make-do "tactics."[77] For other Cubans, meanwhile, a shirt, whatever its modernizing, nationalistic, or egalitarian branding, may have just been a shirt. The populace thereby not only metastasized but also surely metamorphosed and even banalized official discourses and policies.

These observations point to the continued challenge of historicizing material culture from below as well as above. Cuban state agencies in the 1970s couched the production and consumption of new goods in ways both novel and consistent with older socialist values. Yet at the same time, everyday re-inventions and creative solutions, including with leftover presocialist goods, impacted the order imposed from on high. As Reinaldo Arenas explores in his 1971 story "Que trine Eva," some Cubans "responded" to socialist monotony and scarcity by frenetically reproducing foreign fashion styles and novelties.[78] Combining socialist and presocialist, national and foreign, Cubans undoubtedly helped to shape a material order characterized by palimpsests as much as coordinated state design.[79]

Historians and social scientists thus must continue to explore the ways socialist mass goods intermingled with presocialist or contemporary capitalist goods (imported, for example, by Cubans authorized to travel abroad).[80] Some Cubans also "upgraded," modified, or repaired socialist goods with parts derived from capitalist or makeshift material cultures, practicing what the designer and artist Ernesto Oroza calls "technological disobedience."[81] Oroza has documented, for instance, the addition of strips of colored cellophane to black-and-white TV sets to produce a colored image, along with handcrafted and improvised spare parts for electrical appliances fabricated in clandestine workshops. In my own research, I have found evidence of Cubans reproducing foreign styles on fabrics with revolutionary motifs, as well as of young people stitching foreign brand names onto socialist clothes. Paradoxically, by helping to improve the material conditions of individual lives, these practices contributed to the long-term health of Cuban socialism, even as they attested, in part, to the government's material failures.

Nationalistic, democratic, and populist discourses drove consumer reforms and aesthetic movements before and after 1959. This essay has focused on ruptures and continuities attending the transition to Sovietized socialism in the 1970s. This period of material change and ideological ambiguity produced an eclectic social imaginary that continues to resonate in the present. Today, many Cubans still struggle to find—and create—a modern, democratic, and egalitarian nation that can *also* promote material comfort and individual well-being for all. It is precisely this aspiration that unites small business owners, artists, exiles, dissidents, and ordinary Cubans who refuse to accept material comfort as the exclusive prerogative of the select few, whether traditional economic elites or self-proclaimed "revolutionaries."

NOTES

1. Lillian Guerra, *Visions of Power in Cuba: Revolution, Redemption, and Resistance, 1959–1971* (Chapel Hill: University of North Carolina Press, 2012); Louis Pérez, *On Becoming Cuban: Identity, Nationality, and Culture* (Chapel Hill: University of North Carolina Press, 1999).

2. On Cuba's economic performance in the 1970s, see Carmelo Mesa-Lago, *Cuba in the 1970s: Pragmatism and Institutionalization* (Albuquerque: University of New Mexico Press, 1978); Omar E. Pérez Villanueva, ed., *Cincuenta años de la economía cubana* (Havana: Ciencias Sociales, 2010); José L. Rodríguez García, *Desarrollo económico de Cuba 1959–1988* (Mexico, D.F.: Nuestro Tiempo, 1990); Andrew Zimbalist, ed., *Cuban Political Economy: Controversies in Cubanology* (Boulder, CO: Westview Press, 1988).

3. Under the increased influence of cultural dogmatism, starting in 1971 many of Cuba's leading intellectuals were ostracized, barred from doing their work, and even imprisoned. See Carlos A. Aguilera, ed., *La utopía vacía: Intelectuales y Estado en Cuba* (Barcelona: Linkgua, 2008); Lourdes Casal, ed., *El caso Padilla: Literatura y revolución en Cuba* (Miami: Universal, 1972); Duanel Díaz, *Palabras del trasfondo: Intelectuales, literatura e ideología en la Revolución cubana* (Madrid: Colibrí, 2009); Ambrosio Fornet, "El Quinquenio Gris: Revisitando el término," in *La política cultural del período revolucionario: Memoria y reflexión* (Havana: Centro Teórico-Cultural Criterios, 2008); Rafael Rojas, *Tumbas sin sosiego: Revolución, disidencia y exilio del intelectual cubano* (Barcelona: Anagrama, 2006).

4. Guerra, *Visions of Power*. Historians and social scientists have even argued that "the Revolution," as an active process of social upheaval and political change, concluded at some point between the late 1960s and early 1970s, cohering into a state-socialist regime thereafter. See Haroldo Dilla, "La Revolución cubana, a discussion," *Este País* 292 (2015), http://www.estepais.com/articulo.php?id=112&t=la-revolucion-cubana-a-discusion; Marifeli Pérez-Stable, *The Cuban Revolution: Origins, Course, and Legacy* (New York: Oxford University Press, 1993); Rafael Rojas, *Historia mínima de la Revolución cubana* (Mexico, D.F.: Colegio de Mexico, 2015).

5. Djurdja Bartlett, *Fashion East: The Spectre That Haunted Socialism* (Cambridge, MA: MIT Press, 2010), 7.

6. In 1963 the Cuban state began regulating the acquisition of basic mass-consumer goods, namely (though not exclusively), clothing and home goods, first through coupons distributed by work administrations and the Committees for the Defense of the Revolution and, later, through ration cards for the acquisition of industrial goods distributed by the Ministry of Domestic Commerce. See Mesa-Lago, *Cuba in the 1970s*; Margaret Randall, *Women in Cuba: Twenty Years Later* (New York: Smyrna, 1981).

7. Guerra, *Visions of Power*, 316.

8. Mesa-Lago, *Cuba in the 1970s*; Pérez-Stable, *The Cuban Revolution*; Rodríguez García, *Desarrollo económico*.

9. Velia C. Bobes, *Los laberintos de la imaginación: Repertorio simbólico, identidades y actores del cambio social en Cuba* (Mexico, D.F.: El Colegio de México, 2000).

10. On the wider Sovietization of Cuban institutions, economic planning, commerce, and cultural horizons in the 1970s, see Velia C. Bobes, *La nación inconclusa: Reconstituciones de la ciudadanía y la identidad nacional en Cuba* (Mexico, D.F.: FLACSO, 2007); Julio C. Díaz Acosta, "Consumo y distribución normada de alimentos y otros bienes," in Pérez Villanueva, *Cincuenta años*, 333–62; Julio A. Díaz Vázquez, "Gestión y dirección de la economía," in Pérez Villanueva, *Cincuenta años*; Frank T. Fitzgerald, "The 'Sovietization of Cuba Thesis' Revisited," in Zimbalist, *Cuban Political Economy*, 137–53; Jacqueline Loss, *Dreaming in Russian: The Cuban Soviet Imaginary* (Austin: University of Texas Press, 2013).

11. Mesa-Lago, *Cuba in the 1970s*, 72–73. Although it was reformed in 1992, many articles of the 1976 socialist Constitution are still in force today. Different actors and academics have thus called for a general constitutional reform. See Rafael Rojas, Velia C. Bobes, and Armando Chaguaceda, eds., *El cambio constitucional en Cuba* (Mexico, D.F.: Centro de Estudios Constitucionales Iberoamericanos and Fondo de Cultura Económica, 2017).

12. Mayra Espina Prieto and Lilia Núñez Moreno, "The Changing Class Structure in the Development of Socialism in Cuba," in *Transformation and Struggle: Cuba Faces the 1990s*, edited by S. Halebsky and J. M. Kirk (New York: Praeger, 1990), 205–18.

13. On the consumerist and material turn of the 1970s, see Eugenio R. Balari, "The Supply of Consumer Goods in Cuba," in Halebsky and Kirk, *Transformation and Struggle*; Ariana Hernández-Reguant, "The Inventor, the Machine, and the New Man," in *Caviar with Rum: Cuba-U.S.S.R. and the Post-Soviet Experience*, edited by J. Loss and J. M. Prieto (New York: Palgrave Macmillan, 2012).

14. Ernesto Guevara, "La industrialización de Cuba," in *Universidad Popular: Séptimo Ciclo. Economía y planificación*, edited by C. Olivares, L. Soto, R. Anillo, R. Alarcón, and S. Fraile (Havana: Imprenta Nacional, 1961).

15. Luis A. Barreiro Pousa, "Enfoque estratégico de marketing para el comercio minorista de bienes en Cuba," PhD diss., University of Havana, 2002, 62.

16. Susan Eckstein, *Back from the Future: Cuba under Castro*, 2nd ed. (New York: Routledge, 2003), 56.

17. Viviana Togore González and Anisia García Álvarez, "Consumo, mercados y dualidad monetaria en Cuba," *Economía y Desarrollo* 134 (2003): 165–223; Díaz Acosta, "Consumo." The "parallel market," or *mercado liberado* (a Cuban euphemism for "free market"), provided a new alternative for Cubans to spend their salaries outside of the ration system or systems of workplace distribution of material rewards. Initially created in 1971 with the opening of the so-called *casas de regalos*, it was expanded in 1983 after the creation of the Amistad chain of stores.

18. See "Castro Addresses Construction Workers Plenum," December 21, 1971, *Castro Speech Data Base*, http://lanic.utexas.edu/project/castro/db/1971/19711221.html.

19. EMPROVA produced furniture, home goods, and appliances. See Barreiro Pousa, "Enfoque estratégico de marketing"; "Instituto Superior de Diseño," in *EcuRed* (online

encyclopedia), undated entry, http://www.ecured.cu/Instituto_Superior_de_Diseño, accessed July 12, 2016.

20. Fidel Castro, "Castro Addresses Rail Workers, Hails Soviet Aid," January 29, 1975, *Castro Speech Data Base*, http://lanic.utexas.edu/project/castro/db/1975/19750129.html.

21. Fidel Castro, "Castro Inaugurates Units of New Thermoelectric," February 15, 1978, *Castro Speech Data Base*, http://lanic.utexas.edu/project/castro/db/1978/19780215.html; Fidel Castro, "Castro Speaks at Main Commemoration of Builders' Day," December 5, 1978, *Castro Speech Database*, http://lanic.utexas.edu/project/castro/db/1978/19781205-1 .html.

22. Fidel Castro, "Discurso pronunciado por Fidel Castro Ruz, Presidente de la República de Cuba, en la inauguración del Combinado Textil de Santa Clara, celebrada el 2 de diciembre de 1979, 'Año 20 de la Victoria,'" stenographic version of the Council of State, http://www.cuba.cu/gobierno/discursos/1979/esp/f021279e.html. After this textile complex, the government inaugurated the Celia Sánchez Manduley textile complex in Santiago de Cuba. For references to other industrial developments, see *Un pueblo entero* (Havana: Letras Cubanas, 1983).

23. The label CONTEX, short for Confecciones Texiles, or Textile Manufacturing, was registered as a brand in 1981, although it was founded in the late 1970s. It would administer, in 1982, the newly created high-end fashion house La Maison, which catered to the foreign-currency market.

24. *First Congress of the Communist Party of Cuba: Memoirs* (Havana: Department of Revolutionary Orientation of the Central Committee of the Communist Party of Cuba, 1976), 60. In 1978 the Council of Ministers asked ICIODI to come up with a strategy for the elimination of the rationing system.

25. *First Congress of the Communist Party of Cuba*, 39. See also Fidel Castro, "Castro Denies Turning to Capitalism," January 16, 1974, *Castro Speech Data Base*, http://lanic.utexas .edu/project/castro/db/1974/19740116.html.

26. Marie Lavigne, "Advanced Socialist Society," *Economy and Society* 7 (1978): 367–94; Yuri Pavlov, *Soviet-Cuban Alliance: 1959–1991* (Miami: North-South Center Press, 1994), 95.

27. Pavlov, *Soviet-Cuban Alliance*, 112.

28. *First Congress of the Communist Party of Cuba*, 140.

29. Eliseo Alberto, "Los años grises," *Encuentro de la Cultura Cubana*, nos. 53–54 (1996): 33–42. Translation by Jennifer Lambe.

30. Fidel Castro, "Discurso pronunciado por el Comandante Fidel Castro Ruz, Primer Ministro del Gobierno Revolucionario, en el acto de su toma de posesión como Primer Ministro, efectuado en el Palacio Presidencial, el 16 de febrero de 1959," stenographic version of the Prime Minister's Office, http://www.cuba.cu/gobierno/discursos/1959/esp /c160259e.html.

31. Interviewees have identified this brochure as a publication of *Mujeres* magazine, but the booklet itself does not provide editorial information or pagination. A similar brochure from 1979, titled *Moda*, was printed by the Empresa Editorial de la Mujer, the magazine's publisher. This may corroborate the linkage between this publication and *Mujeres* as such.

32. Bartlett, *Fashion East*.

33. On *kulturnost*, see Vadim Volkov, "The Concept of Kulturnost: Notes on the Stalinist Civilizing Process," in *Stalinism: New Directions*, edited by Sheila Fitzpatrick (London: Routledge, 2000), 210–30.

34. Diana Fernández, "Lo cubano en el vestir," *La Jiribilla* 692 (2014), http://www.epoca2.lajiribilla.cu/articulo/8419/lo-cubano-en-el-vestir; Victor Goldgel, *Cuando lo nuevo conquistó América* (Buenos Aires: Siglo Veintiuno, 2013); Pérez, *On Becoming Cuban*; Ismael Sarmiento Ramírez, "Vestido y calzado de la población cubana en el siglo XIX," *Anales del Museo de América* 8 (2000): 161–99.

35. Pérez, *On Becoming Cuban*, 473–74.

36. Omar Fernández Cañizares, *Un viaje histórico con el Che* (Havana: Ciencias Sociales, 2005); Omar Fernández Cañizares, *Primer viaje del Che al exterior: Aniversario 50* (Havana: Ciencias Sociales, 2010); Pérez, *On Becoming Cuban*, 483.

37. Pérez, *On Becoming Cuban*, 483. Traditionally made with linen, this shirt has four front pockets, two vertical strips of *alforza* pleats in the front, and three in the back, among other characteristic details. Though some trace its origins to Mexico, Panama, and the Philippines, the guayabera has been worn in Cuba at least since the beginning of the eighteenth century.

38. In interviews conducted and testimonies published on social media, I have found references to the virtual disappearance of the guayabera shirt from the sartorial imaginary of the mid-1960s. Yet an examination of state practices suggests that, even if with less salience than in the very early 1960s, the guayabera shirt still occasionally came in handy to represent Cubanness. In the mid-1960s, for instance, the MINIL enterprise Moda Cubana created a new brand of guayabera shirts called Criolla.

39. Caridad Abrantes, interview with author, Havana, August 2012 and August 2013. "Cachita," as the CONTEX director was widely known, came up with the idea to transform the guayabera shirt into women's and children's outfits for mass production. However, the brochure *Moda '75, Edición Especial* already includes a drawing of a women's dress inspired by the guayabera shirt.

40. Abrantes interview; Almi Alonso, interview with author, New Jersey, March 2016.

41. EMPROVA designers Gonzalo Córdoba and María Victoria Caignet famously created goods inspired by Cuba's native Taíno culture, notably a dinnerware set. See Lucila Fernández Uriarte, "Cuba: Diseño industrial," in *Historia del diseño en América Latina y el Caribe: Industrialización y comunicación visual para la autonomía*, edited by S. Fernández and G. Bonsiepe (São Paulo: Blucher, 2008), 110–23; Lucila Fernández, "Una isla de diseño," *Revolución y Cultura* 2 (2012): 8–18; Nancy Stout, *One Day in December: Celia Sanchez and the Cuban Revolution* (New York: Monthly Review Press, 2013).

42. This and subsequent information on Cuban brand names was obtained from a 2012 search of the brands registered between 1959 and 1985 at the Oficina Cubana de la Propiedad Industrial.

43. Fernández, "Una isla de diseño"; Fernández Uriarte, "Cuba: Diseño industrial"; Lucila Fernández Uriarte, "Modernity and Postmodernity from Cuba," *Journal of Design History* 18 (2005): 245–55.

44. Fernández, "Una isla de diseño"; Fernández Uriarte, "Cuba: Diseño industrial"; Fernández Uriarte, "Modernity and Postmodernity from Cuba."

45. Abrantes interview; Stout, *One Day in December.*

46. Stout, *One Day in December.*

47. Abrantes interview.

48. Ángel Hernández Gómez, "Características y dinámica de la moda en Cuba," *Demanda* 6 (1984): 3–43; Armando Navarro Vega, *Cuba, el socialismo y sus éxodos* (Bloomington, IN: Palibrio, 2013); Alfredo Llópiz, interview with Janet Vega Espinosa, Havana, July 2015; Carlos Téllez, interview with Janet Vega Espinosa, Havana, July 2015.

49. Quoted in Vladia Rubio and Delia Reyes García, "La cáscara guarda el palo," *Bohemia*, March 2, 2007, http://www.bohemia.cu/2007/03/02/encuba/moda.html.

50. Mesa-Lago, *Cuba in the 1970s*, 106. Also see Anna C. Pertierra, *Cuba: The Struggle for Consumption* (Coconut Creek, FL: Caribbean Studies Press, 2011). As Pertierra argues, this tendency increased following the disintegration of the USSR and Cuba's subsequent economic crisis.

51. "La consistencia de la oferta a la población," ICIODI, Dirección de Investigaciones Globales, 1985, MEP/CH: IG-68; "La ropa exterior de los jóvenes. Los consumidores opinan. Informe No. 2," ICIODI, Dirección de Investigaciones Globales, 1985, IG-56; "Los consumidores opinan. Informe No. 3. El calzado de los jóvenes," ICIODI, Dirección de Investigaciones Globales, 1985, IG-57.

52. Duanel Díaz Infante, "La revolución es el espectáculo," *Diario de Cuba*, August 11, 2012, http://www.diariodecuba.com/cultura/1344672447_694.html; Guerra, *Visions of Power*. Here, my use of the term "strategies" follows Michel de Certeau, *The Practice of Everyday Life* (Berkeley: University of California Press, 1984), understanding it as a symbolic practice of domination performed by the powerful.

53. See the photo reportage of Burt Glinn, *Cuba 1959* (London: Reel Art Press, 2015). See also Guerra, *Visions of Power*, 67–74.

54. In Rafael Fornés, "El gran burgués: Nicolás Quintana entrevisto por Rafael Fornés," *Encuentro de la cultura cubana* 18 (2000): 26.

55. Guerra, *Visions of Power*, 293. This pageant is featured in the documentary *Fidel* (1969), directed by Saul Landau.

56. Camilo Loret de Mola, "Reinas," in *Penúltimos Días* (blog), August 21, 2009, http://www.penultimosdias.com/2009/08/21/reinas/. Similar overdecorated clothes were donned by the finalists of the 1970 pageant. In 1974 the government suspended the celebration of carnival beauty pageants.

57. On the early Bolshevik years, see Bartlett, *Fashion East*, 13–61; Sheila Fitzpatrick, "Cultural Revolution in Russia 1928–32," *Journal of Contemporary History* 9 (1974): 33–52. Also, in this volume, see Elizabeth Schwall's take on the staging of "proletarian" cultural spectacles in 1960s Cuba, such as the ballet *Avanzada*. On Brezhnev-era material culture, see Djurdja Bartlett, "Let Them Wear Beige: The Petit-Bourgeois World of Official Socialist Dress," *Fashion Theory* 8 (2004): 127–64.

58. Jorge Fornet, *El 71: Anatomía de una crisis* (Havana: Letras Cubanas, 2013), 16. Translation by Jennifer Lambe.

59. Mesa-Lago, *Cuba in the 1970s*; *First Congress of the Communist Party of Cuba.*

60. For more on the *actos de repudio*, see Abel Sierra Madero's contribution in this volume.

61. Eloise Linger, "Combining Moral and Material Incentives in Cuba," *Behavior and Social Issues* 2 (1992): 119–36; Muriel Nazzari, "The 'Woman Question' in Cuba: An Analysis of Material Constraints and Its Solution," *Signs* 9 (1983): 246–63. See samples of "Workplace Merits and Demerits" documents and certificates online at *Cuba Material* (blog), http://cubamaterial.com.

62. Randall, *Women in Cuba*, 142n4.

63. Those days, stores opened late and did not close until 11 p.m. See Linger, "Combining Moral and Material Incentives"; Nazzari, "The 'Woman Question.'"

64. S. Fiallo, "Investigación para determinar los lineamientos generales para el diseño de enseres," thesis for the degree of Bachelor in Industrial Design, ISDI, Havana, 1989.

65. Carlos R. Rodríguez, *Discurso pronunciado por el compañero Carlos Rafael Rodríguez en la actividad por el V aniversario de la Oficina Nacional de Diseño Industrial* (1986) (translated by author), archives of the Oficina Nacional de Diseño Industrial, in Havana, Cuba (copy in possession of author).

66. Linger, "Combining Moral and Material Incentives."

67. Linger, "Combining Moral and Material Incentives"; Nazzari, "The 'Woman Question.'" The impact of the system of material rewards in gender relations and in the delineation of professional hierarchies has yet to be studied.

68. Mesa-Lago, *Cuba in the 1970s*, 43.

69. The memoirs of former government insiders, albeit with heavy political overtones, expose double standards and the appetite for luxury among corrupt high-ranking officials and state cadres. See Roberto Ampuero, *Nuestros años Verde Olivo* (Mexico, D.F.: Debolsillo, 2015); Norberto Fuentes, *Dulces guerreros cubanos* (Barcelona: Seix Barral, 1999); Jorge Masetti, *El furor y el delirio* (Barcelona: TusQuets, 1993); José L. Llovio-Menéndez, *Insider: My Hidden Life as a Revolutionary in Cuba* (New York: Bantam, 1988).

70. *Zonas congeladas* were areas in former upscale neighborhoods, vacated as a consequence of the 1960s exodus of Cuba's upper classes, where new political and professional elites often relocated. The awarding or swapping of residences in these areas depended on the approval of Cuban authorities.

71. To cite one example, when the Amistad chain of stores opened in 1983, 13 to 16 percent of the goods for sale in the parallel market had an inconsistent offer, that is, appeared and disappeared regularly in a three-month period; 9 to 15 percent had an irregular offer, that is, appeared and disappeared with no regularity; 8 to 13 percent were affected by an occasional offer, that is, were sold only once or twice in a three-year period; and, finally, 41 percent of goods were never available in a three-year period (this last figure rose to 61 percent in 1985). Moreover 2 to 6 percent of the products available had a low volume of sales due to their elevated prices, and in 2 to 10 percent of cases sales were affected by problems of quality. See "La consistencia de la oferta a la población." See also Díaz Acosta, "Consumo."

72. In 1989 women had access to one meter of "quality A" fabric, one and a half meters of "quality B" material, a uniform skirt, a uniform blouse, one pair of underwear, a pair of work pants, and a work shirt. By comparison, a boy's quota was a shirt produced in

1988 or after, one meter of "quality A" fabric, one and a half meters of "quality B" fabric, a pair of pants or shorts produced in 1988 or after, a pair of uniform pants, a uniform shirt, one item of cotton underwear produced in 1987, one item of knitted cotton underwear, a pair of work pants, and a work shirt. "Investigación de mercado y pronóstico de la demanda nacional de confecciones personales y tejidos hasta el año 2000 (Informe Final)," ICIODI, Departamento de Vestuario y Artículos de Uso Personal, 1990, IM-465, III Eb.

73. Nazzari, "The 'Woman Question,'" 253.

74. Karen Kettering, "'Ever More Cozy and Comfortable': Stalinism and the Soviet Domestic Interior, 1928–1938," *Journal of Design History* 10 (1997): 127. Such mechanisms characterized many Soviet bloc regimes. See Bartlett, "Let Them Wear Beige"; Svetlana Boym, *Common Places: Mythologies of Everyday Life in Russia* (Cambridge, MA: Harvard University Press, 1994); Sheila Fitzpatrick, "'Middle-Class Values' and Soviet Life in the 1930s," in *Soviet Society and Culture: Essays in Honor of Vera S. Dunham*, edited by T. L. Thompson and R. Sheldon (Boulder, CO: Westview Press, 1988), 20–38; Jukka Gronow, *Caviar with Champagne: Common Luxury and the Ideals of the Good Life in Stalin's Russia* (New York: Berg, 2003).

75. Samuel Farber, *The Origins of the Cuban Revolution Reconsidered* (Chapel Hill: University of North Carolina Press, 2006), 68. Also see Alejandro de la Fuente in this volume.

76. Balari, "The Supply"; Bobes, *Los laberintos*; Días Acosta, "Consumo"; Carmelo Mesa-Lago, *Breve historia económica de la Cuba socialista: Política, resultados y perspectivas* (Madrid: Alianza Editorial), 1994.

77. "Tactics" is also used in the sense given by de Certeau, *The Practice*—that is, as resources of the weak to counter the strategies of the powerful.

78. "Que trine Eva" was published in *Viaje a La Habana* (Madrid: Mondadori, 1990). I am thankful to José Quiroga for this reference.

79. For more on the idea of palimpsests in Cuban culture, see José Quiroga, *Cuban Palimpsests* (Minneapolis: University of Minnesota Press, 2005).

80. See Ampuero, *Nuestros años Verde Olivo*; Fuentes, *Dulces guerreros cubanos*; Llovio-Menéndez, *Insider*.

81. See Ernesto Oroza, "Desobediencia tecnológica: De la Revolución al revolico," June 6, 2012, http://www.ernestooroza.com/desobediencia-tecnologica-de-la-revolucion -al-revolico/; Ernesto Oroza and Gean Moreno, "Object as Index: Ernesto Oroza in Conversation with Gean Moreno," June 10, 2008, http://www.ernestooroza.com/object -as-index-ernesto-oroza-in-conversation-with-gean-moreno/.

10. Anniversary Overload?

MEMORY FATIGUE AT CUBA'S SOCIALIST APEX

———

MICHAEL J. BUSTAMANTE

"This flag is discolored and full of stains. It would be a shame if the neighbors saw it in this condition." So complains Ana, the character played by actress Laura de la Uz, at the start of Eduardo del Llano's satirical short film *Aché*, set in 1974. Annoyed, her husband, Nicanor—an affable militant of the Cuban Communist Party—insists that the family heirloom would not be in such bad shape if they hung it outside less often. "But we only hang it on special days," Ana responds. "Riiight," retorts Nicanor, pointing at the calendar. "Because for you 'special' means not only patriotic holidays, but the Storming of the Bastille, the October Revolution, the anniversaries of friendly nations, our wedding anniversary . . . Ah! Look! World Day Against Malaria!" "I am *very* revolutionary," Ana counters, sarcastically (figures 10.1 and 10.2).

Nicanor is not innocent of insincerity himself. When Rodríguez, the head of the local Committee for the Defense of the Revolution (CDR), spots him furtively disposing of the worn flag in accordance with Ana's wishes, a letter of support to secure a coveted scholarship in France suddenly seems in jeopardy. Aware of the importance of appearing "integrated to the [revolutionary] process," Nicanor turns, first, to the black market in search of a substitute, and then to outright theft. The stains on the fabric at the film's start thus reveal themselves to be blots of a metaphorical kind.

Written, filmed, and circulated informally via flash drive in 2010, *Aché* offers a caustic commentary on the excesses of revolutionary loyalism and the

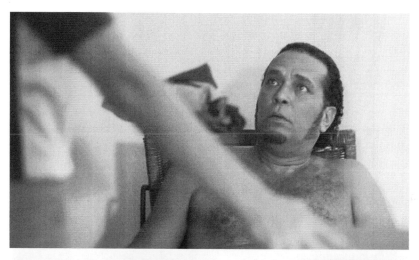

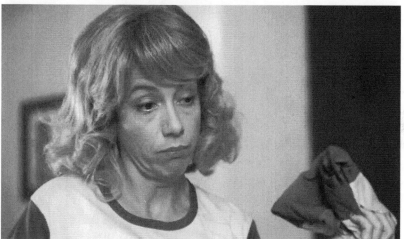

FIGS. 10.1 AND 10.2. Performative patriotism? Fictional characters Nicanor O'Donnell and wife, Ana, debate whether (and how) to secure a new Cuban flag to hang outside of their apartment. Stills from *Aché*, directed by Eduardo del Llano (2010), set in the 1970s.

instrumentalism of nationalistic display.[1] But if the critique targets the *doble moral* (or two-facedness) prevalent in Cuba today, del Llano situates the film in the 1970s in search of the historical roots of pro-forma patriotism. Flipping through state publications of the era, one indeed encounters an anniversary overload akin to that found on Ana's calendar. Between 1972 and 1973, for example, the journal *Revolución y Cultura* included special features on the fifth anniversary of Che Guevara's death, the fifty-fifth anniversary of Russia's October Revolution, the 120th birthday of José Martí, the seventy-fifth birthday of Bertolt Brecht (the East German playwright), and the twentieth anniversary of Fidel Castro's 1953 attack on the Moncada Barracks.[2]

Pomp was nothing new, of course. Dating to before 1959, as Lillian Guerra illustrates in this volume, revolutionary leaders had framed their campaigns as "historic" before they were even complete.[3] In the 1970s, however, commemoration bordered on obsession. With the Revolution's insurgent glory days behind it, memorialization, now sprinkled with Eastern bloc frames of reference, implied an urgent effort to keep the spirit (and loyalties) of the early 1960s alive.

But with commemorative excess, curiously, also came confidence in a modernizing future of Soviet inspiration. As María A. Cabrera Arús notes in chapter 9, the decade began ominously, with economic disarray as a result of the failed ten-million-ton sugar harvest in 1970. Unparalleled political dogmatism set in, enshrined in the pronouncements of the 1971 National Congress of Education and Culture.[4] Nevertheless, in many ways Cuba succeeded in "convert[ing] defeat into victory," just as Castro had pledged.[5] Thanks to integration into the Council of Mutual Economic Assistance in 1972, the island's aggressively subsidized economy grew at an average annual rate of as much as 14 percent.[6] In an environment of improved material conditions and ideological narrowing, the enactment of revolutionary loyalty and hard work could provide a path to trips abroad, home appliances awarded at work, and other forms of political and pecuniary gain.

The onslaught of dates, marches, and references to heroic figures in the 1970s would thus seem to represent ground zero for a performative, even cynical brand of revolutionary citizenship, as del Llano's film proposes. Indeed, both the repetition and *simplification* of state origin stories in this period may have cemented a more passive citizen engagement in state-led memory work, as we will see.[7] Still, ascertaining the degree to which "emblematic" frameworks of national remembrance actually ceased to resonate with personal sentiment presents a challenge.[8] Detailed reports of the attitudes, complaints, and private jokes that greeted daily life during the Revolution's second decade do not abound in the largely closed Cuban archival record.[9] Likewise, documentation of bureaucratic or political negotiations within and between state institutions involved in commemorative activities continues to be inaccessible.

And yet, even within official statements and sanctioned cultural production, one can still trace the evolving contours and contradictions of historical narrations that would have shaped Cubans' own impressions, as well as some surprising clashes over their form. In truth, the wider triumphalist spirit pervading public memory discourse in the 1970s proved a double-edged sword. Short of new events to rekindle the fires of revolutionary hopes, commemorative repetition risked converting the state's grand narratives into empty slogans. Cubans young and old saw signs of relative social progress and prosperity.[10] But they also confronted an epic legend that minimized their contributions in the past, and to which their more modest efforts in the present could hardly compare. Rather than providing fulfillment, the activities expected of citizens—diligent study (for youth), military service (for men), and tireless participation in neighborhood CDRs—might very well have yielded a gnawing sense of frustration. The result, paradoxically, was a cultural climate in which invocations of memory and history appeared everywhere, yet everyday existence could seem unremarkable, *forgettable*—at best the evidence of a future already constructed and a prerevolutionary past left behind.

From the "Time of History" to Futurity's Past

"They asked this man for his time / to be added to the time of History," wrote the poet Heberto Padilla. "They asked him for his lips, / his dry cracked lips, to affirm / and with each affirmation to build up a dream."[11] In the controversial collection *Fuera del juego* (Out of the Game, 1968), Padilla's critical reflections on the binding of individual subjectivity to national epic marked his emergence as an intellectual bête noire within the Revolution's cultural establishment. By 1971 the poet's growing dissidence had culminated in arrest and an internationally denounced public "self-critique."[12] Oddly, however, had Padilla's lines continued circulating, they might have taken on the powers of nostalgic incantation. As reliance on moral mobilization gave way to more mundane patterns of central planning, the true "time of History" for Cubans seemed to have come and gone.

No longer did Cuba's past, present, and future feel quite so immediate, intimately intertwined, or dangerously in the balance. Naturally, the national saga continued to impregnate public rhetoric. In addition to signaling a new age of cultural orthodoxy, the final declaration of 1971's National Congress of Education and Culture insisted that Cubans were living "true history," the era in which "the masses" were the protagonists of social life.[13] Official media likewise cast the bureaucratic "institutionalization" of the state along Soviet lines as a new front of urgent battle.[14] Yet whereas in the 1960s many Cubans *believed* that they were consummating the island's history in real time, by the next decade the joyfully chaotic, unpredictable rallies that characterized the Revolution's first years had long since morphed into routines of mass organization. Thus, when Leonid Brezhnev visited Cuba in 1974—the first Soviet premier to do so—the island's political leadership greeted him with a full military review, a spectacle of state order (not popular euphoria) to seal Cuban-Soviet goodwill.[15]

Officially, any note of retrospective melancholy remained taboo, an oxymoron. The literary giant turned cultural functionary Alejo Carpentier wrote fawningly in 1979, "I have to profoundly thank the Cuban Revolution for the fact that . . . due to its energetic impulse toward the future, I have become immune to the aging, morbid fascination of nostalgia. I have been lucky to belong to a generation of Cubans that, from the first of January 1959, has been cured forever of empty longings, convinced by visible and tangible achievements that, for us, no past was better than the present."[16] Fidel, too, denied that time had sapped the public's spirit. "What has experience taught us?" he asked in 1975. "That [the people's] energy has not fallen, that enthusiasm does not weaken, that if the Revolution had a heroic stage in the fight for liberation and a historic stage in the fight to defend the nation [i.e., the 1950s and 1960s], it also has a very heroic, dignified stage [dedicated to] the work of creation."[17] After a decade of conflict, mass mobilizations, and material shortages, stability might very well have been welcome. Even if plagued with continued problems, long speeches, and the "Sovietization" of Cuban politics and culture, socialist "normalcy" no doubt held considerable appeal.[18]

Still, as the urgency of improvisation gave way to five-year plans, some wistfulness for lived drama may have proved unavoidable. It is telling, for example, that over the Revolution's entire second decade in power, only one event—the notorious bombing of Cubana Airlines flight 455, masterminded by Cuban exiles in October 1976—found a place on the island's national memory calendar.[19] On that occasion, tens of thousands of distraught mourners flooded Revolution Square, waiting in long lines to file past coffins of the deceased. In moments of real crisis, nationalist convictions remained as palpable as ever; the rawness of the tragedy required little embroidery.[20] For the most part, however, older patriotic holidays continued to dominate the commemorative schedule, while anniversaries from the anti-Batista insurgency rounded out the list. Oddly, it was the July 26, 1953, attack on the Moncada Barracks, the ill-fated start to Castro's insurgent career and namesake for his later dominant 26th of July Movement, that remained both the Revolution's most important national holiday and a frequent subject of retrospective hagiography.[21]

The writer Dariela Aquique remembers the month of October as particularly ripe with ritualized, if monotonous, significance during these years.[22] Every October 10, Cubans recalled Carlos Manuel de Céspedes's declaration of war against Spain in 1868, the opening bell in the long struggle for independence and the "100 Years of Struggle" (as Castro famously put it) that followed.[23] The days preceding, however, revolved mostly around recent occasions of national mourning: the memory of Hurricane Flora in early October 1963 (a devastating storm that took twelve hundred Cubans' lives), the "Crime of Barbados" on October 6, 1976 (as the Cubana flight 455 bombing became known), and the death of Che Guevara in Bolivia on October 8, 1967—though, as was later confirmed, his execution actually took place on October 9.[24] At the end of the month thousands of school-children gathered at seashores across the country to recall the mysterious airborne disappearance of the revolutionary hero Camilo Cienfuegos on October 28, 1959, placing flowers atop his presumed maritime grave.[25] Rescue personnel had never located Cienfuegos's remains. By contrast, on July 26, 1970, Fidel tempered his reflections on the failure of the ten-million-ton harvest by revealing that Guevara's hands, severed by his executioners to identify his fingerprints, had been returned "perfectly conserved" to Cuban possession. Next October, he pledged, on the anniversary of Che's death, the government would display the Heroic Guerrilla's preserved appendages in crystal urns to appear as if protruding naturally from his original olive green uniform. A more dramatic totem of revolutionary faith could scarcely have been imagined.[26]

Fortunately, perhaps, this morbid spectacle never came to be. But the 1970s did witness a boom in the construction and expansion of museums across the island. Early on, revolutionary authorities recognized the importance of conserving the history they were making and shaping its telling. Decree-Law Number 17, signed by Raúl Castro on December 12, 1959, authorized the creation of a museum of the Revolution, a modest collection housed first in provisional offices in Havana's Vedado district and still actively seeking donations of material from the public as of 1961. Not until January 4, 1974, however, did *the* Museum of the Revolution formally open its doors, housed in the former Presidential Palace, where it still stands today. As they had so often done since 1959, authorities once again rebaptized a site of "pseudo-republican" infamy into a vessel of revolutionary mythmaking.[27] Two years later the Granma Memorial, displaying Castro's famous yacht under a glass enclosure, opened across the street.[28]

Museums of secondary importance also proliferated. In October 1973 the Museo Casa Natal José Antonio Echeverría, dedicated to the most famous martyr of the Revolutionary Directorate's failed attack on Batista's presidential palace in 1957, officially opened its doors in the city of Cárdenas.[29] Several months earlier the Museo Casa de Abel Santamaría in Havana debuted with similar fanfare and a visit from schoolchildren.[30] Reflecting the extensive cult of Moncada in the year of the attack's twentieth anniversary, a second museum and park dedicated to Santamaría, the most venerated activist to die as a result of the failed assault, also opened on July 26, the anniversary of the attack and his brutal death at the hands of Batista's police.[31] Several days later the panopticon-like Presidio Modelo on Cuba's Isle of Pines (officially renamed the Isle of Youth in 1978) welcomed its first visitors to the refurbished cells where Fidel and other survivors of the Moncada debacle had been imprisoned.[32]

Excluding generalist provincial and municipal museums housed in major towns and cities, of the 154 other functioning museums on the island today, thirty-eight—roughly a quarter—opened in the 1970s. Compare this to the eighteen museums that opened the decade before.[33] All the same, and without knowing who drove this building wave at the national and local levels, one wonders whether these exercises in martyrology, museumification, and literal and figurative "memory prosthesis" (to invoke the case of Che's hands) reflected broader confidence in or a vulnerability of the official historical canon. Allison Landsberg defines "prosthetic memory" as that emerging "at the interface between a person and a historical narrative about the past, at an experiential site such as a movie theater or a museum." "In this moment of contact," she writes, an individual "sutures himself or herself in a larger history."[34] Revolutionary leaders certainly had proven adept at this strategy in the early 1960s, "interpellating [the Cuban] population *both* in the past and in the present" through "a symbolic language that registered with the people, always addressed in the plural," as José Quiroga attests.[35] A decade later, though, authorities needed to connect to a generation that had not been witnesses, let alone protagonists, of the history represented. Though less "tainted" than their parents by prerevolutionary attitudes—or *rezagos* (holdovers)—young people might also have been more likely to take the Revolution's achievements for granted.[36]

On the other hand, more than a defensive effort, the construction of museums may have also represented an expected response to a renewed rhythm of modernization. The French scholar Pierre Nora famously theorized that societies preserve national history in "memory places" like monuments only when the shape of social life makes memory no longer "a real part of everyday experience."[37] Something similar, perhaps, was afoot in Cuba in the 1970s. It was in these years, after all, that early industrialization programs regained force after several years of officially valorized rural asceticism. Following Cuba's insertion into the Council of Mutual Economic Assistance, newly imported mass consumer goods helped resuscitate visions of productive utopias first imagined in the early 1960s.[38] Nonfiction films like 1972's *No tenemos derecho a esperar* (We Don't Have the Right to Wait) took viewers on sweeping tours of infrastructure projects, medical advances, and other social welfare programs finally coming into their own.[39] East of Havana, meanwhile, construction on the planned seaside town of Alamar, and the equally celebrated model settlement of La Yaya in the Escambray, presaged a prosperous residential future made of prefabricated Soviet cement.[40] "Cuba goes forward!" professed one of the more famous songs of the era, as higher standards of living and "material comfort" became legitimizing features of a modest but more stable socialist "dreamworld."[41]

The promise of material plenty, though allowing for the modest consumption distinctions that Cabrera Arús describes in her essay, went hand in hand with admiration for the leveling potential of Soviet technology. Whereas in 1966 "President [Osvaldo] Dorticós declared that communism would not be possible as long as there existed work as brutal as [cutting sugar cane]," by the end of the 1970s mechanized Soviet- and Cuban-designed KTP harvesters (fabricated outside the city of Holguín) accounted for half of all sugar cultivated on the island.[42] In the late 1960s revolutionary officials and authors alike celebrated manual labor in the sugar field as the purifying forge of revolutionary consciousness.[43] Now grandiose "Schools in the Countryside," depicted in Jorge Fraga's film *La nueva escuela* (The New School, 1974), were helping to modernize the backlands as much as expose young urbanites to the rigors of rural life.[44] More dramatically, a celebrated 1976 accord with the Soviets portended Cuba's entry into the nuclear age via the construction of two 440-megawatt reactors on the outskirts of Cienfuegos.[45] And while *Revista Casa de las Américas* once promoted "testing one's bones against underdevelopment" over the arrogance of a Yankee moon landing, by 1978 the Cuban pilot Arnaldo Tamayo was on his way to Moscow to become the first Cuban cosmonaut.[46] In "Introduction to the History of Cuba," the poet Víctor Casaus went so far as to imagine a desacralizing antimonument as the ultimate testament to the age: a housing project that, unbeknownst to residents, covered the hallowed grounds where the bones of Martí and other Cuban political martyrs lay buried. In this view, heretically, the privilege of enjoying the fruits of socialist modernization involved a certain right to forget.[47]

But if such images suggested to Cubans that their lives were already free of worries, Cuba's political leaders constantly reminded citizens—and young people especially—of the sacrifices that had made it possible and against which their efforts would be measured. "If one looks at the age of those who waged the Ten Years War," Castro told members of the Union of Young Communists in 1972,

> the age of Maceo and the great combatants of that era—the ages of revolutionaries of all eras of the history of our country—one would see that they could have been members of the Union of Young Communists if they were living today. That is to say, historically in our country men of your age were the agents and executors of the great revolutions. . . . But today you do not have to fight to take power that the people conquered from the exploiters. You no longer have to shed blood in our country to make a revolution. You have a revolution in your hands![48]

Instead of consigning the past to marble simulacra, "institutionalization" in the Cuban 1970s regimented the place of commemoration in daily life, setting up a series of expectations that all Cubans, and young people in particular, could scarcely hope to meet. "The new generations will have to be superior to the older generations," Fidel intoned.[49] "Run" to the future, the popular singer Silvio Rodríguez advised his idealistic followers, lest it "fall down" without their help.[50] The activities demanded of young people, however, could hardly equal the great deeds students were told to admire. Amid signs of socialist progress, the past could seem more heroic and monumental, but also out of reach.

Origin Stories: Revise and Repeat

Abetting such possibilities for disidentification between ordinary Cubans and political leaders was a subtle but important shift in state discourse itself. Commemorative "surplus" in the 1970s may have repeated familiar storylines and rested on known anniversary markers. But revolutionary officials also began to revise basic elements of that canon in ways that partially wrote everyday Cubans out. By mid-decade the First Congress of the Cuban Communist Party provided the stage for institutionalizing not only the structures of government in a socialist constitution (approved in 1976) but also a newly streamlined narrative of the Revolution's coming-to-be. The resulting account contradicted a previous emphasis on citizen protagonism in the nation's transformations, instead emphasizing the prowess of the Revolution's leaders and suggesting that Cubans had been targets of their premeditated plan.

Since the early 1960s, explanations of the anti-Batista insurrection and the Revolution's subsequent evolution in power had followed a foreseeable script. Starting in late 1961, high-placed intellectuals-cum-politicians like Carlos Rafael Rodríguez, Aníbal Escalante, Blas Roca, and Che Guevara had taken it upon themselves to explain how the revolutionary project had gone from "olive green," as Castro characterized his ideology in 1959, to "red," or openly socialist, by April 1961. This "transition to socialism," Marxist theorists argued, grew out of a process of radicalization forged at the crossroads of domestic class struggle and foreign (read: U.S.) antagonism. The triumph, in other words, of a radical but at first admittedly nonsocialist political project had unleashed both internal and external tensions that eventually took on a logic of their own.[51] In this reading, it was the populace itself and the exigencies of conflict that "pushed" revolutionary officials into casting off lingering bourgeois pretensions. Notably, such views found an echo in Fidel's words during a highly public visit to the Chile of Salvador Allende in late 1971. Seeking to downplay the differences between Cuba's insurgent model and Chile's novel electoral path to socialism, Castro admitted that in 1959 he was "not yet a communist, no. . . . The program of the 26th of July Movement was not yet a socialist program."[52] Cubans, he claimed, understood "that Revolution is a journey, that Revolution is a process." Revolutions, Fidel told Chilean audiences, "could not even be preconceived."[53]

Ironically, though, as the First Congress of the Cuban Communist Party approached, it was precisely a "preconceived" view of Cuba's recent history that began to take hold. Authorities ditched previously dialectical, materialist, if still selective modes of analysis for a more conspiratorial vision. A socialist makeover, voices in the Party now insisted, had been the clear, secretly held desire of the Revolution's core leadership all along.[54] Reflecting upon the significance of the Moncada attack on July 26, 1975, Castro amended his words in Chile four years before. "At the beginning we were few. . . . [And] although our program as the 26th of July movement was not yet a socialist program, *we, the 26th of July, were socialists*" (emphasis added). "Our books were the works of Martí, and Marx, and Engels, and Lenin," he continued, "And these ideas, even in the most difficult of circumstances, brought us to victory."[55] Back in 1961, by contrast, Fidel had been prepared to argue only that "the socialist germ of the Revolution was already present in the Moncada movement." What had once been treated as retrospective revelation had suddenly morphed into a deliberate scheme.[56]

Revolutionary officials also dramatically simplified the history of Cuba's traditional communist party, the Partido Socialista Popular (PSP), one of three main political factions in the revolutionary government after 1959. "And there was also in our country a Communist Party," Castro professed, "and those militant communist revolutionaries were closely united, throughout the struggle, with the combatants of the 26th of July revolutionary movement." Certain members and collaborators of the 26th of July—Raúl Castro, most notably— did have loose ties to the PSP going back to the early 1950s. Officially, though, the PSP leadership not only repudiated Fidel's attack on the Moncada Barracks in 1953 but failed to reach a definitive understanding with his 26th of July Movement until the summer of 1958.[57] After 1959 this legacy made it difficult for many noncommunist rebels to accept the revolutionary government's move to bring them into the fold. Now, in one swift allocution, the Revolution's leader had rendered that history of tension null and void. His words also expunged a sequence of "sectarian" conflicts that had fractured the revolutionary ranks in the 1960s, stemming precisely from pre-1959 competition among anti-Batista groups.[58]

The culmination of such revisionism came at the First Congress of the Cuban Communist Party (PCC) in December 1975. Ironically, what conservative elements of Miami's Cuban exile community had long alleged—that Castro had always been a clandestine communist—became enshrined as official state wisdom. The Revolution of 1959, the Party's widely printed "Historical Analysis of the Cuban Revolution" intoned, "had to be the work of *new* communists, in essence, because they were not known as such." "If it is true that [socialism] was not the general thinking of all of those who initiated the path of revolutionary armed struggle in our country," Fidel backpedaled slightly, "*it was for its principal leaders.*" Isolated, repressed, and politically paralyzed, Cuba's PSP had not been in a position to lead. Only a younger generation, recognizing that "the proclamation of socialism during the insurrectional stage *would not yet have been understood by the people*," proved capable of assuming the undercover vanguard (emphasis added).[59]

The result of these rhetorical gymnastics was a remarkable shift from a dynamic to a more oracular vision of the Revolution's history. Whether a product of Cuba's new strength under Soviet support or residual fears that retrospective what-ifs could prove an ideological Trojan horse, this recasting painted revolutionary socialism as the outcome of premonition and design. "History transpires as a function of objective laws, but men make history," Castro stated at the Party Congress in 1975, curiously inverting the emphasis of Marx's old adage "Men make their own history, but they do not make it as they please."[60] In this case, though, the men making the most consequential history were just a chosen few. Whereas Fidel and other leaders had previously remembered the masses *driving* the revolutionary administration to new ideological heights, now the all-seeing leadership assumed primacy of narrative place and political authorship. No longer the principal agents of revolutionary transformation, the Cuban people now resembled the objects, or at best partners, of a calculated plot.[61]

History as Melodrama, November Doubts

The seeming incontestability of these claims appears dumbfounding from the vantage point of today. Surely many Cubans would have recalled a more complex pattern of historical change. Yet in a decade that was at once past-obsessed and forward-looking, one can almost understand the attractions of amnesia. Besides, save for those paying academic attention to Castro's every word, gradual mutations in public rhetoric registered less powerfully than dramatizations of Cuba's story as consummated epic—particularly on screen. If in audiovisual media the Revolution's true purpose, orientation, and protagonists were represented as broadly unchanging (or unquestioned truths), then the finer points in the state's own shifting narrative on these questions likely passed unperceived.

In this way, arguably the most salient historical narratives available for popular consumption in the 1970s were not the pronouncements of the Communist Party but historical dramatizations in film. The most beloved Cuban movies of the era—all produced by the state-run Cuban Institute of Cinematic Art and Industries (ICAIC)—staged moments of the Revolution's successful conflict against internal and external enemies the decade before.[62] The thriller *El hombre de Mainsinicú* (The Man from Mainsinicú, 1973), for example, famously dramatized the real-life tale of Alberto Delgado, an administrator of a small farm in the Escambray Mountains, a hotbed of counterrevolutionary unrest in the 1960s. After successfully penetrating anticommunist rebel groups on behalf of state security, Delgado was assassinated by insurgents in 1964.[63] Drawing a record 1.9 million viewers, the film stood as a celluloid monument to a national hero fighting off Washington's designs. Director Manuel Pérez may have prepared by speaking with jailed participants from the anti-Castro opposition. Viewers, however, would mostly remember the actor Sergio Corrieri's manly tour de force in the lead role.[64]

Similar blockbuster productions followed. *Patty-Candela* (1976) re-constructed a real CIA plot to assassinate both Fidel and Raúl Castro in July 1961, successfully foiled and revealed to the public thanks to the work of loyal informers.[65] One year later the coming-of-age story *El brigadista* (The Literacy Teacher) revived a familiar symbolic trifecta from the 1960s, linking the Zapata Swamps of Cuba's southern coast, the invasion at the neighboring Bay of Pigs, and the redeeming work of the Literacy Campaign in the area.[66] Because residents of the swamps suffered extreme poverty in the prerevolutionary years, Cuban authorities in 1961 emphasized the potent symbolism of the region's resistance to external attack. In the film, then, it was only appropriate that fifteen-year-old Mario would work as a literacy instructor in the small swamp settlement of Maneadero, transforming from a naïve urbanite into a hardened masculine hero as he successfully fought off counterrevolutionary insurgents supported covertly from abroad.[67] At their best, follow-ups like *Río negro* (Black River, 1977) provided reasonably complex retrospectives on the fine line between revolutionary loyalty and counterrevolutionary betrayal.[68] At worst, sequels like *Guardafronteras* (The Border Guard, 1980) and *Leyenda* (Legend, 1981) substituted melodrama and Hollywood-esque bombast for more serious-minded, if still one-sided historical reconstructions.[69] In all cases, the thread of U.S.-Cuba conflict in the Revolution's history superseded its record of internal divides and shifts.

What the film scholar Michael Chanan has called a "return to the popular" in Cuban cinema in the 1970s—surpassing operatic ICAIC productions of the early 1960s set during the anti-Batista insurrection—built on similar turns in literature, radio, and television.[70] Bolstered by the Ministry of Interior's support for detective fiction as a vehicle for promoting "socialist values," a prolific subgenre of counterespionage paperbacks and audiovisual analogues also emerged.[71] Luis Rogelio Nogueras's award-winning *Y si muero mañana* (If I Die Tomorrow), for instance, recounted the exploits of a secret agent successfully infiltrated into Miami's "Plan Torres," a terrorist plot to attack Cuban shores.[72] Other tales of counterrevolutionary intrigue set in the 1960s, like Enrique Álvarez Jané's *Algo que debes hacer* (Something You Should Do), attracted the attention of, and were remade for, Cuban television.[73] Far and away the most popular example of this kind was 1979's *En silencio ha tenido que ser* (In Silence It Had to Be), starring, once more, Sergio Corrieri (figure 10.3). A joint production of Cuban state television and the Ministry of Interior, the six-part miniseries followed the exploits of a Cuban double agent heroically informing on counterrevolutionaries and the CIA from the early days of 1959.[74] The title and opening credits referenced a passage from Martí's famous last letter

EN SILENCIO HA TENIDO QUE SER

UN NUEVO SERIAL PARA
LA TV CUBANA
VEA PAG. 12

UN
HOMENAJE
DIARIO
A LOS
HEROES
VEA PAG. 11

FIG. 10.3. Debuting in 1979, the TV spy series *En Silencio Ha Tenido Que Ser* was a smash hit, inviting viewers to relive, and mythologize, the Revolution's early Cold War exploits. *El Caimán Barbudo* 135 (March 1979), cover.

before his death. In this way, the show invited audiences to view state intelligence agents as the reincarnation of the Cuban hero's ideas. One reviewer hyperbolically called the series a "work of art," a distillation of the "human stature" and "epic revolutionary inspiration" of Cuban history.[75] A sequel airing in 1980, *Julito el pescador* (Julito the Fisherman), enjoyed similar success and popular appeal.[76]

In the 1960s Carlos Puebla famously sang that Fidel's arrival in Havana had brought all *diversión* (amusement) to a halt.[77] By the 1970s, however, the Revolution had itself become a source of tantalizing entertainment, a past spectacle comfortably, even nostalgically consumed from a movie theater seat. More than a mirror for ongoing social transformations, revolutionary action stories fostered a brand of cultural citizenship akin to that nurtured by Cold War spy sagas of the capitalist world. Films like *Patty-Candela* may have pushed back against depictions of the Caribbean as an exotic backdrop in the style of James Bond. Nonetheless, Cuban contributions to the genre replicated Western discursive codes: the prominence of an "individual masculine protagonist" as "the literal embodiment of state and national interests" and a "semi-documentary narrative style" that "articulated a kind of [passive] civic nationalism linked to the institution of television itself."[78] Such productions called on viewers to become part of a "virtual community . . . of vicarious witness." They fostered a historical common sense, concealing the significance of state leaders' rhetorical shifts, and perhaps even reinforcing feelings of national pride. But the fact that a core group of male actors dominated each and every cast made these productions as much vehicles for depoliticized forms of socialist celebrity as (secret) agents of revolutionary ideals.[79]

Off the screen, meanwhile—back in the present—the question "What now?" remained. Thus even as spectacular portrayals of revolutionary legend provided distraction from the mundane contours of the socialist everyday, less sensationalist reflections on the place of the past in the present did occasionally surface, offering rare windows into simmering doubts. In 1978 ICAIC debuted a film whose complex ruminations on memory and trauma openly contradicted commemorative molds of the time. Shot against the backdrop of the Padilla affair back in 1971, Humberto Solás's *Un día de noviembre* (One Day in November) featured characters struggling to reckon with their histories amid their safely socialist yet somehow ambivalent lives. Because the main characters did not embody stories of proletarian heroism, ICAIC's president Alfredo Guevara opted to preemptively shelve the film for six years.[80] In this sense it represents not just an overlooked oddity in Solás's body of work (best known for classics of revolutionary cinema like 1968's *Lucía*) but an unparalleled meditation on the period's cultural politics.[81]

At the start of the picture, Esteban, a dedicated, though not particularly high-ranking veteran of the anti-Batista urban underground, is diagnosed with an untreatable cerebral aneurysm that could end his life at any moment. Ordered by his doctor to rest indefinitely and confronting his pending mortality, Esteban suddenly feels that his past as an activist and revolutionary lacks the meaning it once held. From his brother and sister-in-law—both selfish types waiting to leave the country for their "little packet of Cornflakes"—to young students at a block party dancing to psychedelic music, the world around him appears superficial. Individuals go through the motions, yet they fail to ap-

FIG. 10.4. Esteban ponders a stagnant present and his revolutionary past. Still from *Un Día de Noviembre*, directed by Humberto Solás (1972).

preciate the struggles of those who came before. "They have it all," agrees his mother, after an exasperating trip to the corner store to pick up subsidized rations alongside grumpy neighbors. "They have work, school for the kids, food, because here no one dies of hunger, and still they complain."

Nonetheless, Esteban remains wracked by self-doubt. Severe headaches prompt flashbacks to the private demons he carries from the anti-Batista struggle. Visits to former collaborators only sharpen his sense of dislocation (figure 10.4). All seem tired of carrying the burden of their "heroism," rejecting, in principle, the idea of resting on their laurels. At the same time, they feel alienated from a newer generation that can never understand or duplicate their sacrifice. Meanwhile, younger Cubans who do strive for a sense of purpose—represented in the film by Esteban's love interest, Lucía—must content themselves with the conviction that their generation "would have done the same." Convinced that life should be about "rebellion, dissatisfaction," she and other characters remain paralyzed because the important political struggles seem to have come and gone.

In the end, Esteban, once prepared to give his life for a cause, cannot fathom that his real death will be "for nothing." A disabled veteran of Cuba's battles against counterrevolutionary "bandits" urges him to "not die while living." But then the ex-soldier catches himself, acknowledging solemnly "how easy it is to give advice" while hiding from his own inner ghosts. Solás may have intended *Un día de noviembre* as a call to intergenerational dialogue, a revolutionary critique of complacency and triumphalism. Yet with Esteban remaining as lost at the film's end as at its beginning, it is difficult to read the story as anything but a pessimistic challenge to narratives equating the Revolution's permanence with a virtual "end of (Cuban) history."

In *Un día de noviembre*, revolutionary Cuba appeared to have reached an imperfect plateau, not a utopia forged on the blood of martyrs. Most troublingly, Solás's Cuba was one in which thoughts, emotions, and private recollections, for all their revolutionary credentials, departed from the optimistic pronouncements of the state. No wonder Roberto José, writing in *El Caimán Barbudo*, called the production "decadent," "in no way constructive," "archival footage"—likely a double entendre referencing the film's history of censorship. The public, José claimed, "has a hard time seeing itself reflected in characters who try to stop time and live on their memories alone."[82] Maybe he was right. The irony, though, is that official media culture in this era, as we have seen, was largely guilty of the same charge.

Conclusion: Memory Surfeit, Memory Absence

Memory and history were ubiquitous in 1970s Cuba, from increasingly simplistic invocations of the revolutionary epic in speeches and films to museums dedicated to venerated heroes. And yet, because the most celebrated campaigns of the 1960s lay firmly in the past, saying what actually *happened* in the Revolution's second decade proved, and remains, difficult. Even in most history books on the island today, these years are cast as interlude.[83] If events, according to Alain Badiou, are defined by their "undecidability" and "ontological disruption," much of the time period examined in this essay was characterized by the opposite.[84] Authorities recast seemingly spontaneous revolutionary events from the 1950s and 1960s as part of a predestined plan. Meanwhile, while there was economic progress, few present-day turning points—especially on the island itself—seemed genuinely capable of firing revolutionary passions anew.[85]

What, though, of the views of everyday citizens, the real-life Nicanors (returning to del Llano's 2010 short) navigating this era's contradictory combination of futuristic confidence and retrospective streamlining? Might they, like Solás, have meditated on history's unresolved dilemmas and stagnated hopes? Or, as in the fictional case of Nicanor, had invocations of patriotic legend become little more than a ticket to getting ahead? "I give you the wine. I eat filet mignon. *Le cordon bleu de rose*," Nicanor's wife, Ana, sings, turning Édith Piaf's "La vie en rose" (made famous in Cuba by the singer Bola de Nieve) into a hilarious paean to dreamed-of French treats.

There is, of course, no simple or uniform answer to these questions. Cuban society has never been monolithic, and archival silence (as Jorge Macle explains) still prevents us from seeing it in its plurality and complexity. *Detrás de la Fachada* (Behind the Façade), one of the most popular Cuban television programs on air at the time, invited Cubans to ignore history entirely, lightheartedly poking fun at daily socialist inconveniences.[86] If that was possible, might one of the government's slogans of the era—"We are happy here!"—have been closest to the truth?[87]

Oral history might seem to provide a work-around. Yet when the object of study is not just the experience of a particular era or event but the shape of popular remembrance *in the past*, interviews conducted in the present are as likely to reveal the nested effects of memory struggles since.[88] Without sufficient insight into popular attitudes and the midlevel negotiations of culture workers in state bodies, one runs the danger of painting Cubans' historical knowledge as the result of a uniform, monolithic, and all-controlling state puppeteer.

But if documenting the everyday doubts of the 1970s remains difficult, a reading of the decade's wider cultural landscape, as this essay suggests, highlights a paradox with which no doubt many Cubans had to privately contend: the simultaneous *surfeit* of public memory and its absence. Commemoration, in other words, was everywhere, but few new domestic milestones appeared worthy of state-sanctioned remembrance in the future. "The Cuban Revolution had been personally lived by the entire population as real experience, excitement, and intimate hope," writes the critic Rachel Weiss. By the end of the 1970s it "had somehow gotten hijacked into the puffery of gray men."[89] Reduced to predictable fable and repetitive, increasingly didactic public transcript, the collective narrative of the state risked opening itself to private notes of melancholy, longing, and regret. For if still capable of inspiration, "the Revolution"—in its successes, shortcomings, and purported omniscience— had also become conspicuously routine.

NOTES

1. *Aché*, directed by Eduardo del Llano (Havana: Sex Machine Productions, 2010).

2. "Testimonios sobre el Che," *Revolución y Cultura* 7 (1972): 43–52; "Suplemento: 55 aniversario de la Revolución de octubre," *Revolución y Cultura* 7 (1972): n.p.; "El pasado 28 de enero," *Revolución y Cultura* 8 (1973): 2; Ulf Keyn, "El legado vital de Brecht," *Revolución y Cultura* 9 (February 1973): 3; Haydée Santamaría, "El Moncada es la vida: Grandeza de los que cayeron y de los que quedaron," *Revolución y Cultura* 12 (July 1973): 26–40.

3. Louis A. Pérez Jr., *The Structure of Cuban History: Meanings and Purpose of the Past* (Chapel Hill: University of North Carolina Press, 2013), 237–84.

4. On the 1971 Congress of Education and Culture, see Jorge Fornet, *El 71: Anatomía de una crisis* (Havana: Letras Cubanas, 2013), 165–86. The term "quinquenio gris" was coined by the Cuban writer Ambrosio Fornet, who himself suffered its consequences; Ambroso Fornet, "Quinquenio gris: Revisitando el término," *Revista Casa de las Américas* 246 (January–March 2007): 3–16.

5. Fidel Castro, "A convertir el revés en victoria," *Con la Guardia en Alto* 9, no. 6 (1970): 18–20.

6. Carmelo Mesa-Lago, *Cuba in the 1970s: Pragmatism and Institutionalization* (Albuquerque: University of New Mexico Press, 1978), 56–58.

7. The notion of collective memory as "work" highlights the active participation normally required—on the part of individuals or institutions—to mobilize resources, attend commemorative events, and vest narratives of history with meaning. As scholars like Jeffrey Olick have insisted, however, when we turn our attention away from "the static aspects of memory" (as a reified "entity") to the "processual aspects of remembering," we can appreciate "collective memory" as a mobile field involving active and passive forms of engagement, as I am suggesting here. See Jeffrey K. Olick, introduction to *States of Memory: Continuities, Conflicts, and Transformations in National Retrospection*, edited by Jeffrey K. Olick (Durham, NC: Duke University Press, 2003), 6.

8. Steve J. Stern defines "emblematic" as opposed to "loose" memory as a "framework for collective remembrance rather than its specific contents," imparting "broad interpretive meaning and criteria of selection to personal memory." Steve J. Stern, *Remembering Pinochet's Chile: On the Eve of London 1998* (Durham, NC: Duke University Press, 2006), 105.

9. Duanel Díaz Infante comments on the underdeveloped study of humor during the Revolution in "¿Humor y contrarevolución?," *Cubaencuentro.com*, November 12, 2009, http://www.cubaencuentro.com/cultura/articulos/humor-y-contrarevolucion-222603.

10. See *El telón de azúcar*, directed by Camila Guzmán (Paris: Luz Films, 2005), a wistful portrait of young Cubans raised in this era.

11. Heberto Padilla, "En tiempos difíciles," in *Fuera del juego* (1968; Miami: Ediciones Universal, 1998), 13. Together with Antón Arrufat's play *Los Siete contra Tebas*, *Fuera del Juego* was awarded a UNEAC prize by an international jury in 1968 but only printed with a foreword noting UNEAC's protest against the "ambiguity" and "anti-historicism" of its contents.

12. For more on the domestic and international implications, see Lourdes Casal, ed., *El caso Padilla: Literatura y revolucion en Cuba* (New York: Ediciones Nueva Atlántida, 1971); Fornet, *El 71*, 147–64; Heberto Padilla, *La mala memoria* (Barcelona: Plaza y Janés, 1989).

13. "Declaración del Primer Congreso Nacional de Educación y Cultura," *Revista Casa de las Américas* 65–66 (March–June 1971): 18.

14. "Cuba: La institucionalziación histórica," *Cuba Internacional*, 1977, supplement.

15. For a visual account of the visit, see *Amistad*, directed by Jorge Fraga (Havana: ICAIC, 1975). Cuban-Soviet relations in the 1960s, while close, had been marked by a

notable substrate of tension—particularly in the aftermath of the Cuban Missile Crisis and as a result of Cuba's support for armed revolution in Latin America. See Jorge Domínguez, *To Make the World Safe for Revolution: Cuba's Foreign Policy* (Cambridge, MA: Harvard University Press, 1989), 61–78.

16. Alejo Carpentier, "Impromptu para un gran aniversario," *Revolución y Cultura* 77 (January 1979): 2. Carpentier first gained literary notoriety in the 1930s and 1940s. Between 1966 and his death in 1980, he served as cultural attaché at Cuba's embassy in Paris.

17. "Discurso pronunciado por el Comandante en Jefe Fidel Castro Ruz, Primer Secretario del Comité Central del Partido Comunista de Cuba y Primer Ministro del Gobierno Revolucionario, en el acto central en conmemoración del XXII aniversario del ataque al Cuartel Moncada, efectuado en la ciudad de Santa Clara, Las Villas," July 26, 1975, http://www.cuba.cu/gobierno/discursos/1975/esp/f260775e.html.

18. Soviet influence—ideologically, politically, culturally—began in the 1960s. The 1970s, however, are generally considered the period when Soviet-inspired economic management, political structures, and material products shaped Cuban society most strongly. "Cuba en la era soviética y post-soviética," panel discussion, 33rd International Congress of the Latin American Studies Association, May 29, 2015, San Juan, Puerto Rico; Jacqueline Loss, *Dreaming in Russian: The Cuban Soviet Imaginary* (Austin: University of Texas Press, 2013).

19. Significant as well was the beginning of "Operación Carlota" in November 1975, commencing Cuba's protracted military involvement in Angola's Civil War. Conducted initially in secrecy, however, Cuba's extended involvement in Angola was not the exclusive focus of a major act of commemoration until 1989, when, as the war neared conclusion, the Cuban government held a national memorial in memory of all of those soldiers who had died on "internationalist missions."

20. For visuals of the public memorial, see *Morir por la patria es vivir*, directed by Santiago Álvarez (Havana: ICAIC, 1976). For a reflection on its impact, by a journalist who was present, see "Steven Kinzer on Cuba in the 1970s and 80s," *Beyond the Sugar Curtain* (blog), n.d., https://www.brown.edu/research/projects/tracing-cuba-us-connections/news/2016/12/stephen-kinzer-cuba-1970s-and-80s.

21. For example, see Marta Rojas, *La generación del centenario en el juicio del Moncada*, 3rd ed. (Havana: Editorial Ciencias Sociales, 1973).

22. Dariela Aquique, "Los octubres de Cuba," *Diario de Cuba*, October 27, 2014, http://www.diariodecuba.com/cuba/1414347485_10981.html.

23. Castro invoked the idea of Cuba's "100 years of struggle" in 1968. See "Discurso pronunciado por el Comandante Fidel Castro Ruz, Primer Secretario del Comité Central del Partido Comunista de Cuba y Primer Ministro del gobierno revolucionario, en el resumen de la velada conmemorativa de los cien años de lucha, efectuada en la Demajagua, Monumento Nacional, Manzanillo, Oriente," October 10, 1968, http://www.cuba.cu/gobierno/discursos/1968/esp/f101068e.html.

24. Guevara was first reported captured and "dead of his wounds" following a battle with Bolivian military forces on October 8. For this reason, the day of his last battle and, for years, presumed death was christened thereafter in Cuba as "The Day of the Heroic

Guerrilla." On the twentieth anniversary of his death, Castro acknowledged publicly that Che was actually executed on October 9. Jon Lee Anderson, *Che Guevara: A Revolutionary Life* (New York: Grove Press, 1997), 740.

25. Lillian Guerra, *Visions of Power in Cuba: Revolution, Redemption, and Resistance, 1959–1971* (Chapel Hill: University of North Carolina Press, 2012), 88–90; "Una flor para Camilo: Hermosa tradición revolucionaria," *Granma*, October 29, 1970, 1.

26. Fidel Castro, "Discurso pronunciado por el Comandante Fidel Castro Ruz, Primer Secretario del Comité Central del Partido Comunista de Cuba y Primer Ministro del Gobierno Revolucionario, en la concentración conmemorativa del XVII Aniversario del Asalto al Cuartel Moncada, efectuada en la Plaza de la Revolución," July 26, 1970, http://www.cuba.cu/gobierno/discursos/1970/esp/f260770e.html; Fidel Castro, "Las Manos del Che," *Bohemia*, July 31, 1970; Bertrand de la Grange, "El insólito viaje de las manos del Che," *El País*, October 14, 2007, http://elpais.com/diario/2007/10/14/internacional /1192312809_850215.html.

27. "Museo de la Revolución festejará su cumpleaños 49," *Juventud Rebelde*, December 10, 2008, http://www.juventudrebelde.cu/cuba/2008–12–10/museo-de-la-revolucion -festejara-su-cumpleanos-49; "Museo de la Revolución" [advertisement], *Revolución*, May 20, 1961, 10. Before opening in 1974 at the former Presidential Palace, the Museum had taken up temporary residence inside the José Martí Memorial in Revolution Square.

28. Ramiro Valdés, "Discurso pronunciado en el acto de inauguración del Memorial Granma, en la Habana, el día 1 de diciembre 1976," *Granma*, December 2, 1976, 3.

29. Hector Hernández Pardo, "En la casa natal de José Antonio Echevarría: Inauguran hoy, en Cárdenas, Museo Regional de Historia," *Granma*, October 10, 1973. Significantly, though José Antonio Echevarría had been incorporated into the revolutionary pantheon since the Revolution's earliest years, members of his own family had long since departed the island for exile.

30. Conchita Pedroso, "Visitan escolares la Casa-Museo donde vivió Abel Santamaría y depositan ante la tarja la primera ofrenda floral," *Granma*, May 28, 1973, 3; "Abren al público como museo, desde mañana, el apartamento de Abel Santamaría en 25 y O, Vedado," *Granma*, June 8, 1973, 1.

31. "Museo Abel Santamaría Cuadrado," Consejo Nacional de Patrimonio Cultural, http://www.cnpc.cult.cu/institucion/526, accessed May 15, 2015; René Camacho Albert, "Seleccionan monumento a Abel Santamaria que erigirán en el parque que lleva su nombre, en Santiago de Cuba," *Granma*, June 27, 1973, 1.

32. Ricardo Bernal Mora, "Inauguran exposición en el antiguo Presidio Modelo de Isla de Pinos," *Granma*, July 30, 1973, 3; Orlando Gómez, "Un museo para la posteridad: El antiguo Presidio Modelo," *Granma*, July 25, 1974, 3. Not mentioned in the displays, conspicuously, was the facility's continued use after 1959 to house counterrevolutionary prisoners, let alone the fates of what one rare text later called the "non-integrated Moncadistas"—that is, the twenty-one veterans of Moncada who had since fallen afoul of revolutionary rule. Centro de Estudio de Historia Militar, Fuerzas Armadas Revolucionarias, *Moncada: La acción* (Havana: Editora Politica, 1981), 2:422.

33. Information culled from the Directorio de Museos, Consejo Nacional de Patrimonio Cultural, http://www.cnpc.cult.cu/directorio-museos, accessed May 14, 2015.

34. Allison Landsberg, *Prosthetic Memory: The Transformation of American Remembrance in the Age of Mass Culture* (New York: Columbia University Press, 2004), 3.

35. José Quiroga, *Cuban Palimpsests* (Minneapolis: University of Minnesota Press, 2005), 2.

36. See, for example, Fidel Castro's reflections on youth and *rezagos* of the past blamed on parents in "Discurso pronunciado por Fidel Castro Ruz, Presidente de la República de Cuba, en el acto de clausura del primer congreso de los CDR en el XVII aniversario de su fundación, en la Plaza de la Revolución, ciudad de la Habana, el 28 de septiembre de 1977, año de la institucionalización," http://www.cuba.cu/gobierno/discursos/1977/esp /f280977e.html, accessed October 23, 2015.

37. Pierre Nora, ed., *Realms of Memory: Rethinking the French Past*, vol. 1: *Conflicts and Divisions*, translated by Arthur Goldhammer (New York: Columbia University Press, 1996), 1.

38. María A. Cabrera Arús, in this volume; *Los bolos en Cuba y una eterna amistad*, directed by Enrique Colina (Paris: RFO/Canal Overseas Productions, 2011).

39. *No tenemos derecho a esperar*, directed by Rogelio París (Havana: ICAIC, 1972).

40. "Terminan obreros industriales los dos primeros edificios construidos en Alamar con plus trabajo," *Granma*, November 2, 1971, 1; Lidice Valenzuela, "El moderno pueblo que los constructores del regional Escambray terminaron en La Yaya, en homenaje al Che Guevara," *Granma*, October 11, 1971, 3.

41. Noel Nicola, Pablo Milanés, and Silvio Rodríguez, "Cuba Va!," on *Grupo de Experimentación Sonora 4*, Areíto Records LD-3482, 1976, LP; Cabrera Arús; Susan Buck-Morss, *Dreamworld and Catastrophe: The Passing of Mass Utopia in East and West* (Cambridge, MA: MIT Press, 2000), as cited in Loss, *Dreaming in Russian*, 6.

42. Lisandro Otero, "Cibernetica: ¿Segunda revolución industrial?," *Revolución y Cultura* 1, no. 11 (1968): 3; Jorge Pérez-López, *The Economics of Cuban Sugar* (Pittsburgh: University of Pittsburgh Press, 1991), 69; Juan Varela Pérez, "Millonarios todos los operadores de combinadas KTP-1 que cortan para los centrales de la Habana," *Granma*, June 5, 1978, 1.

43. For example, see Miguel Cossío Woodward, *Sacchario* (Havana: Casa de las Américas, 1970).

44. *La nueva escuela*, directed by Jorge Fraga (Havana: ICAIC, 1974).

45. Magali García Moré, "Comenzarán a construir la primera central electronuclear en nuestro país en los años 1977–78," *Granma*, February 27, 1975, 1; Jonathan Benjamin-Alvarado, "Cuba's Nuclear Power Program and Post–Cold War Pressures," *Non Proliferation Review* (Winter 1994): 18–26. Dubbed the "Project of the Century," it was mothballed in the early 1990s, incomplete.

46. Arqueles Morales, "Trabajo voluntario," *Revista Casa de las Américas* 60 (May–June 1970): 100–103; "¡Un cubano en el cosmos!," *Granma*, September 19, 1980, 1, 8; Marta Denis Valle, "La gran noticia hacia 30 años: ¡Un cubano en el cosmos!," *Cubadebate*, September 19, 2010, http://www.cubadebate.cu/noticias/2010/09/19/la-gran-noticia -hace-30-anos-¡un-cubano-en-el-cosmos/#.VWEyxouyjwI.

47. Víctor Casaus, "Introducción a la historia de Cuba," *La Gaceta de Cuba* 146 (June 1976): 25.

48. Fidel Castro, "Discurso pronunciado por el Comandante en Jefe Fidel Castro Ruz, Primer Secretario del Comité Central del Partido Comunista de Cuba y Primer Ministro del Gobierno Revolucionario, en la clausura del II Congreso de la Unión de Jóvenes Comunistas, efectuada en el teatro de la CTC-Revolucionaria," April 4, 1972, http://www .cuba.cu/gobierno/discursos/1972/esp/f040472e.html.

49. "Discurso pronunciado por el Comandante en Jefe Fidel Castro Ruz . . . en el Acto Central en Conmemoración del XXII Aniversario del Ataque al Cuartel Moncada, efectuado en la Ciudad de Santa Clara, Las Villas."

50. Silvio Rodríguez, "La era está pariendo un corazón," on *Cuando Digo Futuro*, Areíto and Fonomusic Records, 89.2070/8, 1984 reissue [1977 original], LP.

51. Aníbal Escalante, "Del Grito de Yara a la Declaración de la Habana," *Cuba Socialista* 1, no. 2 (1961): 1–9; Blas Roca, "Nueva etapa de la Revolución Cubana," *Cuba Socialista* 2, no. 5 (1962): 38–53; Rafael Rojas, "Tres relatos sobre el origen del comunismo en Cuba," *Libros del Crepúsculo* (blog), November 21, 2014, http://www.librosdelcrepusculo.net /2014/11/tres-relatos-sobre-el-origen-del.html.

52. "Fidel en la Universidad de Concepción," *Granma*, November 19, 1971, 4.

53. "Fidel en la CUT de Chile," *Granma*, November 23, 1971, 4. Such views would continue to hold purchase in a number of published reflections into the late 1970s and early 1980s. See Carlos Rafael Rodríguez, *Cuba en el tránsito al socialismo, 1959–1963* (Havana: Editora Política, 1979); Antonio Núñez Jiménez, *En marcha con Fidel*, vols. 1–4 (Havana: Editorial Letras Cubanas, 1982).

54. A prior, intermediary point in this shift can be found in Castro's speech on Moncada's twentieth anniversary. On that occasion, he claimed, "Some of us, even before the 10th of March, 1952 [Batista's coup], had arrived at the intimate conviction that the solution to Cuba's problems had to be revolutionary . . . and that the objective had to be socialism." Here, however, Castro did not refer to himself specifically, or even to the attackers at Moncada. Thereafter he repeated the idea that Cuba had "awakened" to a socialist trajectory after 1959. See "Discurso pronunciado por el Comandante en Jefe Fidel Castro Ruz, Primer Secretario del Comité Central del Partido Comunista de Cuba y primer Ministro del Gobierno Revolucionario, en el acto central en conmemoracion del XX aniversario del ataque al Cuartel Moncada, efectuado en el antiguo cuartel convertido hoy en escuela," July 26, 1973, http://www.cuba.cu/gobierno/discursos/1973/esp /f260773e.html.

55. "Discurso Pronunciado por el Comandante en Jefe Fidel Castro Ruz . . . en el acto central en conmemoración del XXII aniversario del ataque al Cuartel Moncada, efectuado en la ciudad de Santa Clara, Las Villas."

56. Fidel Castro, "Editorial: Cuba Socialista," *Cuba Socialista* 1, no. 1 (1961): 3.

57. Raúl Castro was a member of the PSP's Youth League in the early 1950s. President Oswaldo Dorticós, a longtime PSP member, also served as coordinator for the 26th of July in Cienfuegos. For the PSP's declarations on Moncada, see "Batista Opens Terror Drive on Unions, CP," *Daily Worker*, August 5, 1953; "Fascist Terror Grips Cuba; Communists Ask U.S. Labor for Aid," *Daily Worker*, August 10, 1953. After that point the PSP's position on armed struggle wobbled between acceptance and rejection. Caridad Massón Sena, "El Partido Socialista Popular y la Revolución Cubana,"

Revista Caliban 7 (April–June 2010), http://www.revistacaliban.cu/articulo.php?
article_id=82&numero=7#_edn16.

58. Members of the 26th of July and other anti-Batista movements who did not agree
with the alliance with the PSP went on to populate a number of early anti-Castro organizations. Within the political front of the Revolution, meanwhile, the 1962 conflict
over PSP member Aníbal Escalante's *sectarismo*, the 1964 trial of Marcos Rodríguez, and
the 1968 arrests of the so-called *microfracción* (also led by Escalante) all derived from
lingering disputes between PSP leaders and other revolutionary factions. See Lillian
Martínez Pérez, *Los hijos de Saturno: Intelectuales y revolución en Cuba* (Mexico, D.F.:
FLACSO, 2006), 42–45, 64; Miguel Barroso, *Un asunto sensible: Tres historias Cubans de
crimen y traición* (Madrid: Random House Mondadori, 2010); Guerra, *Visions of Power*,
294–95.

59. "Documentos del Primer Congreso del Partido Comunista de Cuba, del Informe
Central del PCC al Primer Congreso, presentado por el Compañero Fidel Castro Ruz,
Primer Secretario del PCC," *Revista Casa de las Américas* 95 (March–April 1976): 13–14.

60. "Documentos del Primer Congreso," 18; Karl Marx, *The 18th Brumaire of Louis
Bonaparte* (1852; Rockville, MD: Wildside Press, 2008), 15.

61. The thesis that Castro was "communist all along" was repeated thereafter on
multiple occasions. See "La estrategia de Moncada," *Revista Casa de las Américas* 109
(July–August 1978): 31. "Before the tenth of March [Batista's coup]," Castro says bluntly
in this published interview, "I was already a communist."

62. Michael Chanan, *Cuban Cinema* (Minneapolis: University of Minnesota Press,
2004), 359.

63. *El hombre de Mainsinicú*, directed by Manuel Pérez (Havana: ICAIC, 1973);
Chanan, *Cuban Cinema*, 359.

64. "Conversando con nuestros cineastas: Manuel Pérez, joven director de El hombre
de Mainsinicú y Río negro," *El Caimán Barbudo* 141 (September 1979): 16–18.

65. *Patty-Candela*, directed by Rogelio París (Havana: ICAIC, 1976). Patty was the CIA's
code name for the operation. "Operation Candela," or "Fire," was the Cuban counterin-
telligence response.

66. *El brigadista*, directed by Octavio Cortázar (Havana: ICAIC, 1977).

67. John Ramírez, "El Brigadista: Style and Politics in a Cuban Film," *Jump Cut* 35
(April 1990): 2.

68. *Río negro*, directed by Manuel Pérez (Havana: ICAIC, 1977).

69. *Guardafronteras*, directed by Octavio Cortázar (Havana: ICAIC, 1980); *Leyenda*,
directed by Rogelio París (Havana: ICAIC, 1981). The latter, for instance, offered a flashy
postmortem on the life of a fictional Cuban double agent in the United States, complete
with a synthesizer-drenched opening theme.

70. Chanan, *Cuban Cinema*, 395.

71. Seymour Menton, "La novela de la Revolución Cubana, fase cinco, 1975–1987," *Revista Iberoamericana* 56, nos. 152–53 (1990): 913–32; Fornet, *El 71*, 93–103; Duanel Díaz
Infante, "Hasta sus últimas consecuencias: Dialécticas de la Revolución cubana," PhD
diss., Princeton University, September 2012, 197–263; Stephen Wilkinson, *Detective Fiction in Cuban Society and Culture* (Bern, Switzerland: Peter Lang International Academic

Publishers, 2006), 109–58. Beginning in 1972 the Ministry of Interior sponsored an annual literary competition devoted to the genre.

72. Luis Rogelio Nogueras, *Y si muero mañana* (Havana: Ediciones Unión, 1978). The book won a UNEAC prize in 1977 and was later turned into a radio novel for Radio Progreso in 1980. The "Plan Torres" is an obvious analogy to Miami's "Plan Torriente" of 1970, a notorious, highly public exile campaign that proved mostly hot air.

73. Enrique Álvarez Jané, *Algo que debes hacer* (Havana: UNEAC, 1977); "Algo que debe ser un homenaje," *Verde Olivo*, November 4, 1979, 58–59.

74. *En silencio ha tenido que ser*, directed by Jesus Cabrera (Havana: Instituto Cubano de Radio y Televisión, Ministerio del Interior, 1979).

75. Víctor Martín Borrego, "En silencio ha tenido que ser: Ejemplo de buena calidad," *El Caimán Barbudo* 138 (June 1979): 24.

76. *Julito el pescador*, directed by Jesus Cabrera (Havana: Instituto Cubano de Radio y Televisión, Ministerio del Interior, 1980).

77. Carlos Puebla y sus Tradicionales, "Y en eso llegó Fidel," on *Canciones Revolucionarias*, Areíto Records EPA-10008, 1965, LP.

78. Michael Kackman, *Citizen Spy: Television, Espionage, and Cold War Culture* (Minneapolis: University of Minnesota Press, 2005), 3, 5. Just as early spy series in the United States counted on the close collaboration of the FBI, Cuban counterparts in the 1970s often counted on the support of the Cuban military and the Ministry of Interior.

79. John Corner, *Television Form and Public Address* (New York: St. Martin's Press, 1995), quoted in Kackman, *Citizen Spy*, 5. In addition to Corrieri, other recurring male leads in this era include Mario Balmaseda and Patricio Wood. For an example of their socialist celebrity, see "Mario, protagonista de Balmaseda," *Verde Olivo*, June 3, 1979, 56–57.

80. *Un día de noviembre*, directed by Humberto Solás (Havana: ICAIC, 1972).

81. The movie's editor later stated that if ICAIC head Alfredo Guevara had screened the picture when it was finished in 1972, Solás and others may have suffered the "parametrización" (a Cuban euphemism for layoffs and ostracism) faced by "troublesome" creative types during the height of the *quinquenio gris*. Fornet, *El 71*, 131.

82. Roberto José, "Un film de archivo," *Caimán Barbudo* 134 (February 1979): 22–23.

83. See the textbook currently used in Cuban high schools, which devotes scarce pages to the 1970s compared to the 1960s: José C. Cantón Navarro and Arnaldo Silva León, *Historia de Cuba, 1959–1999: Liberación nacional y socialismo* (Havana: Editorial Pueblo y Educación, 2009). For a new critical appraisal of the decade, see Emily Kirk, Anna Clayfield, and Isabel Story, eds., *Cuba's Forgotten Decade: How the 1970s Shaped the Revolution* (Lanham, MD: Rowman and Littlefield, 2018).

84. Andrew Robinson, "Alain Badiou: The Event," *Ceasefire*, December 15, 2014, https://ceasefiremagazine.co.uk/alain-badiou-event.

85. Exceptions requiring further research may include Cuba's military intervention in the Angolan Civil War, beginning in 1975, and the 1979 triumph of the Sandinistas in Nicaragua. For a generation of Cuban servicemen well into the 1980s, Angola did prove a revolutionary trial by fire, though one far from home and thus generating trauma as well as pride. The victory of the Sandinistas, meanwhile, sparked revolutionary imagina-

tions, particularly for those Cubans who went to Nicaragua to work. But from home that excitement would have also been vicarious, as events in Nicaragua replayed the early struggles Cubans had already been through. In 1979, another event did arguably shift many Cubans' outlook on the world, though not in a "revolutionary" direction: the visit to the island of 100,000 Cuban exiles, bearing all manner of gifts for their relatives from the capitalist world. See Michael J. Bustamante, "Confronting (and Forgetting) Return: The *Visitas de la Comunidad* of 1979," paper presented at the Annual Meeting of the American Studies Association, Chicago, Illinois, November 9–12, 2017.

86. See, for example, "Los desesperantes" [The desperate ones], *Detrás de la fachada* [Behind the Façade], director unknown (Havana: Instituto Cubano de Radio y Televisión, [1977?]), which includes sketches satirizing the culture of waiting in line to acquire rationed goods. *Detrás de la fachada*, a comedy about relationships between neighbors in a nondescript Havana apartment building, first aired on Cuban television in 1957. After Cuban television was nationalized, the show continued airing with an evolving cast of actors through 1987.

87. Lillian Guerra, "'*Somos felices aquí*': The Revolutionary Theater State and the Mariel Crisis, 1971–1980," unpublished manuscript, 2015.

88. On the challenges of historicizing memory struggle through oral history, see Allistair Thompson, "Memory and Remembering in Oral History," in *The Oxford Handbook of Oral History*, edited by Donald A. Ritchie (Oxford: Oxford University Press, 2011), 77–95.

89. Rachel Weiss, *To and from Utopia in the New Cuban Art* (Minneapolis: University of Minnesota Press, 2011), 33.

11. "Here, Everyone's Got *Huevos*, Mister!"

NATIONALISM, SEXUALITY, AND COLLECTIVE VIOLENCE
IN CUBA DURING THE MARIEL EXODUS

———

ABEL SIERRA MADERO

Get out! Show your feet, worms, and we'll chop them off! Get out,
parasites and scum! My city, so beautiful and clean without lumpens or
queens! Out rats! Be afraid, weaklings, the people have the power! Traitors,
rats, show yourselves, just like that! Our motherland, so clean and clear, get
the trash out of here! Traitors and opportunists, you'd sell your soul for a pair
of blue jeans! Pansies beware—don't mess with the people! Cuba, how
wonderful she is, even more wonderful without those worms!
— "Anthology of the People's Slogans at the
March of the Fighting People"

The inflammatory messages in the epigraph, published on April 23, 1980, appeared in a collection of 100 chants compiled by the newspaper *Granma*, the
official publication of the Cuban Communist Party. They were included as part
of an invitation to a mass assembly to be celebrated on May 1 called the Marcha del Pueblo Combatiente (March of the Fighting People). These slogans
sustained and rationalized a campaign that the Cuban government promoted
to counteract the crisis unleashed by the thousands of Cubans who had recently stormed the Peruvian embassy to request political asylum. After the
Peruvian diplomats refused to hand over those who had entered the embassy,
the Cuban government withdrew its security forces, and in less than forty-

eight hours, more than ten thousand people occupied the facility in the hopes of leaving Cuba. These events initiated an emigration crisis that culminated in the exodus of more than 120,000 Cubans to the United States through the port of Mariel between April 15 and October 31, 1980.

The revolutionary government used the circumstances surrounding Mariel to reinforce processes of national inclusion and exclusion. The "Marielitos" were labeled as nonpatriotic in a narrative that strategically hijacked sexuality, criminality, vagrancy, and other marginalized categories to its advantage. At the same time, the mass exodus provoked suspicion among a sector of the Cuban exile community that distinguished itself from the revolutionary subject on the basis of economic success and social class.

Here, I offer an analysis of the violent, collective actions known as the "acts of repudiation" that were carried out against neighbors, colleagues, and other citizens who demonstrated explicit interest in abandoning the country during the Mariel exodus. Generally the history of these violent actions is relegated to footnotes or reference sections in the books, documentaries, and memoirs that have been published and continue to be published about Mariel. Indeed, academic analysis of the topic has been incredibly scarce. There is no text that deals with the phenomenon of the "acts of repudiation" as its central point of analysis. Such neglect explains the ambiguous ways in which this event has historically been read in and outside Cuba.[1]

In this essay, I consider the acts of repudiation through a more general framework of collective violence—organized by and with the consent of the Cuban state—in order to secure the state's hegemony and manage the crisis generated by the mass exodus. As I will show, these acts patterned a specific type of political violence that differed from that employed by other, concurrent Latin American dictatorships. Even if Cuba did not orchestrate mass disappearances and assassinations as did other countries around the region, we should not underestimate the impact and reach of the acts of repudiation to which thousands of people were subjected during the Mariel boatlift in 1980. Many victims of these attacks, and even eyewitnesses, remember them as horrific and barbaric. By situating these acts of collective violence within a broader framework, we can likewise locate the Cuban case within a larger, more global context.

As the social psychologist Omar Shahabudin McDoom explains, interpretations of collective violence often ascribe a rationale to leaders or elites, while portraying the common people as capable only of spontaneous, emotionally triggered responses.[2] McDoom signals that such an inference tends to privilege the decisions of elites and underestimate the role of the masses in intergroup conflicts. This disregard presumes that elites can strategically manipulate the emotions of the masses but that the populace cannot react in unexpected ways or in opposition.[3] McDoom proposes a synthesis of both focal points because, as he asserts, the rational and the affective are inextricable.

McDoom deploys the concept of "group polarization" to explain how collective violence is almost always preceded by a specific series of processes. As such, he emphasizes intergroup "boundary activation," the construction of an "outgroup negativity," "outgroup homogenization," and "cohesion" among the members of the privileged groups, who are simultaneously required to pass certain tests of loyalty within their own circle.[4] These activities make up the fundamental elements in understanding the psychological foundations of collective violence.

The acts of repudiation that were organized in 1980 against people wanting to flee the country fit into a longer trajectory of political demonization on the island. These violent acts stemmed from a synthesis of biopolitical notions present in official revolutionary ideology. A discourse of animalization dehumanized the thousands of people who wanted to leave the country by representing them as a dangerous species. Simultaneously, homophobic discourse gained momentum, contributing to a feminization and criminalization of the political Other. In both instances, the national political body was being reimagined, its ideological boundaries reconstituted. Even so, the connection between nationalism and sexuality had a long history, stretching back to the 1960s, when it became embedded in the collective imagination. Since then, it had also yielded concrete political initiatives, ranging from the creation of a criminal profile and institutional purges to the founding of forced labor camps that were allegedly designed for rehabilitation and reeducation.

In 1980, confronting a crisis of political legitimacy, the Cuban government began to rely on this formulation of a heteronormative nationalism once more. As in other contexts, extreme circumstances helped to activate the intersection of nationalism and sexuality all the more visibly. The Mariel exodus marked the most significant crisis of legitimacy that the Cuban government had ever confronted.

In this sense, the acts of repudiation constituted a state response to the crisis, and violent actions were justified in a climate similar to a "state of exception" or "state of emergency," which threw the law into temporary limbo.[5] The Cuban government has historically taken recourse to such a state of exception, albeit undeclared, in the context of a Cold War discourse of exceptionality. This status also afforded an important role to the notion of a *plaza sitiada* (state of siege). The "state of siege" idea, a rhetorical response to the battle with the United States, has served to both exacerbate nationalist sentiments and explain away the economic failures of the Cuban model. Likewise, it has served to justify the absence of certain democratic standards in Cuban society and to invalidate internal opposition.

Following this analytical approach, this essay deconstructs the ideological and affective frameworks that grounded the acts of repudiation committed during the Mariel exodus. I am primarily interested in the heteronormative, nationalist discourses that actively intervened in the invention of the Marielitos and contributed to the legitimization of violence as a socially acceptable political practice. As part of that discussion, I will tie together different kinds of sources that complement my analysis of the messages and images that state propaganda generated in response to the crisis.

Few genres simplify and mobilize political discourses as effectively as chants, slogans, and humor, due to the affective and layered meanings that they open up. With this in mind, I will pay special attention to how the comic weekly paper *Palante* covered the events in the Peruvian embassy as well as the slogans utilized in mass mobilizations and acts of repudiation. I will also use a series of interviews conducted in Miami and Havana with people who experienced the mass exodus from different perspectives. Finally, I will address debates in the United States that attempted to explain the crisis and contributed to the polarization of exile politics. I am especially interested in the depictions of the exodus and state-sanctioned homophobia offered by the magazines *Areíto* and *Mariel*, two intellectual projects with very different visions of the 1980 crisis.

Areíto brought together mainly left-leaning Cuban and Cuban American intellectuals and academics. They displayed a romanticized vision of the Revolution and embraced a critical vision of the "historic exile" community that had emigrated to the United States in the 1960s. Members of this earlier migration wave manifested a critical and confrontational approach toward the Cuban government, in some cases due to economic losses stemming from revolutionary directives. *Areíto* members, on the other hand, advocated for a more fluid relationship between the island's government and the Cuban diaspora. Through *Mariel*, intellectuals, writers, and artists who abandoned the country during the boatlift were also able to cohere as a collective. It is impossible to understand the tensions and political controversies attached to the exodus, as well as its impact outside Cuba, without incorporating the discussions and interpretations generated by both groups.

Though it is difficult to trace political practices similar to the acts of repudiation in Cuba before 1959, some sources indicate that acts of collective violence against specific citizens were utilized in several historical moments.

In an article published in the magazine *Cuba Internacional* (September 1988), the journalist Alberto Rubiera recalled that in December 1949 he participated in an "acto de repulsa" (act of repulsion) against a group of Spanish poets in Havana's Ateneo. In that building, which now hosts the Institute of Literature and Linguistics, several Francoist poets, among them Antonio de Zubiaurre, were scheduled to participate in an event. Rubiera recounts that a few leftist students decided to sabotage the occasion. Among them were Antonio Núñez Jiménez and Raúl Valdés Vivó, who gave the following instructions: "We should find some eggs and tomatoes—preferably rotten. Then, dressed as formally as possible—with suit, collar, and tie for men—we should arrive at the Ateneo between 8:15 and 8:30 p.m. and take up different sections of the assembly hall. Of course, in our pockets—or handbags—we will have our foul smelling projectiles."[6] According to Rubiera, it was Valdés Vivó who stood up and shouted several slogans as he "launched an egg and a tomato toward the presiding guests with enviable aim. . . . A full-out battle shortly followed in which we took down the fascists one after another."[7]

During the 1950s, through similar measures taken against politicians and intellectuals, we can trace the act of repudiation as part of a Cuban political tradition. On October 7, 1955, the journalist and politician Carlos Márquez Sterling participated in the program *Ante la Prensa* (Face the Press) on CMQ-Television. When he was finished, he was attacked by a group of youths who threw eggs and other objects at him. In a letter dated October 12, the public relations director of CMQ, Arnaldo Shewerert, sent his apologies to Márquez Sterling for the aggression and attached a statement broadcast the same day in their *Tome Nota* (Take Note) segment to explain what had happened. The statement, referencing a similar assault three years earlier, read, "The assault on CMQ's [radio program] Universidad del Aire—provoked by the events of March 10 [1952]—caused just indignation. Young regime sympathizers went at that time to throw rotten eggs at doctor [Jorge] Mañach. No less indignation is felt today when upon leaving last night from Radiocentro—from the program 'Ante la Prensa,' to which he had been the invited guest—doctor Carlos Márquez Sterling, leader of the Free Ortodoxo Party, was attacked by small groups that launched eggs and other objects at him."[8]

That both Mañach and Márquez Sterling were attacked with eggs is interesting, considering that they were victims of different political groups. This aspect is significant not only because eggs were also used in acts of repudiation during the Mariel boatlift but because it suggests that we cannot assign historical responsibility for developing these types of practices to a specific partisan tendency. In the case of Mañach, the motivation behind the attack must have been his rejection of the invitation extended by Fulgencio Batista to celebrate his arrival to power via a coup d'état on March 10, 1952. However, the attack on Márquez Sterling came from factions of the Ortodoxo Party, part of the opposition to the Batista regime. The note broadcast on CMQ included some of Márquez Sterling's comments, which assured viewers that it was "a rude act of Ortodoxo branches" that were hostile toward him.[9]

One of the first events that can be read as an act of repudiation during the revolutionary period was carried out in June 1959 against one of Cuba's oldest newspapers, the *Diario de la Marina*, which was at odds with the revolutionary government until its closure in 1960. *El Mundo* reported the attack in an editorial: "An incident condemnable in every respect occurred last Monday afternoon as several trucks filled with people arrived in front of the building of our esteemed colleagues at 'Diario de la Marina' hurling slurs against its director and the staff that work there."[10] The text assured the reader that, though the crowd shouted provocations, there was no physical violence against the journalists or staff. Even so, relevant to this discussion, the incident introduced a new mode of state political violence that would become even more visible in 1980.

The journalist Luis Conte Agüero—who had presided over the amnesty committee that pushed for Fidel Castro's 1955 release after the Moncada Barracks attack two years earlier—recalls in his book *America against Communism* that, in March 1959, he tried to read a letter addressed to his former ally in front of the CMQ cameras. In the letter he accused Castro of being a communist and ruining the revolution. According to Agüero, the street where the station was located was then overtaken by Communist Party brigades known as "fuerzas de choque," a few leaders of the 26th of July Movement, and the political police, who moved to prevent his entry into the building.[11] The car that the journalist was traveling in was attacked and he barely managed to escape. Only days later he took asylum in an embassy and then fled the country.

In 1961 Conte Agüero toured various countries in Latin America to offer his critical perspective on the Revolution. However, in many of the forums where he was presenting, he was booed and attacked by protesters sympathetic to Fidel Castro and his Revolution. In Montevideo the newspaper *El Debate* detailed the "lamentable spectacle" that greeted a planned debate about Cuba. Ultimately, the event could not be held because "a group of well-trained sycophants began to whistle and shout insults at the orator."[12] For its part, the newspaper *La Plata* characterized those who shouted at Conte Agüero as a "regimented communist claque" with "known tactics" and chants to shut the speaker up, including exclamations of "To the firing squad!," among others. With the exception of the Communist-affiliated *El Popular*, most press coverage of the incident insisted that such practices belonged to the "uncultured radicals of extremist violence" foreign to "the country's democratic life."[13]

Conte Agüero contended that the actions against him were part of a broader international Communist strategy. The fact that the protesters used practically the same chants and practices in each place was evidence enough for him. These actions suggest that, since the beginning, support for the Cuban Revolution in various regions of Latin America was accompanied by a transnationalization of the act of repudiation as a mode of political agitation and ideological support.[14]

Despite these antecedents, however, the act of repudiation marked a departure from other forms of state violence within both the pre-1959 Republican tradition and the early revolutionary period. The Gerardo Machado (1925–33) and Fulgencio Batista (1952–59) dictatorships, for example, were marked by disappearances, assassinations, and physical torture. In the early 1960s political violence continued to evolve, as in the reliance of the revolutionary government on televised shootings, summary judgments, and institutional purges. In 1980, however, the increasingly prevalent act of repudiation began to move away from other modalities of state violence, as we will see.

"Get Out! Get Out!": Acts of Repudiation and Collective Violence during the Mariel Exodus

After two weeks occupying the Peruvian embassy, the crowd of more than ten thousand began to return to their homes, and the government granted official access to the Mariel port to anyone who wanted to leave the country. Subsequently, and without precedent in Cuban history, public places, work centers, and homes became the sites of a violent crusade carried out with the total consent of authorities. Some testimonies even portray the situation as marked by violence from its very beginning, when a crowd broke into the Peruvian embassy and the building was besieged with people chanting and throwing rocks and eggs at those inside.[15] The violence was such that the Cuban government had to send security to the site to bring the situation under control. Others claim that the acts of repudiation became a type of ritual organized by the Committees for the Defense of the Revolution (CDRs). This institution was designed by Fidel Castro at the beginning of the 1960s to ensure more efficient political control in neighborhoods. The committees surveilled subjects who were considered enemies of the Revolution. This organization functioned as a "lateral power" of the state apparatuses, meddling in even the smallest details of people's daily lives.[16]

Apparently, though, the CDRs' role in the acts of repudiation was grounded in people's relationships with their neighbors. The journalist Mirta Ojito, who left the country as a teenager during the Mariel boatlift, recounts in her book, *Finding Mañana: A Memoir of a Cuban Exodus*, the moment that her family abandoned their house. According to Ojito, the police arrived at their home and proceeded to inventory everything inside. The officials suggested to a neighbor that she find a group to "fix something up for these people." This "something" turned out to be an act of repudiation. The neighbor, however, who was an army lieutenant and belonged to a family of army officials, refused: "No one touches this family. I watched these girls grow up."[17]

Ojito's testimony points to the participation of several different groups in the acts of repudiation. As we will see, this was not an isolated case. Luis Nodarse was president of his local CDR in 1980. In a recent interview, he recounted that a woman raised her hand in a meeting and began to encourage people to go throw eggs at a couple that lived down the block. "I told her to go buy the eggs and throw them, but not to expect me to be there," Nodarse said. It was in that moment that Nodarse became disillusioned with the Revolution. "I believe that is when my rupture with the Revolution began. And I said, 'I won't have anything to do with this.' It was from that moment. That was vile, simply put. They played on the worst human instincts," he concluded.[18]

For Nodarse, the attacks against potential deserters had an antecedent in the policies employed by the Cuban government during the 1960s. At that time, people who wished to leave Cuba were forced to perform labor that authorities deemed appropriate in order to receive their exit permits. Reeducation and rehabilitation laws were put in place to justify these measures, which sent thousands of people to agricultural labor camps or assigned them to scrub floors, sweep streets, clean pig pens, or do construction. Similarly, between 1965 and 1968 many young people who had shown interest in leaving the country ended up in the forced labor camps known as Military Units to Aid Production. About thirty thousand men were sent to these camps—including homosexuals, religious devotees, and criminals—under the law of Obligatory Military Service.

If in the 1960s the rationale for punishing possible deserters centered around rehabilitation, that logic would change markedly during the Mariel exodus. The acts of repudiation and attacks against those who were leaving took the form of symbolic lynchings. Graffiti such as "A traitor lives here!" and "Get out, worms!" appeared on the houses of those wanting to leave, as Marianela Molina relayed in an interview.[19] According to Molina, dolls were used to simulate a hanging. The goal of these symbolic lynchings was to destroy people's reputation and prestige. It was not only state propaganda that fueled those acts; they required the coordinated efforts of political and mass organizations.

Symbolic lynchings sought to intimidate and punish those who were leaving while sending a clear signal to discourage others who wished to do the same. Molina encountered such events in her office, where people carried out acts of repudiation and took their targets "for walks" outside:

> Back then, groups of people took others outside—the targeted person would be walking and a whole whirlwind of people would gather behind them, screaming "Get out, get out." You could see the different groups of agitators in the street, and they would put in eight hours of work just for this. There was another case at my workplace when it was discovered that a female engineer was leaving and an old woman wrote up a poster and, with some others, forced the engineer to tack it onto her chest until she caught the bus, Route 2. I remember it as if it were yesterday. I don't really remember what the poster said, it could have said anything—gusana, traitor. I did go to that act of repudiation. I walked behind the engineer with my heart just breaking.[20]

All signs point to the fact that Party militants and members of the Communist Youth were the first to be compelled to carry out acts of repudiation before the practice became more generalized. This makes sense if we take into account how the revolutionary model had impacted modes of conceiving kinship within a nationalist brotherhood. Ideological ties between militants had supplanted, at least on a symbolic level, those between family and friends.[21] Communist militants, state functionaries, and military personnel had to renounce communication with their relatives abroad in order to maintain economic privileges and job posts. The Communist Party aimed to create a new family sustained by love of the Revolution and hatred of "counterrevolutionaries," which is to say, any political enemy. Consequently, membership in the Party was fundamental to guaranteeing collective intervention during the acts of repudiation. Esperanza Torres, an eyewitness during this historic moment, describes it in this way:

> If you were a Party supporter or in the Youth organization you had to go [to an act of repudiation] or else they would criticize you in the meetings and might even penalize you. At my workplace, not one person ever said no to an act of repudiation. I never said no, but when they came to pick up people, I threw myself into working to pretend like I had really important things going on so I didn't have to go. They came through the departments with a list to look for people and the buses were already outside to take you to an act of repudiation against someone you didn't even know. Every office carried out acts of repudiation on their employees, and neighbors did them in their neighborhoods. Other times, they announced the acts of repudiation when the workday ended. Then they brought in buses to take us to wherever the person lived. When we arrived there, they already had speakers set up and people shouting. The whole thing was barbaric.[22]

In 1980 Esperanza Torres worked in a ministry located on La Rampa, a stretch of one of Havana's most heavily trafficked streets. From her building, Torres claims to have seen several acts of repudiation, but what most impacted her was what the Cuban Institute of Radio and Television (ICRT) arranged for the actress Celeste del Mar: "They put her inside a big vat and rolled her from the ICRT downhill. Mobs followed behind screaming wildly like they weren't even human anymore. They called her 'thug!, traitor!, scum!'—the typical insults of that time. Ah, they came around banging cans and sticks like it was a conga while the poor girl was inside that tank rolling all over the street. After, they walked her back up holding her by the arms. All those acts of repudiation on La Rampa were terrible, but what happened to Celeste del Mar traumatized me for life."[23]

Acts of repudiation could last for days, preventing targeted individuals from leaving their houses for fear of being beaten. On some occasions, crowds would surround their homes and cut off people's access to gas and electricity. "The last days [in Cuba] were very tough," the actress Zobeida Castellanos commented to Jorge Ulla, director of the documentary *En sus propias palabras*

(In Their Own Words). "I couldn't leave the house and, in that way . . . they let us know, right? If we didn't leave the house and we stayed calm, then they wouldn't throw anything at us. Because, before, they were throwing rocks and eggs at us. . . . They were insulting us."[24]

Apparently it was not just unions and the CDRs that supported acts of repudiation. Schools also got involved. José Manuel García was thirteen in 1980 when, after class, the teacher asked the students to participate in one of these violent events at the house of a family that he knew. He described the situation: "I attended for a short time with a deep sense of shame and powerlessness. I felt forced to participate, at least publicly, as part of the crowd, in a brutal action against innocent people, knowing that my family could also be victims when our moment to leave arrived."[25]

The acts of repudiation were designed in such a way so as to create a lack of moral and ethical accountability that permitted mass participation and shared complicity. At the same time, the acts were driven by affective attachments and fidelity to the revolutionary process, activating relations of political favoritism with the state. Many individuals actively engaged in this violence to ensure and accumulate political and symbolic capital within institutions. After families abandoned the country, their houses and belongings were divided up by neighborhood assemblies or the Housing Institute (Instituto de la Vivienda). As such, many of the acts' participants benefited from these partitions.

Several other Caribbean contexts had already seen similar practices of political patronage and exclusion. In the Dominican Republic under Rafael Trujillo, Robin Derby argues, the widespread practice of political denunciation created a liminal, anonymous space, a sort of bureaucracy in the "shadows." Within this parallel theater, citizens could embody and mobilize the state's repressive role to their advantage or simply become spectators of those shameful displays.[26]

What happened in Cuba was similar. The state and its institutions pressured citizens to denounce "counterrevolutionary acts."[27] Citizen informants for the Ministry of the Interior or the CDR were symbolically compensated, and each denunciation was taken into account as a "merit." Participants were distinguished in political and media discourse from the "chivatos" (snitches) who operated during the Batista dictatorship, although in reality they acted very similarly.[28] In Cuba the practice of denunciation, along with the act of repudiation, were constructed as instruments of political domination, a government tactic that contributed to the efficient exercise of power and shored up the hegemony of the governing elite.

In order to counteract images of the thousands of people who had shown interest in leaving the country, the Cuban government needed to mobilize citizens en masse to demonstrate public support for the regime. On April 19, 1980, a few weeks after the initial embassy takeover, the first March of the Fighting People took place. Millions of people paraded in front of the Peruvian embassy carrying posters and chanting well into the night.

Analysis of the chants and posters used during the acts of repudiation provides insight into the ways the national community imagined itself during the Mariel boatlift. If, at the beginning of the revolutionary process, emigrants were depicted as torturers, bourgeois, and exploiters in the media, by 1980 they were described as antisocial, delinquent, and sexual deviants, but above all as traitors and deserters.

It would be impossible to understand the acts of repudiation without taking into account the use of these labels in the political slogans coined during the Mariel exodus. Scholars have noted that slogans constitute a particular form of public discourse that serves to unify the collective voice, polarize public opinion, and simplify messaging to facilitate learning and assimilation.[29] For the scholar Elliott Colla, slogans cannot be read as spontaneous reflections of a collective sentiment; rather they are a strategy to instantiate such thought. Colla suggests that chants and slogans should not be analyzed from a solely textual perspective due to their performative nature—the fact that they are chanted and shouted by people in movement and in a coordinated mode in public spaces. But most important, these movements and demonstrations do not constitute a mere context for the production of meaning, but rather are themselves constitutive of the chants' text and content.[30]

This theoretical approach is fundamental to understanding the function of the slogans within the marches and public protests organized by the Cuban state during the Mariel crisis. In this sense, it is noteworthy that the rallies and acts of repudiation had a kind of soundtrack that heightened their drama and contributed to activating affective registers. One of the songs that accompanied many of the political movements and massive assemblies that the government convened and organized during this time was "Marcha del Pueblo Combatiente" (March of the Fighting People), with lyrics by Pepín Naranjo and music by José María Vitier. Sung by Osvaldo Rodríguez, a songwriter who took asylum in the United States in the 1990s, the song was a sort of war hymn that usually closed out political rallies at the time. According to Rodríguez, the Ministry of the Interior commissioned the song, and they were sent to record it immediately.[31] It included the following lyrics:

> The entire motherland shakes like the raging sea
> Its blood burns with moral rightness
> The courage of its wounded chest roars
> for he who aims to wrest away its life.

> The call to war has sounded
> The toll readies the nation's sons to action
> To fight for all they love
> For Cuba, with Fidel, our flag.
> The enemy always threatens
> to pulverize what we love,
> but fear never reaches our chest
> Here we defeat all tyrants
> and drive our lances into them
> This virile and sovereign nation!

The slogans and acts of repudiation formed part of a process that began with the discrediting of people who occupied the Peruvian embassy. There, the revolutionary government strategically filmed moments of tension provoked by overcrowding and the absence of water, food, and sanitary conditions. The overcrowding reached such a point that people even took over the roof. As days passed, the physical appearance of the occupiers significantly deteriorated and the media focused on criminal activity and people who brandished razors or displayed symbols on their clothes that connected them with the United States, such as American flags. Many of the people who experienced the occupation insist that the Cuban government infiltrated the buildings. Officials, they believed, sent criminals to create chaos and tarnish the image of the occupants.[32]

The Noticiero ICAIC Latinoamericano, a weekly newsreel directed by Santiago Álvarez and produced by the Cuban film institute (ICAIC), also fulfilled an important role in constructing a negative image of the people who stormed the Peruvian embassy. Álvarez closely followed and selectively documented these events. If in only forty-eight hours more than ten thousand people had penetrated the diplomatic mission, the ICAIC newsreel highlighted the fact that more than *one million* Cubans had hit the street in only *thirteen hours* to show support for the Revolution. Their coverage described the people in the Peruvian embassy in a biased way and cut shots of them with dark music and images of rats.[33]

In this way, official propaganda began to export a negative image of those at the embassy while simultaneously injecting content and meaning into acts of violence. For his part, Castro transformed dissatisfaction with his governance into a question of sovereignty and national security. He reactivated revolutionary nationalism, once again grounded in conflict with the United States, and established a connection between deserters and the dark inner workings of the U.S. government. On May 1, 1980, Castro gave a speech in which he thanked the United States for having performed "sanitation" services in receiving the Cuban emigrants.[34] This particular speech rested on three fundamental themes: (1) the military exercises that the U.S. Army was carrying out near the Cuban coast, (2) control of the naval base in Guantánamo, and (3) the cessation of U.S. spy flights carried out with SR-71 planes in Cuban airspace. This rhetoric helped to stoke fear of a perceived American threat among the population and encourage feelings of rejection toward those who wanted to abandon the country. In this context, acts of repudiation were constructed as a necessary defense against an enemy invasion. In some sense, this contributed to the restoration of governmental legitimacy and endowed mass marches and demonstrations of collective violence with a certain logic.

"Here, Everyone's Got *Huevos*, Mister!": Nationalism, Sexuality, and Political Humor

When it came to carrying out acts of repudiation, identifying subjects to target was easy because the Cuban government demanded documentation—safe conduct passes—from people leaving national territory. Such authorizations were obtained through formal applications in police stations, work centers, and processing centers that the government set up for this express purpose. By consolidating this information, the authorities could draft lists that allowed them to quickly enact concrete actions against those seeking exit permits.

However, not everyone who wanted to abandon the country could do so. The government restricted the exit of certain professionals, such as technicians and doctors, while favoring the departure of criminals in order to characterize the exodus as morally corrupt.[35] They released many people from behind bars. In addition, officials pressured citizens with a criminal record or those who were considered a "social danger" to leave.[36] What is more, evidence exists that the authorities took mentally ill patients from hospitals and clinics to force them out of the country.

In the documentary *Más allá del mar* (directed by Lisandro Pérez-Rey), for example, José Scull is interviewed in the American prison where he has been incarcerated since 1983 for murder charges. Scull claims that he was a prisoner in Cuba at the time of the Mariel boatlift and that authorities pressured him into abandoning the country. They released him from prison, he said, and sent him home to wait until he could embark.[37] Similarly, Roberto Saladrigas, another subject in the documentary, notes that the performance of criminality was required in the different centers set up by the government to grant safe conduct passes or exit permits. He says, "You can't just show up and say 'I want to leave, sign me up'—no, there had to be something wrong: my wife is a prostitute, I'm gay, and my daughter is a whore."[38]

Homosexuals were likewise integrated into the antisocial and criminal profiles that the state constructed to portray those who were fleeing. As such, many people who lacked any other reason to obtain exit permits tried to pass as homosexuals, since they allegedly made up the "weak" parts of the national body politic. In a June 14, 1980, speech, Castro detailed the components of this body. By that date, thousands of Cubans had already left for the United States through Mariel port. On this occasion, he insisted:

> There is no reason to be concerned about losing a few of these weak parts. We retain the muscles and bones of the people. This is what we hold on to—the strong parts (APPLAUSE). The people's strong parts are capable of anything. And these strong parts, of which there are many, must be respected because they have impressive force, as was shown during the mass struggles of April and May. We've kept, moreover, the brain and the heart and we still have our feet planted firmly on the ground (APPLAUSE). As for the weak parts, chock it up to plastic surgery (LAUGHTER).[39]

This flattening of the social and the political landscape into one "battlefield" sanctioned collective violence against defenseless citizens. Here, the violent act is compared to cosmetic reconstruction, to a political surgery performed on the national body. "We're talking about a show of force, but not simply for showing off," Castro explained. The leader also categorized the collective actions as a historical imperative. "It was necessary to show force!" he explained, adding, "We had to show the enemy and really teach the enemy that you don't mess with the People. We had to show that you cannot offend the People without punishment."[40]

The metaphor of the "weak" parts outlined by Castro was also used to integrate sexuality into the more general political field. In this rhetoric, homosexuals were categorized not only as deviants and perverts but also as "softies" and "weaklings." Consequently many citizens who could not get a safe conduct pass by other means, perhaps because of their profession, showed up at police headquarters claiming a homosexual identity.

On the affective level, Castro explained that the collective strength displayed during this time stemmed from the "hate that was expressed against the slacker, against the parasite, against the lumpen, against the antisocial."[41] It seems contradictory that hate could be consolidated and transformed into a positive, socially acceptable emotion during this crisis. However, the state-controlled press and media never actually showed the sieges on houses and attacks suffered by alleged deserters. Instead, they celebrated the grand rallies—the Marches of the Fighting People—that Castro often brought to a close with long speeches.

In order to represent and reinforce nationalism, Cuban media tested out a series of images and codified discourses within the sphere of political humor. Such practices aimed to normalize the negative aspects of the period as well as aestheticize state violence. For example, in the film *La marcha del pueblo combatiente* (March of the Fighting People), the filmmaker Santiago Álvarez used Elpidio Valdés, a popular cartoon character created by Juan Padrón. A symbol of *criollo* humor, Elpidio Valdés was a fictional Cuban army colonel who fought against Spain in the nineteenth century. Beginning in the late 1970s, he served as an important didactic and nationalist tool.[42]

"Here, everyone's got *huevos*, mister!" shouts Elpidio Valdés. The declaration, which riffs on the colloquial Cuban term for testicles (literally, "eggs"), is ripe with ideological meaning. It should not be read as peripheral or inconsequential. On the contrary, it codifies an imaginary that repackages masculinity and revolutionary identity while simultaneously representing national Otherness as profoundly feminized. This utterance ascribes moral qualities like bravery, force, and virility to the male sexual organs, here conflated with the entire collective. As such, the assertion of ample "huevos" echoed state doctrines and companion ideological formations, such as the idea of "revolutionary defiance" (*intransigencia revolucionaria*) that defined official domestic and foreign policy.

Besides a discourse of masculinity, the sentence plays with the rationing of food instated in Cuba from 1961 until today. In the commercial language of the island, when a product is "por la libre" it means that its sale is not regulated or rationed. The greater accessibility of such goods is important because eggs (*huevos*) were used repeatedly in acts of repudiation. The very fact that the eggs were charged with so much signifying power—and that *huevos* also connoted national masculinity—explains how well they fit into acts of repudiation. Throwing them at the bodies and homes of those who wanted to leave the country was considered an act of revolutionary affirmation.

FIG. 11.1. "Here, everyone's got *huevos*, mister!" Still from the documentary *La marcha del pueblo combatiente* (1980), special edition of the Noticiero ICAIC, directed by Santiago Álvarez.

Homophobic rhetoric characterized the very earliest press coverage of events at the Peruvian embassy. On April 7, 1980, the newspaper *Granma* published an editorial that noted, "Although in our country homosexuals are neither persecuted nor harassed, quite a few of them have taken up residence in the patio of the Peruvian embassy, alongside gamblers and drug addicts who can't find a good outlet for their vices here [in Cuba]. Exactitude, discipline and rigor are all at odds with softness, delinquency, vagrancy and parasitism."[43] This editorial formulates an ideological equivalency that produces an artificial unity among all occupants of the Peruvian embassy in order to simplify messaging and ease its dissemination and reception in Cuban society. It is not surprising, then, that many slogans and posters used during public demonstrations of support for the Cuban government deployed homophobia as a mobilizing resource.

Homophobic and hateful discourses, often relying on humor and recycled stereotypes, also circulated in other formats. The weekly paper *Palante*, a state-controlled outlet for humor and social critique, fulfilled an important role in this sense. This publication was oriented toward mass consumption, with the idea of filling everything—even people's leisure time—with political

FIG. 11.2. Homophobic cartoon published in *Palante* during the Mariel boatlift. It reads: "No More Competition! There are too many of *us* here, girls!" *Palante*, no. 29 (April 25, 1980): 2.

content. By simplifying political messaging and creating an ideological voice that complemented official rhetoric, *Palante* became not only an instrument of mass entertainment but also an arm of political and social control.

In April 1980 *Palante* joined the national crusade against the occupants of the Peruvian embassy and, once the Mariel port opened, against anyone who wished to leave the country. Homosexuals, though, were one of the fundamental targets of their attacks. On January 18, 1980, one day before celebrating the March of the Fighting People, *Palante* published a supplement entitled, "El ambientoso: Publicación inscripta como papel sanitario en la embajada" (The Troublemaker: Publication Registered as Toilet Paper in the Embassy).[44] The insert's homophobic headline, exploiting similar sounds in *muchas* (many girls/women) and *machos* (macho men), reads, "A la lucha, a la lucha, no somos machos; pero somos muchas" (Fight! Fight! We might not be men *machos*, but, girls, we're many)."

The piece sought to represent the Peruvian embassy as a scatological site: filthy and a world apart from the integrity of the social body. Here, the embassy exists outside the body politic, aligned with all that was outside, discarded, excreted, as Judith Butler might say. Butler notes that the scatological is a discursive strategy "by which Others become shit . . . for inner and outer worlds to remain utterly distinct."[45] The identification of these subjects with excrement and trash would prove a recurrent rhetorical strategy throughout the Mariel period.

Palante also recycled elements of the pervasive biopolitical notions in official discourse, with the aim of dehumanizing those who wanted to leave. From the beginning of the revolutionary process, Castro's speeches were directed toward the animalization of political enemies to portray them as "dangerous species."[46] In this context, the animal is a sort of device or, as Gabriel Giorgi would say, "a point or crossing between languages, images, and meanings from which the frames of signification are mobilized."[47] The transformation of political enemies into worms (*gusanos*), rats, and mosquitoes legitimized policies of social cleansing that were complemented by normative discourses of gender and sexuality.

However, the most prevalent rhetorical turn used in *Palante* and elsewhere during the Mariel boatlift depends on what Ernesto Laclau calls "chains of equivalence." This term is fundamental to understanding how the socialist state constructed its hegemony. For Laclau, the particular ideological formations preferred by these regimes—"the masses," "the people," or "the proletariat"—built on the erasure of strict class antagonisms, even as divergent or opposed interests persisted. To manage these tensions, the political elite implemented discursive strategies to "formally" preserve the class-based character of the construct (proletariat), while still creating a relation that exceeded class bounds (the people).[48] Among these discursive strategies, Laclau highlights "enumeration." Through enumeration, "chains of equivalence" are forged around opposite poles, contributing to the construction of antagonism between sectors.

The practice of enumeration can be found in Castro's speeches; it practically constitutes their rhetorical base. In this way, the people who wished to depart the country—like those who dissented from the revolutionary project—were integrated into a chain of equivalence also including vagrants, criminals, drug addicts, prostitutes, and homosexuals. This discourse condoned state-sponsored physical and symbolic violence wielded by the collective. Eventually—and still today—it came to function as a strategy of social and political control.[49]

Laclau argues that the construction of equivalences has a performative character. In this, the creation of unity between different sectors is not a mere discursive ornament but rather the very core of a political project.[50] Communist discourse used the symbolic figure of the "New Man" to link the revolutionary cause with an intrinsically "positive" chain of equivalence. In turn, a negative chain of equivalences tied together a symbolic national Otherness that deployed the term "lumpenproletariat" as its foundation.

Susana Peña, author of *¡Oye Loca! From the Mariel Boatlift to Gay Cuban Miami*, claims that many Cuban men utilized the figure of the *loca*, the dramatically effeminate gay man most persecuted within the Cuban political sys-

FIG. 11.3. Caricature published in the humor weekly *Palante*, which constructs a negative chain of equivalence around the occupants of the Peruvian embassy. The site and its inhabitants are identified with the scatological, with that which should be flushed away. *Palante*, no. 28 (April 18, 1980): 3.

tem, in order to get out of the country. As Peña notes, these men turned up in police stations dressed in tight pants and bright, extravagant garments, often with dyed hair and ostentatiously effeminate gestures.[51] The gay writer Reinaldo García Ramos, a founder of one of the most polemical cultural projects of the 1960s (Ediciones El Puente), recounts that, when he went to a police station to ask for an exit permit, there was a line of more than thirty people pretending to be gay in order to obtain safe conduct passes.[52]

This performance of homosexuality, however, did not go over the heads of Cuban authorities. It did not even escape Castro, who in a speech on May 1, 1980, referenced the topic: "Some little pansy like someone said (LAUGHTER), some scoundrel in disguise. You all know, the CDRs know this better than anybody, they know that some people like that lined up also, [and] by the way, those are the ones who are most irritating, the fakers."[53] In exporting "undesirables," the Cuban government wanted to prove that the mass exodus was not at all connected with a failure of the socialist model. This would also reinforce an image of Cuba as a virile, revolutionary nation and would prevent future conflict with such stigmatized groups.[54]

It is interesting that the performance and simulation of a homoerotic identity was used as a strategy by heterosexual men who wanted to get off the island and again by many who later found themselves in refugee camps in the United States. According to some sources, many homosexuals started to get out of refugee camps much earlier than other groups. This was largely due to the work of organizations that supported sexual freedom, including, among others, the Metropolitan Community Church, the National Gay Task Force, Gay Rights Advocates, Parents and Friends of Gays, Integrity (a gay Episcopalian organization), Dignity (a gay Catholic organization), and the Gay Community's Cuban Refugee Project. These organizations sought out funding in order to help gay Cubans.[55]

According to Michael Bergeron, editor in chief of *Gay Life*, these groups provided support by searching for sponsors who could offer employment, food, clothing, furniture, English lessons, or housing.[56] When single heterosexual men without sponsors found out that homosexuals got out of the camps faster, they started to simulate and claim a false gay identity. "Some straight refugees are overdoing it. In their eagerness to appear gay, they make themselves more flamboyant than the actual gays, who are in turn more flamboyant than their American counterparts," said a Metropolitan Community Churches official.[57]

From the Other Side of the Pond: The Mariel Generation and *Areíto* Magazine in the Representation of the Exodus and State Homophobia

Many of the Cuban refugees kissed American soil once they disembarked from their boats, thinking that the worst was behind them. They did not imagine that they would once again find themselves under automatic suspicion. The Cuban government's campaign to depict the refugees as criminals, delinquents, and "undesirables" had impacted American perceptions. One survey by the *Miami Herald* showed that only 17 percent of non-Hispanic whites thought that the arrival of the Cubans would benefit Miami-Dade County, while 68 percent thought the local impact would be negative.[58] It is within this context that the term "Marielito" appears—a category devised by the American press and the Cuban exile community to distance and differentiate themselves from the recently arrived refugees. Voices from the American academy contributed to the construction of this criminological and delinquent profile, largely reproducing the views of the Cuban government.

The Cuban (American) magazine *Areíto* was one such space that publicized this vision of the Mariel boatlift. In the mid-1970s *Areíto*, published in the

United States, brought together leftist Cuban and Cuban American intellectuals and academics. According to Román de la Campa, who formed part of the first cohort, the members of *Areíto* had become "resentful of the 1960s Cuban exile community, critical of U.S. imperial policies, and, at the same time, soft on the Revolution."[59]

That attitude carried over to *Areíto's* coverage of Mariel. In its pages, contributors argued that the Mariel exodus had nothing to do with a political or social crisis in Cuba, but was instead caused by external factors. As such, the publication helped to prevent damage to the image of the Revolution and its legitimacy. The acts of repudiation, for example, were presented as spontaneous actions sparked by the indignation of the masses. Lourdes Casal, a professor at Rutgers University and one of the most important participants in the *Areíto* project, explained them in this way: "Meanwhile, in the general population, an attitude of great indignation was developing against those who had camped out [in the Peruvian embassy] and particularly against those who, up until just weeks before, behaved as if they were true revolutionaries. These feelings generated the rallies of repudiation when the occupants returned to their houses. It was even necessary to warn against physical violence in those rallies, through the Committees for the Defense of the Revolution and other organizations—such was the population's state of mind and the hostility they harbored against those who decided to leave the country."[60] While trying to play down the violent content of the acts of repudiation, Casal also ignored the level of organization that went into them, preferring to think of them as spontaneous popular demonstrations.

Casal's analysis misses the fact that the mass mobilizations and demonstrations she describes were executed under the auspices of political organizations. Even today, these types of initiatives are subject to state decisions about the use of public resources. Without access to public transport, for example, none of these events could have succeeded. The level of organization was such that *Granma*, the official publication of the Cuban Communist Party, provided direction for the March of the Fighting People. The newspaper published maps, directions, and guidelines from the Organizing Commission, where they specified locations for participants to be picked up by state buses as well as particular messages to be chanted and clothing to be worn.[61]

In 1980 mass transportation was entirely run by the Cuban state, rendering the quick movement of masses of people a matter of official importance. Moreover, the state was Cuba's only employer at this time, which meant that collective participation in political rallies or acts of repudiation depended on bureaucratic calculation. Political officials selected workers who would participate in order to minimize economic and salary disruptions. From the design and printing of posters, to the sound system that broadcast speeches and chants; press, radio, and television coverage and the music used as a soundtrack—everything was orchestrated by government agencies. The acts of repudiation, therefore, cannot be imagined without the direct intervention of state power.

In contrast, Casal's *Areíto* article purposefully sought to defend the government's management of the crisis and construct a negative image of the people who occupied the Peruvian embassy. According to her account, the government at first tried to provide food for all of the embassy's occupants with dishes prepared by the luxurious kitchen at the Tropicana cabaret. She adds, "Many people went hungry because the behavior of the occupants began to deteriorate and criminals started to take over. The strongest, most violent men—the most lumpen subjects—were in control of the patio where the food arrived and took control of it, too."[62] This statement contrasts with the testimonies of various occupants of the Peruvian embassy. Many insist that the food offered by the government was not only bad but so scarce that many ended up eating whatever they could find, from mango leaves to raw potatoes.[63]

Areíto's support for the Cuban government became more militant when writers who had abandoned the country during the exodus—Reinaldo Arenas, Ana María Simo, René Cifuentes, and Reinaldo García Ramos, among others—began to gain visibility in the United States and cohere as a literary generation. These intellectuals founded the magazine *Mariel*, a literary and cultural project that debuted in the spring of 1983 and ran until the end of 1985. The leading article in the first issue of *Mariel* argued that the social content and political significance of the exodus had been erased by government propaganda, with "the enormous weight of terror and human discontent borne by the Mariel refugees . . . overshadowed by the most simplistic characterization of a tiny minority of them."[64]

A text from the first issue by García Ramos deserves special attention, since it can be read as a reply to various articles about the exodus published in the United States, such as "The CILC and the Mariel Generation" by Marifeli Pérez-Stable (*Areíto*, 1982). In her text, Pérez-Stable presents both the recently formed Committee of Intellectuals for the Liberty of Cuba (CILC), which aimed to draw attention to violations of human rights on the island, and the Mariel generation as members of a political lobby, aligned with projects that courted the Reagan administration in the political war against the Cuban Revolution.[65] "The ideological assumptions of CILC and the Mariel 'generation' are extraordinarily fragile," Pérez-Stable points out, since they lack the "political personality" that would bestow credibility on their arguments and guarantee their "influence beyond the present situation."[66]

García Ramos's answer to this text was directed to Pérez-Stable, but more generally to the *Areíto* group and its positioning vis-à-vis the Cuban Revolution:

> For them, Cuba isn't a nation, but a "charisma": an authoritarian and definitive voice that fills a pathetic void in need of flagellation. For them, Cuba is Fidel Castro. . . . If the fatherland is equivalent to the obligation to serve as a spokesperson for Fidel Castro, I do not have a fatherland and I don't want one. If the only way to be Cuban is to proclaim Fidel Castro as an intrinsic, eternal condition of our being, I was not born and did not live for 36 years in the same country where Miss Pérez-Stable wants to spend her ideological vacation.[67]

This would not be the last point of friction between *Areíto* and *Mariel*. Another conflict surfaced in October 1983, when the magazine *New York Native* published a dossier titled "Gay Latins" in which they included texts by Reinaldo Arenas and René Cifuentes about homophobia in Cuba. Both texts were preceded by a short essay titled "The Easy Convenience of Cuban Homophobia," signed by Ruby Rich, a journalist and member of the New York State Council on the Arts, and Lourdes Argüelles, a Cuban collaborator with *Areíto*. Rich and Argüelles insisted that the migration of gays turned political only during the Mariel exodus and that homophobic laws in the United States were relaxed for Cubans as a result of Cold War politics. Within the United States, they emphasized, "the stories that gay Cuban emigrants carry with them serve to feed 'Cubaphobia,'" thereby partaking in a "dirty Cold War." Rich and Argüelles accused the "new Mariel generation, composed by right-wing intellectuals," of using homophobia as "ammunition in the Cold War." Recognizing the possibility of antigay activity, they nonetheless minimized its extent: "We've heard of repression, suppression, and persecution for simply being gay, of jailing and discrimination. Some of these stories are undoubtedly true, at least in part."[68]

The text sought to remind the international community that, under U.S. law, refugee status was obtained on the basis of demonstrating political persecution in one's native country. "Cuba was and is a profoundly homophobic society; but people aren't jailed solely for homosexuality, they go to jail for common crimes, for robbery," the authors added.[69] These types of arguments have been consistently utilized to diminish and delegitimize the testimonies of Cuban refugees and to contest a characterization of the Revolution as totalitarian. Nonetheless, Rich and Argüelles did correctly argue that homosexuality was punishable by law in the United States at that time and could be an obstacle to entry into the country as well as to obtaining U.S. citizenship. Immigration policy evolved to receive gay Cuban refugees, in recognition of the fact that they came from a communist country, while other refugees—such as Haitians fleeing François Duvalier's dictatorship—were not afforded the same privileges.[70]

In the spring of 1984 *Mariel* published an issue dedicated to homosexuality in Cuba in which the editors hoped to include Rich and Argüelles's text. According to Ana María Simo and Reinaldo García Ramos, the editors proposed to translate and publish the article in its entirety along with *Mariel's* response, but Rich and Argüelles would not give their authorization. "It is really telling that these writers," Simo and García Ramos noted, "felt a certain inclination to talk about Cubans but not to Cubans . . . and they don't feel confident enough that their argument will hold for people who were actually born in Cuba, those who suffered the diverse forms of persecution that Castro eagerly enacted."[71]

However, in a recent conversation, Argüelles commented that, despite her support of *Areíto*, she was not "very close to the magazine's editorial team." She maintained some ideological differences with them because, in her words, "their knowledge of capitalism and American politics was very limited." "I was more radical," she added, "but I also had a critical vision of the Cuban Revolution, that was not accepted by some members of *Areíto* and made me feel out of place." These differences escalated to such a point, she claims, that some of her work on the topic of homophobia and homosexuality in Cuba was censored, never to be published in the magazine. Along these lines, she points to her text "Homosexuality, Homophobia, and Revolution: Notes toward an Understanding of the Cuban Lesbian and Gay Male Experience, Part I," written collaboratively with Rich and published by *Signs* in 1984. This article was first written in Spanish at the end of the 1970s for publication in *Areíto*. She believes, however, that "the text was rejected because it contained a critical vision of the Revolution."[72]

According to Argüelles, another article written at the peak of the Mariel exodus that critiqued the methods employed by the Cuban government, including the acts of repudiation, also went unpublished in *Areíto*. She concluded, "Those texts became problematic, both for those who had a more militant position in support of the Revolution and the right-wing exiles who attacked me for being communist, even though I was really an anarchist who critiqued both governments. Later on I came to understand that it's impossible to please God and the Devil at the same time."[73]

Epilogue

"Anyone who doesn't have Revolutionary genes, who doesn't have Revolutionary blood, who doesn't have a mind fit for Revolutionary ideas, who doesn't have a heart fit for Revolutionary effort and heroism: we don't want them, we don't need them in our country," Castro declared on May 1, 1980, during the March of the Fighting People.[74] In that speech, Castro deployed a series of biopolitical notions to construct affective and symbolic borders between those who were leaving and those who stayed. In this way, political belonging was defined by only two actions: stay or leave. No other option existed. Those who left automatically became traitors and were vulnerable to physical or symbolic attacks in public demonstrations and acts of repudiation.

Though thirty-five years have passed since then, we have recently seen how these acts have been recycled and implemented against dissenters and activists from the island's independent civil society. The act of repudiation, though deeply rooted in the revolutionary political imaginary, cannot be read solely as a tool of social control wielded by the Cuban state. It also speaks to the absence of democratic institutions and laws that would punish violence mobilized as political practice. Currently, these actions do not maintain the mass character they developed in 1980, but they continue to be organized by political organizations under the supervision of the Department of State Security at the Ministry of the Interior. The *brigadas de respuesta rápida* (rapid-response brigades), made up of an increasingly diverse group of people, still operate with total impunity and receive broad logistical and material support—just like during the dark days of the Mariel exodus.

NOTES

Editors' note: The editors thank Ian Russell for his assistance with the translation of this essay.

Epigraph: "¡Que se vayan! ¡Gusanos, si sacan los pies se los cortamos! ¡Que se vayan los parásitos y la escoria! ¡Mi ciudad más limpia y bonita sin lumpens ni mariquitas! ¡Fuera las ratas! ¡Qué tiemblen los flojos, el pueblo entró en acción! ¡Gusanos, ratones, salgan de los rincones! ¡Nuestra patria limpia y pura, que se vaya la basura! ¡Gusano, lechuza, te vendes por pitusa! ¡Que tiemblen los flojos, el pueblo está actuando! ¡Cuba, que linda es Cuba, sin los gusanos me gusta más!" Printed in "Antología de las consignas del pueblo en la marcha del Pueblo Combatiente," *Granma*, April 23, 1980, 4.

1. Documentaries about the Mariel exodus that reference the acts of repudiation include *Más allá del mar / Beyond the Sea* by Lisandro Pérez-Rey, USA/CUBA (2003), 80 min. (in Spanish with English subtitles). In addition, see *Voices from Mariel* (2011), NFocus Pictures, produced by Adriana Bosch and directed by James Carleton. In José García, *Voces del*

Mariel: Historia oral del éxodo cubano (Miami: Alexandria Library Publishing House, 2012), several testimonies are included that describe the acts of repudiation.

2. Omar Shahabudin McDoom, "The Psychology of Threat in Intergroup Conflict: Emotions, Rationality, and Opportunity in the Rwandan Genocide," *International Security* 37, no. 2 (2012): 120. Although this work is based on the Rwandan conflicts of the 1990s, I consider his framework to be much more useful in understanding processes of collective violence and the tools that activate them in other, more general contexts. Here the aim is not to establish comparisons between one case and the other but rather to locate the foundations of collective violence in Cuba within a more universal frame.

3. McDoom, "The Psychology of Threat," 121.

4. McDoom, "The Psychology of Threat," 122.

5. On the "state of exception" with respect to biopolitics, see Giorgio Agamben, *State of Exception* (Chicago: University of Chicago Press, 2005).

6. Alberto Rubiera, "Puntos suspensivos," *Cuba internacional*, August 1988, 96. Taken from a scrapbook put together by Antonio Núñez Jiménez, the article is found in a section of the scrapbook titled "University Struggles." This album makes up volume 35 of his personal collection that is located in the Fundación Antonio Núñez Jiménez (Havana). Thanks to Lillian Guerra for this reference.

7. Rubiera, "Puntos suspensivos."

8. Sheet No. 114 of the section "Take Note" from CMQ's news broadcast, transmitted October 7, 1955, at 5:56 p.m. Document originally located by Lillian Guerra.

9. Sheet No. 114 of "Take Note." By this time Márquez Sterling had already separated from the Orthodoxo Party founded by Eduardo Chibás to create the Ortodoxia Libre. The groups referred to here were from the branch of his old party, aligned with Castro, with whom Márquez Sterling had significant differences. He believed in suffrage as a path to resolve the country's political crisis and avoid civil war, while Castro favored armed resistance. As we now know, Castro's vision triumphed. Since the mid-1950s Castro had tried to end the political career of Márquez Sterling, who, on January 4, 1959, was detained with his family and remained under house arrest until March of the same year, when he managed to leave Cuba.

10. "Coacción al 'Diario,'" *El Mundo*, June 24, 1959.

11. Luis Conte Agüero, *América contra el comunismo* (Miami: Anti-Communist Christian Front, 1962), 129. I thank Jennifer Lambe for the reference to this text.

12. "La hostilidad de una claque regimentada impidió al Dr. Conte Agüero exponer su pensamiento," *La Plata*, March 17, 1961, cited in Conte Agüero, *América contra el comunismo*, 115.

13. "Editorial," *El bien público*, Saturday, March 18, 1961, cited in Conte Agüero, *América contra el comunismo*, 118.

14. Numerous examples can be cited on the transnationalization of the act of repudiation by the Cuban government, using embassies and delegations to convene and organize demonstrations in academic, political, and cultural forums against those who display a critical vision of the official narrative. One of the most scandalous acts of repudiation took place in Panama during the celebration of the Summit of the Americas

in April 2015. On that occasion, the Cuban delegation, together with the Venezuelan, boycotted debate forums and verbally and physically attacked some Cuban dissidents invited to the event. For more information, see Nora Gámez Torres, "Cumbre de las Américas: Las frases memorables, los actos de repudio y lo que no sucedió," *El Nuevo Herald*, April 13, 2015, http://www.elnuevoherald.com/noticias/mundo/america-latina /article18459476.html#storylink=cpy.

15. These testimonies are taken from the documentary by Lisandro Pérez-Rey, *Más allá del mar / Beyond the Sea*. In the documentary *La marcha del pueblo combatiente*, directed by Santiago Álvarez, the massive demonstrations in front of the Peruvian embassy are also visible. These materials provide the tone of the chants and cries of the demonstrators.

16. Michel Foucault, *La verdad y las formas jurídicas* (Barcelona: Editorial Gedisa, 1996), 97.

17. Mirta Ojito, *Finding Mañana: A Memoir of a Cuban Exodus* (New York: Penguin, 2005), 174–75.

18. Interview with Luis Nodarse, Havana, June 3, 2015.

19. Interview with Marianela Molina, Havana, June 5, 2015.

20. Interview with Marianela Molina.

21. Louis Smith and Alfred Padula, *Sex and Revolution: Women in Socialist Cuba* (New York: Oxford, 1996), 144.

22. Interview with Esperanza Torres, Miami, January 12, 2015.

23. Interview with Esperanza Torres.

24. Zobeida Castellanos's testimony in the documentary *En sus propias palabras* by Jorge Ulla. For more information, see Jorge Ulla, Lawrence Ott Jr., and Miñuca Villaverde, *Dos filmes de Mariel: El éxodo cubano de 1980* (Madrid: Editorial Playor, 1986), 30–31.

25. José Manuel García's testimony in García, *Voces del Mariel*, 30.

26. Lauren Derby, "In the Shadow of the State: The Politics of Denunciation and Panegyric during the Trujillo Regime in the Dominican Republic, 1940–1958," *Hispanic American Historical Review* 83, no. 2 (2003): 301.

27. The CDRs played an important role in the denunciations. They have maintained this approach since the organization's founding through the present day. In September 2015 the newspaper *Juventud Rebelde*, the official publication of the Union of Young Communists (UJC), reported on a meeting of the organization's leadership. Participants agreed to "strengthen" links between the UJC and the CDR and the latter's system of "denunciations for preventing and confronting illegalities, crimes, and social indisciplines." "Instan a mantener el contacto directo con los cederistas," *Juventud Rebelde*, September, 17, 2015, http://www.juventudrebelde.cu/cuba/2015–09–17/instan-a-mantener-el -contacto-directo-con-los-cederistas/.

28. The term *chivatos* was frequently used in Cuba during the 1950s to refer to those citizens who gave up people who conspired or fought against the Batista dictatorship to the police.

29. Robert Denton, "The Rhetorical Functions of Slogans: Classifications and Characteristics," *Communication Quarterly* 28 (1980): 10–18.

30. Elliott Colla, "In Praise of Insult: Slogan Genres, Slogan Repertoires and Innovation," *Review of Middle East Studies* 47, no. 1 (2013): 37–48.

31. Abel Sierra Madero and Lillian Guerra, interview with Osvaldo Rodríguez, Miami, August 14, 2015.

32. Taken from testimonies gathered by Lisandro Pérez-Rey in *Más allá del mar / Beyond the Sea.*

33. Santiago Álvarez, *La marcha del pueblo combatiente* (1980), special edition of the Noticiero ICAIC, https://www.youtube.com/watch?v=mov4hoQ3nJc.

34. Fidel Castro, "Discurso pronunciado . . . en la plaza de la Revolución 'José Martí,' el 1º de mayo de 1980," http://www.cuba.cu/gobierno/discursos/1980/esp/f010580e.html.

35. In both documentaries, *En sus propias palabras* by Jorge Ulla and *La ciudad de las carpas* by Miñuca Villaverde, interviewees testify to these discriminatory policies. For more information, see Ulla et al., *Dos filmes de Mariel.*

36. The idea of "social danger" or pre-criminality comes from the field of criminology and criminal law and was very influential at the end of the nineteenth century. Such a notion judges the individual to have a proclivity for committing crimes a priori and not for actually having committed any crime. In Cuba this condition (the *estado peligroso*) was included in the Code of Social Defense during the first half of the twentieth century (article 48). After 1959 the government recuperated this concept, integrating it into the Penal Code, where it remains today. People with a criminal record or a "dangerous" profile can be detained and arrested by police at any moment without warning. This criminal figure has been inflected with political content in its mobilization against dissidents and the opposition movement. For more information see Law No. 62 de 1987, in *Código Penal Cubano* (Havana: Editorial del MINJUS, 2003).

37. According to the American Immigration and Naturalization Services, 19 percent of the 124,789 refugees from Mariel—23,970 emigrants—admitted to having been in prison in Cuba. This figure includes 5,486 political prisoners. However, 70 percent of those who were imprisoned on the island had been taken in for crimes so minor that they did not even count in the United States. Paul Montgomery, "For Cuban Refugees, Promise of U.S. Fades," *New York Times*, April 19, 1981.

38. Roberto Saladrigas's testimony in Lisandro Pérez-Rey's *Más allá del mar.*

39. Fidel Castro, "Discurso pronunciado en la inauguración del complejo de la salud Ernesto Guevara, en la provincia de Las Tunas, el 14 de junio de 1980," http://www.cuba.cu/gobierno/discursos/1980/esp/f140680e.html.

40. Fidel Castro, "Discurso ofrecido en el acto conmemorativo del primero de mayo, efectuado en la Plaza de la Revolución," http://www.cuba.cu/gobierno/discursos/1980/esp/f010580e.html.

41. Castro, "Discurso ofrecido en el acto conmemorativo del primero de mayo." The term "lumpen" is analogous to the word "delinquent" and originates in Marxist-Leninist philosophy, transformed into state doctrine under Joseph Stalin. It was used in the Soviet Union, the socialist Eastern bloc, and China to contrast with the "New Man," the symbolic ideal of these regimes. In Cuba the term "lumpen" was used a great deal in both political and media discourse to describe those subjects who did not adhere to the values of the ideal revolutionary citizen.

42. The Elpidio Valdés character began to circulate in comic strips at the end of the 1970s in several magazines around the country, including *Pionero* and DDT. In 1979 the character arrived in the animated world with a feature film, *Elpidio Valdés*, produced by ICAIC. By 1980 the character enjoyed a great deal of popularity.

43. "La posición de Cuba," *Granma*, April 7, 1980, 1.

44. "El ambientoso: Publicación inscripta como papel sanitario en la embajada," *Palante*, no. 28 (April 18, 1980), 11. *Ambientoso*, here translated as "troublemaker," was a popular term for criminals.

45. Judith Butler, *Gender Trouble: Feminism and the Subversion of Identity* (New York: Routledge, 1990), 170.

46. Through thorough analysis of Castro's speeches between 1959 and 1980, I have concluded that he most often used the terms "worm" (*gusano*), "parasite," "lumpen," "slacker," "yankee," "counterrevolutionary," and "bourgeoisie," among others, to refer to subjects who did not fit into the revolutionary project.

47. Gabriel Giorgi, *Formas comunes: Animalidad, cultura, biopolítica* (Buenos Aires: Eterna Cadencia, 2014), 12.

48. Ernesto Laclau and Chantal Mouffe, *Hegemonía y estrategia socialista: Hacia una radicalización de la democracia* (Madrid: Siglo XXI, 1987), 152, 73.

49. On current acts of repudiation, consult the documentary *Gusano* (2013), produced in Havana by the opposition group Estado de SATS. Dozens of videos of acts of repudiation against members of the Cuban opposition can be found on their YouTube channel.

50. Laclau and Mouffe, *Hegemonía y estrategia socialista*, 74.

51. Susana Peña, *¡Oye Loca! From the Mariel Boatlift to Gay Cuban Miami* (Minneapolis: University of Minnesota Press, 2013), 487.

52. Interview with Reinaldo García Ramos, Miami, May 16, 2015.

53. Castro, "Discurso pronunciado . . . en la Plaza de la Revolución 'José Martí,' el 1º de mayo de 1980."

54. Susana Peña, "'Obvious Gays' and the State Gaze: Cuban Gay Visibility and U.S. Immigration Policy during the 1980 Mariel Boatlift," *Journal of the History of Sexuality* 16, no. 3 (2007): 490.

55. For more detailed information on the role of gay activism in the United States with respect to Cuban refugees, see Julio Capó Jr., "Queering Mariel: Mediating Cold War Foreign Policy and U.S. Citizenship among Cuba's Homosexual Exile Community, 1978–1994," *Journal of American Ethnic History* 29, no. 4 (2010): 78–106.

56. Barbara Brotman, "Gay Cuban Refugees Get Boost to Freedom," *Chicago Tribune*, August 11, 1980.

57. Brotman, "Gay Cuban Refugees."

58. Alex Brummer, "How Fidel Gave Jimmy Another Disaster," *Guardian*, May 23, 1980.

59. Román de la Campa, "Revista Areíto: Herejía de una nación improbable," *Revista Encuentro*, no. 40 (2006): 140.

60. Lourdes Casal, "Cuba, abril–mayo 1980: La historia y la histeria," *Areíto* 6, no. 23 (1980): 16.

61. "Orientaciones de la Comisión Organizadora," *Granma*, August 18 and 30, 1980, 1. The maps appear on the back cover.

62. "Orientaciones de la Comisión Organizadora," 16.

63. From testimonies gathered by Jorge Ulla in his documentary *En sus propias palabras*.

64. Editorial, *Mariel* 1, no. 1 (1983): 2.

65. Marifeli Pérez-Stable, "El CILC y la 'Generación' del Mariel," *Areíto* 3, no. 29, (1982): 21.

66. Pérez-Stable, "El CILC," 22.

67. Reinaldo García Ramos, "Mariel en tres mentes," *Mariel* 1, no. 1 (1983): 28.

68. Ruby Rich and Lourdes Argüelles, "The Easy Convenience of Cuban Homophobia," *New York Native* 3, no. 23 (1983): 34, 35. Even though the authors recognize that the North American authorities adjusted immigration law to assimilate homosexual Cubans, they fail to mention the activism of gay organizations in the United States that also played a key role in this process.

69. Rich and Argüelles, "The Easy Convenience," 35.

70. For a more detailed study of these tensions, see Capó, "Queering Mariel," 78–106.

71. Ana María Simo and Reinaldo García Ramos, "Hablemos claro," *Mariel* 2, no. 5 (1984): 9.

72. Telephone interview with Lourdes Argüelles, September 10, 2015. The interview was made possible thanks to Eliana Rivero.

73. Interview with Lourdes Argüelles.

74. Castro, "Discurso pronunciado . . . en la plaza de la Revolución 'José Martí,' el 1º de mayo de 1980."

PART III
Concluding Reflections

12. Cuba 1959 / Haiti 1804

ON HISTORY AND CARIBBEAN REVOLUTION

ADA FERRER

In 1962 the historian Eric Hobsbawm suggested that the Russian Revolution was to the twentieth century as the French Revolution to the nineteenth. The analogy represented less a direct comparison than a suggestive juxtaposition. From the executions of the French king and the Russian czar to the destruction of the nobility, the rise of novel state forms, and the institutionalization of new ideas, both revolutions represented a radical—if never total—break with the past. Whatever continuities historians may continue to identify between the ancien régimes and the revolutions they produced, there was, in some sense, a *before* and an *after* 1789/1917. As the Cuban novelist Alejo Carpentier wrote about the French Revolution, "The world had seen so many changes that the storyteller's 'once upon a time' had been replaced by the phrases 'before the Revolution' and 'after the Revolution.'"[1] He might have said the same about the Russian case.

Hobsbawm's juxtaposition of the two great European revolutions finds fertile ground (or bountiful waters) in the Caribbean, home to two of its own world-historical revolutions: the Haitian Revolution of 1791 and the Cuban Revolution of 1959. The argument that the Cuban Revolution was to the twentieth century as the Haitian was to the nineteenth is patently compelling, highlighting—as Hobsbawm's original formulation did—the radical nature of two discrete revolutions and the significance of each beyond its temporal and geographic boundaries.

The link between the Haitian and Cuban revolutions was perhaps first made by C. L. R. James. In his appendix to the 1963 edition of the *Black Jacobins*, James casts the two revolutions as part of a greater Caribbean, or West Indian, revolution. The project begun by Toussaint Louverture in revolutionary Saint-Domingue, writes James, lived on in the revolutionary state created by Fidel Castro in Cuba. James actually says very little specifically about the Cuban Revolution in that appendix, choosing instead to compose a rapid-fire survey of Caribbean history to argue that both revolutions had the same root causes in the legacies of the sugar plantation and racial slavery. The Haitian Revolution's challenge to the plantation system continued and was being realized in Cuba in the early 1960s. "In a scattered series of disparate islands," James explains, "the process consists of a series of uncoordinated periods of drift, punctuated by spurts, leaps and catastrophes. But the inherent movement is clear and strong."[2]

James knew, of course, that the fact that the struggles of the Haitian Revolution still needed to be fought a century and a half later highlighted the possibility that a revolution's promise guaranteed no outcome. The appendix itself highlights some of the external sources of the Haitian Revolution's undoing in the actions of colonial and neocolonial interests powerfully arrayed against revolution. In a lecture delivered a few years later, James elaborated on internal sources of conflict that are present but not fully developed in *The Black Jacobins*, namely struggles among the rank and file: "This was a genuine historic part of every revolution."[3] Yet the 1963 appendix left all that aside. James was less interested in discussing the Cuban Revolution itself then in narrating a broad history that linked the struggles of the Haitian Revolution to those of the Cuban, "whatever its ultimate fate."[4]

However brief James's consideration of the Cuban Revolution in the appendix that bore its name, other sources suggest that he thought about the parallels and connections between the two revolutions deeply over a long period of time: in 1958–59, as he read about the Revolution's seizure of state control; in 1962–63, as he penned the famous appendix to *The Black Jacobins*; in the late 1960s, as he traveled to Cuba to participate in cultural congresses and as he followed news of Che Guevara's death; and in the early 1970s, as he lectured to black activists and intellectuals in the U.S. South. Writing in 1967 to the Cuban novelist Edmundo Desnoes, James shared some of his thoughts on the Cuban Revolution:

> Unfortunately, I do not know Spanish and therefore am unable to be in as close touch with the revolution as I would like to be. But I have a

pretty good idea of the way the revolution was moving. . . . I know the British, French, the Russian Revolution pretty well, and as you know the Haitian. I therefore seem to understand the things I read about the Cuban Revolution not only instinctively but often as if I were reading about things at which I was present or in which I was taking part. I understood what you were saying strangely enough as though I had been seeing it before.[5]

James conveys an almost intuitive sense of Cuba's Revolution. But what exactly might he have deemed so familiar based on his extensive knowledge of the Haitian Revolution?

This brief essay does not provide an exhaustive answer to that question; much less is it an in-depth comparison of the Haitian and Cuban revolutions. It is, rather, a short reflection—from someone who has worked extensively on Cuba and on revolution but not on the Cuban Revolution—that seeks to juxtapose two of the hemisphere's most transformative and interesting revolutions. That juxtaposition, I hope, may lead us to some compelling convergences. Those convergences, in turn, challenge us to think about the Cuban Revolution as something other than singular or exceptional, to think of it— James's appendix notwithstanding—as highly contingent.

Juxtaposed Histories

Despite the century and a half that divides the Haitian and Cuban revolutions, the parallels between the two are striking. Aside from the significance of a towering and seemingly sui generis leader in both cases, perhaps the most obvious parallel is the profound rupture in each society's economic structure. In Haiti the Revolution destroyed slavery—the principal economic and social institution of French Saint-Domingue. Whatever forms of coerced labor reemerged later, no person could legally hold another as property after 1793. As a whole, the colony's propertied class lost not only its human property but also its immovable assets—a loss that was codified with independence in 1804 and with Article 12 of the country's first constitution in 1805, which forbade ownership of property by whites. The old ruling class was entirely displaced. The plantation system that had made the French colonists and metropolitan state so wealthy was not entirely destroyed (particularly in the North), but its successor in postindependence Haiti was significantly smaller in scale; it had a new class of owners, and its agricultural laborers—as all workers—were juridically free.[6]

The economic rupture in Cuba following 1959 was equally dramatic. Increasingly radical agrarian reforms, nationalizations, and expropriations through 1968 eliminated most private property on the island. Large private landholdings disappeared, and in their place stood nationalized farms and state-run cooperatives. American companies—Esso, United Fruit, Standard Oil, Chase Manhattan, Texaco, and others—were nationalized in August and September 1960. Cuban-owned businesses were expropriated in the months that followed. Many former property holders left the island; others accepted compensation and stayed on, as state employees rather than proprietors and employers. Then, on the eve of the Bay of Pigs invasion in April 1961, Castro proclaimed the socialist character of the Revolution. Article 1 of the 1976 constitution codified it: "Cuba is an independent and sovereign socialist state of workers." By then, as in Haiti, the prerevolutionary propertied class had ceased to exist as such.

Radical projects often produce ambitious—sometimes euphoric, sometimes quixotic—schemes that generate a powerful sense of possibility. Something akin to what Lynn Hunt calls a "mythic present" prevailed in both places.[7] The changing of Saint-Domingue's name to Haiti (the local indigenous word for "mountainous land") was in that vein: a powerful, symbolic gesture that ostensibly wiped away the French past and marked the start of a completely new era. Even after the war, citizens were mobilized to rise in case of a French threat; cannons were moved up into the mountains, and ordinary citizens were called to do the work, the loads apportioned according to their strength and the hiring of others prohibited. In Cuba the population was mobilized as well. Citizen militias were trained to combat potential U.S. attacks. Adolescents fanned into the mountains en masse—a militia armed with paper and pencil—to battle against illiteracy. Ordinary citizens were charged with the authority to watch neighbors. It was not just the revolutionary states that were new and unprecedented: so too were their citizens—new revolutionary subjects, new men and new women, at least in theory.

Because both revolutions unleashed such profound changes, they also provoked equally dramatic reactions. The historian R. R. Palmer once claimed that one could calculate the intensity of a revolution by counting its exiles. In both Haiti and Cuba revolution produced major diasporas. Seymour Drescher calculates the number of exiles for Haiti as 20 per thousand, as compared to 5 per thousand in France. For Cuba, the equivalent number is significant, if lower than Haiti's. For example, in 1980, the year with the highest number of émigrés (due to the Mariel exodus), that number was 14.6 per thousand. Each of these diasporas—French and Cuban—was produced, of course, in a different historical moment. The diaspora created in the context of the Cuban Revolution unfolded in a context of major Latin American and Caribbean migration to the United States. For example, the percentage of people leaving Puerto Rico without a revolution is much higher than Cuba's.[8] Yet even as migration became a major historical force elsewhere, in Cuba it was experienced as an inherent part of the drama of revolution.

What the numbers in and of themselves do not reveal is the extent to which migration and exile were central to the social, political, and emotional experience of revolution. In both Haiti and Cuba, out-migration helped the new revolutionary state consolidate its rule and legitimacy. The first documents produced by the Haitian state paid particular attention to people of color who had left or been expelled, proposing laws and policies designed to facilitate their return. Meanwhile, the question of what would happen to the enemies of the Revolution who had stayed was a prominent matter of state (and object of rumor) in the immediate aftermath of Haitian independence.[9] In Cuba the possibility of leaving (or being left) became part of everyday life, and weighty decisions about whether to stay or go shaped the individual calculus and experience of revolution. Loved ones applied for passports, neighbors left their valuables with neighbors to safeguard them, and many Cubans confessed that they tired of the farewells. The disaffected (and sometimes just the weary) left, in the process making the label "enemy" (or the epithets *gusano*, *escoria*, *vendepatria*) easier to invoke. But notwithstanding the pervasive and in many ways accurate association of exile with counterrevolution and the right, Miami today, as I have written elsewhere, "is full of children of the Revolution."[10]

Yet a clear difference exists between the revolutionary diasporas of Cuba and Haiti. At the turn of the nineteenth century a young U.S. government was wary of the revolutionary exiles, who, U.S. leaders feared, might bring the ferment and tumult of France and its colony to a not yet consolidated and tenuous United States.[11] The Cold War context of Cuba's Revolution meant that the U.S. government welcomed and aided people leaving Cuba as a way to make a point about the failures of communism. What began as a trend in 1959 became a matter of policy in 1966 with the Cuban Refugee Adjustment Act, which accelerated the nationalization process for refugees from the island. The welcome offered to Cuban refugees (particularly if they were white) was thus significantly smoother and more generous than that given to other refugees. In 1994 thousands of Cubans *and* Haitians took to the sea in makeshift vessels and headed to U.S. soil. The contrast between the U.S. government's response to the Cuban and Haitian refugee crises—happening at the same time and on the same waters—could not have been starker. The Cubans were treated as political refugees from Castro's Cuba and, initially, were rescued at sea and welcomed on land with more or less open arms. The boundary between political and economic refugees is, of course, a blurry one, but in 1994, in the midst of the severe economic crisis of Cuba's Special Period, the majority of the Cuban refugees were principally economic migrants. Meanwhile, the thousands of Haitians who began arriving in the immediate aftermath of the 1991 military coup against Jean-Bertrand Aristide, though arguably political refugees, were picked up, treated as economic refugees, denied or not considered for political asylum, and returned to Haiti (and later, Guantánamo). Ultimately, the unjustifiable difference led the Clinton administration to begin taking Cuban rafters rescued at sea to Guantánamo as well.[12]

Another international response confronted both new revolutionary states: formal diplomatic isolation. In the case of Haiti, no foreign power recognized the new state. At the insistence of the United States, Haiti was barred from attending the Congress of Panama, the 1826 meeting of the hemisphere's independent nations—this notwithstanding Haiti's place as the earliest non--U.S. American state to win independence and notwithstanding the financial and strategic assistance it had given to some of the very states attending the meeting. Almost a century and a half later, in 1962, the revolutionary Cuban state would also be barred from membership in that Congress's successor, the Organization of American States.[13]

Exclusion from formal organizations and formal diplomatic isolation did not preclude more violent acts of war. After January 1, 1804, the French government authorized its citizens (on the eastern third of the island, or formerly Spanish Santo Domingo) to fan into Haitian territory and kidnap, enslave, and kill Haitians.[14] On a more massive scale, the United States invaded Cuba in April 1961. The intention was to stage "an unspectacular landing" of U.S.-trained Cuban exiles, who would then be joined by locals to wage war on Castro and his government. Needless to say, the unspectacular landing was a spectacular failure, serving to consolidate Castro's popularity and legitimacy. In a secret meeting between Che Guevara and President Kennedy's aide Richard Goodwin in Montevideo a few months after the invasion, Che thanked the United States for the invasion, stating, as Goodwin recalled, that "it had been a great political victory for them—enabled them to consolidate—and transformed them from an aggrieved little country to an equal."[15] David had bested Goliath.

While postrevolutionary Haiti did not have to confront a military invasion on the scale of the Bay of Pigs, it was forced to confront France's enmity on another front. In 1825, with French ships in the harbor threatening to invade, Haitian president Jean-Pierre Boyer accepted France's offer of recognition. In exchange, however, his country paid dearly. The price was an indemnity of 150 million francs (later reduced to 60). To pay it Haiti contracted a crippling debt that it would continue to pay well into the twentieth century. Indeed, as late as 1914, 80 percent of Haiti's budget went to paying the indemnity and related fees.[16] France's indemnity-for-recognition policy might be understood as a form of economic warfare against the new revolutionary state, a possible parallel to the economic embargo pursued by the United States against the Cuban state for over fifty years.

The world's hostility to revolution in both cases was not the same, but in both cases it was potent. But so too was the inspiration that communities outside Haiti and Cuba drew from each revolution. The "idea" of Haiti had enormous power among enslaved and free people of color across the Atlantic World. In colonial Cuba, for instance, Haitian revolutionary figures served as models for would-be black revolutionaries seeking to topple the slave regime at various moments in the island's history. The inverse is also true. After 1959 it was the Cuban model that attracted anti-Duvalier activists in Haiti. Elsewhere too opponents of military dictatorship and advocates of decolonization, civil rights, and other radical and progressive causes the world over looked to Cuba as a model and potential source of practical support. Both states encouraged that identification explicitly, through specific policies as well as through what we might call media strategy.[17]

One policy pursued in both places was the embrace of fugitives from hostile states. The early Haitian state did this in two dramatic ways. It received (and provided asylum and material aid) to Latin American revolutionaries seeking to win independence from Spain—Simón Bolívar the most famous among them. Second, Article 44 of the 1816 Constitution of the Republic offered nationality and citizenship to Africans (and indigenous Americans) and their descendants who stepped foot on Haitian soil. The policy drew enslaved people from neighboring regions to Haitian shores.[18] The Cuban state likewise welcomed fugitives, including men and women fleeing right-wing military dictatorships in South America and African American activists fleeing U.S. racial capitalism and the FBI. Among the latter was Assata Shakur, who characterized her flight and residence in Cuba as akin to marronage, implicitly equating Cuba, like Haiti, to a maroon state writ large. For the Cuban state, the analogy was perhaps a bit uncomfortable.[19]

Indeed, the question of race is one area where the parallels between the revolutions become significantly murkier. In Haiti the revolutionary state validated blackness explicitly in its founding documents. That is evident most clearly in Dessalines's 1805 Constitution, which declared all Haitians to be black, but also in Pétion's 1816 Constitution, which offered citizenship to black foreigners who arrived in Haiti. Beyond the law, early national intellectuals repeatedly cast Haitian independence as a precursor to the redemption of Africa. These proclamations did not, of course, preclude racial strife internally, and, indeed, a recurring and complicated theme in the postindependence history of Haiti is the tension between citizens identified as black and those identified as mulatto.[20]

In Cuba the race and revolution question unfolded quite differently. While it was not a major focus of the revolutionary movement's platform before 1959, black activists and their allies pushed it onto the national agenda almost immediately after the revolutionary seizure of power. But the state itself was cautious on the issue, preferring to address racial inequality indirectly, as an economic issue. By 1962 it had rejected most talk of racial injustice and redress as divisive.[21] So, unlike in Haiti, in Cuba there was no explicit or defiant embrace of blackness, at least domestically. Internationally, however, the state seemed much more willing to address questions of race and blackness explicitly. It became intimately involved in military and political conflicts on the African continent and proudly invoked a "Latin-African" identity in the 1970s, as Christabelle Peters describes in this volume.[22] At a time of intense cultural and political ferment around race globally—especially during the late 1960s—the Cuban state welcomed the solidarity of black activists from across the world, especially from the United States. In much the same way that the U.S. government pointed to its Cuban refugees to highlight the failures of communism, so too did the Cuban state welcome African American activists to highlight the power of racial injustice and violence in the United States. On the domestic front, however, the Cuban state sought to limit contact between international black activists and intellectuals who arrived on the island and the Afro-Cuban ones so eager to talk to them.[23]

In both Haiti and Cuba, then, the revolutions and the states they created had an outsized international presence. They prompted spectacular hostility from former colonial (or neocolonial) powers. At the same time, they inspired admiration, and sometimes emulation, from subaltern communities. That dual, crosscutting influence accounts, in part, for the polarized responses to and analyses of the revolutions in both cases.[24]

Ultimately, however, both revolutions share a set of troubled relationships at their core. An obvious one is the thorny relationship between past and present. In theory, revolutions represent a definitive break with the past. In Haiti a new name for the country signaled that break. The "time of the French" had ended. New times even called for the physical elimination of remaining French in order to guarantee that the past would never encroach on the present. The construction of massive fortresses in the mountains would serve as additional insurance against the return of an unwanted past.[25]

In Cuba any number of projects—on scales grand and mundane—speak to this drive to overcome a past of mediated sovereignty, injustice, and underdevelopment. On a minor scale were things like the tax on "society" items in newspapers, plans to eliminate the silent h in Spanish as elitist, the removal of the word "God" from national currency, the creation of a revolutionary calendar, the organization of mass weddings and registrations of births, and the ritual burial of U.S. companies (Esso, United Fruit, etc.) and old Cuban newspapers (*Diario de la Marina*). On a major scale were mass mobilizations for far-reaching and well-known projects such as the agrarian reform, the literacy campaign, popular militias, neighborhood watch programs for national defense, and the fevered campaign to produce a 10-million-ton harvest in 1970, the achievement of which would represent the Revolution's defeat of underdevelopment forever. Much less known was a series of ambitious and quixotic projects to physically transform Cuba's landscape in the service of revolutionary development, examined by Reinaldo Funes Monzote in this volume. Indeed, revolutionary initiatives, laws, and programs were so incessant and ubiquitous that even a cursory survey of any good chronology of the first years of the Cuban Revolution reminds one of the notion of revolutionary, accelerated, or mythic time.[26]

Yet, no matter how fervently revolutionary leaders heralded the arrival of new times and the resounding defeat of the past, the past seemed always present—and not just as prologue, either. I refer here to what Jeremy Adelman has called the "problem of persistence" and Steve Stern "the tricks of time" in Latin American history. In this volume, Alejandro de la Fuente perceptively suggests that "still" and "yet" may serve as something like keywords of the Cuban Revolution.[27]

In both Cuba and Haiti even the most transformative projects contained within them elements of the very past they were designed to overcome. For example, to build the fortresses that would safeguard Haiti's new revolutionary present and to grow the crops that would sustain its army, authorities relied not on the legal slavery of old but on forms of coerced labor not always clearly distinguishable from its predecessors. Workers in chains carried stones to the fortress under construction; *agriculteurs* were formally attached to plantations and faced stringent limits on their mobility; and corvée systems produced needed workers for state projects.[28] In Cuba, meanwhile, ambitious designs to transform the countryside and with it the economy continued to reproduce vital features of the past, most notably sugar monoculture and dependency on a single foreign market. On the cultural front, the effort to make "new men" often reproduced patriarchal habits and assumptions about gender, among other things. The point here is not to look for continuities with the past as a way to diminish the power of the revolutions but rather to look at transformation and continuity as historians generally do—to understand the ways in which change itself is informed by patterns, institutions, and practices central to the societies that produced the transformations in the first place.[29]

If the Haitian and Cuban revolutions exhibit this complex tension between past and present, and between continuity and change, both also encompassed a troubled relationship between the revolution *within* and the revolution *without*. Put another way, revolution abroad was not always the same thing as the revolution at home. The welcome Haiti offered fugitive slaves did not mean that local people did not face the harsh reality of forced labor, nor did the welcome Cuba offered U.S. black activists necessarily translate into support for black activism locally. In Haiti and Cuba, as in perhaps all revolutions, the story of how revolution destroys particular forms of domination prompts other critical questions about how new—and sometimes not so new—forms of domination emerge out of those very same processes.

Conclusion

In their introduction to this volume, Jennifer Lambe and Michael Bustamante aptly call for writing histories of the Cuban Revolution "from within." Among other things, they urge us to write those histories precisely *as* histories, and not as teleology or ideology. The work of the historians in this volume, and others not in this volume, goes a long way to advance that project.[30] It is my hope that this brief juxtaposition of the Haitian and Cuban revolutions adds to that call a reminder to cast our nets widely and to consider comparative, connected, and transnational histories as central to the endeavor of writing these new histories. Indeed, some of the essays in this volume—including those by Christabelle Peters and Alejandro de la Fuente—do just that. We do well, also, to look at the work of Haitian and Haitianist historians and scholars over the past two or so decades.[31] Their scholarship took the Haitian Revolution—an event earlier relegated to the margins—to the very heart of new perspectives on the Atlantic World and the Age of Revolution. As historical work on the Cuban Revolution becomes, finally, more prevalent both on and off the island, we do well to do as Haitianist scholars have done: to take "our" revolution into domains beyond the Cuban. As the vast new scholarship on the Haitian Revolution and its international impact reminds us, our work must focus on both internal and external aspects of the revolution. Indeed, it should work precisely to challenge traditional boundaries between those two realms. Doing so helps us better bring into view the revolution's histories—always in the plural.

NOTES

1. Eric Hobsbawm, *The Age of Revolution* (New York: Vintage, 1996); Alejo Carpentier, *Explosion in a Cathedral*, translated by John Sturrock (New York: Noonday, 1963), 336.

2. C. L. R. James, *The Black Jacobins: Toussaint Louverture and the San Domingo Revolution* (New York: Vintage, 1963), 391–418.

3. C. L. R. James, "How I Would Re-write *The Black Jacobins*," *Small Axe* 8 (September 2002): 104–8.

4. James, *The Black Jacobins*, 391.

5. C. L. R. James to Edmundo Desnoes, London, October 29, 1967, Box 1, Folder 3, C. L. R. James Papers, Columbia University Archives. The collection includes other correspondence related to James's relationship with Cuba. See also Andrew Salkey, *Havana Journal* (New York: Penguin Books, 1971).

6. On this history in general, see Laurent Dubois, *Haiti: The Aftershocks of History* (New York: Henry Holt, 2012).

7. Lynn Hunt, *Politics, Culture, and Class in the French Revolution* (Berkeley: University of California Press, 1984), 27.

8. See Seymour Drescher, "The Limits of Example," in *The Impact of the Haitian Revolution in the Atlantic World*, edited by David Geggus (Columbia: University of South Carolina Press, 2001), 10; on Cuba, Philip Peters, "Migration Policy Reform: Cuba Gets Started, U.S. Should Follow," Lexington Institute, December 2012, http://www .penultimosdias.com/wp-content/uploads/2012/12/CubanMigration.pdf. Peters's figures are drawn from Cuba's National Office of Statistics.

9. See the essays in Julia Gaffield, ed., *The Haitian Declaration of Independence: Creation, Context, and Legacy* (Charlottesville: University of Virginia Press, 2015).

10. See, for example, [?] to Nnene, February 26, 1962, and V. to Japonesa querida, March 16, 1962, letters 7 and 8, Folder 1, Cuban Letters Collection, Tamiment Archives, New York University. The subject of farewells is prominent in the novel *Inconsolable Memories* by Edmundo Desnoes, which served as the basis for Tomás Gutiérrez Alea's classic film *Memories of Underdevelopment*. The theme resurfaced powerfully during the Special Period. See especially the work of two Havana-based novelists: Wendy Guerra, *Todos se van* (Barcelona: Bruguera, 2006), and Alejandro Hernández Díaz, *La milla* (Havana: Pinos Nuevos, 1996), as well as the work of the Havana-based poet Reina María Rodríguez, *Otras cartas a Milena* (Havana: Ediciones Unión, 2003). The final quote is from my essay "Listening to Obama in Cuba," NACLA, March 28, 2016, http://nacla.org /news/2016/03/28/listening-obama-cuba.

11. See Ashli White, *Encountering Revolution: Haiti and the Making of the Early Republic* (Baltimore: Johns Hopkins University Press, 2010).

12. On the Cuban 1994 rafter crisis, see the digital archive created at the University of Miami, *The Cuban Rafter Phenomenon*: http://balseros.miami.edu. For a comparison of the two cases, see Thomas David Jones, "Human Rights Tragedy: The Cuban and Haitian Refugee Crises Revisited, A.," *Georgetown Immigration Law Journal* 9, no. 3 (1995): 479–524.

13. On the international response to Haitian independence, see especially Julia Gaffield, *Haitian Connections in the Atlantic World: Recognition after Revolution* (Chapel Hill: University of North Carolina Press, 2015); Rayford Logan, *The Diplomatic Relations of the United States with Haiti, 1776–1891* (Chapel Hill: University of North Carolina Press, 1941). The literature on U.S.-Cuban relations is vast. For an introduction, see Lars Schoultz, *That Infernal Little Cuban Republic: The United States and the Cuban Revolution* (Chapel Hill: University of North Carolina Press, 2011).

14. Graham Knessler, *An Island-Wide Struggle for Freedom: Revolution, Emancipation and Reenslavement in Hispaniola, 1789–1809* (Chapel Hill: University of North Carolina Press, 2016), ch. 5; Ada Ferrer, *Freedom's Mirror: Cuba and Haiti in the Age of Revolution* (New York: Cambridge University Press, 2014), 189–99.

15. See U.S. Department of State, *Foreign Relations of the United States, 1961–1963: Cuba*, vol. 10, https://history.state.gov/historicaldocuments/frus1961-63v10/d257; Richard Goodwin, Memorandum for the President, August 22, 1961, National Security Archive, http://www2.gwu.edu/~nsarchiv/bayofpigs/19610822.pdf.

16. See Dubois, *Haiti*, 7–8, 97–105.

17. On the use of "media" by the revolutionary state in Haiti and Cuba, respectively, see Deborah Jenson, *Beyond the Slave Narrative: Politics, Sex, and Manuscripts in the Haitian Revolution* (Liverpool: Liverpool University Press, 2011); Lillian Guerra, *Visions of Power in Cuba: Revolution, Redemption, and Resistance, 1959–1971* (Chapel Hill: University of North Carolina Press, 2012).

18. Ada Ferrer, "Haiti, Free Soil, and Atlantic Antislavery in the Revolutionary Atlantic," *American Historical Review* 117, no. 1 (2012): 40–66.

19. On the Latin American left in Cuba, see Jorge Castañeda, *Utopia Unarmed: The Latin American Left after the Cold War* (New York: Knopf, 1993). On the U.S. black left in Cuba, Van Gosse, *Where the Boys Are* (New York: Verso, 1993).

20. David Nicholls, *From Dessalines to Duvalier: Race, Colour and National Independence in Haiti* (New Brunswick, NJ: Rutgers University Press, 1996), chs. 2–3; Michel Rolph Trouillot, *Haiti, State against Nation: The Origins and Legacy of Duvalierism* (New York: Monthly Review Press, 1990); Dubois, *Haiti*, 86–87.

21. Alejandro de la Fuente, *A Nation for All: Race, Inequality, and Politics in Twentieth-Century Cuba* (Chapel Hill: University of North Carolina Press, 2001), ch. 7; Devyn Spence Benson, *Antiracism in Cuba: The Unfinished Revolution* (Chapel Hill: University of North Carolina Press, 2016).

22. On Cuba's African involvement, see Peters's essay in this volume, as well as her book *Cuban Identity and the Angolan Experience* (London: Palgrave Macmillan, 2012); two volumes by Piero Gleijeses, *Conflicting Missions: Havana, Washington, and Africa,*

1959–1976 (Chapel Hill: University of North Carolina Press, 2003) and *Visions of Freedom: Havana, Washington, Pretoria, and the Struggle for Southern Africa, 1976–1991* (Chapel Hill: University of North Carolina Press, 2013).

23. See the special issue "Black Power," *Pensamiento Crítico* 17 (1968); Salkey, *Havana Journal*; Carlos Moore, *Pichón: Race and Revolution in Castro's Cuba. A Memoir* (Chicago: Chicago Review Press, 2008); Henry Louis Gates Jr., interview with Eldridge Cleaver, *Transition* 49 (1975).

24. Much has been written on the polarization in Cuban analyses of the Revolution; see Lambe and Bustamante's introduction in this volume. For an introduction to the Haitian case, see Michel-Rolph Trouillot, *Silencing the Past: Power and the Production of History* (Boston: Beacon Press, 1995), ch. 3.

25. See Gaffield, *The Haitian Declaration of Independence* (especially the essays by Jean Casimir, Jeremy Popkin, and Erin Zavitz); Dubois, *Haiti*, ch. 1; Ferrer, *Freedom's Mirror*, 189–99.

26. For historical work on these campaigns in the first years of the Revolution, see especially María del Pilar Díaz Castañón, *Ideología y revolución: Cuba, 1959–1962* (Havana: Editorial de Ciencias Sociales, 2004); Guerra, *Visions of Power in Cuba*; and both authors' contributions to this volume. The extended chronology in the appendix to Díaz Castañon's *Ideología y revolución* (300–326) is especially useful, as well as fascinating to compare to the very different, and equally extensive, chronology in Emeterio Santovenia and Raúl Shelton, *Cuba y su historia* (Miami: Rema Press, 1965), 305–47. Rafael Rojas in this volume also touches on the notion of "revolutionary time."

27. Jeremy Adelman, ed., *Colonial Legacies: The Problem of Persistence in Latin American History* (New York: Routledge, 1999), 1–13; Steve Stern, "The Tricks of Time: Colonial Legacies and Historical Sensibilities in Latin America," in Adelman, *Colonial Legacies*, 135–50; De la Fuente in this volume.

28. Dubois, *Haiti*, 53–54, 65–67, 105.

29. For an excellent example of this kind of work for the Haitian Revolution, see Malick Ghachem, *The Old Regime and the Haitian Revolution* (Cambridge: Cambridge University Press, 2012), which exams legal continuities between the *ancien* and revolutionary legal histories of Saint-Domingue/Haiti. For the Cuban Revolution, in addition to essays in this volume by Reinaldo Funes Monzote, Abel Sierra Madero, and Alejandro de la Fuente, see Michelle Chase's *Revolution within the Revolution: Women and Gender Politics in Cuba, 1952–1962* (Chapel Hill: University of North Carolina Press, 2015), which examines the ways in which prerevolutionary civil society shaped the mass organizations established by the state after 1959.

30. The list of historians not in this volume whose work represents part of this emerging wave of writing on the Revolution would include, among others, Oscar Zanetti, Marial Iglesias, Ricardo Quiza, Michelle Chase, and Rachel Hynson.

31. The literature is too vast to cite here. For a very selective, English-language sample, see the work of Michel-Rolph Trouillot, Laurent Dubois, David Geggus, Carolyn Fick, Malick Ghachem, Jeremy Popkin, Julia Gaffield, and myself.

13. *La Ventolera*

RUPTURES, PERSISTENCE, AND THE HISTORIOGRAPHY
OF THE CUBAN REVOLUTION

—

ALEJANDRO DE LA FUENTE

To Cubans it was a familiar image, one embedded in our experiences and understandings of "La Revolución." Attitudes, spaces, economic activities, and cultural expressions that did not conform to our expectations of what La Revolución was supposed to represent and incarnate were conceptualized as leftovers, remnants of a surviving past. La Revolución was an all-encompassing phenomenon, one that had taken over—had saturated and occupied—every imaginable interstice of national life. The few remaining spaces still colonized by the past would capitulate in due course to the inexorable push of the new order. The new revolutionary order was like an avalanche, a flood that would reach and domesticate every inch of our lives.

Except that it didn't. Precisely because the past was conceived as all that had not changed yet, it was still in fact everywhere. "Still" and "yet" became the keywords of La Revolución. They explained economic practices that were thought to be incompatible with the new order but were in fact inseparable from the new economic system, like the so-called black market; a political culture that, despite radical departures, refused to move beyond traditional logics and networks of patronage; the much diminished but still standing churches; the doggedness of racial and gender ideologies; the prevalence of ancestral cultural practices; our endless fascination with the United

States and with U.S. culture; crime. It was a language used frequently by Fidel Castro himself. When, for instance, tens of thousands of Cubans got ready to leave their country in the summer of 1980 during the Mariel boatlift, the leader of La Revolución explained it through the metaphor of incomplete change: "Even though unfortunately we *still* have lumpen, even though we *still* have declassed elements, that we *still* have antisocial elements . . ."[1]

The rhetoric of a vanishing past (still) and a soon-to-be future (yet) speaks to one of the defining features of any social revolution: change. Scholars of social revolutions may not agree on what constitutes, precisely, a social revolution, but fundamental change (be it in political and economic structures, in social relations, or in value systems) is always part of the equation.[2] By conceptualizing actions, values, and activities that did not conform to the "new" as leftovers of the past, revolutionary authorities and intellectuals reinforced the association between radical transformations and La Revolución. Persistence was defined as the no-revolution, social relations located outside the revolution.

Logically, then, the history of La Revolución is by definition the history of successful change—"la revolución triunfante"[3]—as anything else does not fall within the subject of study. Historians of the Cuban Revolution (or any other) must penetrate through the dense fog created by these associations and categories to explain the complex, contradictory, and overlapping processes that constitute a revolution, including those that undermine the logic of successful change. These processes cannot be comprehended in a linear logic of changes and continuities, as they occur in overlapping but disjointed scenarios and time lines. To put it differently, in order to reconstruct the history of La Revolución, historians need to pay serious attention to the "outside," what La Revolución defines as no-revolution.

Some of these questions about change, persistence, multiplicity of time lines, and history came into sharp focus in the 1990s, as La Revolución faced its most formidable crisis. In the 1990s Cuba looked like a society that was moving forward—toward the 1950s. This is why Rafael Rojas remarked in *El Estante Vacío* that in the 1990s the whole history of Cuba, *la historia entera*, had suddenly fallen over the island.[4] The past turned into future, a future that was, could only be nostalgic. Things deemed disappeared from the Cuban postrevolutionary landscape, from golf courses and prostitution to racism, became ubiquitous and omnipresent. Foreign investors were welcomed back. U.S. dollars became legal tender. The old Havana Biltmore Yacht and Country Club, the first club of the bourgeoisie nationalized by the revolutionary government and transformed into a "workers' circle" in 1960, reopened its doors, as a private club again, in 1997. It is now called Club Habana. The traditional idioms of change—*still, yet*—were not useful to describe these new/old phenomena. A new language, new metaphors were required to understand, from the vantage point of the 1990s, La Revolución.

This new language has been slowly articulated in a new historiography of the Cuban Revolution. This new body of scholarship tends to place the revolutionary process in a time frame that is not bounded by the traditional chronology of insurrection and triumph—what Marifeli Pérez-Stable graphically defines as the 1959 divide—and rescues processes, time lines, and actors that were otherwise obscured by the blinding effects of January 1959.[5] In this brief reflection, I suggest that the very existence of this historiographic turn, as well as the questions and problems it seeks to address, are best comprehended by looking at other bodies of historiography and by placing the Cuban revolutionary experience—and its historiography—in a comparative perspective. In this sense, I readily dispense with any fantasies of Cuban exceptionalism, except to note that all revolutions promote themselves by claiming to be unique, particularly in relation to the pasts that they help create, only because such pasts have been supposedly transcended.

A Historiographic Turn

The economists were among those who first identified and discussed how much of old Cuba remained alive in socialist Cuba, decades after 1959. In key areas of the economy, despite massive changes in ownership, economic planning, and state control over economic affairs, some deep, structural traits of traditional Cuba remained intact. Cuban authorities in the 1960s had frequently criticized monoculture and promised industrialization and diversification as the only antidotes against underdevelopment. By the late 1980s sugar (one is tempted to insert "still" here) represented 74 percent of Cuba's total exports, and the industrialization fantasies of the 1960s had evaporated. Revolutionary authorities disparaged Cuba's dependence on foreign markets and promised to break with it. Yet by 1987, 72 percent of Cuba's total trade happened with just one partner, the Soviet Union. Cuba's foreign trade concentration had actually increased compared to 1958. As the economist Carmelo Mesa-Lago wrote in 1993, although the Cuban Revolution was a process of "profound and totalizing transformation . . . there are elements of the past that have persisted, such as the notable dependency on sugar exports and the concentration on a single commercial partner." The author described this "persistence" as "surprising."[6]

The issue of the possible "persistence" of economic structures, social relations, and cultural practices in revolutionary Cuba relates to an older historiographic debate concerning the radicalization of the Revolution. For decades, scholars have wondered about the causes of radicalization and have tried to make sense of the drastic economic, social, and institutional changes that took place in just a few years in the 1960s. Scholars of an older historiographic generation pointed out that none of the factions fighting against Batista advocated the destruction of capitalism and therefore tended to explain the subsequent radicalization of the revolutionary process by highlighting the importance of Fidel Castro's leadership. In its crudest form, this argument claimed that Fidel Castro had betrayed the ideals of the Revolution.[7] Echoes of this explanation are still found in recent scholarship. To mention one significant example, the importance of Castro's leading role in the radicalization of revolutionary politics is a central analytical element in Samuel Farber's *The Origins of the Cuban Revolution Reconsidered*. Farber devotes a chapter to the question of whether the Revolution was driven "from above or from below" and argues that "the masses of revolutionary followers" played a limited role in defining policies and programs: "The claim that mass pressures from below, particularly during 1959 and early 1960, left Castro no other option but to stay the radical revolutionary course is not credible." In his view the radical shift "moved from the leaders to the masses rather than the other way around." In this process, the author concludes, "the Cuban masses have remained the objects rather than the subjects of history."[8]

Most explanations, however, center on some combination of popular mobilization and leadership action, although which groups mobilized and for what purposes continues to be open to various interpretations.[9] Recently the historian Lillian Guerra has argued that revolutionary politics and rituals of participation and redemption resulted in an authoritarian political culture that can be described as a "grassroots dictatorship," a concept that seeks to move beyond radicalization debates as being propelled from "above" or "below."[10] Other authors emphasize the importance of external factors such as the hostility of the United States or plain imperial blindness.[11] The role played by Cuban communists, organized in the Partido Socialista Popular, has also elicited interest, as radicalization is frequently linked to the implementation of a "communist"-inspired program.[12]

This debate centers on the nature, the actors, and the forces that drove the process of radicalization and revolutionary change in Cuba, but radicalization and revolutionary change, two concepts that are used more or less interchangeably, are not questioned. This has been one of the few points of consensus in the historiography about the Cuban Revolution.[13] In the words of the historian Oscar Zanetti, "The transcendence of the revolution is so huge, that from the point of view of history it establishes a before and after for everything."[14] The most recent historiography, however, has begun to raise serious questions about the narratives of radicalization and change. Most of these new works study figures, institutions, cultural practices, and processes across the 1959 divide. They adopt temporal and conceptual frames that turn 1959 and the changes ushered by the Revolution into (admittedly significant) moments in wider historical processes. For Rafael Rojas, for instance, La Revolución is a process that goes from the mid-1950s through the mid-1970s.[15] An approach of this sort makes it at least possible to explore threads and continuities that a view of 1959 as the source of a historical "before" and "after" would obscure. This new historiography explicitly challenges the narrative that the Revolution was just a process of "true rupture" with a clearly demarcated past, or that the Revolution defined a before and an after in every area of the country's life.[16]

Jenny Lambe's recent work on Cuba's premiere mental health institution (Mazorra), and on the treatment of psychiatric patients in Cuba, illustrates this new trend. Mazorra is an excellent case to study the Revolution's impact, as it represents precisely one of those institutions that are frequently associated with radical change following the Revolution—a paradigmatic example of a total and unqualified break with prerevolutionary Cuba. As an official history of the hospital states, before 1959 the patients were "herded up in insalubrious wards, naked and hungry, lacking hygiene and the necessary food. . . . The hospital was still managed just like a jail." That was before 1959. "Happily for our nation all that horrible nightmare ended with the triumph of the Revolution."[17]

Lambe's work shows, however, that the one therapy hailed as a prime example of change in the hospital's therapeutic regimen—*ergotherapy*, or occupational therapy—was in fact widely practiced in the institution long before the Revolution of 1959. Work may have acquired new meanings after 1959 as a constitutive element of revolutionary subjecthood, but work has been a constant theme in the history of the hospital. The author thus concludes "that paradigms of change and continuity centered exclusively on the 1959 Revolution are not adequate to the task of narrating the complex and rarely linear story of Mazorra."[18]

There are other examples. A recent study about tuberculosis, for instance, shows that the creation of a public health system is a contribution not of the Revolution but of state-building practices in republican Cuba. Citizens' expectations concerning state responsibilities in the area of public health predate 1959, so one of the paradigmatic successes of the Cuban Revolution is rooted in narratives of republican rights, citizenship, and national belonging.[19] Threads of continuity are likewise evident in another area of model change: the elimination of slums and urban poverty under the Revolution. According to a recent study, the program articulated by a young Fidel Castro during his Moncada attack trial to solve the acute housing problem in Cuba was essentially the housing program that Fulgencio Batista was trying to implement. "A revolutionary government would solve the housing problem by cutting all rents in half . . . by tearing down hovels . . . and by financing housing all over the island on a scale heretofore unheard of," Fidel Castro asserted. Batista could not have agreed more. In a public speech just a few months before Castro's defense, Batista asserted that "state initiative" was "on the march" and promised exactly what Fidel Castro would promise later. "Decent, healthy, comfortable lodging for families of scarce resources occupies our highest attention," Batista declared. The way to achieve that was, precisely, to cut rents, to build workers' housing, and to eliminate shantytowns. And both Batista and Castro further agreed on two important points. First, that shantytowns represented a social shame incompatible with Cuba's standing as a nation; second, that their elimination was a responsibility of the Cuban state.[20]

Prerevolutionary practices, expectations, and institutions percolated throughout postrevolutionary society in other ways. Ecological interventions by the revolutionary state were conceptualized in the name of socialism, but as Reinaldo Funes Monzote shows in his study in this volume, such interventions were informed by older developmental understandings of well-being and nature. In the area of culture, again one of the paradigmatic areas of change, as the creation of a new culture was sine qua non to the construction of a new man and a new order, historians detect important continuities across 1959. For instance, recent work shows that the Cuban republican state was already implicated, in profound and consequential ways, in the production of a national culture. Beginning in the 1940s state support for various forms of cultural production was widespread, as was the creation of regulatory bodies and mechanisms dealing with national culture.[21] (Elizabeth Schwall's essay in this volume touches on some of these through-lines in the case of ballet.) Public debates and policies in the area of race relations, another important arena of revolutionary change, took place within preexisting, long-term discursive boundaries that left little space, as in the past, for Afro-conscious thinkers, activists, and intellectuals to exist and voice their own perspectives. They continued to be marginalized or stigmatized, just as they had been in pre-1959 Cuba. Early antiracist policies, campaigns, and efforts frequently reproduced traditional images of blacks in subservient roles or used visual cues and idioms linked to racially charged representations of people of African descent.[22]

Scholars of political culture have also identified important continuities in Cuban political language, practices, and performances. They have argued, for instance, that Fidel Castro's "declassed political leadership" was grounded in a populist tradition that, while politically militant, was programmatically and theoretically vague. As a result, Castro's ideological vagueness and his ability to reach agreements with various social groups at different points are presented not only as congruent with Cuban political culture but in fact as a product of such culture—a culture that lived on after 1959.[23] This is not very different from Sergio López Rivero's characterization of the Revolution as a process draped with a rather old wardrobe. In his graphically titled book *El viejo traje de la Revolución*, López Rivero argues that Cuban nationalism is at the very foundation of the Cuban revolutionary process, which managed to transform what had been a vague feeling into a political movement.[24] The main author of this transformation was none other than Fidel Castro. And if the Revolution, which was, after all, the epitome of change, wore an old and familiar suit, so did the counterrevolution. A recent study about anticommunism argues, not surprisingly, that opposition to the growing political visibility and relevance of the communist Partido Socialista Popular in 1959 was articulated by actors, institutions, and media that were hardly new in Cuba's cultural and political scenarios.[25]

Although scholars of political culture continue to obsess over Fidel Castro's leadership, most of the recent scholarship on the Revolution looks at nonelite actors and how they shaped policies through everyday actions. The new scholarship is populated by schoolteachers, shantytown residents, mental patients, medical personnel, and musical performers—in other words, by ordinary people. Indeed, as historians expand their work into the "terra incognita" of daily life, the nature, extent, and very existence of the changes with which the Revolution is always associated become less clear. Such changes cease to be a foregone conclusion and become empirical questions, topics to be explored and researched, almost always with new sources. In this new scholarship the centrality of Fidel Castro's leadership recedes to the background—a major engine of historical change no longer. And threads of continuity are located precisely in areas—health care, urban poverty, race relations, culture—where change was supposed to be the greatest.

There are several bodies of scholarship that may help us think through questions of revolutionary change and of social, economic, and cultural threads of continuity. One of these bodies refers to what we could call, following Jeremy Adelman's lead, the "problem of persistence."[26] The idea that Latin Americans are inevitably trapped by their colonial past—the idea that past is destiny—has informed the historiography of the region in important ways and was particularly evident in the historiography built on the dependency school. Interpretations centered on deep structures of cultural or economic flavor pose serious problems, however, as they tend to exclude "local human agency" from the story.[27] Since revolutions are by definition processes of rupture and change, there is much to be learned from those who seek to problematize persistence by carefully analyzing long-term and contingent obstacles and how people act on them. The insight that Latin American histories can follow "several overlapping time lines" can be usefully applied to our studies about revolutionary change, precisely because different areas of social life (and sometimes different areas within a country or even a city) follow their own, overlapping, different time lines.[28]

It is useful to think of the Cuban case in light of the findings, debates, and concerns that animate another body of scholarship: the historiography on the Mexican Revolution. There are, to begin with, significant similarities between the revolutionary mythmaking processes of Mexico and Cuba, among other things because revolutions are always built on the construction and explicit repudiation of "the" past, as if such thing—a single, totalizing past—existed in fact. In other words, in order to negate them, revolutions invent their own pasts. In the case of Mexico, the various revolutionary factions disagreed on many fundamental things, but they all agreed that what started in 1910 was a real revolution and that it was a revolution connected to previous efforts to build an independent and prosperous Mexico. As the historian Thomas Benjamin has written, the Revolution was "presented as the third stage of an ongoing revolutionary tradition in Mexico that began with the insurgency in 1810 and the reform in the 1850s," a process that sounds remarkably similar to Cuban revolutionaries' own efforts to portray themselves as the heirs of José Martí and of the *mambises* who fought for independence in the nineteenth century—the epic of the "100 años de lucha."[29] Mexican revolutionaries had to invent their "familia revolucionaria" out of the various conflicting factions, just as the Cubans had to invent a history of the Revolution in which divisions and factionalism played no role. Institutionally the Mexicans dealt with this problem through the creation of the Partido Nacional Revolucionario in 1929, while the Cubans created the Partido Unido de la Revolución Socialista in 1962, which was called "unido" precisely because it was not. In Cuba, as in Mexico, La Revolución became a living, self-referential, acting subject that seemed to take a life of its own.

There are interesting parallels between the emergence of a critical, revisionist historiography of the Mexican Revolution in the 1970s and 1980s and recent developments in the historiography of the Cuban Revolution. Following widespread disenchantment with the Partido Revolucionario Institucional and its institutional revolution, several historians questioned the extent of economic and social change that actually took place in Mexico. The revisionist interpretation stressed the importance of structural continuities and the inability of popular movements such as those led by Zapata and Villa to produce lasting and effective change. The historian John Womack summarized the revisionist interpretation in his well-known essay for the *Cambridge History of Latin America*: "For all the violence this is the main historical meaning of the Mexican Revolution: capitalist tenacity in the economy and bourgeois reform of the state."[30]

The Cuban Revolution has not produced a similar body of revisionist historiography, but some of the recent works discussed above may well be the initial salvos of a historiographic turn. It surely is no coincidence that this new historiography builds on the disenchantment with the official revolutionary project—with the institutional revolution, to put it in Mexican but fully understandable terms—that followed the so-called Special Period, the crumbling of the socialist welfare state, and the increasing visibility of targeted but widespread repression against critics and dissidents of various kinds.

Critical historians of the Cuban Revolution may turn to the study of the Mexican historiography not only to identify comparable processes and methodological opportunities but also to reflect on how changing economic and political circumstances produce shifts in historiography and on the production of new, relevant pasts. Since many of the historians now working on the Cuban Revolution are familiar with the historiography of Mexico, these borrowings are taking place already. For instance, it is probably not a coincidence that the emergent revisionist literature about the Cuban Revolution is much more sensitive to popular initiatives and actions than Mexican revisionists were. Those working on Cuba have the advantage of hindsight and have clearly incorporated methodological insights from the vast literature on everyday forms of state formation in postrevolutionary Mexico, a body of scholarship that reincorporates popular agency into the history of the Revolution.

As Gil Joseph and Daniel Nugent argue in their magisterial edited volume, an unfortunate consequence of the revisionist emphasis on the rise of the Mexican revolutionary state after the 1920s was to relegate popular participation to a subordinate, almost inconsequential role.[31] By studying how grassroots movements and cultures shaped state institutions and policies, postrevisionist historians of Mexico insisted on the need to study popular movements and cultures and their impact on day-to-day state actions and configurations, but also raised important questions about the state itself, especially about the power and reach of the revolutionary state. Some regional studies—those dealing with Yucatán immediately come to mind—show that the power of the revolutionary state was not without limits, although those studies also show that this does not mean that people in the area did not experience the Revolution.[32]

With its attention to the construction and functioning of the revolutionary state, the historiography of the Mexican revolution connects with the work of political scientists who have studied the state in other revolutionary societies. The question of state reach is of great importance to students of the Cuban Revolution, who frequently assume that, particularly after the defeat of the armed opposition at Girón (the Bay of Pigs) and the Escambray (site of an antigovernment insurgency between 1960 and 1965), the power and reach of the Cuban state were essentially unhindered. This assumption is not without foundation. The so-called mass organizations in neighborhoods, workplaces, and schools did provide the Cuban state with a capillary reach, to put it in Foucauldian terms, that is nothing short of impressive. Coupled with a process of "unambiguous centralization of political power" the government bureaucracy "succeeded in claiming greater control over both society and the economy."[33] But how this centralization was experienced, negotiated, and perhaps contested at the local level requires careful empirical study. Taking advantage, again, of Mexican historiography, the historians of Cuba need to treat the coherence and effectiveness of the revolutionary state as empirical questions rather than assumptions.[34]

If Cuban historiography is experiencing a Mexican moment, however, its influence appears to be confined almost exclusively to scholars working on Cuba outside the country. In conversations with junior historians in Cuba, they unanimously and emphatically denied the existence of a critical historiographic turn that questions the centrality of 1959 within the island.[35] They asserted that Cuban historians continue to see the Revolution as the divide that clearly separates socialism from the republican past. Whether this is due to the weight of an official rhetoric that reduces La Revolución to successful change, or to the limitations of a nationalist university training that pays limited attention to the historiographies and debates of other revolutionary processes, such as the Mexican, remains to be studied. In any case, part of the problem is the dearth of serious research about postrevolutionary Cuba within the island. Studies about this period are particularly susceptible to political and personal concerns, as many of the protagonists are still alive. That is why these studies frequently adopt a testimonial form or offer interpretations that are "often superficial, even schematic."[36]

In this discussion the two contributions included in this volume by Cuba-based scholars offer a graphic and provocative contrast. On the one hand, as mentioned earlier, Funes Monzote shows that the developmentally inspired ecological interventions of the revolutionary government were of republican manufacture and had clearly discernible republican roots. Cuban geographers linked environmental, economic, and social concerns and spoke of agrarian reform, industrialization, and planning (even in the USSR), since at least the 1950s. In other words, Funes Monzote's contribution seems to contradict the assertion that the 1959 divide continues to be central to Cuba-based historians. Funes Monzote, however, is a Cuba-based scholar with privileged and exceptional access to international academic markets. A frequent visitor to American and European universities, his scholarship engages with the voluminous work on Cuba that is produced outside the island and partakes in transnational historiographic conversations in ways that are not easily accessible to most Cuba-based historians, particularly those at the start of their careers.

María del Pilar Díaz Castañón's chapter in this volume may represent a better illustration of historiographic developments within Cuba concerning the Revolution. Her novel and useful analysis of the language used in print advertisements supporting revolutionary figures and programs, such as the agrarian reform, shows an important shift, "a transit" from republican citizens' demands (*pedir*) to the revolutionary engaged citizens' language of participation and sharing (*dar*). She explores the difficulties involved in a nuanced assessment of change, but change is nonetheless at the center of the story. This is the case even though Díaz Castañón is in fact attentive to issues of persistence and continuity, as illustrated by the strategies followed by the Asociación Nacional de Hacendados de Cuba, which were steeped, as she notes, in republican traditions and styles. Other elements in her work also point to issues of persistence. The willingness of landowners to cooperate with "the new government and the new strongman" followed deeply ingrained political practices, as illustrated by the limited opposition that Batista faced after the 1952 coup. Even the signature economic transformation promoted by the revolutionary government in Year 1, to use Díaz Castañón's graphic expression, agrarian reform, was a well-established, widely shared republican goal.

La Ventolera

As we write the new histories of the Cuban Revolution, it is perhaps important to remember the obvious: the Revolution did produce profound and significant change. Changes may not have been as complete, totalizing, and radical as once conceived, but changes were nonetheless significant. People experienced them as real and consequential. As we rewrite the histories of revolutionary Cuba, I find myself increasingly concerned not with the weight of the past but rather with the overwhelming, blinding weight of our present. We study the Revolution—very much like the Mexican historians of the 1970s and 1980s did—from a perspective of disenchantment and skepticism about La Revolución. We write from and at a time when it is easy to miss the numerous alternatives, the paths half-taken, the multiplicity of futures made possible by the collapse of the Batista regime. Those alternatives, paths, and possible (even plausible) futures are part of the history of the Revolution as well, for the Revolution proceeded along disjointed time lines, at different speeds, and in a regionally uneven fashion. "Still" and "yet" do not exhaust the history of the Revolution, but they do convey something (many things, actually) about La Revolución.

This is exemplified in the state's contradictory approaches to popular cultural forms. We know that in the late 1960s, as Cuban authorities extolled the virtues of the Revolution's "new man," several state institutions took steps to control, discourage, and even repress Afro-Cuban religious practices such as Palo Monte, Santería, and Abakuá. These practices were characterized, much to the chagrin of Afro-Cuban intellectuals, as remnants of a past of colonialism and ignorance that had no place in Cuba's socialist society. Afro-Cuban religions were presented as savage, primitive practices incompatible with socialism and progress. The initiation of youngsters was prohibited; gatherings and the performance of ceremonies were placed under police control.[37]

There was nothing particularly revolutionary or new about the Cuban state's efforts to wipe out Afro-Cuban cultural practices. State authorities had sought to eradicate those religious practices for decades. Practitioners could also turn to a rich history of resistance, simulation, and adaptation to cope with such efforts. One of the things they probably knew best is that governments come and go, but the *orishas* stay forever. Some practitioners describe measures taken to hide their altars, their beliefs, and the colors of their saints from authorities, pretty much as they had done since colonial times. By the 1990s, when the number of Santería followers seemed to explode, it became clear that, as in the past, the efforts of the Cuban state to eradicate these religions had met with modest success at best. In fact scholars of Santería have argued that it is under the atheist Revolution that Santería has been transformed into Cuba's national religion.[38]

It is tempting to construct a linear connection between republican and contemporary Cuba in this area and to reduce both state eradication efforts and the growing popularity of Santería to the category of continuities. But that would tell us very little about how practitioners and other people experienced the Revolution, how their actions helped shape state policies in this area, or how systematic or coherent state efforts to eliminate Afro-Cuban religious practices were to begin with. A narrative of continuity flattens a contentious process that was full of contradictions and ambiguities, for continuities acquire historical meaning only when studied in relation to the indeterminacies and alternatives they encountered. A notion of continuity ignores, for instance, that the 1990s were a particularly favorable conjuncture for the expansion of Santería and other religious practices. It misleadingly projects a 1990s development to the 1970s and 1980s. To put it differently, a narrative of continuity in this area obliterates stories, experiences, and attitudinal changes that did take place during the early decades of the Revolution.

Nor are state eradication efforts captured by a narrative of continuity. Post-1959 state policies concerning Santería and other African-based religions were uneven, contradictory, and ambiguous. The revolutionary government opposed Afro-Cuban religions but sought at the same time to turn Afro-Cuban cultural expressions into the foundations of a new, popular revolutionary national culture. Institutions such as the Conjunto Folklórico Nacional, Danza Nacional de Cuba, and the Museo de Guanabacoa, all created in the 1960s, sought to secularize Afro-Cuban religious practices but in fact helped to reinvigorate and valorize such religions as key elements of a popular, radical national identity. By the late 1960s, just as the National Revolutionary Police were trying to control Santería gatherings and *bembés*, young visual artists such as Manuel Mendive, Rafael Queneditt, Leonel Morales, Clara Morera, Rogelio Rodríguez Cobas, and Ramon Haití were openly celebrating the orishas and African religiosity in their works, with state support and in state-run galleries. Queneditt's first solo exhibit in 1969 was titled *Motivos Yoruba*, and his first engraving, a beautiful chalcography, *Eleguá*. The three best-known pieces of

Mendive from the period are titled *Babalu Ayé*, *Obba*, and *Oyá*.[39] The state may have sought to secularize Afro-Cuban religions, but its support for popular music and art probably contributed to the expansion of Santería and helps explain why Santería's following is today fully cross-racial. Christine Ayorinde claims, "Instead of Afro-Cuban religions disappearing into secularized folklore, as had been hoped, the secular [became] incorporated into popular belief."[40] So much, then, for continuities. The expansion of Santería in the 1990s is surely connected in some ways to the vitality of these religious practices in prerevolutionary Cuba, but the linearity of such connection is an illusion.

In his award-winning novel *Adire y el Tiempo Roto*, published in 1967, the Afro-Cuban writer Manuel Granados captured the puzzling mix of ruptures and continuities that take place in a revolutionary society. "La gente no cambia por dentro," he wrote, "tiene que venir la ventolera. . . . Así y todo quedan grandes pedazos con raíces profundas que luchan por brotar" (People don't change inside. A strong wind has to blow. . . . Even then, there are deep roots that remain and struggle to resurface).[41] As we continue to study the Cuban Revolution, it is important to analyze those deep roots, the big chunks that remain, but let us not forget that the Cuban Revolution was as powerful and strong a wind as winds can be.

NOTES

1. Fidel Castro, "Discurso pronunciado por el Comandante en Jefe Fidel Castro Ruz," May 1, 1980, http://www.cuba.cu/gobierno/discursos/1980/esp/f010580e.html. My translation and emphasis.

2. In addition to the paradigmatic volume by Theda Skocpol, *States and Social Revolutions: A Comparative Analysis of France, Russia, and China* (New York: Cambridge University Press, 1979), see Jack A. Goldstone, *Revolutions: A Very Short Introduction* (New York: Oxford University Press, 2014), and Eric Selbin, *Modern Latin American Revolutions* (Boulder, CO: Westview Press, 1998).

3. Mario Mencía, "Gracias a la revolución por existir y subsistir," *La Jiribilla*, Año X (February 18–24, 2012).

4. Rafael Rojas, *El estante vacío, literatura y política en Cuba* (Barcelona: Editorial Anagrama, 2009), 57.

5. Marifeli Pérez-Stable, *The Cuban Revolution: Origins, Course, and Legacy* (New York: Oxford University Press, 1993), 5.

6. Carmelo Mesa-Lago, *Breve historia económica de la Cuba socialista* (Madrid: Alianza Editorial, 1994), 9–10.

7. An early and graphic inquiry about the nature and radicalization of the Cuban Revolution is Theodore Draper, *Castro's Cuba: A Revolution Betrayed?* (New York: New Leader, 1961).

8. Samuel Farber, *The Origins of the Cuban Revolution Reconsidered* (Chapel Hill: University of North Carolina Press, 2006), 69, 114.

9. Pérez-Stable, *The Cuban Revolution*.

10. Lillian Guerra, *Visions of Power in Cuba: Revolution, Redemption, and Resistance, 1959–1971* (Chapel Hill: University of North Carolina Press, 2014).

11. Thomas G. Paterson's *Contesting Castro: The United States and the Triumph of the Cuban Revolution* (New York: Oxford University Press, 1994) provides convincing evidence to sustain this view. For an opposing view, see Vanni Pettinà, *Cuba y Estados Unidos, 1933–1959: Del compromiso nacionalista al conflicto* (Madrid: Catarata, 2011).

12. Guerra, *Visions of Power*, 18, 77–88.

13. One telling exception is the work of Carlos Moore, who conveyed a certain skepticism about the existence of a true revolution in Cuba since the 1960s in his "Le peuple noir a-t-il sa place dans la Révolution Cubaine?," *Presence Africaine* 52 (1964): 177–230.

14. Oscar Zanetti Lecuona, "Medio siglo de historiografía en Cuba: La impronta de la Revolución," *Cuban Studies*, no. 40 (2010): 84.

15. Rafael Rojas, *Historia mínima de la Revolución cubana* (Mexico City: Turner, 2015).

16. Mencía, "Gracias a la revolución por existir y subsistir."

17. *Memory of the Psychiatric Hospital of Havana* (Havana: Cuban Book Institute, 1971), n.p. I thank Jenny Lambe for sharing this source with me.

18. Jennifer Lambe, "A Century of Work: Reconstructing Mazorra, 1857–1959," *Cuban Studies* 43 (2015): 90.

19. Kelly Urban, "The Sick Republic: Tuberculosis, Public Health, and Politics in Cuba, 1925–1965," PhD diss., University of Pittsburgh, 2017.

20. Jesse Horst, "Sleeping on the Ashes: Slum Clearance in Havana in an Age of Revolution, 1930–1965," PhD diss., University of Pittsburgh, 2016.

21. Cary A. García Yero, "The Arts, the Artists, and the State: Cultural Policy in 1940s Cuba," paper presented at 33rd International Conference of the Latin American Studies Association, San Juan, Puerto Rico, 2015.

22. Devyn Spence Benson, *Antiracism in Cuba: The Unfinished Revolution* (Chapel Hill, University of North Carolina Press, 2016).

23. Farber, *The Origins of the Cuban Revolution Reconsidered*, 168.

24. Sergio López Rivero, *El viejo traje de la revolución: Identidad colectiva, mito y hegemonía política en Cuba* (Valencia: Universidad de Valencia, 2007).

25. Fabio Fernández Batista, "Alergia al rojo: A propósito del anticomunismo en Cuban durante el año 1959," *Debates Americanos* (forthcoming). I thank the author for sharing this text with me.

26. Jeremy Adelman, ed., *Colonial Legacies: The Problem of Persistence in Latin American History* (New York: Routledge, 1999).

27. Stuart B. Schwartz, "The Colonial Past: Conceptualizing Post Dependentista Brazil," in Adelman, *Colonial Legacies*, 189.

28. Jeremy Adelman, "Introduction: The Problem of Persistence in Latin American History," in Adelman, *Colonial Legacies*, 12.

29. Thomas Benjamin, "The Mexican Revolution: One Century of Reflections, 1910–2010," in *The Mexican Revolution: Conflict and Consolidation, 1910–1940*, edited by Douglas Richmond and Sam Haynes (College Station: Texas A&M University Press, 2013), 214.

30. John Womack, "The Mexican Revolution, 1910–1920," in *The Cambridge History of Latin America*, edited by Leslie Bethell (New York: Cambridge University Press, 1986), 5:82.

31. Gilbert Joseph and Daniel Nugent, eds., *Everyday Forms of State Formation: Revolution and the Negotiation of Rule in Modern Mexico* (Durham, NC: Duke University Press, 1994).

32. For a distinguished example, see Paul Eiss, *In the Name of el Pueblo: Place, Community, and the Politics of History in Yucatan* (Durham, NC: Duke University Press, 2010).

33. Jorge I. Domínguez, *Cuba: Order and Revolution* (Cambridge, MA: Belknap Press, 1978), 137.

34. These questions have also preoccupied scholars of the Chinese Revolution, such as Vivienne Shue, *The Reach of the State: Sketches of the Chinese Body Politic* (Palo Alto, CA: Stanford University Press, 1988).

35. I am grateful to David Domínguez, Laura Vázquez, and Fabio Fernández Batista for their comments about this topic during our meeting in Havana, July 3, 2015. Fernández Batista's article on anticommunism, "Alergia al rojo," however, appears to fit within the new historiography.

36. Zanetti Lecuona, "Medio siglo de historiografía en Cuba," 95.

37. I deal with this issue in *A Nation for All: Race, Inequality and Politics in Twentieth-Century Cuba* (Chapel Hill: University of North Carolina Press, 2001), 290–95.

38. Christine Renata Ayorinde, *Afro-Cuban Religiosity, Revolution, and National Identity* (Gainesville: University Press of Florida, 2004).

39. On the work of these visual artists, see Alejandro de la Fuente, ed., *Grupo Antillano: The Art of Afro-Cuba* (Pittsburgh: University of Pittsburgh Press, 2013).

40. Ayorinde, *Afro-Cuban Religiosity*, 135–36.

41. Manuel Granados, *Adire y el tiempo roto* (Havana: Casa de las Américas, 1967).

14. Whither the Empire?

JENNIFER L. LAMBE

There is a specter that haunts the pages of this book; any scholar or observer of Cuban history may already be feeling its absence. These chapters have admittedly little to say about the imperial behemoth, the Goliath to Cuba's David: in short, the U.S. government, which has played such an outsized role in shaping Cuba's national—and even revolutionary—destiny. The peripheral role of the United States here may seem surprising considering the long history of intervention in its sovereign neighbor to the south. Nonetheless, in closing, this essay explores why we have chosen to invert the normal order of emphasis, at times perpetuated even in official revolutionary discourse. That is, instead of affording the United States a starring place, we have chosen to frame this project around histories of the Cuban Revolution elaborated primarily from *within*, and on Cuban terms. In so doing, we have sought to push back on the historical politics of imperial obviousness, perhaps the most enduring grand narrative that has shaped the telling of Cuban history.

The United States has unquestionably exercised enormous influence—military, political, economic, and cultural—over the course of Cuban history. Yet Cuban histories written through and exclusively in reference to the United States risk hyperbolizing and even reifying that power. As I explore below, U.S.-centrism, even when critical and well-intentioned, has sometimes run dangerously close to rewriting Cuban history in its own political and ideological image. Far from a recent trend, this tendency was born in the crucible of imperial extension, as the United States began to parse its relationship to the revolutionary island over which it had come to exercise dominance, if not control.

At the turn of the twentieth century, the protracted flirtation of U.S. policymakers with their Caribbean neighbors came to fruition in a late intercession in Cuba's war for independence—what would thereafter be known, speciously, as the Spanish-American War. Though the Teller Amendment (1898) prevented the United States from turning Cuba into an outright colony, a military occupation, followed by the imposition of the Platt Amendment, significantly curtailed the degree of sovereignty enjoyed by the new nation. When U.S. occupiers finally departed in 1902, the island would begin to exercise a strange sort of self-determination: theoretically inviolable and popularly lionized, but riddled by imposed legal loopholes.[1]

Cuba's opaque political status thus left room for doubt and dialogue long after the formal achievement of independence. It was precisely this issue that students across the United States would take up in a 1907–9 intercollegiate debate on the prospect of Cuban annexation. In the context of yet another U.S. military occupation of the island (1906–9),[2] a Minnesota student named Ezra Englehart argued strenuously in favor of annexation. "Cuban Independence is a myth," he declared. Even compared to others in his camp, Englehart's assessment was dire. Cuba, he continued, "may have been independent when discovered by Columbus," but the arrival of "civilization"—in the form of Europeans—had since guaranteed its political subjection. The "interchange of products," or, in short, capitalism ascendant, seemed to have condemned Cuba to the perpetual condition of economic, and therefore political, "dependence." U.S. intervention, Englehart determined, had done little to change this essential equation.[3]

Englehart's conclusion displays the willful solipsism of imperialist thinking: the assumption, shared by high school students and policymakers alike, that Cuba might be structurally fated for external domination. We might read his endpoint as an expression of a cultural consensus and in some respects an omen, presaging the decades of U.S. intervention and aggression to come. Certainly, by 1909 the argument for U.S. oversight had acquired a tinge of obviousness. As Cuba emerged from yet another military occupation, many politicians in the United States (and some on the island) had only dug their heels in further. Cuba, they had concluded, was simply unprepared for the burden of independence. That determination was often framed in the language of moral imperative. "Cuba needs but one thing," another high schooler, Fred Warber, argued in favor of annexation, and "we can give the one thing needed. Cuba has suffered, will continue to suffer for want of freedom. That freedom she can only get through American citizenship, which will come through annexation."[4] This was the essence of the paradigm thereafter known as "Plattism," wherein the political fate of Cuba was ineluctably bound to that of the United States.

Intercollegiate debate might seem a poor synecdoche for public sentiment, yet there is a historical and historiographical obviousness to these arguments, too. It seems indisputable that any history of Cuba, distant or recent, should include the United States as a starring player—*the* starring player, even. It seems self-evident, too, that Cuban political paradigms should be constructed around the affliction of Plattism: rarely embraced, often repudiated, and occasionally subsumed, anthropophagically, in the cultural realm.[5] The long arc of Cuban historiography bears the mark of this original duality; "Cuba does not owe its independence to the United States," proclaims the title of a classic nationalist work by the historian Emilio Roig de Leuchsenring.[6] Since 1898 many Cuban politicians, reformers, and revolutionaries have concluded the same. For each political generation, the rejection of Plattism has offered an ideological platform for nationalists of all stripes, a unifying glue where no other common ground was available. The power of anti-Plattism survived and even swelled following the 1934 abrogation of the Platt Amendment, possible thanks to the anti-imperialist militancy bound up in Cuba's 1933 Revolution.[7]

Finally, the 1959 Revolution brought anti-Plattism to its political apotheosis, as Cubans united against yet another U.S.-backed tyrant (Batista) and, after his ouster, combated subsequent U.S. efforts to arrest the Revolution's leftward turn. Though debates about Fidel Castro's original ideology (or lack thereof) have reached something of a stalemate, nationalism was undoubtedly one motor of its formidable appeal.[8] Revisionist accounts of Cuba-U.S. relations, particularly those focused on the cultural sphere, have often departed from the political framing of this paradigm, but similarly validated its effects. Where the nationalist canon saw the unilateral imposition of imperial authority, U.S.- and island-based historians have captured some of the essential ambivalence of this relationship, grounded in love and hate, neocolonial influence and Cuban agency and creativity.[9]

So where is the United States in this book's accounts of the Cuban Revolution? Or, to put it more baldly, why has it been so absent in these pages? Recent scholarship on U.S.-Cuba relations has undoubtedly contributed to shaping new understandings of the Revolution as well as political events beyond historiographical doors. One such work of note is William LeoGrande and Peter Kornbluh's fascinating *Back Channel to Cuba: The Hidden History of Negotiations between Washington and Havana* (2014). The book chronicles the often thwarted efforts of politicians on both sides to repair relations between the two countries and, following its release, entered into a kind of metatextual relationship with the process of diplomatic normalization. Undoubtedly, work in this vein, drawing when possible on newly declassified official sources, will go a long way toward grounding and nuancing political events at hand, alongside new social and cultural histories of the U.S.-Cuba relationship since 1959.[10]

Without diminishing in any way the trailblazing work of LeoGrande, Kornbluh, and others, we have nonetheless taken a different path here, at some distance from the well-trod territory of U.S.-Cuba relations. We have chosen to feature work that probes the *inner* workings of revolutionary state and society, alternative routes of international inflection and influence, and, above all, the sui generis Revolution forged not only through the rejection of Plattism and the adoption of socialist and Soviet influence but also on its own terms. Diplomatic isolation from the United States imposed many hardships on Cuba, but it also opened up new opportunities. In decolonizing Africa, within the Soviet bloc, but fundamentally in the nationalist archetypes of its own historical tradition, Cuban leaders and citizens found fertile ground to construct new political and social imaginaries.

Many did not depend on the United States for their power or transcendence, even as Washington represented a frequent imperial foil. Meanwhile, U.S. cultural influence persisted in other arenas, a muted but vital contribution to revolutionary transculturation. To reduce the history of the Cuban Revolution to a series of skirmishes with the United States runs the risk of missing the point. If the Cuban Revolution indeed sought to break with the Plattism that preceded it (even if it perhaps reified it in other forms), new histories of the Revolution must also, we believe, take up this challenge.

Yet the Plattist peril lives on. Roughly a century after the notion first entered our political vocabulary, it was given new life by the political and economic transformations attached to the normalization process undertaken by Raúl Castro and Barack Obama. Much as during the post-Soviet Special Period, Cuba was once again caught in a flash of media attention, imbued with and driven by the allure of the island's past-in-present anachronism.[11] The appeal of Cuba's liminality appeared ever more tantalizing in light of its presumably imminent disappearance, a fetish that drew its power from "our" role—as Americans, that is—in both creating and now destroying the fragile ecosystem of a society without McDonald's and Wal-Mart.[12] In the spirit of an ostensibly progressive ambivalence about "self," U.S. commentators began to "mourn" what "[we ourselves had] transformed."[13] Voyeuristically, we indulged doomsday prophesy in depicting the encroachment of late industrial capitalism into a site of socialist alterity, the "touristic heterotopia that gathers economies and temporalities."[14] That presentism was an unmistakably self-referential discourse and a commercial one, too: the touristic analogue of "natives" dressing up in traditional garb for the preening anthropologist's eyes. As journalists and talking heads fantasized about revisiting Cuba's icons of past-in-present, it was hard to avoid the feeling that we were experiencing what amounted to a collective imperialist regression, of a piece with the European and Canadian tourists who have long rambled around the Plaza de la Revolución in fashionably clunky cars. This act of discursive appropriation silenced Cuban history itself, transposing "our" past onto "their" evanescent present.

Recent imperialist resurgences harken to the most prominent trope in Cuba's history: that Cuba's past, present, and (presumably) future should be understood as a mere subtext of or footnote in the history of the United States. The allure of this story has been hard to resist for many on and off the island who have looked to the United States to forge new political and economic opportunities for a vulnerable late socialist Cuba. Yet the affect of empire sometimes trumps even economic interest; the allure of Cuba's difference has always coexisted uneasily with the potential boon it presented to U.S. business. That difference has long exercised an analytically magnetic effect, luring tourists and researchers alike into a germinal space of (hyper-)cross-cultural contact. And so, as Cuba reacquired the trappings of a space "suddenly" within our sights, Americans once again turned to a process of self-education about their geographically proximate yet politically distant neighbor. Normalization drove a frenzy of Cuba reporting and musings characterized by excruciating self-centeredness—Where are "we" in Cuba? What of Netflix, Beyoncé, and Obama?—but also evident sincerity.

That U.S.-centrism has found a surprising counterpoint in Cuban political and popular culture. Cuban officials seem to have harbored hopes that normalization might light a path out of the economic woes that face Cuba absent the patronage of Venezuela, its most important backer in recent years. Some began to cautiously court U.S. business leaders and politicians even as others continued to mobilize *against* U.S. cultural influence. And here official warnings were less paranoid than they might seem. The process of normalization unleashed and magnified pro-U.S. sentiment in the Cuban popular imaginary. The effects thereof were immediately visible on the island, where leggings adorned with the American flag and popular adoration for former President Obama (at least until he lifted the "wet foot, dry foot" policy) were omnipresent. If U.S. hegemony was revivified in the aftermath of normalization, its effects were not unilaterally imposed on Cuba, but rather conditioned and even advanced by Cuban officials and popular audiences alike.

From the vantage point of yet another twist in U.S. presidential politics, however, this discursive regime can suddenly appear both quaint and ephemeral. The fragility of normalization was rarely reckoned with in the months leading up to the death of Fidel Castro and the surprise election of Donald Trump. Yet both events highlight the contingency of Cuba's path forward and its dependence on U.S. economic and political tides. With the gradual disappearance of Cuba's historical revolutionary leaders—including Raúl Castro's partial step back from political authority—a Trump-ordained reversal in the process of rapprochement may threaten Cuba's economic survival. The dramatic swing in Cuba politics, from détente under Obama to escalating hostility under Trump, nonetheless lands once and again on the disproportionate influence of the United States *and* the self-centered terms of its engagement.

A century ago, things were, perhaps, not so different, even if the late revolutionary state seems quite distant from the early postcolonial state it strangely mirrors. Take, for example, the debate with which I began. As students and teachers all over the country prepared to discuss the prospect of Cuban annexation, the War Department had found itself besieged by requests for information, data, and documents. "This is a question which is greatly discussed in my county and it has raised quite a sensation among some of the college students," Robert P. Moss wrote Secretary William H. Taft in January 1908. Issuing an urgent request for educational materials, Moss added that the "majority" was quite opposed to Cuba's annexation.[15] Indeed, the prompt had led one Kentucky State student to write President Theodore Roosevelt himself, gingerly suggesting, "Under obligation of our promise and the Platt amendment, we would not be justified in establishing our permanent rule over or in Cuba without first the legally expressed consent or request of her people to such an action."[16]

Nonetheless, many of those students and teachers who wrote to the U.S. government sought not only an answer but information: a bibliography—or an archive—that might help them resolve the question of Cuba's fate. On the first score, government officials invariably demurred; per Major Frank McIntire, assistant to the chief of the Bureau of Insular Affairs, "it would hardly be proper for an official of an executive department of this government to express an opinion."[17] For a time, they also balked at the second, suggesting that the Bureau of Insular Affairs had not issued any such publication that could be easily parsed for clues. In sporadic admissions, however, Bureau officials began to disclose the architecture of such an archive, composed exclusively of U.S. voices, and official ones at that (congressional debates, speeches, and "great power" communications). In order to determine, then, whether annexation would serve the welfare of *Cuba*—the original framing of the question—it seemed obvious to most to consult only sources on and from the *United States*.

The question of archival presence and absence is a critical one for any scholar of Cuba, especially for the period after 1959. Many of us—again, both on the island and off—have made frequent recourse to U.S. sources in order to understand the Revolution, due in no small part to the challenges of accessing Cuban archives, as Jorge Macle Cruz describes in his contribution to this volume. Yet archival exigencies need not overdetermine our analytical frameworks. I have lingered on the case of the annexation debate to remind us of the historiographical stakes attached to the imperialist master narrative: that when Cuban history is debated in U.S. terms, "we" tend to emerge at the center of "their" story—or "they" tend to see themselves in "our" terms.

So what, we might ask, can revisionist accounts of the Cuban Revolution offer as an alternative? How can they avoid becoming merely another self-referential archive, particularly when published in English for a (largely) North American audience? Undoubtedly, the obstacles are not only intellectual and political but also structural. We have thus made every effort to feature our island colleagues here, while acknowledging, per Alejandro de la Fuente, that the search for new perspectives may itself spring from largely external historiographical roots.

Still, the intellectual dividing lines run deeper. The inherent dualism of Cuban history—that is, the prominent role played by and afforded to the United States—may be, in some respects, unavoidable. That does not mean, though, that it is necessarily unidirectional. To paraphrase John F. Kennedy, that most complicated and often despised figure in the history of U.S.-Cuba relations, what if we were to ask not what the United States can do for Cuba (politically, socially, historiographically) but how the history of the United States might look if we were to put the Cuban Revolution at its center? What unexpected stories, what counter- and antinarratives might result from inverting the imperialist politics of historical obviousness?

Perhaps they would render visible and transparent the presence of imperialism itself. Recent historical scholarship seems to point in exactly this direction, with respect to Cuba and more broadly. New research highlights the long engagement of U.S. progressive communities with Cuba, as a complex object of ideological inspiration on one hand and exoticist fascination on the other.[18]

This work speaks to and builds on a formidable tradition of transnational and diplomatic history charting the "intimate" and often fraught connection between the small island and its powerful northern neighbor.[19]

In this salutary attention to the central place of empire in U.S. history, especially vis-à-vis Cuba, there nonetheless looms a familiar proximate danger: that of always repositioning the United States at the center of a Cuban story. It is thus equally encouraging to witness the ever more plural field of transnational Cuban history, in which connections with Latin America, the socialist camp, and the decolonizing world have come to assume their rightfully central place (chapters in this book by Christabelle Peters, María A. Cabrera Arús, and Ada Ferrer represent novel contributions in this regard).[20] As historians explore lateral and South–South spheres of Cold War influence, they coincide with U.S.-Cuba scholars in highlighting the significant weight attached to Cuba's revolutionary inspiration, while also affording Cuba a more consequential agency in shaping the postcolonial and nonaligned world of the 1960s, 1970s, and 1980s.

Yet the "transnational turn" is not equally available to all. It is worth pausing to point out the obstacles faced by Cuban historians, especially those based on the island, in pursuing the kinds of peripatetic research agendas attached to geographically pluralist projects. In this, practical disparities collide with epistemological problematics.[21] Scholars in the global North enjoy disproportionate access to budgets and archives compared to their counterparts in the South. Meanwhile, Cuban scholars must also contend with imposing political barriers to their mobility, as determined by both their own government and those of the countries in which they seek to conduct research.

But the pursuit of transnational history is not simply conditioned by differential access to resources. We must also be attentive to the ideological assumptions embedded in a desire for a "multi-sited historiography" of the Cuban Revolution.[22] As postcolonial scholars have warned, transnationalism may ultimately reify imperial assumptions about core and periphery, with respect to both intellectual substance and academic structures. At its least self-aware, it tends to reimagine the formerly colonized world as a foil and stage for historical process among the former imperial powers. That dubious inversion of scholarly priorities registers as particularly galling in a place as invested in nationalist politics as revolutionary Cuba.

While indulging evocative flirtations with transnational contexts, this volume has thus insisted on a Cuba-centric account of the revolutionary period. Without marginalizing the disproportionate influence the United States has exercised on the island, I have argued that its rightful place here is that of a supporting player. U.S. imperialism may have done much to determine the historical conditions with which Cuban actors contended in articulating a nationalist response. To do justice to their story, however, we must be careful not to construct yet another self-referential archive. Ultimately, Cubans were the authors, however constrained, of the island's revolutionary futures. New histories of the Cuban Revolution would do well to follow their lead.

NOTES

1. See Louis A. Pérez, *Cuba and the United States: Ties of Singular Intimacy* (Athens: University of Georgia Press, 1997), *The War of 1898: The United States and Cuba in History and Historiography* (Chapel Hill: University of North Carolina Press, 1998), and *Cuba in the American Imagination: Metaphor and the Imperial Ethos* (Chapel Hill: University of North Carolina Press, 2008).

2. On the second U.S. occupation of Cuba, see Allan Reed Millett, *The Politics of Intervention: The Military Occupation of Cuba, 1906–1909* (Columbus: Ohio State University Press, 1968); Teresita Yglesia Martínez, *Cuba: Primera república, segunda ocupación* (Havana: Editorial de Ciencias Sociales, 1976); Jorge Ibarra, *Cuba, 1898–1921: Partidos políticos y clases sociales* (Havana: Editorial de Ciencias Sociales, 1992); Lillian Guerra, *The Myth of José Martí: Conflicting Nationalisms in Early Twentieth-Century Cuba* (Chapel Hill: University of North Carolina Press, 2005).

3. Paul M. Pearson, ed., "Annexation of Cuba," in *Intercollegiate Debates: Briefs and Reports* (New York: Hinds, Noble and Eldredge, 1909), 391, 392.

4. Pearson, "Annexation of Cuba," 396.

5. See Louis A. Pérez, *On Becoming Cuban: Identity, Nationality, and Culture* (Chapel Hill: University of North Carolina Press, 2008) and *The Structure of Cuban History: Meanings and Purpose of the Past* (Chapel Hill: University of North Carolina Press, 2013).

6. Emilio Roig de Leuchsenring, *Cuba no debe su independencia a los Estados Unidos* (Havana: Editorial Ediciones La Tertulia, 1950). The continued salience of this text is evident in its having been reissued on multiple occasions in Cuba, including in 1961 and 1975.

7. The literature on the Platt Amendment and its final elimination is vast, including a two-volume work by Emilio Roig de Leuchsenring: *Historia de la enmienda Platt* (Havana: Oficina del Historiador de la Ciudad, 1961). For a discussion of this work, see Louis A. Pérez, *Essays on Cuban History: Historiography and Research* (Gainesville: University Press of Florida, 1995), 125–26.

8. See Thomas G. Paterson, *Contesting Castro: The United States and the Triumph of the Cuban Revolution* (New York: Oxford University Press, 1994).

9. See, for example, Pérez, *On Becoming Cuban*; Marial Iglesias Utset, *Las metáforas del cambio en la vida cotidiana: Cuba, 1898–1902* (Havana: Ediciones Unión, 2003); Ricardo Quiza, *Imaginarios al ruedo: Cuba y los Estados Unidos en las Exposiciones Internacionales (1876–1904)* (Havana: Ediciones Unión, 2010); Steve Palmer, José Antonio Piqueras, and Amparo Sánchez Cobos, *State of Ambiguity: Civic Life and Culture in Cuba's First Republic*

(Durham, NC: Duke University Press, 2014); Michael E. Neagle, *America's Forgotten Colony: Cuba's Isle of Pines* (New York: Cambridge University Press, 2016).

10. The archival diplomacy of Peter Kornbluh and others at the National Security Archives has been exemplary; see, for example, Peter Kornbluh, ed., *Bay of Pigs Declassified: The Secret CIA Report on the Invasion of Cuba* (New York: New Press, 1998); Laurence Chang and Peter Kornbluh, eds., *The Cuban Missile Crisis, 1962: A National Security Archive Documents Reader* (New York: New Press, 1992). Meanwhile the CIA has continued to fight political battles over when and how to declassify information about the Bay of Pigs in its own official history of the event. In Cuba, historians with special access to classified Cuban documents have also made important contributions to this history while maintaining a strong emphasis on U.S. sources; see, for example, Elier Ramírez Cañedo and Esteben Morales Domínguez, *De la confrontación a los intentos de "normalización": La política de los Estados Unidos hacia Cuba* (Havana: Editorial de Ciencias Sociales, 2011). On U.S.-Cuba relations, see Jana Lipman, *Guantánamo: A Working-Class History between Empire and Revolution* (Berkeley: University of California Press, 2009); Anita Casavantes-Bradford, *The Revolution Is for the Children: The Politics of Childhood in Havana and Miami, 1959–1962* (Chapel Hill: University of North Carolina Press, 2014); John A. Gronbeck-Tedesco, *Cuba, the United States, and Cultures of the Transnational Left, 1930–1975* (Cambridge: Cambridge University Press, 2015); Devyn Spence Benson, *Antiracism in Cuba: The Unfinished Revolution* (Chapel Hill: University of North Carolina Press, 2016). New scholarship on Cuban migration after 1959 has also made important contributions in this area; see, for example, Julio Capó, "Queering Mariel: Mediating Cold War Foreign Policy and U.S. Citizenship among Cuba's Homosexual Exile Community, 1978–1994," *Journal of American Ethnic History* 29, no. 4 (2010): 78–106; Jana Lipman, "'The Fish Trusts the Water, and It Is in the Water That It Is Cooked': The Caribbean Origins of the Krome Detention Center," *Radical History Review* 115 (Winter 2013): 115–41; Susana Peña, *Oye loca: From the Mariel Boatlift to Gay Cuban Miami* (Minneapolis: University of Minnesota Press, 2013); Jana Lipman, "A Refugee Camp in America: Fort Chaffee and Vietnamese and Cuban Refugees, 1975–1982," *Journal of American Ethnic History* 33, no. 2 (2014): 57–87; Teishan Latner, "Take Me to Havana! Airline Hijacking, U.S.-Cuba Relations, and Political Protest in Late Sixties' America," *Diplomatic History* 39, no. 1 (2015): 12–30; Michael Bustamante, "Anti-Communist Anti-Imperialism? Agrupación Abdala and the Shifting Contours of Cuban Exile Politics, 1968–1986," *Journal of American Ethnic History* 35, no. 1 (2015): 71–99. See also my new digital humanities project, *Beyond the Sugar Curtain: Tracing Cuba-U.S. Connections since 1959*, www.brown.edu/sugarcurtain.

11. Ana María Dopico, "Picturing Havana: History, Vision, and the Scramble for Cuba," *Nepantla: Views from South* 3, no. 3 (2002): 451–93.

12. Michael Moynihan, "Castro's Hipster Apologists Want to Keep Cuba 'Authentically' Poor," *Daily Beast* (blog), December 18, 2014.

13. Renato Rosaldo, "Imperialist Nostalgia," *Representations* 26 (Spring 1989): 108.

14. Dopico, "Picturing Havana," 487.

15. Letter from Robert P. Moss to Secretary William H. Taft, January 27, 1908, Box 273, Item 47, Bureau of Insular Affairs, General Classified Files, 1868–1945, RG350, National Archives, Washington, DC.

16. Letter from Beverly Todd Towers to Theodore Roosevelt, March 20, 1907, Box 273, Item 47, RG350, National Archives, Washington, DC.

17. Letter from Frank McIntire to Robert P. Moss, February 3, 1908, Box 273, Item 47, RG350, National Archives, Washington, DC.

18. See, for example, Van Gosse, *Where the Boys Are: Cuba, Cold War America and the Making of a New Left* (London: Verso, 1993); Timothy B. Tyson, *Radio Free Dixie: Robert F. Williams and the Roots of Black Power* (Chapel Hill: University of North Carolina Press, 1999); Ian Lekus, "Queer Harvests: Homosexuality, the U.S. New Left, and the Venceremos Brigades to Cuba," *Radical History Review* 89 (2004): 57–91; Frank Guridy, *Forging Diaspora: Afro-Cubans and African Americans in a World of Empire and Jim Crow* (Chapel Hill: University of North Carolina Press, 2010); Devyn Spence Benson, "Cuba Calls: African American Tourism, Race, and the Cuban Revolution, 1959–1961," *Hispanic American Historical Review* 93, no. 2 (2013): 239–71; John Gronbeck-Tedesco, *Cuba, the United States, and Cultures of the Transnational Left, 1930–1975* (New York: Cambridge University Press, 2015); Peter Hulme, "Seeing for Themselves: U.S. Travel Writers in Early Revolutionary Cuba," in *Politics, Identity, and Mobility in Travel Writing*, edited by Miguel A. Cabañas, Jeanne Dubino, Veronica Salles-Reese, and Gary Totten (London: Routledge, 2015); Abel Sierra Madero, "Fidel Castro, el Comandante 'Playboy,'" *Letras Libres*, December 1, 2016, http://www.letraslibres.com/espana-mexico/politica/fidel -castro-el-comandante-playboy; A. Javier Treviño, *C. Wright Mills and the Cuban Revolution: An Exercise in the Art of Sociological Imagination* (Chapel Hill: University of North Carolina Press, 2017); Teishan Latner, *Irresistible Revolution: Cuba and American Radicalism, 1968–1992* (Chapel Hill: University of North Carolina Press, 2018).

19. For a few exemplary works, see Roig de Leuchsenring, *Historia de la enmienda Platt*; Emilio Roig de Leuchsenring, *Los Estados Unidos contra Cuba libre* (Santiago de Cuba: Editorial Oriente, 1982); Pérez, *Cuba and the United States*; Paterson, *Contesting Castro*; Pérez, *The War of 1898*; Pérez, *On Becoming Cuban*; Eduardo Sáenz Rovner, *The Cuban Connection: Drug Trafficking, Smuggling, and Gambling in Cuba from the 1920s to the Revolution* (Chapel Hill: University of North Carolina Press, 2008); Pérez, *Cuba in the American Imagination*; Lars Schoultz, *That Infernal Little Cuban Republic: The United States and the Cuban Revolution* (Chapel Hill: University of North Carolina Press, 2009); Lipman, *Guantánamo*; Soraya M. Castro Mariño and Ronald W. Pruessen, *Fifty Years of Revolution: Perspectives on Cuba, the United States, and the World* (Gainesville: University Press of Florida, 2012); Esteban Morales Domínguez and Elier Ramírez Cañedo, *Aproximaciones al conflicto Cuba–Estados Unidos* (Havana: Editora Política, 2015).

20. A small sampling of relevant works: Thomas C. Wright, *Latin America in the Era of the Cuban Revolution* (New York: Praeger, 2000); Piero Gleijeses, *Conflicting Missions: Havana, Washington, and Africa, 1959–1976* (Chapel Hill: University of North Carolina Press, 2002); *Todos iban a ser reinas*, directed by Gustavo Pérez, 2006; Yinghong Cheng, "Sino-Cuban Relations during the Early Years of the Castro Regime, 1959–1966," *Journal of Cold War Studies* 9, no. 3 (2007): 78–114; *Freddy Ilanga: Che's Swahili Translator*, directed by Katrin Hansing, 2009; Kepa Artaraz, *Cuba and Western Intellectuals since 1959* (New York: Palgrave Macmillan, 2009); Tanya Harmer, *Allende's Chile and the Inter-American Cold War* (Chapel Hill: University of North Carolina Press, 2011); Christabelle Peters, *Cuban*

Identity and the Angolan Experience (New York: Palgrave Macmillan, 2012); Piero Gleijeses, *Visions of Freedom: Havana, Washington, Pretoria and the Struggle for Southern Africa, 1976–1991* (Chapel Hill: University of North Carolina Press, 2013); Anne Luke, "Listening to *los Beatles*: Being Young in 1960s Cuba," in *The Socialist Sixties: Crossing Borders in the Second World*, edited by Diane Koenker and Anne E. Gorsuch (Bloomington: Indiana University Press, 2013); Jacqueline Loss, *Dreaming in Russian: The Cuban Soviet Imaginary* (Austin: University of Texas Press, 2013); Renata Keller, *Mexico's Cold War: Cuba, the United States, and the Legacy of the Mexican Revolution* (New York: Cambridge University Press, 2015); Anne Gorsuch, "'Cuba, My Love': The Romance of Revolutionary Cuba in the Soviet 1960s," *American Historical Review* 120, no. 2 (2015): 497–526; Robert Karl, "Reading the Cuban Revolution from Bogotá, 1957–62," *Cold War History* 16, no. 4 (2016): 337–58; Jonathan C. Brown, *Cuba's Revolutionary World* (Cambridge, MA: Harvard University Press, 2017).

21. See Lara Putnam, "The Transnational and the Text-Searchable: Digitized Sources and the Shadows They Cast," *American Historical Review* 121, no. 2 (2016): 377–402.

22. Per Sebastian Conrad, adapted in Andrew Zimmerman, "Africa in Imperial and Transnational History: Multi-sited Historiography and the Necessity of Theory," *Journal of African History* 54 (2013): 331–40.

CONTRIBUTORS

MICHAEL J. BUSTAMANTE is an assistant professor of Latin American history at Florida International University. His writing on Cuban and Cuban American history has appeared in *Journal of American Ethnic History*, *Latino Studies*, and *Cuban Studies*, among other publications.

MARÍA A. CABRERA ARÚS teaches at the Gallatin School of Individualized Studies and is a former postdoctoral fellow at the King Juan Carlos I of Spain Center, both at New York University. Her writing on Cuban fashion has appeared in *Theory and Society* and *Cuban Studies*. She is the creator of the blog *Cuba Material*, and in 2015 she co-curated the exhibition *Pioneros: Building Cuba's Socialist Childhood* at the Parsons School of Design.

MARÍA DEL PILAR DÍAZ CASTAÑÓN is a professor of philosophy and history at the University of Havana. Her books and edited collections include *Ideología y Revolución: Cuba, 1959–1962* (2001), *Éditos inéditos: Documentos olvidados de la historia de Cuba* (2005), and *Prensa y Revolución: La magia del cambio* (2010).

ADA FERRER is the Julius, Roslyn, and Enid Silver Professor of History and Latin American and Caribbean Studies at New York University. She is the author of *Freedom's Mirror: Cuba and Haiti in the Age of Revolution* (2015) and *Insurgent Cuba: Race, Nation, and Revolution, 1868–1898* (1999).

ALEJANDRO DE LA FUENTE is the Robert Woods Bliss Professor of Latin American History and Economics and the director of the Afro-Latin American Research Institute at Harvard University. He is the author of *Havana and the Atlantic in the Sixteenth Century* (2008) and *A Nation for All: Race, Inequality, and Politics in Twentieth-Century Cuba* (2001). He is the editor of the journal *Cuban Studies*.

REINALDO FUNES MONZOTE is a professor of history at the University of Havana, director of geohistoric research at the Antonio Núñez Jiménez Foundation (Havana), and the Henry Hart Rice Foundation Visiting Professor at the MacMillan Center for International and Area Studies at Yale University. He is the author of *From Rainforest to Cane Field in Cuba: An Environmental History since 1492* (2008) and *El despertar del asociacionismo científico en Cuba (1876–1920)* (2004).

LILLIAN GUERRA is the Waldo W. Neikirk Professor of Cuban and Caribbean History at the University of Florida. She is the author of several books, including *Visions of Power in Cuba: Revolution, Redemption, and Resistance, 1959–1971* (2012) and, most recently, *Heroes, Martyrs, and Political Messiahs in Revolutionary Cuba, 1946–1958* (2018).

JENNIFER L. LAMBE is an assistant professor of Latin American and Caribbean history at Brown University. She is the author of *Madhouse: Psychiatry and Politics in Cuban History* (2017).

JORGE MACLE CRUZ, a geographer by training, is the former curator of the maps collection at the National Archives of Cuba, where he directed the digitization of documentary sources and the project "History of Cuban Cartography." He has published articles on archival standardization and in the field of geosciences. He was a visiting fellow at the Newberry Library in Chicago in 2015.

CHRISTABELLE PETERS is a lecturer in Latin American cultural/political history at the University of Bristol and a former postdoctoral scholar at the University of Warwick. She is the author of *Cuban Identity and the Angolan Experience* (2012).

RAFAEL ROJAS is a professor of history at the Centro de Investigación y Docencia Económicas in Mexico City and the author of over twenty books on the intellectual, cultural, and literary history of Cuba and Latin America. In 2011–12 he was a Global Scholar at Princeton University, and in 2018 he served as a Presidential Visiting Scholar at Yale University.

ELIZABETH SCHWALL earned her doctorate in history from Columbia University and has taught at Northwestern University and the University of California, Berkeley. Her writing on Cuban dance has appeared in *Hispanic American Historical Review* and is forthcoming in *Dance Chronicle*, *Cuban Studies*, and the volume *The Futures of Dance Studies*.

ABEL SIERRA MADERO is a PhD candidate in literature at New York University, having previously earned a doctorate in history at the University of Havana. He is the author of *Del otro lado del espejo: La sexualidad en la construcción de la nación cubana* (2006) and *La nación sexuada: Relaciones de género y sexo en Cuba, 1830–1855* (2002).

INDEX

Note: Page numbers in italics refer to illustrations.

Ministry of Foreign Investment, 52–53
Ministry of Industries, 52
Ministry of Information, 68
Ministry of Light Industry (MINIL), 194, 198
Ministry of the Interior, 230, 255–56, 269
Ministry of the Revolutionary Armed Forces, 53
Mirabal, Elizabeth, 15
Mi Solar (musical), 161
Moda '75, Edición Especial (brochure), 195, 196
modernization, 41
Molina, Marianela, 252
Moncada Barracks, attack of, 36, 38, 68, 72, 223, 224, 295
Montané, Magaly, 80
Montesquieu, Baron de, 125
Moore, Carlos, 10
Mora, Anita, 83
Mora, Eusebio, 83
Morales, Leonel, 302
Moreno Fraginals, Manuel, 8
Morera, Clara, 302
Morley, Morris, 13
Morray, J. P., 35
Moss, Robert P., 311
Motivos Yoruba (Queneditt exhibit), 302
Motorcycle Diaries (Guevara), 172
Movimiento Patriótico de Apoyo Económico a la Reforma Agraria y el Desarrollo Industrial (MPAERA), 104
MPAERA. See Movimiento Patriótico de Apoyo Económico a la Reforma Agraria y el Desarrollo Industrial
MPLA. See Popular Movement for the Liberation of Angola
Mundo, El (newspaper), 249
Museo Casa de Abel Santamaría, 224
Museo Casa Natal José Antonio Echeverría, 224
Museo de Guanabacoa, 302
museums, 223–25

Naranjo, Pepín, 255
Nasser, Gamel Abdel, 174
National Archive of Cuba: access restrictions, 53–54, 56, 58–59, 312; challenges of, 51–55; on Cuban Revolution, 21–22, 47–49; declassification process, 56; document manage-

ment practices, 54–55, 59; erasure of, 48; historians' strategies on, 55–58; legislation, 49–55, 58–59; marginalization of archival science and, 59; principles for future, 58–59
National Assembly of People's Power, 53
National Association of Agronomy and Sugar Engineers, 52
National Atlas of Cuba, 132
National Bank of Cuba, 52
National Botanical Garden, 133
National Commission for the Promotion and Defense of Tobacco, 52
National Commission of Expert Control, 51
National Commission of the Cuban Academy of Sciences, 128, 131
National Congress of Education and Culture, 220, 221–22
National Council of Culture, 57–58, 131
National Customs Office, 52
National Exporting and Importing Company for Primary and Secondary Materials, 52
National Gay Task Force, 264
National Institute for the Stabilization of Sugar, 52
National Institute of Agrarian Reform, 52, 127
National Institute of Hydraulic Resources, 135
nationalism, 43, 72, 197–202, 210–11, 218; sexuality and, 246, 257–64
nationalization of industry, 149
National Liberation Front of Angola (FNLA), 181
National Museum of Fine Arts, 130
National Office of Free Trade Zones, 52
National Revolutionary Police, 302
National Treasury, 52
National Union for the Total Independence of Angola (UNITA), 181
National Zoo, 133
Nazzari, Muriel, 209
Neto, Agostinho, 181, 184
Network of Historical Archives, 50, 52, 53–54
New Left, 43
New York Native (magazine), 267
New York Times (newspaper), 69, 71
Nietzsche, Friedrich, 33
Nipe Bay, 135
Nkrumah, Kwame, 174, 186n16
Nodarse, Luis, 251
Nogueras, Luis Rogelio, 230